CAMBRIDGE STUDIES IN AMERICAN LITERATURE AND CULTURE

Re-making it new

# Re-making it new

Contemporary American poetry and
the modernist tradition

LYNN KELLER
University of Wisconsin, Madison

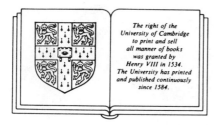

The right of the
University of Cambridge
to print and sell
all manner of books
was granted by
Henry VIII in 1534.
The University has printed
and published continuously
since 1584.

CAMBRIDGE UNIVERSITY PRESS
Cambridge
New York   New Rochelle   Melbourne   Sydney

Published by the Press Syndicate of the University of Cambridge
The Pitt Building, Trumpington Street, Cambridge CB2 1RP
32 East 57th Street, New York, NY 10022, USA
10 Stamford Road, Oakleigh, Melbourne 3166, Australia

© Cambridge University Press 1987

First published 1987

Printed in the United States of America

*Library of Congress Cataloging-in-Publication Data*
Keller, Lynn, 1952–
Re-making it new.
(Cambridge studies in American literature and culture)
1. American poetry – 20th century – History and
criticism.   2. Modernism (Literature)   I. Title.
II. Series
PS310.M57K45   1987      811'.52'091      85–33452

*British Library Cataloguing in Publication Data*
Keller, Lynn
Re-making it new: contemporary American
poetry and the modernist tradition. –
(Cambridge studies in American literature
and culture).
1. American poetry – 20th century –
History and criticism
I. Title
811'.54'09      PS323.5

ISBN 0 521 33283 4

For my mother, Kathleen Clear Keller,
and in memory of my father,
Joseph Michels Keller, 1911–1970

# Contents

vii

# Acknowledgments

Many teachers, colleagues, and friends have helped make this book possible. Robert von Hallberg directed the dissertation from which it grew, and to him – along with the other readers, James E. Miller, Jr., and Richard Strier – I owe my first and heartfelt thanks. Ronald Wallace has read several more recent versions, and I cannot thank him enough for all the guidance and generous support he has provided. I am also grateful to others who have read parts of the manuscript and given their advice: Walter Rideout, Eric Rothstein, Cyrena Pondrom, Susan Friedman, Betsy Draine, Michael Hinden, Robert Ferguson, Elizabeth Abel, Cristanne Miller, and Elizabeth Hirsh. For her painstaking work checking the manuscript, I thank Elizabeth Wyatt. Most of all, I am grateful to Duncan Carlsmith, who provided love and encouragement through it all.

I am indebted to the Whiting Foundation for a fellowship that supported me during the early stages of this project. The National Endowment for the Humanities and the Graduate School of the University of Wisconsin–Madison provided summer support which freed me to write. I also thank the Institute for Research in the Humanities at the University of Wisconsin for providing a semester's research support.

My thanks to James Merrill, John Ashbery, and Robert Creeley for allowing me to quote from their letters, and to John Hollander for allowing me to quote from his conversation. Patricia Willis of the Rosenbach Foundation and Lisa Brower of Vassar College Library were wonderfully helpful when I needed to examine unpublished materials by Moore and Bishop. Thanks also to Alice Methfessel for permission to examine Elizabeth Bishop's letters and to Clive E. Driver for permission to examine and quote from Marianne Moore's letters.

Chapter 1 originally appeared in a different version as " 'Thinkers

Without Final Thoughts': John Ashbery's Evolving Debt to Wallace Stevens" in *ELH*, 49 (Spring 1982): 235–61, © 1982 by The Johns Hopkins University Press. Chapter 5 appeared in a different version as "Lessons from William Carlos Williams: Robert Creeley's Early Poetry" in *Modern Language Quarterly*, 43 (December 1982): 369–94.

# Introduction:
# "Unless there is / a new mind there cannot be a new / line": the modernist inheritance

## I

From the prophetic chants of the Beats to the terza rima of the formalists, from the dreamscapes of the surrealists to the intellectualized constructions of Black Mountain, from the whimsical games of the New York School to the emotional dramas of the confessional writers – in the last thirty five years, American poets have poured forth a rich variety of powerful poetry. Even when one considers only the poetry written by those who came of age in the years immediately surrounding World War II, both the quantity of fine work and its formal diversity are astonishing. One way in which we may understand this plenitude and identify common trends within this heterogeneity is by considering contemporary work in the context of the earlier modernist achievements. Because modernism was central to the literary tradition inherited by poets born in the 1910s and 1920s, their volumes trace various ways of coming to terms with that modernist inheritance.

This is a study of four contemporary poets whose first collections appeared shortly after World War II – John Ashbery, Elizabeth Bishop, Robert Creeley, James Merrill – and of how modernism operates as a tradition in their work. No four poets can fully represent the diversity of contemporary writing, but each of these four, besides being a major figure in his or her own right, represents a significant trend or "school" in contemporary poetry. Consequently, patterns observed in the works of these four poets point to broad trends in contemporary poetry and clarify the relation of recent work to the work of the major modernists.

John Ashbery is the most notable voice in the "New York School" (others include James Schuyler, Kenneth Koch, Barbara Guest, Frank O'Hara, Ted Berrigan), a group closely tied to what is arguably the century's last true avant-garde, the abstract expressionist school of painting. Also linked to the American abstract expressionists, but less drawn to continental influences and more drawn to Californian ones, were the Black Mountain poets, including Charles Olson, Robert Duncan, John Weiners, Ed Dorn (and, tangentially, Denise Levertov, A. R. Ammons, LeRoi Jones [Baraka], W. S. Merwin); they are represented here by Robert Creeley. At the opposite pole from the organic forms of the Black Mountain projectivists are the works of James Merrill, the most elegant of formalists. In this study he represents a number of poets who choose the constraints of traditional verse forms – among them, Anthony Hecht, John Hollander, Marilyn Hacker, May Sarton, Richard Howard. Elizabeth Bishop belongs to no school. Yet her semiformalist orientation, in which traditional craft is modified, disguised, and understated as strict form blends with informal language and rhetoric, is widely shared, not only by older figures such as Robert Lowell, John Berryman, and Randall Jarrell, but also by Louis Simpson, James Wright, Richard Hugo, Adrienne Rich (for a time), Maxine Kumin, and Galway Kinnell.

Since the work of each of these four poets shows close affinities with that of a particular modernist, I have chosen to consider each in relation to a particular predecessor: Ashbery with Wallace Stevens, Bishop with Marianne Moore, Creeley with William Carlos Williams, and Merrill with the representative of a slightly later modernist generation, W. H. Auden. One has only to think of Ashbery's meditative manner, Bishop's descriptions, Creeley's free verse prosody, and Merrill's rhymed pageantry to recognize the influence operating within these pairs. In addition, influence has been confirmed by the testimony of each of the younger poets, and three of the four pairs (Ashbery and Stevens being the exception) enjoyed significant personal contact. Yet, while influence helped determine my selection of pairs, influence per se is not the focus of my inquiry. I share Robert Pinsky's belief that

> the idea of influence, insofar as it emphasizes the irresistible force of one personality upon another, is a Romantic tradition, implying that poetry expresses unique internal forces rather than imitating an objective world by technical means which may be shared. For me, the neutral terms "affinity" and "tradition" offer ways to discuss how a poet may have been affected by other poets . . .[1]

My intention is to examine the historical transmission and modification of modernist poetic techniques. The pairings I employ provide a methodological frame that makes manageable an inquiry into the continuities between generations; the pairings also establish an inductive base for speculations about the distinguishing traits of contemporary poetics. Though I devote little space to the contemporary poets' debts to other poets, whether premodern, modern, or contemporary, many other influences are certainly present. Merrill was influenced by Stevens, Yeats, and Proust, among others; Ashbery by Auden, Bishop, Hölderlin, and Reverdy; Creeley by Campion, Pound, and Olson; Bishop by Herbert, Hopkins, and Auden, and so on. Nonetheless, the pairings I have chosen seem of primary importance in charting the operation of modernism as a tradition.

In using these pairs to suggest generalizations about the modernist inheritance, I presuppose that, despite the differences between Williams, Stevens, and Moore, and between their works and those of Pound and Eliot, the former three are nonetheless representative of modernism. (Auden is a special case, to be considered separately.) Admittedly, no single poet's work possesses all the traits usually considered modern; nor is any poet likely to be entirely consistent in his or her apparent modernity. Moore, for example, is typically modernist in her emphasis on exact presentation of the object, in her use of abrupt juxtapositions, prose rhythms, and inconspicuous rhymes, but her fondness for moral propositions seems archaic. Stevens' irony and wit, his impersonality, and his idiosyncratic diction follow modernist principles, but his poetry often operates on a high level of abstraction. Williams' interest in colloquial diction and local material, his use of collage, and his delight in the concrete image place him firmly in the center of modernism, but his manner and voice are much more personal and less ironic than the other modernists'. Eliot and Pound, though they were the movement's most important theoretical spokesmen, were far more involved with resuscitation of past cultures and with esoteric allusion than were the others. Still, it is reasonable to treat any one of these figures as representative of modernism because of shared fundamental aims and beliefs beneath their diverse priorities and practices.

Although the exact boundaries of modernism are still in dispute, its territory is generally familiar. Since this study does not propose to revise critical understanding of early modernism, a quick survey will provide adequate background: Anglo–American poetic modernism took shape in the years immediately preceding and following World War I, when a number of young poets were struggling to revitalize the techniques of their art, or in Ezra Pound's words, to "make it new." Born in the 1880s and influenced directly or indirectly by such thinkers as Henri Bergson, T. E. Hulme, and Rémy de Gourmont, these revolutionary artists shared a sense that people had become displaced from reality by conceptual, social, and linguistic conventions. They were confident that the artist need not be bound by those conventions and could therefore disclose new aspects of reality, unveiling the flux of immediate experience that habitual forms of thought and articulation had masked. Loosely associated through the new network of little magazines such as *Poetry*, *Others*, and *The Dial*, they believed themselves to be participating in an artistic renaissance that would throw off the conventions of the past, allowing them and their readers to "step barefoot into reality."[2]

The conventions that the Anglo-American modernists were most determined to overthrow were those of their immediate literary predecessors, representatives of the "Genteel Tradition."[3] The avant-garde poets of the early twentieth century were opposed to lofty vagueness and to what Pound termed "emotional slither,"[4] both of which they associated with late Romantic and Victorian poetry.[5] They reacted against "poeticized" treatment and against narrow conceptions of the subject matter suitable for poetry. Mistrusting abstractions and generalized statements, they tended to focus on accurate, particularized treatment of concrete things, and attempted to express ideas in terms of sensory impressions.

Of course, the modernist revolution was a response to other conditions beyond those purely literary. The litany of historical pressures is in the main no less valid for being familiar:

> [Modernist literature] is the art consequent on Heisenberg's 'Uncertainty principle', of the destruction of civilization and reason in the First World War, of the world changed and reinterpreted by Marx, Freud and Darwin, of capitalism and constant industrial acceleration, of existential exposure to meaninglessness or absurdity. It is the literature of technology. It is the art consequent on the disestablishing of communal reality and conventional notions of causality, on the destruction of traditional notions of the wholeness of individual character, on the linguistic chaos that ensues when public notions of language have been discredited and when all realities have become subjective fictions. Modernism is then the art of modernization.[6]

Contemporary developments in archeology, philology, and the visual arts – not specifically mentioned above – were also among the forces impelling these changes. Thus, Hugh Kenner has argued that the uncovering of a real Troy and of miraculously fresh cave paintings by Magdalenian artists gave ancient art an immediacy and actuality that put an end to the nineteenth-century "romance of time."[7] The discovery of tattered Alexandrian papyrus manuscripts may, he claims, have led to the new focus on fragments, on diction rather than syntax, and on "non-consecutive arrays."[8] Advances in comparative philology and etymology drew

attention to continuities between different modern languages and between modern and ancient languages. As etymological dictionaries revealed the origins and histories of words, single terms came to seem
charged with metaphoric significance. The techniques of cubism and collage showed how fragments might be juxtaposed in modern art so as to
offer simultaneous perception of multiple perspectives, multiple times;
the spirit of dadaism encouraged unrestrained experimentation.

As is well known, in poetry the result of all this was a proliferation of
bold formal experiments. The avant-garde poets of the early twentieth
century shared a belief that the modern era demanded for its expression
new poetic styles and fresh techniques. Consequently, free verse became
popular; traditional meters, when used, appeared in unconventional or
irregular ways. Some poets sought to replace traditional narrative method
with what Eliot termed the "mythical method," by "manipulating a
continuous parallel between contemporaneity and antiquity."[9] For all,
parataxis and ellipsis became crucial structural devices, and metaphor assumed an essential role as a juxtaposing technique by which new relations could be revealed while retaining the modern standards of com-
pactness, concreteness, and precision. Striving to bring poetry closer to
modern life (and in so doing, following what we can now recognize as a
Romantic program), the modernists adopted prose syntax and colloquial
diction and presented subjects that were often small and ordinary rather
than grand and beautiful.

The modernist revolution in poetry came to full fruition in the early
1920s with the publication of such works as Eliot's *The Waste Land* (1922),
Williams' *Spring and All* (1923), Stevens' *Harmonium* (1923), Moore's *Observations* (1924), and Pound's *A Draft of XVI Cantos* (1925). Soon after
the appearance of *The Waste Land* the movement entered a new phase
which some among the avant-garde regarded as a severe setback. William Carlos Williams later recalled:

> [*The Waste Land*] wiped out our world as if an atom bomb had
> been dropped upon it and our brave sallies into the unknown
> were turned to dust. . . . Eliot returned us to the classroom just
> at the moment when I felt we were on the point of an escape to
> matters much closer to the essence of a new art form itself.[10]

While Eliot surged into prominence and became the dominant figure
determining poetic practice and critical principles for the next two decades, the other modernists remained by and large outside the mainstream. (As I shall explain in a moment, their exclusion contributed to
their usefulness for later poets.) In addition, a split emerged between
those who chose to live in Europe, aligning themselves with the Euro-

pean cultural heritage – notably, Pound and Eliot – and those who remained in America. Yet it is fair to consider them under the single rubric "modernist," since all were working to develop a poetry that would unite the emotions and the intellect, that could include the prosaic, the obscure, the unrefined; all of them felt that poetic techniques and language itself must be altered – cleaned, pruned, reshaped – and that expected continuities must be violated for poets to represent reality, whether internal or external; all believed in writing as renewal and self-consciously strove to discover a new idiom.

Although most of the poets we now regard as major modernists continued refining their innovations in new volumes of poetry until well after World War II, the tremendously optimistic energy of the movement had dispersed long before. Poets coming of age in the late thirties and the forties therefore encountered modernism not as an enthusiasm still in the making, but as something essentially made – an accomplished body of literature already part of the literary tradition they inherited.

It is not mere chance that in this study Williams, Moore, and Stevens are the ones who represent modernism as a force shaping contemporary poetry; the work of these figures has been more useful to recent poets than that of Eliot or even Pound. When the younger artists began to publish, Eliot's work had for twenty years provided an established model of modern poetic practice particularly favored by academic critics and readers. Sharing Pound's sense that "no good poetry is ever written in a manner twenty years old, for to write in such a manner shows conclusively that the writer thinks from books, convention and cliché, and not from life,"[11] the postmodern generation sought an alternative to Eliot's modes. They therefore looked to lesser known figures, who seemed to stand apart from the current establishment, to suggest other manners and techniques. Moreover, the contemporary avant-garde by and large was not drawn to Pound's and Eliot's quest for hidden springs of knowledge and ordering structures in ancient myths and languages, buried cultures, or foreign lands. Like those modernists who stayed in America, most recent poets have chosen to focus on the world immediately before them in the present, and not to regard materials inherited from past cultures as bearing special truth or deserving special reverence.[12]

W. H. Auden came to America precisely to escape from the constraints of continental traditions, and his own iconoclastic beginnings enhanced his appeal as a model for the younger generation. In other ways, however, he is an intentional anomaly in this study, a reminder that literary history does not occur in tidy generations any more than it develops in a single direction. He was born nearly twenty years later than the high modernists, and, as Chapters 7 and 8 will demonstrate, the American

Auden did not aspire to "make it new"; yet his highly individualistic style and manner – developed partly through his own battles with the influence of Yeats and Eliot – provided another alternative to Eliotic modernism that has shaped contemporary writing.

Born in 1907, Auden was of the first generation able to recognize that the modernists, while insisting on the necessity of liberation from conventions of the past, themselves created new conventions of language and technique. Those born later than Auden have been even more aware that the process of "making it new" to which the modernists devoted themselves is in constant need of updating if poets are to continue to capture the immediate data of experience and to bring freshness to familiar realities. Thus, contemporary poets have encountered in modernism a polarized inheritance. On the one hand, the poems of the great modernists are impressive models offering a body of powerful techniques that invite further development and extension. On the other hand, modernist attitudes and principles encourage the contemporary poet to reject the methods of his or her immediate predecessors, just as the modernists rejected those of the late Victorians and decadents who preceded them.

As Walter Jackson Bate and Harold Bloom have argued, this kind of tension can develop in any literary inheritance, particularly a post-Miltonic one;[13] any conventions may grow stifling, and any past achievements may come to seem challenges that must be outdone. Subsequent generations may feel compelled to reject as well as to emulate. Yet a particularly forceful, immediate, and necessary polarization between continuity and divergence is built into modernism's operation as a tradition. The modernists' loud insistence on revolution – on the necessity of revitalizing the language and of discovering a poetry consonant with each new era – combined with their awesome poetic achievements, exacerbate for their descendants the usual conflict between imitation and rebellion.

This study is structured to reflect both impulses – toward continuity and toward discontinuity – which modernism, acting as a tradition, provides. Two chapters are devoted to each contemporary poet; in each case, the first investigates the nature of the affinities between the paired poets of the two generations, while the second delineates the ways in which the later poet diverges from his or her predecessors, striving, in Ashbery's words, to "re-make it new."[14] Because the modernists were concerned with the renewal of language and its poetic usage, the central innovations of modernism involve technique more than content, motif, or theme. Consequently, in examining recent poets' debts to the modernists, I have focused less on what poems say than on how they say it.

However, the poems' philosophical and thematic contents have proved particularly useful in my comparisons to the extent that the poetry is reflexive, taking the nature and limitations of art or of language as its subject.

This structure should not suggest an illusorily sharp demarcation between continuities and discontinuities. It is often difficult to discriminate between a new practice and a modification of an old one, between a new perspective and an earlier one become newly popular. Thus, the tradition of indeterminacy that Marjorie Perloff has traced from Rimbaud through Pound, Stein, Williams, Beckett (and on to Cage, Ashbery, Antin) is *a* modernist tradition, but one not prominent in America between the wars.[15] Similarly, Ashbery's discovery of dadaist and surrealist ideas and techniques appeared to him more of a divergence from modernism than now seems historically accurate. (Williams' *Kora in Hell* [1920], for instance, was powerfully influenced by the automatic writing of the surrealists.) Yet even if explorations of chance and the unconscious were important to modernist art, the absorption of surrealism and the pervasive exploitation of chance in recent poetry may add up to something qualitatively different from modernism, perhaps best labeled postmodernism.[16] Further complicating such questions of periodization is the development undergone by the modernists themselves during their own lengthy careers; some attitudes expressed and embodied in late works such as *Four Quartets*, "The Auroras of Autumn," or "An Ordinary Evening in New Haven" may appear more characteristic of post-World War II aesthetics than of high modernism. Thus, a young poet's divergence from the important twenties work of a major modernist may follow the development of that same modernist's later poetics. And, of course, diverging from a particular practice of one modernist may have little or no generational significance if it means converging with the practice of another.

How radically *has* contemporary poetry diverged from modernist poetry? Since 1960 critics have been debating whether modernism is still going on in some modified form, or whether modernism "was" and is no longer.[17] The position one takes depends largely on which aspects of modernism one chooses to emphasize in defining that movement and naming its central practitioners. Too often "postmodern" is employed as a narrow evaluative label applied with either scorn or approbation to experimental works whose aggressive emphasis on textuality and on the web of society's semiotic codes may be linked to poststructuralist criticism. It is my belief that "postmodern" may more usefully serve as a general period term encompassing a broad spectrum of work that both follows after and depends upon modernism. Contemporary literature's genuine distinction from modernist literature need not depend upon extreme or dramatic disruption of modernist aesthetics. I am far less interested in classifying contemporary creations as late modernist, neomodernist, or postmodernist than in appreciating contemporary works and in identifying developmental trends in twentieth-century literature. In this study of the careers of four markedly different poets, of their affinities with high modernism and their divergence from it, some general trends do emerge. Focusing on these trends rather than on any classifying label, the remainder of the introduction provides a brief summary of the directions in which I see contemporary poetry evolving.

## II

The modernists were conscious of participating in a sweeping aesthetic revolution, and their ambitions for poetry were immense. They seemed willing to dare anything both in technique and in vision, believing that − despite the artist's separation from society at large − changes in the arts could transform people's conceptions of themselves and their world, perhaps ultimately transforming society. For contemporary poets, the sense of an avant-garde has been more elusive, and the optimism with which the modernists experimented has dimmed. Post-World War II writers see in the modernists sobering examples of how quickly novelty fades, of how rapidly bold new techniques can become lifeless prescriptions. Perhaps, too, the younger poets have been intimidated by the rapid canonization of their immediate forebears. Examination of four poets will suggest, however, that recent writers' more modest aspirations do not simply reflect a discouraged sense of belatedness. Contemporary poets' pervasive sense of limitation must be positively distinguished from the despair we hear in the late works of, say, Eliot or Pound, where the modernists acknowledge the limits of the powers of the human mind and the language it has created, the limitations of their art. Contemporary poets differ in tending not to battle against limits but rather to play with them, not to abhor chaos or lament the arbitrariness of order but to accept each as intriguing possibility. Rather than seeking that precisely faceted central crystal, whose image recurs as radiant ideal in modernists' late works, they choose to explore the marginal, what Ashbery terms "the central perimeter / our imaginations' orbit" (*The Double Dream of Spring*, p. 82). Contemporary poets' revisions of modernist approaches thus represent a conscious critique of modernist aims and assumptions, reflecting an altered sense of what it means for art to be close to life.

Bringing art close to immediate reality was a principal goal of the modernists and was responsible for their expanding the diction and subject matter available to poetry. Poets of subsequent generations have continued these efforts at inclusiveness, and have gone even further in incorporating into poetry the low, the common, the trivial, the random, the prerational. "[G]aswork smokestack whistle tooting wisecracks" must come into the poem, David Ignatow explains, not "because we like it that way, / but because we find it outside our window each morning" ("Get the Gasworks").[18] The modernists, in attempting to penetrate the film of custom obscuring perception of the minute and familiar particulars of reality, also attempted to create larger structures in which these freshened perceptions might be meaningful. Although intensely conscious of humankind's "dispossession . . . in the cosmic scheme,"[19] they nonetheless were able to discern or construct grand coherence in historical patterns, in the "rhyme" of luminous human achievements, in experiences of religious revelation, or in the "supreme fictions" that the human imagination substituted for religious mythologies. Eliot celebrated the "mythical method" precisely because it offered "a way of controlling, of ordering, of giving a shape and a significance to the immense panorama of futility and anarchy which is contemporary history."[20] Recent poets appear more suspicious of sweeping patterns. While sharing the modernists' awareness that stable patterning is absent from the external world, later generations doubt the value of constructing order and creating controlling patterns. In their eyes the modernist insistence on coherence constitutes an evasion of the immediate experience that art is to capture.

Rather than trying to tame chaos as the modernists did, Ashbery, Bishop, Creeley, and Merrill (like others of their generation) strive, in their various ways, to accept it, believing that events are "only connected by 'and' and 'and,' " that even such patterns as cause-and-effect evade confrontation with the disjunction and contingency of reality. They are intensely conscious of chance (though only Ashbery and Creeley imitate the abstract expressionists in allowing contingency to shape their creations); they seek to illustrate the opacity of experience and to highlight the artificiality and autonomy of linguistic or artistic structures. Increasingly wary of imaginative projection, they insist on the impenetrability of external reality and they resist the modernist desire to project cohesive orders there. As A. R. Ammons explains in "Corsons Inlet":

> in my sayings
> swerves of action
> like the inlet's cutting edge:
> there are dunes of motion,
> organizations of grass, white sandy paths of remembrance
> in the overall wandering of mirroring mind:

but Overall is beyond me: is the sum of these events
I canot draw, the ledger I cannot keep, the accounting
beyond the account:

in nature there are few sharp lines:

In the contemporary poets' perspective, whatever is meaningful exists
apart from any large metaphysical frame and must be discovered within
the jumbled ordinary world, glimpsed – perhaps completely by chance
– within the flux of an ongoing present. Thus Ammons continues a few
lines later, "so I am willing to go along, to accept / the becoming /
thought, to stake off no beginnings or ends, establish no walls," and at
the end of the poem he affirms his will to "[enjoy] the freedom that /
Scope eludes my grasp."[21]

Contemporary artists are even more preoccupied than their predecessors with temporal flux. This is an outgrowth of a conflict inherited from
the Romantics via the modernists – that between the fixed, conventional,
and abstract nature of language and the fluid, instantaneous, and particular nature of experience.[22] The dominant modernist solution was to
avoid abstractions and focus on concrete particulars; these particulars,
revealed through startling metaphors, were usually assembled using collage techniques. Recent poets have concentrated more on fluidity, and in
attempting to bridge the gap between their medium and their experience,
have sought more inclusive ways of rendering what Stevens called "the
mind in the act of finding." Dramatically extending a modernist tendency, they take increasing interest in art and verbalization as processes
rather than products, even if that results in diminished intensity. Thus,
Ashbery's meandering meditations, like Merrill's self-revising and contradictory cosmology, exemplify a desire to capture the complexity of
the mind's workings. Creeley's rejection in the late 1960s of art that is
tidily conclusive and finished, and his substitution of casual journal-like
formats demonstrate that he became more intrigued with the process of
having thoughts than with the significance of their content. Similarly, as
Bishop's career progressed she redefined the nature and function of descriptive writing, focusing less on identifying exact verbal analogues for
phenomena, internal or external, and more on following the ongoing
process of attention, its inevitable approximations and continual modifications.

These contemporary poets have largely lost interest in metaphor as a
means of momentarily suspending an object outside the flux, of perfectly
uniting intellect and emotion in a realm of timeless truth. As Ashbery
puts it, "One cannot guard, treasure / That stalled moment. It too is
flowing, fleeting" (*Houseboat Days*, p. 70). Hence, metaphor may again
serve a simply – or playfully – ornamental function. More generally,

contemporary poets appear less confident than their immediate predecessors that the poet can effectively cleanse language so that it can accurately reveal the contours of experience. It is now common to think, as Robert Hass says, "that / because there is in this world no one thing / to which the bramble of *blackberry* corresponds, / a word is elegy to what it signifies" ("Meditation at Lagunitas").[23] The modernists' presentational strategies seem no closer to unmediated presence and sensation than the discursive, propositional modes deprecated by the modernists. Contemporary poets, though still valuing exactitude and freshness, have far less faith in the potential precision of language, and they doubt whether markedly individualized usage – if it is possible – is the most effective means of communicating one's sense of immediate reality. They therefore tend more than the modernists to work within the flat and worn language of our immediate daily experience. Of course, such modernists as Pound and Williams enjoyed creating colloquial, even prosaic, voices, but they did so without abandoning a sense of the privileged nature of the artist's perception and language. Contemporary poets doubt the writer's ability to stand free of conventions. They employ clichés, banal expressions, and dully discursive manners non-ironically, implying that mundane language, however slack, at least has the advantage of keeping art close to the untransformed and ordinary present, the now in which human interactions, and connections, occur.

To the extent that their verbal medium will allow, these contemporary poets attempt to immerse themselves in the dynamic present and to disclose direct psychological experience. Focusing on the processes of epistemology rather than on achieved knowledge, they portray the mind engaging itself in the world and attending to events, without imposing fixed interpretations on that experience.[24] Poets today do not believe they can or should eradicate the human propensity to entertain organizing systems and stabilizing fictions, but they have revalued those organizing tendencies – regarding them not as glorious powers especially well developed in the artistic imagination, but simply as inevitable outgrowths of human need. They frequently explore the ways in which their minds invent patterns – through dreams, fantasies, observations, memories, occult constructs, linguistic conventions, or supposedly rational analyses. But they demystify these patterns (though not necessarily the processes by which the patterns emerge), presenting them as obviously provisional and self-created. Their poetry, in consequence, is more obviously subjective than the modernists', and in many ways more personal.[25]

In presenting personal experience and private emotions without the mask of a persona or pretense of objectivity, contemporary poets show an affinity with the nineteenth-century Romantics. It is hardly surprising that this generation should feel free to adopt some techniques of the Romantics that the modernists, because of their place in literary history, felt compelled to reject. Spared the rigors of a major revolutionary period, contemporary poets can relax into a freer eclecticism. Predictably, in this skeptical era, most have not returned to the Romantics' transcendental perspective or to the Romantic dream of humans at home in nature (Snyder, Kinnell, Wright are among the exceptions). The postmodernist generation has maintained Stevens' sense of a world "That is not our own and, much more, not ourselves," while refusing to offer Stevens' consolation of an alternate secular mythology.

There are, however, novel consolations offered by these poets because their works dissolve distinctions and polarizing categories conventional to Romantics and modernists alike. These divisions and hierarchies are not just the products but also the generators of anxious graspings after order. Dissolving divisions in a spirit of accommodation and acceptance, recent poets attempt the dissolution of categories that generate many of our anxieties. Most fundamentally, as already discussed, the postmodernists challenge the distinction between order and chaos. But virtually all dichotomies are suspect – high/low, male/female, real/fictive, self/other, reason/imagination, noise/music, presence/absence (as well as the divisions between literary genres) – and are made to blur in the fluidity or the labyrinthine reflexivity of postmodernist poems. Once again, Ammons' propositions in "Corsons Inlet" apply:

> I have reached no conclusions, have erected no boundaries,
> shutting out and shutting in, separating inside
>                    from outside: I have
>                    drawn no lines:

These, then, are some major tendencies one can observe in the poetry that grows out of the modernist tradition, present in varying degrees and combinations in four paradigmatic poets: an intensified interest in art and verbalization as processes rather than products, and a consequent re-evaluation of the function and power of metaphor; an eclectic approach to literary tradition (and to the traditions of the nonliterary arts), including an exploitation of Romantic subjectivity; a desire to embrace and play with both the limitations of language and the disorder or contingency of experience; a distrust of imposed orders and thus an interest in dissolving the rigid categories of conventional dichotomous thinking. Ashbery, whose work I shall examine first, may well be the most thoroughly and obviously postmodern – most concerned with indeterminacy, with process, and most determined to embody his ideas about the radical uncertainties of language and experience in the diction and movement of his poems. Yet Bishop and Merrill, who are far more conventional in their approach to poetic forms and subjects, also participate in these developments. Because they are not avant-garde writers, it is their participation in these trends that argues most persuasively for a genuine periodization – not a crude chronological demarcation of a particular year as the beginning of the postmodern period, but a significant shift in attitudes and approaches shared by the majority of poets writing in America during the last thirty years.

I shall return to the issue of periodization in the Conclusion, where I shall also evaluate the achievements and the importance of my contemporary subjects. The intervening chapters examine the historical relation between modernist and postmodernist poetry as it is manifest in the work of four pairs of poets, each of whom demands consideration not according to an imposed theoretical structure but on his or her own terms.

# 1 "Thinkers without final thoughts": the continuity between Stevens and Ashbery

## I

Defending the "studious imitations" of an earlier artist in the work of a contemporary collage-maker, John Ashbery once remarked that "a profound impulse received from another artist has to work itself out as the sincerest form of flattery before the business of self-discovery can begin."[1] A comparable process in which obvious imitations of a master precede the evolution of a distinct personal style is evident in Ashbery's own "working out" of the impulse he received from Wallace Stevens.

It seems fitting that Ashbery, a poet fascinated by chance, should have begun to write poetry – and should have encountered the work of Wallace Stevens – because of a chance occurrence: Although he knew little about current events, Ashbery as a high school student was "good enough at guessing" to win a *Time* current events contest for which he was awarded Louis Untermeyer's anthology of modern poetry.[2] The anthology immediately sparked his interest in the works of Stevens and Auden and, to a lesser extent, other moderns such as Crane, Williams, and Moore; inspired to be a poet, Ashbery "went through a period of paying [his] dues and writing like them."[3] The relatively long period when Ashbery's poetry often sounded like Stevens' was crucial to his development. Ashbery's early published works employ many of Stevens' tricks of language and syntax while they explore Stevens' attitudes toward the imagination and toward the nature and function of poetic creation. Examined chronologically, Ashbery's early volumes trace a shift in orientation from Stevens' earlier to his later works that accompanies the young poet's progress toward more subtle and selective adaptations of Stevens' techniques as he discovers his own voice and style.

15

Ashbery's first major collection,[4] *Some Trees* (1956), unabashedly adopts both Stevens' theories and Stevens' modes, particularly those of his first volume, *Harmonium*. *Some Trees* rarely evokes the voice of the late meditative Stevens; instead, it echoes the more fantastic creations of Stevens the ringmaster and clown, inventor of the paltry nude, the Emperor of Ice Cream, the Prince of Peacocks. "The Thinnest Shadow," for example, could almost be mistaken for an early poem by Stevens. Like a number of poems in *Harmonium*, it is a brief narrative about an emblematic fantastic character and is written in short lines reminiscent of nursery rhymes. Here are the first two quatrains:

> He is sherrier
> And sherriest.
> A tall thermometer
> Reflects him best.
>
> Children in the street
> Watch him go by.
> "Is that the thinnest shadow?"
> They to one another cry.    (ST 43)

In Stevens' fashion, the fanciful adjectives "sherrier" and "sherriest" seem to have been chosen, or invented, as much for their sound as for their meaning (possibly, associations with a sherry-drinking social class). The strangeness of these words calls attention to the sing-song rhyme, as does Stevens' rhyming of "Scaramouche" and "barouche" (CP 61)[5] or "negress" and "egress" (CP 71). Ashbery's delineation of character follows Stevens' habit of using obesity to indicate vitality and imaginative fertility, and thinness to connote the absence of those qualities.[6] The grotesque fascination with death evident beneath the playful surface of "The Thinnest Shadow" is very like that of similarly short-lined poems by Stevens, such as "The Worms at Heaven's Gate," "The Jack-Rabbit," and "Cortège for Rosenbloom." Even the same rhyme of "cold" and "mo[u]ld" appears in the final stanza (also four lines long) of Stevens' "The Man Whose Pharynx Was Bad."

While few poems in *Some Trees* fit as neatly into a Stevensian mold as does "The Thinnest Shadow," unmistakable echoes of Stevens' diction and syntax, or even of specific lines by Stevens are generously scattered throughout. One cannot read the closing lines of "Glazunoviana" – "In the flickering evening the martins grow denser. / Rivers of wings surround us and vast tribulation" (ST 22) – without thinking of the parallel syntax and imagery of "Sunday Morning":

And, in the isolation of the sky,
At evening, casual flocks of pigeons make
Ambiguous undulations as they sink,
Downward to darkness on extended wings.  (CP 70)

Though Ashbery in his later works rarely calls attention to alliteration and assonance, as Stevens consistently does in *Harmonium, Some Trees* does contain passages that emphasize sound play, e.g., "I went into the mountains to interest myself / In the fabulous dinners of hosts distant and demure. / The foxes followed with endless lights" (ST 70). Stevens' infatuation with the exotic is evident in Ashbery's diction and imagery throughout the volume – e.g., "connoisseurs of oblivion," "a novice was sitting on a cornice," "naked as a roc's egg," "watching her glide aloft in her peplum of bright leaves." Some of Ashbery's more outlandish titles, such as "Meditations of a Parrot" and "Glazunoviana," also follow Stevens' example.

The resemblances between Ashbery's early work and Stevens' poetry penetrate deeper, however, than these surface delights. A number of poems in *Some Trees* explore Stevens' subject matter, and they do so using the rhetoric and syntax of what Helen Vendler has identified as Stevens' most characteristic mode, that of "qualified assertion."[7]

One such poem is "The Instruction Manual," Ashbery's most exuberant poem demonstrating the joys of imaginative flight. Its protagonist, like Stevens' Ordinary Women, flings monotony behind him and escapes to a richly detailed imagined world. His mind roams in a realm of pleasing, colorful images, like Stevens' mind-moth in "Hibiscus on the Sleeping Shores." The blatantly clichéd romantic figures he envisions – earnest young lovers, proud mothers, modest young wives – call attention to the artificiality of this Guadalahara, as does the cinematic manipulation of the point of view – "Let us take this opportunity to tiptoe into one of the side streets" (ST 16). Such techniques create an effect comparable to that of Stevens' "lingua . . . jocundissima" (CP 397); both poets' methods of exaggeration are simultaneously self-indulgent and self-mocking, at once gaily playful and ironically self-protective. They underline the fictive nature of the imaginative world while emphasizing the sheer pleasure of such ventures. Thus Ashbery humorously identifies Guadalahara as the "City I wanted most to see, and most did not see, in Mexico!" (ST 14).

Yet at the end of "The Instruction Manual," the speaker draws back from his imagined experience, reminding us that such flight is "limited" and this place only a temporary refuge. In the closing lines, the church tower reverts into an office building in which a bored employee is confined. This movement of qualification follows a pattern typical of Stevens, evident, for example, in "Hibiscus on the Sleeping Shores," where the last lines remind us of the tedious reality of "stupid afternoons" to which we inevitably return.

A similar movement of qualification occurs in "Illustration" (ST 48–50), this time accomplished in part by the use of Stevensian syntax. Like "The Thinnest Shadow," this poem presents a *Harmonium*-like third-person narrative about an emblematic character – the female "novice" who jumps from "a cornice / High over the city." The story is delivered playfully, punctuated by puns – "begging her to come off it" – and comical details – "A mother offered her some nylons / Stripped from her very legs." But the theme is serious, as it is in most of Stevens' apparently playful poetry. The novice's ceremonial suicide, motivated by a desire to "move // Figuratively," illustrates the universal need for an imaginative vision of grander human potential. Ashbery's "novice," then, is a version of Stevens' "figure of capable imagination" (CP 249) or "major man" (e.g., CP 387), the exponent of a noble idea of humanity to which others may aspire. The ceremonial nature of her behavior recalls Stevens' sense of poetry as a necessary replacement for religion as well as a form of apotheosis (CP 378).

Like much of Stevens' poetry dealing with the human desire to "resemble a taller / Impression of ourselves" (ST 49), this poem employs the tentative syntax which Vendler has identified as characteristic of Stevens' "search for a middle route between ecstasy and apathy."[8] Part II of "Illustration" opens with a generalized proposition that explains the meaning and value of the suicidal gesture. Employing the normative and optative "must" and "may," its phrasing is distinctly like Stevens'. Drawing an analogy between the woman and moths attracted to a flame, Ashbery then asserts that those who foolishly destroy themselves for imaginative enrichment do not lessen the stature of we who behave more prudently; in fact, "we twinkle [flame-like] under the weight / of indiscretions." After that point, however, the poem calls this affirmation more and more into question, as Ashbery progressively weakens the link between the "novice" and the "we" of speaker and audience. The optative mood now carries implications of failure; while "we might have soared from earth," uplifted by her exemplary liberating gesture, it is not clear that we did in fact do so. Moreover, the woman is now reduced in stature to "only an effigy / Of indifference." Just as Stevens' poems often close with a comparison that asserts *as if* rather than *is*, "Illustration" closes with an analogy – "a miracle // Not meant for us, as the leaves are not / Winter's because it is the end" – that severs the connection between the woman and the audience, qualifying radically the image in part I of genuine spectator involvement in this ceremonial.

In "The Mythological Poet" (ST 34–6), Ashbery uses a more abstract emblematic figure to explore another common theme of Stevens: the poet's role in combatting the pressure exerted by reality or "the world of things" on the ideal world of art. The "fabulous and fastidious" poet – Stevensian language and alliteration – described in part II fits Stevens' vision of a poet whose imagination is grounded in "things as they are" and who can discover Olympia in the crusty smokestacks of suburban Oxidia (CP 182). After revealing in part I the corruption and disruption of ideal beauty by the world of things, Ashbery offers in part II the possibility that the poet who remains "Close to the zoo, acquiescing / To dust, candy, perverts" can reestablish harmony and reveal beauty in the mundane. Once again, Stevens' themes are approached with Stevensian rhetoric; Ashbery struggles to affirm the power of the imagination, yet does so with tentative syntax. More longing than certainty emerges from Ashbery's urgent questions: "For isn't there, / He says . . .?" "And oh . . . might not . . .?" Here Ashbery's rhetoric, lacking the disguises provided by Stevens' strings of appositives and by his extended syntax, is more obviously one of doubt and longing than that of his modernist predecessor.

The many poems in *Some Trees* (including those already discussed) that are written in dramatic and descriptive modes, using self-protective and self-mocking exaggeration, exotic diction, and elaborate sound play, establish a clear link between the early work of Ashbery and Stevens. By adopting Stevens' celebratory indulgence of the imagination, by imitating his aural, and occasionally his visual, extravagance, Ashbery enabled himself to pursue any flight of fancy without feeling tied to particular subjects or to a particular formal program. Stevens' early work was a liberating model for Ashbery at the outset of his career.

Stevens' later poetry moves away from the buoyant sensuality and dramatic character of *Harmonium* toward more discursive, dialectical, and explicitly philosophical modes. This more meditative and linguistically austere Stevens is the more significant one for Ashbery's later works. Occasionally one feels the presence of the later Stevens in *Some Trees*; "*Le livre est sur la table*" (ST 74–5), more than any other poem in this volume, anticipates the Stevensian character of Ashbery's later poetry.

In "*Le livre*," Ashbery displays Stevens' fondness for propositional language and for seemingly logical argument. The poem opens with a grand and abstract proposition: "All beauty, resonance, integrity, / Exist by deprivation or logic / Of strange position." The idea expressed is central to Ashbery's aesthetics, since his poetry "exists" by ellipses or

"deprivation" and by juxtaposition, or "logic / Of strange position."
Then a phrase indicating deductive reasoning, "This being so," introduces a particular example: "We can only imagine" the woman who
exemplifies "beauty, resonance, integrity." "Yet we know what her breasts
are" – that is to say, this imagining is a form of genuine knowledge –
"and we give fullness / To the dream." As Stevens frequently does, Ashbery here asserts the importance of the imagination's contribution to reality, the value of "The difference that we make in what we see" (CP
344). Two examples of "giv[ing] fullness" follow: We perceive and speak
as if tables support books and as if inanimate objects such as pens willfully aid us in our endeavors. In selecting for examples such common
objects as a book, a table, and a pen, Ashbery was, according to a statement he made in 1973, "half-consciously imitative of Stevens." He cites
"An Ordinary Evening in New Haven" as an example of the kind of
"meditative verse" he had in mind, in which "the things in a room and
the events of everyday life can enter and become almost fossilized in the
poems."[9] These examples, while apparently furthering the logical argument, actually introduce its qualification and shift the poem into a less
confident mood, since "the plume leaps in the hand" is far-fetched enough
to make us question the authenticity of such imaginative domination.

The questions that conclude the first section of "*Le livre*" make more
explicit Ashbery's qualification of his initial proposition: "But what //
Dismal scene is this? the old man pouting / At a black cloud, the woman
gone / Into the house, from which the wailing starts?" Like Stevens,
Ashbery presents observations in the form of questions,[10] here demonstrating that human beings have no control over a harsh and indifferent
cosmos and that the imagination is powerless to prevent suffering. Antithetical propositions lie at the heart of this poem, as they do in much of
Stevens' work: It is true both that the mind has dominion over the world
and that the world controls the mind. The poem gives the appearance of
logical argument, while in fact it represents an exploration in search of
some middle way in which logical distinctions may be blurred and the
paradox resolved. This moderating tendency, the desire to blur distinctions between polarized concepts or categories, besides being characteristic of Ashbery's later work, is characteristic of Bishop, Creeley, and
Merrill as well.

The second section of "*Le livre*" continues to investigate the relationship between mind/art and reality, now using Stevens' symbol of the sea
to represent material reality. Granting "The maker's rage to order words
of the sea" (CP 130), Ashbery's poem questions whether it might have
been only "the dark voice of the sea / That rose" (CP 129) or whether
"all the secrets vanish[ed] when / The woman left" (ST 75). Young Ash-

bery will not assert, as Stevens did in "The Idea of Order at Key West," that "She was the single artificer of the world / In which she sang" (CP 129); less confident, or less willing to proclaim what may be merely a projection of human desire and need, he will only remind us of the questions we must keep asking.

This pseudological discursive mode of later Stevens acquires a permanent place in Ashbery's work. However, Ashbery subsequently abandoned some of Stevens' later techniques with which he experimented in *Some Trees*. Like many other beginning poets refining their craft in the fifties, the young Ashbery sometimes worked in strictly regulated poetic forms. Those he favored tended to require repetition of words or phrases, thereby creating an effect very like that of Stevens' less regulated repetition of key words. Stevens makes some use of repetition in *Harmonium*,[11] but his more characteristic repetitions appear in the later works, where common terms recurring in different positions or relations lend an appearance of simplicity to the presentation of complex and abstract ideas. Typical is the opening of "Description Without Place," which announces the possibility that reality may be simply the appearances we perceive and, further, that perception altered by imagination may alter reality:

> It is possible that to seem – it is to be,
> As the sun is something seeming and it is.
>
> The sun is an example. What it seems
> It is and in such seeming all things are.
>
> Thus things are like a seeming of the sun
> Or like a seeming of the moon or night
>
> Or sleep. It was a queen that made it seem
> By the illustrious nothing of her name.
>
> Her green mind made the world around her green.
> The queen is an example . . . This green queen
>
> In the seeming of the summer of her sun
> By her own seeming made the summer change.   (CP 339)

Though his subject is epistemological, Stevens eschews all philosophical terminology, preferring almost comically simple monosyllables – sun, moon, queen – that one would expect to find in a children's tale. Ashbery's reiteration of concrete and ordinary terms in the three sestinas in *Some Trees*, and the patterned restatement of lines and words in "Pantoum" and "Canzone" create a similar aura of particularity and clarity in difficult and even mystifying poems. At times the mystification seems to result from Ashbery's intending only to investigate what meaning might emerge from placing a limited number of words in variously arranged proximity (something he investigates further in *The Tennis Court Oath*). At other times, Ashbery, like Stevens, is interested in conveying sophisticated concepts while restricting himself to a small and simple vocabulary.

This is the case in "The Painter" (ST 54–5), another Stevens-like third-person narrative, another poem in which the sea symbolizes reality. Stevens' themes abound: the artist's frustrated desire to capture "things as they are" (cf. CP 165, II); the problem of solipsism (is all art self-portraiture?); and the recurrent question from "The Idea of Order at Key West," whether the sea or the self shapes art's order. Some of the ideas, of course, are distinctly Ashbery's; for example, the final whiteness of the canvas on which the painter has captured the sea's portrait reflects Ashbery's notion that "putting it all down" leads ultimately to the same end as "leaving all out" (TP 3). Nonetheless, the writing has a consistently Stevensian character, largely because of the word repetition, which is not limited to the recycling of end-words required in a sestina. "Sea," for instance, not one of these end-words, appears six times; "paint," "painter," and "imagine" also recur. The vocabulary of this poem thus seems as limited, as lean, as that of, say, "Sketch of the Ultimate Politician," which begins:

> He is the final builder of the total building,
> The final dreamer of the total dream,
> Or will be. Building and dream are one.
>
> There is a total building and there is
> A total dream. There are words of this,
> Words, in a storm, that beat around the shapes.
>
> (CP 335)

Since Stevens here intends only to "sketch" his vision of major man as creative political leader, he appropriately limits himself to a few words providing the barest outlines. Similarly, Ashbery appropriately employs a lean vocabulary in creating his brief parable about the experimental artist. "The Painter" concludes with an evasive simile – "the sea devoured the canvas and the brush / As though his subject had decided to remain a prayer" – a final Stevens-like touch that allows the poet to convey the sense of an explanation, a truth glimpsed, without in fact asserting that it is the truth.

Many of the traits that link *Some Trees* to *Harmonium* are not characteristic of Ashbery's later work. The flamboyant language and the emblematic personifications, for example, disappear as Ashbery develops his own more subdued manner and quieter voice. Progressing from his early wholehearted adoption of Stevens' ideas about poetry and the poet, the maturing Ashbery selects those he finds genuinely congenial. He discards some of Stevens' principles, such as his conception of the poet's hieratic role, or his reverence for the poet's "rage to order." Others Ashbery qualifies; for example, Stevens' "necessary fiction" becomes in Ashbery's works an inescapable fiction which is not always a desirable condition of human perception. Still other principles, such as Stevens' desire for poetry to escape stiffening formulations and to capture the activity of consciousness, Ashbery reinforces and extends so that they guide his development of innovative poetic methods.

## II

Ashbery has described the poems in his second volume, *The Tennis Court Oath* (1962), as "automatic poetry": "I wasn't satisfied with the way my work was going and I felt it was time to just clear my head by writing whatever came into it . . . and I think it helped me along."[12] The dramatic shift away from the Stevensian imitations of *Some Trees* (a shift I shall examine in Chapter 2) does seem to have freed Ashbery to get on with "the business of self-discovery," though the volume itself is his least successful. In his next collection, *Rivers and Mountains* (1966), he has discovered his own voice and his own thematic emphases, and manages more subtle manipulation of techniques and principles adapted from Wallace Stevens.[13] Ashbery has moved toward a more discursive mode, employing longer lines grouped in more extended clusters. "Into the Dusk-Charged Air" (RM 17–20) exemplifies Ashbery's modification of the linguistic experiments of *The Tennis Court Oath* in order to create a more communicative poetry, and his adaptation of Stevens' themes to uses distinctly his own.

This playful poem is shaped by the apparently arbitrary requirement that each line mention at least one of the world's rivers. Each river is named only once and is described in a simple coherent sentence. With this amusing device Ashbery jokingly demonstrates the potential for endless variety within the limits of a given framework, as Stevens does in "Sea Surface Full of Clouds." Both poems focus on an aspect of reality that is fluid and moving; but while Stevens demonstrates the limitless inventive power of the fertile imagination, Ashbery exhibits a less flamboyant and more mundane means of enriching one's experience.

Grounding his art in American speech, Ashbery avoids the extravagant ornamentation of Stevens' diction and imagery. The tone of "Into

the Dusk-Charged Air" is matter-of-fact; its lines are often prosaic –
"The Mississippi / Is one of the world's longest rivers, like the Amazon.
/ It has the Missouri for a tributary" – and its figures are frequently trite
– "the Rhine sings its eternal song." Yet the poem shows how much
variety is available within the confines of such familiar language. Ashbery's diction ranges from the formal – "Fat billows encrusted the
Dniester's / Pallid flood" – to the technical – "the Arkansas erodes / Anthracite hummocks" – to the banal – "People walk near the Trent" – to
the colloquial – "The Parana stinks." Even when the poem comes closest
to Stevens' ostentatious sound play – "If . . . the Albany / Arrest your
development, can you resist the Red's / Musk, the Meuse's situation?" –
Ashbery avoids the recherché terms and exaggerated sensuality of "Sea
Surface" – "Like damasks that were shaken off / From the loosed girdles
in the spangling must" (CP 101). Using a predominantly common vocabulary, Ashbery simply varies his sentence structure in order to demonstrate that ordinary language is as variable as the world's rivers, and,
at least potentially, as interesting.

   "Into the Dusk-Charged Air" is only one of a number of poems from
*Rivers and Mountains* demonstrating Ashbery's progress in finding the
kinds of diction that are most meaningful for him. Ashbery's diction,
like Stevens', is varied and widely inclusive, and both poets continually
juxtapose the abstract against the concrete, the formal against the casual.
By the time he was writing *Rivers and Mountains*, however, Ashbery had
established his own range of diction, which descends farther down the
scale of colloquialism than Stevens' – "I'd like to bugger you all up, /
Deliberately falsify all your old suck-ass notions" (RM 41) – and ascends
less high into the realm of elaborate decoration. Stevens believes "that in
poetry bigness and gaity are precious characteristics of the diction" (NA
152), and he therefore tries to bring new life to fancy words that have
disappeared into dusty lexicons. By contrast, Ashbery, in his mature work,
strives to revitalize the worn prosaic language of clichéd discourse and
folk aphorisms. Recently he explained: "I am interested very much in
debased and demotic forms of expression. . . . They often seem so much
more moving than something that is beautifully phrased and composed,"
and he went on to describe their use, in modernist terminology, as an
attempt "to sort of purify the language of the tribe."[14]

   A tongue-in-cheek manner, a campiness whose self-mockery almost
disguises sincerity, usually accompanies Ashbery's most heavy-handed
clichés. Yet these exaggeratedly trite statements are almost always mixed
with or closely followed by less conventional formulations reinforcing
the same notions; thus the reader cannot mistake the poet's underlying
seriousness. For example, in "The Ecclesiast" (RM 21–2) Ashbery pre-

sents the lamentable universality and "humdrum"-ness of suffering in language that is not only proverbial, but also so heavily overlaid with clichés that one might be tempted to dismiss as disdainful mockery the third verse paragraph: "For the shoe pinches, even though it fits perfectly. / Apples were made to be gathered, also the whole host of the world's ailments and troubles." One cannot do so, however, since the bleak perspective of these lines is legitimized (as well as alleviated) in the movingly direct lines that follow: "and across the sunlight darkness is taking root anew / In intense activity. You shall never have seen it just this way / And that is to be your one reward." Though no more enamored of stale formulas from the past than were the modernists, Ashbery recognizes that "when people are trying desperately to communicate some deep feeling they usually do it rather awkwardly and clumsily; this has a pathos built into it that some more literary form of expression wouldn't have";[15] his poetry capitalizes on that aspect of our speech. By slightly modifying hackneyed phrases or by mixing clichés with less banal diction, he infuses fresh energy into worn expressions, highlighting the meaning they do in fact carry.

Ashbery's most earnest declarations of feeling are now usually distinguished by slack syntax and casual diction – "What is agreeable / Is to hold your hand. The gravel / Underfoot. The time is for coming close" (RM 14) – sometimes interspersed with simple lyricism –

> I prefer "you" in the plural, I want "you,"
> You must come to me, all golden and pale
> Like the dew and the air.
> And then I start getting this feeling of exaltation.     (RM 26)

Expressing his more private feelings in language that slides easily into cliché not only approximates emotionally charged speech; it also allows Ashbery to control a complex dual tone in which he simultaneously makes a sincere statement and comments wryly upon it. For instance, the lines "You must not, then, / Be very surprised if I am alone: it is all for you, / The night, and the stars, and the way we used to be" (RM 14) contain a genuine lament, but their ironic humor indicates that the speaker has some perspective on his own self-indulgence, and on the commonness of his situation.

The refined control of shifting tones and the increasing sureness of voice in *Rivers and Mountains* accompany the appearance of those subjects which predominate in Ashbery's later work. (I use "subjects" loosely, since, as the poet has stated, "There are no themes or subjects in the usual sense, except the very broad one of an individual consciousness confronting or confronted by a world of external phenomena.")[16] *Rivers and*

*Mountains* is the first volume in which Ashbery's interest in poetry as a record of mental process is clearly apprehensible. Here again Stevens is surely a guide, for it is he who defined modern poetry as "The poem of the mind in the act of finding / What will suffice" (CP 239) and who emphasized that poetry is a process in a constantly advancing present. Ashbery's central interests diverge from Stevens', but they stem from the same sources and look to many of the same ends. Both men are content to be "Thinkers without final thoughts / In an always incipient cosmos" (OP 115), or, in Ashbery's words, "continuing but ever beginning / My perennial voyage" (RM 44).

Ashbery's "subject" revolves around broad epistemological questions to which he, like Stevens, offers varied and often contradictory answers. Since both poets paradoxically identify flux as the only constant in the universe, both are intent on being true to ever-changing perceptions rather than trying to establish any fixed truths. Truth, for which they do search, is a relative matter, more locatable in the process of searching than in any point reached:

> Each moment
> Of utterance is the true one; likewise none are true,
> Only is the bounding from air to air, a serpentine
> Gesture which hides the truth behind a congruent
> Message, the way air hides the sky.   (RM 27)

Ashbery has found striking ways to embody in his poetic techniques this conviction that what most closely corresponds to truth can be mirrored only in the motion between one moment of consciousness and the next. In the late 1960s Ashbery explained that the characteristic devices of his verse – "ellipses, frequent changes of tone, voice (that is, the narrator's voice), point of view" – are intended "to give an impression of flux."[17] Eliminating many of the clues by which readers customarily link particular passages to earlier and later ones, these techniques serve to bind the reader to the immediate moment in the poem. The reader is thereby forced to participate in the poet's metaphysical stance, to "[have] / the progression of minutes by accepting them, as one accepts drops of rain / as they form a shower, and without worrying about the fine weather that will come after" (RM 32). In Ashbery's mature work there is an insistence, both thematic and technical, on the certitude of continual change, on the irreducible complexity of experience, and on the necessity of accepting both these conditions.

The constant evasion of perception and articulation by protean reality or truth is the thematic focus of "Clepsydra" (RM 27–33), the poem that

marks Ashbery's full entrance into the meditative and abstractly metaphysical mode of late Stevens. The poem's opening demonstrates that
Ashbery is further developing Stevens' method of giving fullness to abstractions by referring frequently to concrete objects and ordinary phenomena; both poets describe realms that are at once "mysterious and
near" (RM 28). The question that opens "Clepsydra," "Hasn't the sky?"
would seem to arise from a specific context, as if abstracted from the
middle of a particular dialogue. The narration and explanation that follow also seem tied to an actual moment and landscape; but because all
antecedents are missing, the concrete terms take on a metaphorical quality without their figurative reference being clear. Not until the tenth line
is it apparent that "Hasn't the sky?" is a truncated form of the perennial
human query about the nature of the "basic principle operating behind"
the universe. We are then told that the answer is as ungraspable as a
mirage, as obscure as the motion of river fronds, as unfixable as a waterfall that is perpetually descending to another level.

The poem is a mimetic representation of that figurative waterfall or
waterclock (a clepsydra is a waterclock); the movement of its "stream"
of consciousness might be temporarily allayed by a solipsistic stance –
we "are / The reply that prompted the question" – but this peace is as
ephemeral as all other "truths." Momentary flashes of insight are the
most one can hope for: "it was these / Moments that were the truth,
although each tapered / Into the distant surrounding night." As the poem
goes on to explore the nature of these moments, the question of their
permanence and coherence, and the meaning of the time that surrounds
them, its remarkably extended syntax reflects the uninterrupted flow of
a searching consciousness. Stevens' syntax is most certainly a model here,
since one of Stevens' most distinctive skills is his ability to draw out a
single sentence over as many as eighteen lines (see, for example, CP 466,
II) by using appositives and qualifications. Moreover, Stevens' use of
extended syntax reflects the same concerns that apparently motivate Ashbery's: a desire to capture the world's undulation in one's syntax, and a
belief that an object or experience can be rendered most accurately by an
inclusive portrayal in which the whole can be understood from the "sum
of its complications" (NA 87).

Good examples of Ashbery's typical methods of syntactic elaboration
and suspension are provided by two consecutive sentences from "Clepsydra" (RM 29, ll. 16–36). The first of these, which begins, "There was
only a breathless waste," is ten lines long. The second and third lines are
an apposite description of "breathless waste," developing Ashbery's revision of the Biblical proposition, "In the beginning was the Word." The

next four lines qualify the idea presented in the previous three, beginning with the mock-academic formulation, "Though one must not forget that the nature of this / Emptiness, these previsions, / Was that . . ." Again, terms are expanded in figurative appositives typical of Stevens before moving into a further qualification introduced by "except that . . ." Ashbery extends the second of these sentences over eleven lines by using a protracted simile that describes the way "an imaginary feeling" "protected its events and pauses" in terms of a telescope's "protection" of a distant mountain vista. He develops the simile in such detail that the mountain scene, originally merely a tangential comparison, becomes the object of focus. On the next page he offers an alternative simile, again elaborated for a number of lines until a slight shift in the poem's focus again takes place. In these ways, Ashbery recreates the meandering of human consciousness in a world without fixed truths. Even where the sentences are shorter, Ashbery relies heavily on logical terms of contradiction and qualification, such as "but" and "although." This reflects his epistemological faith that the most lasting and truthful perspectives are those which are "complicated like the torrent / In new dark passages" – literary as well as geological.

Because Ashbery tries to render the complexity of individual consciousness as he finds it, paradox is as prevalent in his work as it is in Stevens'. Some of these paradoxes are simple and rather common, being based on the mind's ability to entertain contradictory emotions simultaneously – e.g., "a feeling, again, of emptiness, but of richness" (RM 30). Others are conceptually more difficult; for example, it is the "egotistical" "blindness" of what I take to be two lovers (though they might be two aspects of one consciousness) "turned in on each other" to the exclusion of the rest of the world which allows them access to clear visions of that world. These moments of clarity, in turn, are ephemeral and ungraspable yet permanent, isolated yet joined. What happens in any moment is distinct, intended for that moment alone; nonetheless that present is impossible to locate, scarcely called into being before it is gone. Like Stevens' paradoxes, and his proliferating resemblances and metaphors, Ashbery's paradoxes point ultimately toward an affirmation of essential unity in the cosmos.[18] Ashbery's universe is like a mobius strip – a "single and twin existence" – and by accepting the twists of paradox the poem is able to speak affirmatively: "In this way any direction taken was the right one, / Leading first to you, and through you to / My self that is beyond you and which is the same thing as space" (RM 32).

Ashbery shares some of Stevens' "passion for yes" (CP 320), but the contemporary poet, typical of his generation, restricts his affirmation within narrower limits. Though there may be a "sphere of pure wisdom," according to Ashbery we shall never see in it more than groping shadows, and even this reductive experience we shall retain only as if it were the impression left by a powerful dream. Unable to celebrate presences, Ashbery takes comfort in "non-absence" (RM 27).

The semantic content of Ashbery's lines therefore tends to reinforce the doubting aspect of Stevens' qualified assertions. Comparing Ashbery's uses of Stevensian linguistic patterns in *Rivers and Mountains* to those in *Some Trees*, one is more conscious of the absence of buoyant optimism in the later volume. There is nothing particularly cheering about statements like these from "Clepsydra":

> There should be an invariable balance of
> Contentment to hold everything in place, ministering
> To stunted memories, helping them stand alone
> And return into the world

or

> It may be assumed that you have won, that this
> Wooden and external representation
> Returns the full echo of what you meant

or

>       and you
> Must wear them like clothing, moving in the shadow of
> Your single and twin existence, waking in intact
> Appreciation of it, while morning is still and before the
>     body
> Is changed by the faces of evening.

Yet the very moderation of such statements gives them an aura of authority and wisdom that is nonetheless reassuring and affirming.

Ashbery shares with Stevens, or rather with Stevens at the sober wintry end of his polarized vision, a sense of humanity's isolation in the cosmos. Both poets regard poetry as an attempt to bridge the gap between consciousness and the world. While Ashbery is more conscious of the limits of what words or imagination can accomplish – of "the dividing force / Between our slightest steps and the notes taken on them" (RM 32) – both men concur that "From this the poem springs: that we live in a place / That is not our own and, much more, not ourselves / And hard it is in spite of blazoned days" (CP 383). This painful sense of alienation provides the impulse for "The Skaters," the long poem that culminates *Rivers and Mountains*.

The themes explored in "The Skaters" overlap those that Stevens usu-

ally investigates – the value of the imagination, the artist's "rage to order," the necessity that art discard old forms and replace them with fresh
ones. A more sophisticated version of "The Instruction Manual," "The
Skaters" centers on the playful presentation of imaginative voyages. But
this more philosophical poem is less concerned with the realms to which
the imagination transports us than with the processes of voyaging and
returning, of integrating imaginative experience into ordinary experience, and of relating the order established in art to the order or disorder
of reality. The structure and style of the poem reflect the complexity and
fluidity of these ideas and of the experiences from which they derive.

Like Stevens' later long poems, which are structured to follow the
movement of the thinking mind, "The Skaters" does not progress from
a particular starting point to a climactic finish. Instead, its form is like a
musical theme and variations in which the same ideas recur, though examined from varied perspectives and in different styles as by a mind
attempting to refine its understanding. Thus the four numbered sections,
though distinct, are more complementary than progressive. Section I focuses primarily on memories of childhood attempts to escape boredom
and loneliness through imaginative adventure.[19] Section II is a collage of
visions of adult travel – some remembered, some imagined – which appear and collapse, creating a sense of disconcerting impermanence and
wondrous inventive fertility. Section III presents a generally more propositional and analytic examination of imaginative voyaging. Section IV
provides an acceleration of shifting scenes, images, and voices, until from
the spinning fragments of life, real and imagined, arises a momentary
vision of perfect (artificial) order. These sections are interdependent in
motifs as well as themes; the perspective lines and the skaters' lengthening arches of section I appear repeatedly in later sections. Moreover, each
section, like the waterfall of "Clepsydra," perpetually "Drums at different levels" (RM 27) as the narration shifts from academic exposition, to
lyrical description, to metaphysical elaboration, to clichéd visions in archaic diction, to reflexive commentary on the poem itself or of the poet's
voices upon each other.

The whole poem moves like the skaters who

> elaborate their distances,
> Taking a separate line to its end. Returning to the mass,
>     they join each other
> Blotted in an incredible mess of dark colors, and again
>     reappearing to take the theme
> Some little distance.    (RM 37)

Therefore what is important, as Ashbery declares, is not an individual passage or even the impression made by the whole, but rather the action by which it is created and the structure in which it unfolds. What is of interest is the mind in the act of finding – "The rhythm of the series of repeated jumps, from abstract into positive and back to a slightly less diluted abstract" (RM 39).

Given their shared preoccupation with change and process, it is not surprising that Stevens and Ashbery rely heavily on a common group of images and metaphors, notably ones involving weather and climate – sun, snow, clouds, etc. – and the stages within temporal cycles – day and night, winter and summer, morning and afternoon. In Stevens' work these terms can be grouped into orderly systems so that certain mental states, ideas, colors, and places are linked to particular seasons.[20] Ashbery is not interested in such neatly arranged correspondences, but "The Skaters" demonstrates that by the mid-sixties Ashbery was using terms denoting environmental conditions in extended metaphors for inner states.

Though Ashbery develops key metaphors over the course of the entire long poem, he does not, as Stevens does, sustain them on a consistent metaphorical plane. Believing that if a poem "keep[s] harping on this traditional imagery[,] the reader will not have been taken in" (RM 58), Ashbery keeps one step ahead of his reader by ostentatiously shifting back and forth between the literal and metaphorical. "The Skaters," like Stevens' "The Comedian as the Letter C," relies on the ancient trope by which a voyage represents both the progress of life and the process of self-discovery. Aware that his readers will be familiar with this convention, Ashbery calls attention to his own artifice by providing obvious clues for distinguishing literal from imaginative and metaphorical voyaging. Presenting so many scenes as pure fantasy to begin with, Ashbery's anticipatory deflation forestalls his readers' feeling smug or bored when they recognize, for instance, that a rainy day is a projection of the speaker's dampened spirits, and an alligator-infested swamp his slough of despond (RM 45). Making these meanings obvious challenges the reader to examine more closely the mysterious mental process that brings the speaker to the point where "again the weather is fine and clear" and the journey "is on."

Humorously calling attention to the conventional nature of his figures, Ashbery implies that images are fun-filled decoration, not exact revelation. "The human brain, with its tray of images / Seems a sorcerer's magic lantern" (RM 36), and Ashbery takes pleasure in sleight of hand. By transforming the "maple seed pods . . . spattering down" into "birch pods . . . clattering down," into "magnolia blossoms" that "fall with a plop" in section IV, Ashbery pursues Stevens' principle that the "motive for metaphor" is to provide the "exhilaration of changes" (CP 288). Ashbery entertains his reader by exhilarating shifts in his images, any of which can exemplify – but may also modify – a single governing process.[21]

Ashbery has an additional reason for undercutting the more clichéd figures he uses, and that is genuine ambivalence; clichés are both true and dangerous, useful and inadequate. For Ashbery, all verbal formulations are "a kind of flagellation, an entity of sound / Into which being enters, and is apart" (RM 34). That is to say, words become an essential part of the experience they signify, yet there is an unavoidable gap between expression and experience. Words are valuable since they do "[bring] down meaning," but they offer a dangerous temptation to falsify in accordance with "wishful thinking."

Ashbery often links this "wishful thinking" with traditional patterns of language and thought. When he wishes to emphasize that an attitude is particularly reductive in its simple optimism, he often uses diction and syntax that are not only clichéd but archaic:

> And away they pour, in the sulferous sunlight,
> To the aqua and silver waters where stands the glistening
>     white ship
> And into the great vessel they flood, a motley and happy
>     crowd
> Chanting and pouring down hymns on the surface of the
>     ocean.   (RM 46)

In so doing, Ashbery stresses that comfortably traditional perspectives, here dramatized by the insipidly happy crowd "pouring down hymns," are too familiar and too easy; the contemporary poet, by contrast, "is best / Face to face with the unsmiling alternatives of his nerve-wracking existence. / Placed squarely in front of his dilemma, on all fours before the lamentable spectacle of the unknown" (RM 40–1). This conviction is in line with modernist principles, as is Ashbery's dictum that the world should be purged of all trash from the past (RM 37, 49). To accomplish this "general housekeeping" Ashbery here institutes the poetic "flame fountain" in which conventional scenes appear only momentarily "in the gaps in the smoke" before they are effaced.

Nonetheless, as we saw in "Clepsydra," Ashbery's hopes concerning the power of poetry are somewhat less sanguine than Stevens'. Despite Ashbery's desire for novelty and freshness, the scenes he paints remain essentially conventional. Moreover, he no longer shares Stevens' confidence in the artist's ability to shape words in new ways that will enlarge people's thinking and enable them to attain more noble, more heroic stature. The poet's attempts to develop new, more sophisticated forms of "finer expression" are frustrated because "The human mind / Cannot retain anything except perhaps the dismal two-note theme / Of some sodden 'dump' or lament" (RM 34). The poet therefore finds himself trapped: "So back we go to the old, imprecise feelings, the / Common knowledge, the importance of duly suffering and the occasional glimpses / Of some balmy felicity" (RM 40). Words, like the painter's perspective lines, provide only a seeming order. Speaking of the ordering effect of these and, by extension, of poetic lines, Ashbery says they provide

> some comfort after all, for our volition to see
>     must needs condition these phenomena to a
>     certain degree.
> But it would be rash to derive too much confidence
>     from a situation which, in the last analysis,
>     scarcely warrants it.
> What I said first goes: sleep, death, and hollyhocks
> And a new twilight stained, perhaps, a slightly
>     unearthlier periwinkle blue,
> But no dramatic arguments for survival, and please
>     no magic justification of results.   (RM 53)

While Stevens asserts that "A candle is enough to light the world. / It makes it clear" (CP 172), Ashbery will only go so far as to declare that the poet's task is "to hold the candle up to the album" (RM 41).[22] He makes no proclamations about the clarity of that small illumination, nor does he strike a hieratic pose. Nonetheless, as one who colors the sky a "slightly unearthlier" shade, Ashbery is carrying on, in chastened form, the Romantic tradition in which the poet acts as private interpreter of the heavens. Ashbery's Romantic roots, which are also Stevens', are most apparent in his next volume, *The Double Dream of Spring* (1970).

## III

Some of the ways in which Ashbery's work grows out of the Romantic tradition have already been suggested: his dissatisfaction with inherited forms and restrictions within which one (supposedly) cannot accurately reflect reality; his aspiration toward originality;[23] his use of materials from common life and ordinary speech; his probing of individual experience; his focus on the imagination, on its place and powers in a world unlike itself. Ashbery's awareness of the division between his own conscious nature and the unconscious world that surrounds him suggests, as Pinsky has noted (speaking not just of Ashbery but of contemporary poetry in general),

> a continuity between contemporary and modernist poetry – and, beyond that, a continuity with the Romantic poetry of the nineteenth century. Monumental and familiar, the conflicts are between conscious and unconscious forces within the mind: between the idea of experience as unreflective, a flow of absolutely particular moments, and the reality of language as reflective, an arrangement of perfectly abstract categories.[24]

Pinsky demonstrates that these broad conflicts have been inherited by virtually every modern poet, and that "it sometimes seems hard to find a modern poem which does not touch on the problem at least glancingly, as a kind of second subject."[25] What is striking about *The Double Dream of Spring*, however, is the number of its poems in which these conflicts are the primary subject. Furthermore, the volume is notably more lyrical than those preceding, and rural settings are more frequent. In typical Romantic fashion, a landscape or a particular scene often provides the stimulus for the speaker's meditation; his private problems present occasions for exploring universal dilemmas. The poet/speaker is repeatedly presented as a quester or pilgrim advancing into the unknown, seeking to understand his place in a mysterious cosmos. The passage of time, the role of memory, and the relation of the individual's past to his present and future are dominant themes. The poems of *Double Dream* demonstrate that Ashbery's modifications of Romantic techniques and ideas are extensions of the modifications that Stevens imposed.

Most of the nineteenth-century English Romantics and their American transcendentalist counterparts valued the imagination as a unifying or reconciling power through which one could perceive the unity of one's mind with the divine power governing and infusing nature. The imagination was itself godlike, being, in Coleridge's words, "a repetition in the finite mind of the eternal act of creation in the infinite I AM."[26] Stevens' theory of the imagination involves a shift in emphasis appropriate to a more thoroughly skeptical age; for him what the imagination provides is explicitly a substitute for the divine, rather than a connection with or reenactment of divine creation. "After one has abandoned a belief in god," Stevens says, "poetry is that essence which takes its place as life's redemption" (OP 158). The imagination's role is to produce the supreme fiction that "must take the place / Of empty heaven and its hymns" (CP 167). Stevens celebrates the artist's ability to renew "the fiction of an absolute" (CP 404). In his opinion, "The final belief is to believe in a fiction, which you know to be a fiction, there being nothing else. The exquisite truth is to know that it is a fiction and that you believe in it willingly" (OP 163).

Ashbery, who shares Stevens' skepticism about the existence of any nonfictive ordering ideal, is less "willing" – or less desperate – to believe in the imagination's fictive replacement. If imaginative perception of beauty and order does not accord with external reality, why grasp after absolutes? Though he himself may live in part according to fictions which assign meaning and impose order, he seems to feel more ambivalence about the fantastic nature of these supports than Stevens does. Humankind, Ashbery states, is simply "fond of plotting itineraries" and "our foreshortened memories will keep us going" (DD 31–2). What remains for him to celebrate is that people *do* keep going, even when they are conscious that, in fact, "There was never any excuse for this" (DD 32).

Although frequently undercutting or mocking imaginative embellishment or organization of reality, Ashbery acknowledges the need for fictions that allow us to feel at home and in control: "But the fantasy makes it ours, a kind of fence-sitting / Raised to the level of an esthetic ideal" (DD 18). He freely concedes that his aesthetic practices rest on a falsifying base, one that he nonetheless accepts because it tempers harsh experience and helps us in "learning to accept / The charity of the hard moments as they are doled out" (DD 19).

Such "fence-sitting" is evident in the volume's attitudes toward language and perception. The Romantics strove to portray their feelings accurately by binding themselves to careful description of their own immediate perceptions. In order to replace received truths with original and private ones, or at least with original formulations, they looked to the particulars of experience. Stevens, too, was attuned to the "difference between the and an" (CP 255) and claimed that poetry conveys knowledge of reality through its attention to "things" (a central modernist doctrine). Despite the notable abstraction of his poetry, Stevens sought an "abstraction blooded" and tried to root his poetry in observations made "with a clinging eye." Like Stevens and the Romantics, Ashbery values particularity, but he lacks faith in the mind's ability to hold or convey authentic details. Moreover, the language available to Ashbery as a contemporary poet is not suited to conveying fresh perceptions of the physical world.

This is made clear in "Definition of Blue" (DD 53–4), a mock-academic, but nonetheless serious, statement about the problems encountered by a post-Romantic postmodernist poet who is committed to the inherited values of individuality and originality. His society is one in which "mass practices have sought to submerge the personality," and irremediable "packaging" has "supplanted the old [i.e., immediate, particular] sensations." Moreover, "today there is no point in looking to imaginative new methods / Since all of them are in constant use." The contemporary poet is condemned to work with timeworn or debased language and techniques. But Ashbery affirms that this medium can nonetheless contribute not only to the accuracy of art's general portrait of "all being" but also to the understanding of "the exact value" of the individual in his or her particular time and place:

> The most that can be said for them [i.e., the methods
>     in use] further
> Is that erosion produces a kind of dust or exaggerated pum-
>     ice
> Which fills space and transforms it, becoming a medium
> In which it is possible to recognize oneself.

Thus the apparently parodic versions of traditional motifs – such as those involving quest and pilgrimage – and of traditional lyric forms – such as the aphoristic rhymed couplets of "Some Words" – are seriously, as well as mockingly, intended. The element of parody, indicating the author's half-apologetic embarrassment, protects him against charges of sentimentality while allowing him to use these formulas as genuine expressions of his ideas.[27]

At the same time, "fence-sitting" Ashbery does not abandon his attempts to "make it new" and to strip his poetic language of what Shelley termed the "veil of familiarity."[28] "For John Clare" (DD 35–6) and "French Poems" (DD 37–40) – both concerned with the difficulty of taking in, retaining, and expressing the particulars of experience, and the danger of missing the world's "indescribable fineness" through perceiving only "infinite quantities" – exemplify two of the methods by which Ashbery attempts to freshen poetic language.

The lyric addressed to the minor Romantic poet Clare exploits the resources of prose as a flexible vehicle for creating new effects. The prose is jagged, full of sentence fragments and ellipses, but its rhythms and diction convey the effect of speech idiom:

> There ought to be room for more things, for a spreading out, like. Being immersed in the details of rock and field and slope – letting them come to you for once, and then meeting them halfway would be so much easier – .

Casual syntax and colloquial language are mixed with more academic formulations and vocabulary – "it is possible that finally, like coming to the end of a long, barely perceptible rise, there is a mutual cohesion and interaction" – and with vivid description – "The pollarded trees scarcely bucking the wind . . . Clabbered sky." Such prose (which Ashbery will explore more fully in his next volume, *Three Poems*) has strong affinities with Stevens' discursiveness, though Ashbery's mild voice avoids the magisterial tone prevalent in Stevens' late work. Stevens, too, relies heavily on prose rhythms and prose syntax. Nominative constructions, such as "it is possible that," or "there is," are common in his poetry also. Stevens often uses academic rhetoric, which, though sometimes mockingly presented, nonetheless propounds his own doctrines.[29] And of course, as we have noted, Stevens too favors conditional terms such as "ought" and "would." Most importantly, both poets rely on varied voices and varied diction to give authenticity to conglomerates formed from "sacked speech" (CP 530).

"French Poems" demonstrates a different tack Ashbery sometimes takes in attempting linguistic renewal. As stated in the notes at the end of the volume, he first wrote these pieces in French and then translated them into English "with the idea of avoiding customary word-patterns and associations." Though the poems are arranged in verse lines, their syntax suggests elegant prose, and the generally lengthy sentences flow smoothly. Yet there is an unfamiliarity, a slight stiffness in the sentence construction: "But the existence of all these things and especially / The amazing fullness of their number must be / For us a source of unforgettable questions." In addition, the similes and explanatory elaborations in "French Poems," though employing concrete terms, are elusive and give a quality of strangeness to familiar words and ordinary syntax:

> All kinds of things exist, and, what is more,
> Specimens of these things, which do not make themselves
>     known.
> I am speaking of the laugh of the squire and the spur
> Which are like a hole in the armor of the day.

Similar surprising details and unexpected words or constructions appear in many poems that are not translations, so that Ashbery's language often appears almost divorced from a referential function. Stevens' exotic diction and his propensity for sound-symbolic words give a similar, if less extreme, autonomy to his poetic language; "It is a world of words to the end of it" (CP 345).

The aesthetic and epistemological principles behind Ashbery's idiosyncratic choice of terms and images are largely the same as those determining the strange terminology in which Stevens outlines his "mundo." Both poets are attempting to refine and redefine concepts that have been evolving for centuries; the oddness of their formulations grows naturally from their desire for an accuracy which they believe lacking in conven-

tional patterns of expression. This is why critics who insist on translating
Stevens' terms risk distorting, and often do distort, his ideas. This is why
Ashbery as art critic reserves his highest praise for those whose work
cannot be explained in any terms other than its own. In discussing the
work of Brice Marden, for instance, Ashbery declares, "To create a work
of art that the critic cannot even begin to talk about ought to be the
artist's chief concern"; reviewing an exhibit of work by Jasper Johns, he
remarks, "Johns is one of the very few young painters of today whose
work seems to defy critical analysis, and this is precisely a sign of its
power – it can't be explained in any other terms than its own, and is
therefore necessary"; analyzing why "the twentieth century, whatever
else it may be, is the century of Matisse, Picasso, and Gertrude Stein,"
and why the adventurous works of Stein and Picasso remain so tremendously exciting, Ashbery explains, "Both Picasso and Gertrude Stein
manage to escape critical judgement by working in a climate where it
simply could not exist. Picasso sets up new forms whose newness protects them from criticism: there are no standards by which to judge them
except the painter's own as gleaned from other works by him."[30] Not
surprisingly, Ashbery is fond of quoting Stevens' phrase, "a completely
new set of objects," as the goal of an artist's creation.[31]

Like many twentieth-century artists, Ashbery and Stevens strive for
an art that is rooted in the ordinary and banal while revealing the world's
awesome mysteriousness – "The extreme of the known in the presence
of the extreme / Of the unknown" (CP 508). However, when deriving
the ordinary materials of their poetry from autobiographical sources, these
two are notably more impersonal than most of their contemporaries.
Stevens writes poems about the cities he knows best, New Haven and
Hartford, about the Connecticut River, about his Zeller ancestors, and
occasionally about specific autobiographical events such as an afternoon
spent bathing in a stream (CP 371). But in so doing he allows his readers
little insight into his own personality, his private life, or his personal
positions on political or social issues. Instead, he uses his own environment and experience to exemplify the most universal conditions. Thus
the Connecticut River, while retaining its local identity, becomes something of ultimate value, as indicated by the phrase "river of rivers" which
echoes the Nicene creed's "deum de deo, lumen do lumine" (CP 533).

Ashbery may draw more on personal, especially erotic, relationships,
but he maintains a comparable veil over his experiences: "What I am
trying to get at is a general, all-purpose experience – like those stretch
socks that fit all sizes."[32] Steering widely clear of the confessional, Ashbery favors the impersonalized pronoun "he" which, as Bloom points
out,[33] may have been adopted from Stevens. (Auden's example would

also encourage this choice.) His experiences, if discernible, are merely occasions for universalizing meditations. "The Bungalows" (DD 70–2) provides a good example of Ashbery's use of what might be autobiographical material. From the opening verse paragraph we may piece together the outlines of a particular situation: a possibly autobiographical "we" are on their way to a rural vacation spot where they are to stay in bungalows. Though they are beyond the city's "gray steel towers," their destination is not yet in view, and they are eagerly anticipating viewing that landscape and being joined by some friends. Knowing that their impatience is profitless, "we" are trying, with little success, "to stay in immediate relation" to the tangible things around them. After the opening lines this situation is not referred to, except as a symbol. The "presumed landscape" of the bungalows becomes an emblem of the universal "dream of home," which leads into commentary on contemporary society's destructive alienation from natural objects of desire. This in turn leads into a debate on the proper role of art in this culture – whether art should continue to uphold traditional ideals or reflect the triviality of contemporary reality.

The personal "we" disappears in all this, being replaced by a general societal "we" –

> During Coca-cola lessons it becomes patent
> Of noise on the left, and we had so skipped a stage that
> The great wave of the past, compounded in derision,
> Submerged idea and non–dreamer alike

– or the editorial "we" of an assumed pompous voice – "We shall very soon have the pleasure of recording / A period of unanimous tergiversation in this respect." "You" is used to address society at large – "you who were directionless," "you have gone into your houses and shut the doors." By the final verse paragraph the poet has withdrawn into his own mind; he reflexively examines his art ("you even avoided / The monotony of perfection by leaving in certain flaws"), now using the second person pronoun to address an aspect of himself. While such a "you" might include the reader, here the ironic presentation of "you" as one who tries to satisfy both critical camps presented earlier, carefully planning his art's development while building into that plan the appearance of directionlessness, has a distancing effect. The poem concludes with a backing off movement typical of Stevens' qualification. Compare, for example, "From oriole to crow, not the decline / In music. Crow is realist. But, then, / Oriole, also, may be realist" (CP 154) with "For standing still means death, and life is moving on, / Moving on towards death. But sometimes standing still is also life" (DD 72).

"Fragment," the 500–line poem that concludes *The Double Dream of Spring*, provides an even more striking example of Ashbery's depersonalizing of personal materials.[34] For Ashbery, far more than for Stevens, human love and sexuality, the tremendous value and the terrible difficulty of human contact, are recurrent themes. His own love affairs and friendships can frequently be glimpsed in his poetry, but the glimpses are brief, the situations immediately generalized into larger abstractions. In "Fragment," the ending of a relationship and the consequent beginning of a new stage in life prompt the poet's elaborate, sometimes impenetrable, ruminations on one's need to feel in control of one's life, on the human propensity for ordering experience, on the problematic relationship between one's internal world and external phenomena. Yet the poem is never less opaque in its personal revelations than in the following passage referring to an "incident" that is never identified:

> Gradually old letters used as bookmarks
> Inform the neighbors; an approximate version
> Circulates and the incident is officially closed.
> And I some joy of this have, returning to the throbbing
> Mirror's stiff enclave, the sides of my face steep and over-
> run.

>                                                          (DD 84)

Pronouns shift apparently at random so that the narrator retains no distinct identity, and "we are somehow all aspects of a consciousness giving rise to the poem."[35] The autobiographical situation (if it is one) remains an emblem, evidence "that two people could / Collide in this dusk" (DD 90), that human contact, though rare and fleeting, is nonetheless possible.

Ashbery, then, is like Stevens in that, as Kenner said of the older poet, his work takes "little interest in the bared heart."[36] Nonetheless, a distinction must be drawn between them here, since Ashbery does convey a sense that his ideas grow out of private events and interactions, even though the events and their agents remain undisclosed. Intimate contexts, and a confidential relationship with the reader, are implicit in much of his mature poetry. Many of the most moving and successful poems in *Double Dream* derive their emotional power and their air of sincere engagement from strategic limited use of a quite personal tone or of apparently private experience. For example, "Rural Objects" (DD 43–5), a troubled examination of how "Even at the beginning the manner of the hourglass / Was all-severing," is sometimes addressed to a "you" for whom the speaker seems to care deeply – "This is why I look at you / With the eyes you once liked so much in animals." "Summer" (DD 20), which is concerned with the inevitable gap between an event and "the sobering 'later on,' / When you consider what a thing meant, and put it down," also occasionally seems addressed to a close friend – "just as life is divided up / Between you and me, and among all the others out there." Feeling addressed as that "you," readers listen more attentively, responding as if to an act of trust. Again in "Evening in the Country" (DD 33–4) – reminiscent of "Tintern Abbey" – general topics such as the "corruption of the city" or "the process of purification" assume the interest of personal concerns because the poem's context is one of personal emotion: "I am still completely happy."

Ashbery's controlled use of personal elements conveys a sense of sincere urgency which Stevens attains largely through exclamation and exhortation. Since the scope of Ashbery's affirmations is vastly reduced from Stevens', the magisterial pose and noble proclamation of Stevens' late work would be unsuitable. At the same time, Ashbery's use of the personal furthers the impression that he is accurately rendering mental processes, including the inevitable weaving of private experience into reflection.

Having evolved many of his own techniques from the works of Stevens, Ashbery since *The Double Dream of Spring* has diverged increasingly from his modernist mentor. Nonetheless, Stevens' idiom can be heard in undertones throughout much of Ashbery's later poetry. Moreover, Stevens' desire to represent "the act of the mind" has been a guiding principle for all Ashbery's more recent experiments. The mental process that most interested Stevens, however, was that of the imagination creating a fiction which "mediates between the requirements of desire and the conditions of reality."[37] Thus, as Helen Vendler has pointed out, although it was Stevens' "announced intent to remain the poet of reality, to 'hasp on the surviving form / Of shall or ought to be in is,' " nonetheless "again and again, he found himself seduced away to what ought to be, forsaking all description and reporting of present and past in favor of the normative and the optative, the willed and the desired."[38] In Ashbery's effort to be a poet of reality, as subsequent volumes will demonstrate, he strenuously resists such seduction. Without any naive pretense that fictive mediation is finally escapable, he nonetheless strives to hold his poems to the present by attempting to illustrate in them the mundane yet mysterious processes by which the world is immediately apprehended.

# 2 "We must, we must be moving on": Ashbery's divergence from Stevens and modernism

"There is no real alternative to innovation," Ashbery has declared, "and the artist, if he is to survive, cannot leave art where he found it."[1] "In art . . . any change has to be for the better, since it shows that the artist hasn't yet given in to the ever-present temptation to stand still and that his constantly menaced vitality is emitting signals."[2] Ashbery's own vitality – his energetic "will to discover" and his engagement in the "discovery of new forms"[3] – is chronicled in eleven collections of poems to date, each documenting his commitment to artistic experimentation.

This innovative spirit is part of the modernist inheritance, epitomized in Pound's dictum, "Make it new." But while the modernists provided Ashbery with a theory propelling him toward innovation, obviously they could not provide techniques he might use in rejecting or transforming their own example; to use Ashbery's paradoxical phrasing (actually a paraphrase of Busoni), "the best way to follow a great example is by turning away from it, since its importance is in its singularity, and that is by definition inimitable."[4]

In the late 1940s Ashbery's need to "turn away from" the modernists was compounded by the academic establishment's codification of modernist practices (particularly those of Eliot and Pound) into a set of prescriptions.[5] He was determined not to be ensnared by these rules: "No one with a sense of adventure," he has recalled, "was going to be drawn to the academic poetry that flourished at that time."[6] Because of his historical situation, Ashbery's task was to "re-make it new"[7] – his phrase (used to describe the work of de Kooning) acknowledging both debt to the modernists and movement beyond them. For practical assistance Ashbery looked to a part of modern tradition which is anti-literary and anti-artistic, and which goes back to Apollinaire and the Dadaists, to the collages of Picasso and Braque with their perishable newspaper clippings, to Satie's *musique d'ameublement* which was not meant to be listened to.[8]

That is, he turned to a heterogeneous collection of recent or contemporary musicians (e.g., Ives, Cage), painters (the abstract expressionists), and continental writers (Roussel, de Chirico, the surrealists) who provided alternative examples of the "singularity" or "uniqueness"[9] he hoped in his own way to achieve, and whose attacks upon orthodox conceptions of art provided models for the liberation he sought. By and large, their aims and practices did not contradict those of Ashbery's primary modernist model, Wallace Stevens; rather, Stevens' aesthetics presented more conservative versions of the radical principles pursued by the "anti-artistic" tradition.

Unlike Stevens, Ashbery belongs to a generation that "'grew up Surrealist' without even being aware of it."[10] We may now give little thought to Breton's manifestos of 1924 and 1930, but according to Ashbery, "very little of the meaningful art of today could have been possible without what the poet Henri Michaux once described as 'the great permission' Surrealism gave artists 'to put down anything that came into their heads.' "[11] Ashbery's description of what pleases him about Stevens' work – "its unique amalgamating of the power of the unconscious mind (imagination, surrealism, or whatever you want to call it) with that of the conscious, ordering mind"[12] – links the modernist's aims to the surrealists'; nonetheless, Ashbery's profound interest in "resolution of the states of dream and reality . . . in a sort of absolute reality" – he paraphrases Breton – led him to experimentation more obviously surrealist in technique than Stevens'.

A similarly strong yet limited continuity exists between Stevens and the abstract expressionists, as is evident from Harold Rosenberg's use of quotes from Stevens' poems to introduce action painting and make its principles accessible to his readers (December 1952). According to Ashbery, during the late forties and the early fifties, when "the poem was a moribund form[,] . . . the 'action' was in Action-Painting"[13] naturally Ashbery and other young poets such as Frank O'Hara took inspiration from the visual arts.[14] Particularly influential was the painters' "idea of being as close as possible to the original impulse to work, which somehow makes the poem, like the painting, a kind of history of its own coming into being."[15] As Rosenberg explains, the painting was conceived of as an "event," and the canvas not as the place where the mind records its contents, but rather as "itself the 'mind' through which the painter thinks by changing a surface with paint."[16] This processive conception of art coincides with Stevens' notion of modern poetry as "the poem of the mind in the act of finding." However, painters such as Pollock, Kline, and de Kooning went further than Stevens in their liberation "from Value – political, aesthetic, moral."[17] Their sense of the painting as a moment in the painter's life involved emancipation not only from traditional subject matter and representation, but also from the restrictions of taste or relevance imposed by social mores and aesthetic conventions. Only the act of painting mattered. Stevens, by contrast, believed the artist responsible for upholding aesthetic and moral value; he regarded the imagination as the source of "our spiritual height and depth" (NA 34) as well as of aesthetic pleasure.

The action painters, by opening their work to the accidental, went further than Stevens in breaking down the distinction between art and life. Like them, contemporary avant-garde musicians were exploring the artistic possibilities of chance events in ways that powerfully affected Ashbery, for whom "la grande permission" came from the music of John Cage. Ashbery has often singled out his first exposure to Cage's music – a performance of "Music of Changes" he attended with O'Hara on New Year's Day, 1952 – as a crucial event in his poetic career. The concert jolted him out of several years of unproductivity, a period of "intense depression and doubt," by prompting the realization "that I could be as singular in my art as Cage was in his."[18] Ashbery was especially captivated by Cage's aleatory method of composition: "What mattered was that chance elements could combine to produce so beautiful and cogent a work."[19] Overall, Cage's compositions are dramatically experimental applications of many of the notions essential to Ashbery's poetry: the concern with processes rather than finished products; the desire to explore new possibilities and to question traditional definitions, procedures, and values; and, most notably, the interest in making available for art whatever appears or happens in the environment. Although Cage's ideas harmonize with Stevens' conceptions of reality as flux and art as process, Ashbery's testimony that "Cage taught me the relevance of what's there"[20] suggests one important way in which Cage's example counters that of Stevens. According to Stevens, "the poetic process is psychologically an escapist process" (NA 30) because "the poet gives to life the supreme fictions without which we are unable to conceive of it" (NA 31); the imagination serves to "[press] back against the pressures of reality" (NA 36). Consequently, his is poetry of the optative mood.[21] Though never simply an idealist, Stevens believes that the poet mediates between the actual and the ideal.

Like Stevens, Cage seeks to enhance our appreciation of the world around us and to expand the range of experience that art can present. But his method, unlike Stevens', involves no imaginative transformation of what comes in from our environment. Cage admits no opposition between order and chaos; what was formerly regarded as "noise" he embraces as music. "Our intention," Cage states, "is to affirm this life, not to bring order out of chaos or to suggest improvements in creation, but simply to wake up to the very life we're living."[22] This dissolution of the division between chaos and order, the abandonment of art as a *higher* form of reality, is characteristic of postmodern art. Ashbery's interest in accepting and including in his poetry the entire field of the world as it is actually apprehended, rather than as it might or should be seen, distinguishes his work from Stevens' and identifies his art with that of the contemporary avant-garde.

## II

As the title's allusion to the French Revolution implies, Ashbery's second volume, *The Tennis Court Oath* (1962), dramatizes in its experiments his rebellion against tradition and the literary establishment.[23] Ashbery was reexamining his notion of poetry – "sort of tearing it apart with the idea that I would put it back together"[24] – and the methods of the "anti-artistic" tradition were useful tools in this demolition.

Much of the volume is automatic poetry like that of the surrealists, in which words and phrases spill onto the page without the conscious mind imposing syntactic or semantic coherence. The results are not to be "understood," though they may evince a mysteriously persuasive power like that of dreams.[25] Thus, while the diction of these poems derives largely from common experience and refers to ordinary objects, the shattered syntax and the bizarre juxtapositions in the imagery preclude communication of particular ideas or depiction of recognizable situations. The preponderance of images related to death, disease, darkness, destruction, and inanimate objects, however, lends a unifying mood of bleakness or grotesquerie to many of these poems. Their fragmentation conveys a sense of the world as a "heap of detritus" (TCO 22), a junkyard of misplaced objects, severed limbs, and ineffectual actions.[26] *The Tennis Court Oath's* jarring discontinuities build upon and transform the modernists' appreciation of surprising juxtapositions, unexpected images, and witty contrasts as means of freshening our perceptions; for Ashbery (perhaps taking his lead from Apollinaire via de Chirico) surprise is "the one essential ingredient of great art."

However, consistent surprises soon cease to astonish and grow tiresome. A critic can add little to elucidate lines as relentlessly fractured as the following (or rather, a critic's interpretation appears as obviously subjective and associative, as arbitrary, as the passage itself):[27]

> The arctic honey blabbed over the report causing darkness
> And pulling us out of there experiencing it
> he meanwhile . . . And the fried bats they sell there
> dropping from sticks, so that the menace of your prayer
>     folds . . .
> Other people . . .          flash
> the garden you are boning
> and defunct covering . . . Blind dog expressed royalties . . .
>                         (TCO 33; poet's ellipses)

Even Ashbery has dismissed these automatic poems as works he no longer finds particularly interesting.[28]

Elsewhere in *The Tennis Court Oath* Ashbery plays with the techniques of *assemblage* and with the use of the "ready-made." Like many of his contemporaries in the other arts, he seeks a complete liberty of inclusion, indicating that the act of discovery or of casual choice is itself of interest without regard to the uniqueness or aesthetic quality of what is discovered. The volume's long poem "Europe," for instance, contains a number of passages lifted from a World War I novel, *Beryl of the Bi-Plane*, which Ashbery happened to discover in a bookstall on a Parisian quay. The novel's fragments frequently are identifiable either by their subject matter – war, engines, aviators, flight courses – or by the romantic clichés they contain – "her lover's strong clean-shaven face" (TCO 70), "plot to kill both of us, dear" (TCO 83). However, placed in a disorienting context of surrealistic associations, descriptions of the poet's immediate situation ("The snow has begun to fall on Paris [where Ashbery was living] / It is barely noon" [TCO 81]), and snippets from newspapers ("he was sent to the state senate" [TCO 78], "Lenin de Gaulle three days later" [TCO 75]), the "ready-made" bi-plane bits appear more mysterious than trite. Hints of the bi-plane plot assume in their enigmatic appearances and disappearances a resonance and complexity more like the tangled events we actually live than like the predictable patterns to which we escape in pulp fiction. Ashbery transforms the dime novel into something analogous to life as we experience it: "life, which always seems to be taking place somewhere else . . . whose perceived fragments are tantalizing clues to what the whole might be but whose climax might easily go unperceived."[29] The poem's line, "He had mistaken the book for garbage" (TCO 65) may well describe Ashbery's (or the bookseller's) initial misjudgment of *Beryl of the Bi-Plane*, and may serve as a somewhat admonitory Cagean invitation to be more attentive to whatever we find around us.

*The Tennis Court Oath* demonstrates that Ashbery himself was giving renewed attention to how words generate meaning and how we find order in words. Since spatial arrangement affects our understanding of collections of words, in several poems Ashbery tries using space as a form of accident. No conceptual or emotional logic determines, for example, the spatial organization of the following lines from "Rain":

> The storm coming –
> Not to have ever been exactly on
> this street with cats
> Because the houses were vanishing behind a cloud
> The plants on the rugs look nice
> Yet I have never been here before

> Glass

> regime    (TCO 31)

Instead of using the spatial field to chart the ordered progress of his ideas, as Charles Olson or Robert Creeley would, Ashbery dramatizes an absence of links in the unpredictable, distractable, even random, motion of mind.

Nonetheless, our experience of the poem is limited and shaped by its arrangement; our own responses are not haphazard. By confronting us with such defamiliarized spatial arrangements of words, Ashbery forces us to be more conscious of our habitual reliance on space to order our perceptions and, more generally, of the arbitrariness of the conventions by which we determine meaning. We find ourselves disoriented by structures that defy the conventions of progressive indentation toward the righthand margin. Made aware of our assumption that words that stand out – either to the far left ("Because the houses . . .") or in isolated centrality ("Glass") – are important, we remain unsure whether these poems allow any privileged positions. Such works are a far cry from Stevens' "maker's rage to order." Ashbery exhibits a rage to disorder, though his final purpose may be to reveal the futility of trying to distinguish order from chaos, since some sort of order seems to arise inevitably in the human act of apprehension.

To test the limits of the human ability to perceive chaos or tolerate meaninglessness, Ashbery also investigates whether groupings and juxtapositions in themselves generate meaning.[30] For example, in "To the Same Degree" (anticipating his 1979 long poem "Litany") Ashbery exploits the tensions between two independent columns of writing; their parallel placement invites a simultaneous attention that may lead to the discovery of accidental but nonetheless meaningful relations between the two columns. This parataxis differs from the modernists' surprising metaphorical juxtapositions, which were intended to allow insight into a reality usually veiled by the conventions of language and perception. For Ashbery there may well be no such core; there is only language, whose "center / Keeps collapsing and reforming" (SP 41).

While *The Tennis Court Oath* is more strikingly obscure than Ashbery's other volumes, its opacity is of the same general nature. He regards his poetry as "a kind of mimesis of how experience comes to me. . . . What I am probably trying to do is illustrate opacity and how it can suddenly descend over us, rather than trying to be willfully obscure."[31] And again: "The difficulty of my poetry isn't there for its own sake. It's there to reflect the difficulty of living, the everchanging, minute adjustments that go on around us and which we respond to from moment to moment – the difficulty of living in passing time, which is both difficult and automatic, since we all somehow manage it."[32] As in his later volumes, in *The Tennis Court Oath* Ashbery is trying both to illustrate "the dilemma of understanding"[33] and to explore the impact of that dilemma on human existence.

Thus, the frustration of partially blocked communication and incomplete contact with one's world is the thematic focus of the volume's more intelligible poems. In " 'How Much Longer Will I be Able to Inhabit the Divine Sepulcher . . .,' " for example, life itself is a tomb. In its dark and often suffocating encasement, the individual is cut off from insight into himself and his surroundings:

> Who are you, anyway?
> And it is the color of sand,
> The darkness, as it sifts through your hand
> Because what does anything mean.   (TCO 27)

Though needing to be released, he remains trapped by his own fear of the light and love that exist "terribly near us." In "A Last World" our society is self-destructively galloping into the flames because of "the weight of an inconstant universe" where "the truth is cold" and "the passions are locked away," where we find ourselves "lost by our comrades / Somewhere between heaven and no place" (TCO 58). And in "The Suspended Life" the perspective of a sedated traveler for whom the world appears prepackaged and blank hardly differs from that of people nominally "at home": Wherever one is, others seem far away, and one experiences primarily absence and the failure to make contact:

> Do you see
> The difference between weak handshakes
> And freezing to death in a tub of ice and snow
> Called a home by some, but it lacks runners,
> Do you? When through the night
> Pure sobs denote the presence
> Of supernatural yearning you think
> Of all those who have been near you
> Who might have formed a wall
> Of demarcation around your sorrow,
> Of those who offered you a coffee.   (TCO 37)

Ashbery's sense of the isolating dislocation of human experience, as well as his interest in how chance and order operate in human perception and communication do not change dramatically after this early volume; but here, as Ashbery admits, he did not succeed in "keep[ing] meaningfulness up to the pace of randomness."[34]

## III

After "taking poetry apart to understand how it works" in *The Tennis Court Oath*, Ashbery produced two volumes in which he "was trying to fit it back together."[35] As we saw in the preceding chapter, *Rivers and Mountains* and *The Double Dream of Spring*, although far more traditional than *The Tennis Court Oath*, were nonetheless enriched by that volume's questioning and dismantling of traditional writing. Ashbery's next book, *Three Poems* (1972), marks a second period of radical experimentation, this time involving "prose poetry in which the ugliness of prose would be exploited and put to the uses of poetry."[36]

The challenge Ashbery sets himself in this volume is to "put it all down" (TP 3), which is to say that his goal is an inclusiveness more thorough than simply admitting into art fragments picked at random from the environment. He was finding that the division of poetry into lines was "interfering" with "the processes of [his] thought as [he] was writing,"[37] and he believed prose would allow a closer approximation of the uninterrupted flow of consciousness, without inhibiting rapid transitions between the abstract, the concrete, and the imagistic. In embracing the "ugliness of prose," Ashbery allows dry, analytic, and pseudo–philosophical language to predominate. Motivating his linguistic inclusiveness is a Cagean desire to attach us more firmly to the elusive present:

> But meanwhile I am to include everything: the furniture of this
> room, everyday expressions, as well as my rarest thoughts and

> dreams, so that you may never become aware of the scattered
> nature of it, and meanwhile you *are* it all, and my efforts are
> really directed toward keeping myself attached, however dimly,
> to it as it rolls from view, like a river which is never really there
> because of moving on someplace. (TP 14–15)

He identifies the "grid of everyday language" (TP 33) as what prevents
one from slipping helplessly into the past. Thus Ashbery's use of banal
expression, though somewhat parodic and often amusing, is far from
satirical; he treasures whatever yokes us to our immediate world.

"What moves me," he has said, "is the irregular form – the 'flawed
words and stubborn sounds' as Stevens said, that affect us whenever we
try to say something that is important to us. . . . The inaccuracies and
anomalies of common speech are particularly poignant to me. This essence of communication is what interests me in poetry."[38] *Three Poems*
echoes the flawed speech of our mundane world "of provocative but
baffling commonplace events" (TP 31) with the awkward wordiness and
automatic formulas of conversation, journalese, lazy academic or business discourse. Yet Ashbery triumphs over ordinariness; in the context
of his work, flaccid banality yields something intriguing and fresh.

Sometimes Ashbery accomplishes this transformation simply by shifting from impersonal analytical formulations to more evocative metaphorical ones – either extended comparisons or, as in the following passage, a single sharp image:

> Perhaps what I am saying is that it is I the subject, recoiling from
> you at ever-increasing speed just so as to be able to say I exist in
> that safe vacuum I had managed to define from my friends' dis-
> interested turning away. As if I were only a flower after all and
> not the map of the country in which it grows. (TP 15)

Elsewhere Ashbery lends elegance to his prose through syntactic and
rhythmic balance, though the phrases themselves may be hackneyed. For
instance, in the following passage he constructs an elaborate symmetry
by employing parallel clauses ("out of . . . out of," "as far above . . . as
it was beneath"), by dividing larger syntactic units into two halves, and
by using a number of paired words or phrases linked by "and" ("to and
fro," "everything and everybody," "earth and heaven"). The resulting
linguistic structure mirrors the beautiful crystallization being discussed:

> He thought he had never seen anything quite so beautiful as that
> crystallization into a mountain of statistics: out of the rapid
> movement to and fro that abraded individual personalities into a
> channel of possibilities, remote from each other and even re-

moter from the eye that tried to contain them: out of that river of humanity comprised of individuals each no better than he should be and doubtless more solicitous of his own personal welfare than of the general good, a tonal quality detached itself that partook of the motley intense hues of the whole gathering but yet remained itself, firm and all-inclusive, scrupulously fixed equidistant between earth and heaven, as far above the tallest point of the earth's surface as it was beneath the lowest outcropping of cumulus in the cornflower-blue empyrean. Thus everything and everybody were included after all. (TP 48–9)

Generally, in attempting to imbue his prose with textural interest and surprise, Ashbery combines disparate images and allusions with assorted levels of diction while extending syntax to unexpected lengths and in unforeseen directions.

Ashbery's innovations erode the barrier between art and life by creating what he regards as a form of representation truer than those he inherited – one which approaches as nearly as possible the acceptance of all things, insistently denying that a selective focus is a necessary condition for meaningfulness. What he seeks is a Supreme Non-Fiction. Hence he explains his interest in the long poem in the following terms: "[Long poems] are in a way diaries or logbooks of a continuing experience or at any rate of an experience that continues to provide new reflections and therefore it gets to be much closer to a whole reality than the shorter ones do."[39] In "The New Spirit," for example, he tackles the question of what constitutes personal identity by slowly "tak[ing] apart the notion of you so as to reconstruct it from an intimate knowledge of its inner workings" (TP 19–20); the poem's "half-hearted, seemingly lazy way of moving forward," which permits continuing reexaminations and qualifications, imitates the extended, often dilatory, process of self-discovery.

As a further development of this new kind of realism, Ashbery tries to place chance in a more balanced perspective than he had in *The Tennis Court Oath*. He still regards life as "a series of accidents complete in themselves and as components fitting into one big accident" (TP 24) and therefore allows his poems a less determinate movement and a more chaotic assortment of images than the modernists would employ. But he also acknowledges, with a particularly comforting image, that "our shared apprehending of the course as plotted turns it into a way, something like an old country road" (TP 24). The "new spirit" that the poem affirms involves "assuming the idea of choosing." In other words, it paradoxically admits the rightness of selectivity, though that selection is of a particularly contemporary variety: "a new kind of arbitrariness" (TP 9) in which it doesn't matter what is selected. "Everything is a way, none more suitable nor more accurate than the last. . . . This despite the demonstrable rightness of the way we took" (TP 17–18). At the poem's conclusion the speaker declares that in order to deal with "the major question that revolves around you, your being here . . . you have got to begin in the way of choosing some one of the forms of answering that question" (TP 51). This amounts to an admission that despite his insistence on an all-inclusive mimesis and on art constituted from untransfigured materials of life ("pedestrian turns of phrase,"[40] clichés, proverbs, and other ready-made forms of language), Ashbery's art, as an outgrowth of human consciousness, inevitably imposes artificial bounds upon experience through an inescapable "narrowing down process." In a parallel admission of art's limitation, Ashbery concedes that no art can in fact "leave all out": "forget [i.e., leave out] as we will, something soon comes to stand in their place. Not the truth, perhaps, but – yourself" (TP 3). Even without a conscious "rage to order," ordering and selection are unavoidable.

Ashbery does not deceive himself about the artist's practical ability to reach such polemical goals as liberation from Value (the goal itself a value), from imposed order, from selectivity – and this knowing yet uncynical self-awareness adds to the intellectual appeal of his work. He also admits that art may be incapable of fulfilling the multiple, often contradictory demands readers place upon it:

> Any reckoning of the sum total of the things we are is of course doomed to failure from the start, that is if it intends to present a true, wholly objective picture from which both artifice and artfulness are banished: no art can exist without at least traces of these. . . . Perhaps no art, however gifted and well-intentioned, can supply what we were demanding of it: not only the figured representation of our days but the justification of them, the reckoning and its application, so close to the reality being lived that it vanishes suddenly in a thunderclap, with a loud cry. (TP 113)

Here again he diverges from Stevens, who came far closer to believing that art *could* present "not ideas about the thing but the thing itself." Stevens regarded even the abstractions in his poetry as firmly grounded in objective reality; his "river of rivers" is "in Connecticut," "a local abstraction" (CP 533). He saw poetic truth as analogous to empirical knowledge (NA 54). Like the Romantics before him, Stevens believed that the gap between human consciousness and external reality could be bridged via "the *mundo* of the imagination," though not "the gaunt world of the reason" (NA 57–8). For Ashbery, however, the Romantic opposition between the rational and imaginative faculties as well as the Romantics' faith in the superiority of the imagination for producing "an agreement with reality" (NA 54) no longer seems particularly relevant; in attempting his foredoomed "reckoning of the sum total of the things we are" Ashbery is therefore free to employ rational and overtly abstract structures.[41]

Ashbery's reliance on the rational faculties is particularly apparent in the longest of *Three Poems*, "The System," an investigation of epistemology in the present age when the fixed system of truths accepted "in those days" no longer seems viable. The speaker, skirting the "too well rehearsed" facts commonly regarded as truth or history, explores instead a new frontier provided by "the living aspects" of "a fiction that developed parallel to the classic truths" (TP 55). This unmapped "other tradition" of knowledge is comparable to the "anti-artistic tradition" within which Ashbery places his poetry as a whole. His rhetoric and methods in "The System" resemble those of the philosopher: He proposes theories, entertains hypothetical assumptions, offers alternative explanations or solutions, and evaluates their adequacy in dialectical debate. The poem's tone is far less tentative than that of "The New Spirit"; using "pedantic, philosophical language" and phrases emphasizing orderly or causal relations ("thus it was that," "hence," "it is certain that," "so"), Ashbery intentionally endows this prose poem with a "lecturing quality."[42]

Delineating tidy classifications within the apparent confusion of experience, the professorial speaker lists three possible methods for attaining intellectual understanding – "reason, sense, or a knowing combination of both" – and asserts that "only the first has some slim chance of succeeding through sheer perversity, which is possibly the only way to succeed at all" (TP 68). He then examines two theories of the growth of knowledge: one is the "great careers" approach, according to which fixed lessons are slowly accumulated; the alternative, preferable but far from ideal, is the " 'life-as-ritual' concept" (TP 70), in which each stage of living is considered in itself without reference or comparison to the past. In addition, he distinguishes two kinds of happiness: "frontal," in which happiness is fully achieved for an epiphanic moment through "grace as chance"; and "latent or dormant," which though immediately withheld seems always about to start. Furthermore, he identifies our senses and the "facts" they convey – rather than imaginative revelation – as providing the certainty we need about the authenticity of our moments of understanding. The poem, then, moves by a highly rational process of division and analysis.

This process paradoxically results in a cyclical return to the faith in unity and connection embodied in the old system:

> Having begun by rejecting the idea of oneness in favor of a plu-
> rality of experiences, earthly and spiritual . . . you gradually be-
> came aware that the very diversity of these experiences was en-
> dangered by its own inner nature, for variety implies parallelism,
> and all these highly individualistic ways of thinking and doing
> were actually moving in the same direction and constantly
> threatening to merge with one another in a single one-way mo-
> tion toward that invisible goal of concrete diversity. For just as
> all kinds of people spring up on earth and imagine themselves
> very different from each other though they are basically the same,
> so all these ideas had arisen in the same head and were merely
> aspects of a single organism: yourself, or perhaps your desire to
> be different. So that now in order to avoid extinction it again
> became necessary to invoke the idea of oneness, only this time if
> possible on a higher plane . . . so that each difference might be
> taken as a type of all the others and yet remain intrinsically itself,
> unlike anything in the world. (TP 100–1)

None of the roads rationally evident to the speaker could lead him beyond the dilemma that prompted his inquiry: "you began to realize that
the two branches were joined together again, farther ahead; that this place
of joining was indeed the end, and that it was the very place you set out
from" (TP 90). One is left knowing only that one must somehow "learn
to cope with the onrushing tide of time and all the confusing phenomena
it bears in its wake" (TP 90), and that they must be approached as a
unified whole.

Ironically, such an approach is possible through that supremely nonrational act, love. The "invisible web" that connects your eyes to those
of "the beloved" also connects "both of you to the atmosphere of this
room" and these filaments operate as organizing "guidelines" for living
(TP 95). Yet this reversal does not amount to a satirical attack upon
reason. Despite some playful mockery, Ashbery does not belittle the reasoning process which brought him to his final realization, even if that
was only a reconfirmation of the place where he started. Reason, a human faculty, is simply limited; we are destined to receive only "fragments of the true learning" (TP 79). Ashbery always manages to find
something positive to say for things as they are, if only "because there is
no escaping them" (TP 67). In this case he optimistically affirms that
while we cannot know the key word or secret principle that orders life,
we can know its effects. To know more "would be to know too much.
Meanwhile it is possible to know just enough" (TP 95).

The largest truths (and death is surely among them) are "unimaginable, in a word."

And would you believe that this word could possibly be our salvation? For we are rescued by what we cannot imagine: it is what finally takes us up and shuts our story, replacing it among the millions of similar volumes that by no means menace its uniqueness but on the contrary situate it in the proper depth and perspective. At last we have that rightness that is rightfully ours. But we do not know what brought it about. (TP 104–5)

Rescue is not brought about by privileging either the imagination or reason, reality or fantasy; but that unimaginable salvation does seem related to the passage of time. For Ashbery, the only genuine and crucial choice we face is how we relate to time. We must not remain fixed, nor allow ourselves to be sucked into the past, but must flow with the tumultuous current of an ever-changing now. The problems posed by the passage of time become the focus of the volumes that succeed *Three Poems*.

## IV

*Three Poems* may well be Ashbery's most optimistic volume. Each part of the trilogy enacts a rewarding process of discovery or problem-solving and ends with a low-keyed yet fervent affirmation and resolution. The discovery of the "new spirit" amounts to the birth of a new being,[43] and in the subsequent poems this new person identifies a perspective on knowing that frees us to move into the "kinetic future," using our windows on the past only "to stay on an even keel in the razor's-edge present" (TP 102). This volume provides the clearest demonstration of one of Ashbery's most extraordinary powers as a poet: In an era when celebratory optimism would be highly suspect, he is able to affirm with quiet certainty and fullness the very limited good that urban dwellers of the late twentieth century *can* acknowledge as genuine. Beneath all his qualifications lies a profound faith in the value of "casual moment[s] of knowing" (TP 69) and of an exceedingly limited but nonetheless real progress – a gradual "synthesis of very simple elements in a new and strong . . . relation to each other" in which the old "blend[s] inconspicuously with the new in a union too subtle to cause any comment" (TP 117–18). One of the pleasures Ashbery's poetry provides is the conviction that there is real worth, even glory, in participating in that muted spectacle.

Yet the resolutions achieved in a world of flux cannot be fixed and must be "rethought each second" (TP 61). Therefore it is not surprising that *Self-Portrait in a Convex Mirror* (1975) goes over much of the same thematic and conceptual territory mapped out in *Three Poems*, usually taking a more somber point of view. It is as if the initial excitement of discovery has passed and the poet, faced with the problem of making his home on the new frontier, finds it difficult to hold onto the acceptances achieved in the preceding volume.

*Self-Portrait* contains no prose poems and, until the concluding title poem, Ashbery returns to an art that depends on "knowing what important details to leave out," while allowing their absence to invoke their presence so that in fact they are "all over the page" (SP 5). Thus the title of the first poem, "As One Put Drunk into the Packet-Boat," evokes the "left out" context of Andrew Marvell's poem from which it derives. The poem is "Tom May's Death," and it begins:

> As one put drunk into the Packet-boat,
> *Tom May* was hurry'd hence and did not know't.
> But was amazed on the Elysian side,
> And with an Eye uncertain, gazing wide,
> Could not determine in what place he was.

These absent lines announce the dominant perspective and themes of Ashbery's volume. The speaker in these poems finds himself continually "hurry'd hence" by time and struggles, "with an eye uncertain," to determine where he is at each moment. His perspective is usually that of an alienated spectator or passive victim bewildered by passing time and change. His experience is dominated by a sense of incompleteness or partial fulfillment, as if he were "sitting in a place where sunlight / Filters down, a little at a time, / Waiting for someone to come" (SP 1). Life feels like an "interminable" "curtain-raiser" (SP 18); waiting seems to be the essence of the human condition. The ultimately significant event which will "orchestrate" the shapeless fragments of one's life into a "great, formal affair . . . that takes in the whole world" (SP 1) is endlessly postponed. Instead of this apocalyptic event, what does arrive as a recurrent motif is a crucial cryptic message or letter which one is not there to receive or to which one cannot respond:

> One day a man called while I was out
> And left this message: "You got the whole thing wrong
> From start to finish. Luckily, there's still time
> To correct the situation, but you must act fast.
> . . . Much besides your life depends on it."
> I thought nothing of it at the time.
>                    (SP 3, ellipsis added; see also SP 18, 45)

Since the speaker so often feels cut off from his world and from those around him, it is fitting that the poems should rely heavily on ellipsis and on movement that reflects the fragmentation of human experience and attention. The verbosity and syntactic coherence of *Three Poems* have been preserved in *Self-Portrait*, but the easily inclusive and smooth progress of prose has been replaced by a more erratic and less clearly directed "movement of the caravan away / Into an abstract night, with no / Precise goal in view" (SP 16).

Continuing his progressive divergence from Stevens' apotheosis of the imagination, Ashbery in *Self-Portrait* appears particularly troubled by the "escapist" (NA 30) nature of Stevensian imaginative process, and wary of the exotic sensual music that eases such transport.[44] In the Stevensian echoes of such lines as

> There are still other made-up countries
> Where we can hide forever,
> Wasted with eternal desire and sadness,
> Sucking the sherbets, crooning the tunes, naming the names,
>
> (SP 33)

we hear a combination of longing and disillusionment indicative of Ashbery's ambivalence as he tries throughout *Self-Portrait* to assess the limitations of language and art. He is more candid than before about his nostalgia for the soothing order depicted in the art of the past, including Stevens' poetry, while resolutely resisting the temptation to "hide" there.

Ashbery's attraction to tradition's purely imaginative and fantastic worlds is evident even in the volume's titles: "Märchenbilder," "Hop o' My Thumb," "Robin Hood's Barn," "Scheherazade." In "Scheherazade" (SP 9–11) he depicts the seductive beauty of the imagination's fertile landscape, where "an inexhaustible wardrobe" of words and dreams "has been placed at the disposal / Of each new occurrence" so that, decked in appropriate costume, each "can be itself now." The decorative lushness associated with the storyteller Scheherazade is reminiscent of Stevens, who also cultivated "colored verbs and adjectives" and "loved the particles [referring to the parts of speech] / That transform objects of the same category / Into particular ones, each distinct." Ashbery feels a nostalgic warmth for these old fictions that restore our good humor by portraying a world of merciful balances in which good is rewarded, evil punished, and errors exonerated. "The songs protect us, in a way"; that is, the archetypal patterns of myth and romance – such as the dwarfs, wicked brothers, daring rescues, and happy endings which he uses to tell his story in "Oleum Misericordiae" – impose design on our splintered experience so that we can see "some reason for having come / . . . so far alone, unasked" (SP 67). Nonetheless, Ashbery is keenly aware that the "possibilities are limited" in this art so removed from immediate experience.

For Ashbery, the essential shortcoming of such fiction is that it is outside time and therefore cannot encompass the processive nature of experience and consciousness. The moment an event assumes its Scheherazadian fictive costume, it is fixed and without vitality:

> but all [in Scheherazade's mental landscape]
> Was wariness of time watching itself
> For nothing in the complex story grew outside:
> The greatness in the moment of telling stayed unresolved
> Until its wealth of incident, pain mixed with pleasure,
> Faded in the precise moment of bursting
> Into bloom, its growth a static lament.   (SP 10)

Ashbery has acknowledged that "the passage of time is becoming more
and more *the* subject of my poetry as I grow older,"[45] and, despite the
respite provided by imaginative fiction à la Scheherazade, such art does
not help us confront the challenge of remaining attached to the ever-
fleeting present. Real history is "disorganized, lackluster," and today's
art must reflect this honestly. The richly embellished particularity that is
accessible to Scheherazade, or even to Stevens, is often beyond Ashbery's
reach because he is committed to capturing a world sluiced by time:

> It's getting out of hand.
> As long as one has some sense that each thing knows its
>     place
> All is well, but with the arrival and departure
> Of each new one overlapping so intensely in the semi-darkness
> It's a bit mad. Too bad, I mean, that getting to know each
>     just for a fleeting second
> Must be replaced by imperfect knowledge of the featureless
>     whole,
> Like some pocket history of the world, so general
> As to constitute a sob or wail unrelated
> To any attempt at definition.   (SP 16)

Even the movement of Stevensian process, which we can equate with
"getting to know each for a fleeting second," is too slow and stately to
serve the poet of the 1970s.

Modernist poetry reflects a Bergsonian belief in the temporal character
of consciousness, with its streaming sensations inaccessible to the conventional poetic language of preceding eras.[46] In order to capture this
primary experience, the modernists tried to pierce the veil of habitual
perception by focusing on immediate sensations and immediately perceived objects, and by describing these with fresh metaphors and sur-

prising juxtapositions that were to reveal new relations. The poet's task
was to render experience exactly as it crystallized for him at each moment. Like the modernists, Ashbery participates in what Hugh Kenner
has called an "aesthetic of glimpses."[47] But his is an era of even more
accellerated change, and external changes seem to affect one's internal
sense of time. Contemporary Americans tend to perceive the problem of
capturing immediate experience, of being in the present, as more difficult
for them than for previous generations; the innovations in Ashbery's poetry reflect this heightened anxiety characteristic of the second half of the
twentieth century.

If Ashbery's art is to keep pace with the "grand galop" of contemporary urban culture, he can seldom afford the luxury of imaginative invention; the best he can provide is straightforward notation of mundane
trivia ("And today is Monday. Today's lunch is: Spanish omelet, lettuce
and tomato salad, / Jello, milk, and cookies" [SP 14]). More generally,
if his art is to attach us to the present, then any traditional elements,
which would be cherished and repeated in Scheherazadian creation, can
be threatening. Thus, "Voyage in the Blue" closes with the archaic structure of a castle "weigh[ing] its shadow ever heavier" on the young couple and their dog presently floating down life's river (SP 27). And in
"Ode to Bill," Ashbery explicitly rejects tradition's idyllic pastoral:

> One horse stands out irregularly against
> The land over there. And am I receiving
> This vision? Is it mine, or do I already owe it
> For other visions, unnoticed and unrecorded
> On the great, relaxed curve of time,
> All the forgotten springs, dropped pebbles,
> Songs once heard that then passed out of light
> Into everyday oblivion? . . .
>
> . . . . . . . . . . . . . . . . . . . . . . . . . . . . . . . . . . . . . . . . . .
> . . . Him too we can sacrifice
> To the end of progress, for we must, we must be moving on
>                                      (SP 50–1, ellipses added)

Here, then, is the dilemma Ashbery faces at this point in his career: If
he adopts traditional methods of arranging and describing experience, he
risks confusing fresh realities with the quite different ones of the past.
Yet he is now unsatisfied with art which merely reenacts the directionless
drift of experience. Thus he complains in "Grand Galop":

> But I was trying to tell you about a strange thing
> That happened to me, but this is no way to tell about it,
> By making it truly happen. It drifts away in fragments.

And one is left sitting in the yard
To try to write poetry
Using what Wyatt and Surrey left around,
Took up and put down again
Like so much gorgeous raw material.[48]    (SP 19)

Needing to liberate himself from traditions that he finds in many ways compelling, Ashbery makes no bones about his bitterness that the ancient, charming visions are currently such distortions:

Surrey, your lute is getting an attack of nervous paralysis
But there are, again, things to be sung of
And this is one of them, only I would not dream of intrud-
        ing on
The frantic completeness, the all-purpose benevolence
Of that still-moist garden where the tooting originates:
Between intervals of clenched teeth, your venemous
        rondelay.                                              (SP 20)

Fortunately, the kind of poetry he is seeking "does sometimes occur / If only in creases in forgotten letters / Packed away in trunks in the attic – things you forgot you had" (SP 19), though one must plow through masses of trivia to find "a gasp of new air / Hidden in that jumble" (SP 20). The "one thing that can save America now" – the authentic mode of contemporary artistic communication – is neither grandly historical nor richly imaginative. It lies hidden in the most ordinary moments, in the "lumber of life"; it surfaces in the rather private, shared perceptions of commonplace events occuring "in cool yards, in quiet small houses in the country . . . in fenced areas, in cool shady streets" (SP 44–5).

Current vernacular and pedestrian language – the diction of the commonplace – help Ashbery attach himself to this level of experience. He does not share the modernists' interest in etymology, in the past traditions and cultures single words can evoke. Instead he places special value on demotic words or speech patterns unavailable to Wyatt and Surrey – perhaps unacceptable even to the modernists – limited as these words may be:

So there is whirling out at you from the not deep
Emptiness the word "cock" or some other, brother and sis-
        ter words
With not much to be expected from them, though these
Are the ones that waited so long for you and finally left,
        having given up hope.
There is a note of desperation in one's voice, pleading for
        them.                                                 (SP 19)

Consequently the diction of *Self-Portrait* tends to be as slack (and slightly more colloquial) and the phrasing as verbose as that of *Three Poems*:

> The streets
> Offered a variety of directions to the foot
> And bookstores where pornography is sold. (SP 18)

> "A nice time," you think, "to go out:
> The early night is cool, but not
> Too anything." (SP 15)

> "Once I let a guy blow me.
> I kind of backed away from the experience.
> Now years later, I think of it
> Without emotion. There has been no desire to repeat,
> No hang-ups either. (SP 22)

As a new formal development reflecting Ashbery's desire to hold onto "the gap of today filling itself" (SP 7), in "Tenth Symphony" (SP 46–7) and "Lithuanian Dance Band" (SP 52–3) he tries taking advantage of the immediacy of the epistolary form. The grand title of the former half-jokingly points to Ashbery's faith in the significance of the informally talky and digressive. The poem purports to be a letter to a friend with whom the poet hasn't communicated in years, yet instead of offering a summary of his life during that interim Ashbery opens with what is most immediately in his thoughts:

> I have not told you
> About the riffraff at the boat show.
> But seeing the boats coast by
> Just now on their truck:
> All red and white and blue and red
> Prompts me to.

(Such impersonality is typical of Ashbery's poetry; feeling that "to talk about myself would be immodest," he believes "the circumstances of my own life are of no compelling interest to other people.")[49] From there Ashbery moves by association (what one has not told another) to the most sweeping questions – "Why you love me, why we love you and just exactly / What sex is" – and then asserts, "There is some connexion . . . among this." This playful procedure reflects serious tenets of Ashbery's aesthetics: "Art is, after all, what is happening now; the past, Bach and Chekhov, can always fill itself in as it is needed. The important thing is to start from the beginning, that is, the present."[50] "Lithuanian Dance Band" pushes the epistolary form ("I write you to air these few thoughts feelings") even closer to the immediate texture of events by eliminating

punctuation, thereby capturing in its long lines the flood of multiple simultaneous events comprising the "worldly chaos in which we struggle."

The letter is particularly suited to expressing Ashbery's values because
its assumed purpose is contact and communication with another person.
It represents an attempt to alleviate one's aloneness, or at least make it
"more human" by acknowledging the reality of another's equally lonely
life. Ashbery regards human contact as life's most meaningful and precious experience. Thus "Fear of Death" expresses with poignant directness the poet's terror of "growing old / Alone, and of finding no one at
the evening end / Of the path except another myself"; he dreads the
foreseen end to dialogue, when "silence is the last word" (SP 49). And
in "No Way of Knowing" (SP 55–7) he praises popular songs (sample
lyrics: "Why must you go? Why can't you / Spend the night, here in my
bed, with my arms wrapped tightly around you?") because of their enduring spirit of "camaraderie." These songs create a "mood" true to our
overall sense of the "bits and pieces of knowledge we have retained" –
e.g., memories of "favorite friendships" – and give continuity to the
"chain of lengthening days."

Moments of human contact are particularly precious because when
they are occurring it is easy to be fully in the present. The satisfaction of
such "being here now" is reflected in the playful exuberance of "On
Autumn Lake." After clowning with Chinese-American pronunciation
and syntax of the "Confucius say" variety, Ashbery reveals as the source
of his very immediate happiness his sense of lively communication and
intellectual community among friends:

> I do not think that this
> Will be my last trip to Autumn Lake
> Have some friends among many severe heads
> We all scholars sitting under tree
> Waiting for nut to fall. Some of us studying
> Persian and Aramaic, others the art of distilling
> Weird fragrances out of nothing, from the ground up.
> In each the potential is realized, the two wires
> Are crossing.[51]                                    (SP 48)

Ashbery also grounds himself and his poetry in the present by drawing
our attention to the thoughts he is having about writing while writing.
We are never allowed to forget that these poems are merely "ideas about
the thing," not "the thing itself," that they are produced by a limited
individual using a medium that can yield only clumsy approximations of
the meaning he intends. Within the poems we find, for instance, the
following:

                    last month
      I vowed to write more. What is writing?
      Well, in my case, it's getting down on paper
      Not thoughts, exactly, but ideas, maybe:
      Ideas about thoughts. Thoughts is too grand a word.
      Ideas is better, though not precisely what I mean.
      Someday I'll explain. Not today though.   (SP 50)

      I know that I braid too much my own
      Snapped-off perceptions of things as they come to me.
      They are private and always will be.   (SP 44)

      *Es war einmal* . . . No, it's too heavy
      To be said. Besides, you aren't paying attention any more.
      How shall I put it?   (SP 59; poet's ellipsis)

In "The Tomb of Stuart Merrill" Ashbery even self-mockingly includes a fragment of a letter he received commenting on his work:

> "I have become attracted to your style. You seem to possess within your work an air of total freedom of expression and imagery, somewhat interesting and puzzling. After I read one of your poems, I'm always tempted to read and reread it. It seems that my inexperience holds me back from understanding your meanings." (SP 38)

Such self-deprecating irony, habitual for Ashbery, shatters the smooth surface of traditional artistic illusion. He reminds us of his art's limitations because he does not want to offer a rarefied never-never land, nor seem to promise more guidance or fulfillment than poetry can in fact deliver (Stevens can be accused of both). Allowed no false hopes, his readers will not be disappointed. (Ashbery's ambitions, of course, are great nonetheless: Protected by modesty of voice and manner, he can offer generalizing pronouncements on the great literary themes and hope that his poetry, like "night, the reserved, the reticent, gives more than it takes" [SP 2].)

     Despite all the techniques through which he aims to capture the experience and outlook of his time, Ashbery, well-versed in the traditions of both the visual and verbal arts, neither wishes nor pretends simply to discard the art of the past. By basing the volume's culminating title-poem upon a direct and intimate confrontation with an ancient artwork, Ashbery addresses directly the questions of how artifacts from the past are true or untrue, useful or hindering in the present.[52]

     The image of a convex mirror had first appeared in a passage in "The System" describing the human tendency to use the beloved for egocentric purposes:

the individual will . . . sallies forth full of ardor and *hubris*, bent on self-discovery in the guise of an attractive partner who is *the* heaven-sent one, the convex one with whom he has had the urge to mate all these seasons without realizing it. (TP 57)

As artist, Ashbery has discovered his "convex one" in a literally convex self-portrait which the sixteenth-century mannerist, Francesco Parmigianino, painted on a hemisphere of wood. Because the painter rendered the rounded reflecting surface of the mirror with such care, looking at the portrait inevitably creates the illusion of looking into a mirror at a reflection of oneself: "it is a metaphor / Made to include us, we are a part of it and / Can live in it as in fact we have done, / Only leaving our minds bare for questioning" (SP 76). While the modernists deplored what Pound called "explanatory metaphor," Ashbery generally treats metaphor as a means of explication rather than swift revelation. Nowhere is this divergence more apparent than in his intellectualized ramblings refiguring Parmigianino's metaphor.

Ashbery regards the old portrait's ordering techniques as in many ways indistinguishable from our own, and he laments their falsifying egocentrism:

> I see in this only the chaos
> Of your round mirror which organizes everything
> Around the polestar of your eyes which are empty,
> Know nothing, dream but reveal nothing.
> I feel the carousel starting slowly
> And going faster and faster: desk, papers, books,
> Photographs of friends, the window and the trees
> Merging in one neutral band that surrounds
> Me on all sides, everywhere I look.    (SP 71)

Still-used "laws of perspective," which derive from the painter's fear that the uncharted moment will be chaos without them, organize the painting. A similar self-protective "mistrust" leads us, too, to impose design – "a weak instrument though necessary" (SP 72) – on our perceptions. The ideal forms that result are projections of timeless human dreams; these fantasy structures are important because they "nourish a dream which includes them all" (SP 73) – that is, they allow us a comprehensive harmonizing epistemology (a supreme fiction). In addition, the portrait feeds into "the nostalgia of a collective past": its viewers think they recognize their own sensations portrayed and are soothed knowing "that others felt this way / Years ago" (SP 77).

Though Ashbery himself uses art in these (in his view) self-indulgent ways, he does not condone them. He declares – and this is a radical notion with far-reaching consequences for traditional ideas such as organic form – that in the final analysis what matters in any artwork is that something was included which was totally foreign to the artist's intention. The artist may blame himself when "he finds / He has omitted the things he started out to say / In he first place," but in so doing he is simply

> "unaware that necessity circumvents such resolutions.
> So as to create something new
> For itself, that there is no other way,
> That the history of creation proceeds according to
> Stringent laws, and that things
> Do get done in this way, but never the things
> We set out to accomplish and wanted so desperately
> To see come into being.    (SP 80)

This mysterious necessity is what insures the genuine value of art; it forces the artist to include an "otherness" (not a mirroring of oneself) that "chang[es] everything / Slightly and profoundly" (SP 81) so that unintentionally he creates something new.

The artist's conscious attempt to fix his experience in his artwork is a "life-obstructing task." As a reflection of Parmigianino's speculations about the relation of self and soul, inner and outer, art and life, his painting can offer his viewers only "second-hand knowledge." And while we, faced with bewilderingly shapeless experience, may be tempted to rely on this as on the laws of perspective, "Yet I know / That no one else's taste is going to be / Any help, and might as well be ignored" (SP 82). The value of an artwork – and here we return to the theories behind action painting – lies in the moment and process of creation; it is only during the "movement / Out of the dream into its codification" that "Something like living occurs" (SP 73).

Yet Ashbery recognizes that in addition to offering subsequent generations the dangerous temptation of "exotic / Refuge within an exhausted world," the painting can more constructively push us into the present:

> I think it is trying to say it is today
> And we must get out of it even as the public
> Is pushing through the museum now so as to
> Be out by closing time. You can't live there.    (SP 79)

We are in a position to recognize that an artwork seen from a later age is mortified, a "frozen gesture,"

A convention. And we have really
No time for these, except to use them
For kindling. The sooner they are burnt up
The better for the roles we have to play.    (SP 82)

Thus at the climax of the poem Ashbery bravely struggles free from the past. He addresses the painter, "Therefore I beseech you, withdraw that hand, / Offer it no longer as shield or greeting," and immediately Francesco's image "fall[s] back at a speed / Faster than that of light to flatten ultimately / Among the features of the room" (SP 82). In the poem's closing lines Ashbery turns to his own world. Fully in the present, he aches with disappointment and loneliness, knowing now the narrow limits of the help we can obtain from an art museum's, or a library's, "cold pockets / Of remembrance" (SP 83).

## V

By the 1970s, when Ashbery was writing *Three Poems, Self-Portrait*, and his next collection *Houseboat Days* (1977), a quarter-century had elapsed since his first avant-garde explorations, and the situation of experimental artists in our society had changed dramatically. No longer a tiny neglected minority, the avant-garde by the late 1960s had become the center of attention in the art world. Lecturing at Yale in 1968, Ashbery voiced his concern that the "avant-garde can now barely exist because of the immense amounts of attention and money that are focused on it." He posed the question,

> What then must the avant-garde artist do to remain avant-garde? For it has by now become a question of survival both of the artist and of the individual. In both art and life today we are in danger of substituting one conformity for another. . . . Protests against the mediocre values of our society such as the Hippie movement seem to imply that one's only way out is to join a parallel society whose stereotyped manners, language, speech and dress are only reverse images of the one it is trying to reject.

He answered that avant-garde artists must fight even harder now than in 1950 to preserve their individual identities:

> Before they were fighting against general neglect, even hostility, but this seemed like a natural thing and therefore the fight could be carried on in good faith. Today one must fight acceptance which is much harder because it seems that one is fighting oneself.

Always gently affirming, Ashbery offered the hopeful conclusion that the present climate, while not ideal for discovery, still is "conducive to it" because it forces the artist to "take steps he hadn't envisaged."[53]

Believing that "most reckless things are beautiful in some way, and recklessness is what makes experimental art beautiful," Ashbery, even as a widely recognized and middle-aged artist, has pushed himself to continue taking new risks and unenvisioned steps.[54] In 1976, describing the self-imposed challenge of trying to write the "quite short poem," Ashbery declared, "There is no intrinsic value in doing one thing or the other, but in doing the recalcitrant thing. That is my present form of experimenting."[55]

But for a mature poet, is the formal variation of shortening or lengthening one's poems really experimentation? To use James Merrill's refrain: yes and no. Such changes allow Ashbery to feel that he has not "knuckled under and gone on turning out the same product all these years."[56] So long as he experiences a form's recalcitrance as a fresh challenge, then it serves its purpose of renewal. Yet Ashbery admits that he is "not really very successful" in avoiding repeating himself. The reader familiar with Ashbery's earlier work and looking for something strikingly new in recent volumes would likely feel disappointed. Ashbery's sensibility, linguistic resources and style, taste and opinions have not altered much. In 1972 he described his poems as "trying to get at . . . a general, all-purpose experience . . . something in which anybody can see reflected his own private experiences without them having to be defined or set up for him."[57] In 1982 he depicted his poetry in nearly identical terms, as presenting "paradigms of common experience which I hope other people can share."[58] His concern with transcribing the processes of conception and perception has been consistent throughout his career; he is still intrigued by the awkwardness, the clumsy quirks of American speech and American landscape, still resisting the single voice, still seeing life as motion, still determined to make the best of whatever life has to offer.

For many readers the most compelling changes in Ashbery's mature works occur in tone, theme, and preoccupation, not in form or style. *Houseboat Days* (1977), for instance, stands out as the first volume in which Ashbery seems fully comfortable with his work's relation to the language and conventions of the past. Sounding more confident than in *Self-Portrait*, Ashbery now dwells less on his sense of passivity in the face of passing time and events and is no longer content to see himself or his world "as though reflected / In streaming windowpanes" (HBD 28). Instead, he is determined to build his own "bridge like that / Of Avignon, on which people may dance for the feeling / Of dancing on a bridge.

I shall at last see my complete face / Reflected not in the water but in the worn stone floor of my bridge" (HBD 28). No longer waiting for the mailman to deliver the crucial message, he recognizes that it is he who "had been carrying the message for years / On my shoulders like Atlas, never feeling it / Because of never having known anything else" (HBD 53). After the exorcism of "Self-Portrait in a Convex Mirror," he no longer fears that he will be sucked into the past by what has been left behind. He trusts that "the present has done its work of building / A rampart against the past, not a rampart, / A barbed wire fence" (HBD 19). This leaves him free to enjoy the view between the wires. His inclusiveness consequently gains a fuller range in literary history; the "pyrography" of this volume and those that succeed it is often fed by the "kindling" of tradition. Stevens' colorful fantasies and rich linguistic play, as found in *Some Trees*, are among the fragments of our past that Ashbery reassimilates.

"Daffy Duck in Hollywood" demonstrates and discusses Ashbery's new liberty with historical materials. This "fabulation" is a wild and comical conglomeration of diction, syntax, and fictional characters from many eras, particularly from current comic strips and their archaic equivalents in popular entertainment, ancient romances. The merging of these worlds demonstrates how past culture infuses present civilization. Daffy Duck listens to characters from the late fifteenth century who can whistle popular tunes of recent decades as well as operatic adaptations of chivalric romances. And Daffy's comparably hetereogeneous vocabulary is one that even Stevens' Comedian as the Letter C would envy: "mutterings, splatterings, / The bizarrely but effectively equipped infantries of happy-go-nutty / Vegetal jacqueries, plumed, pointed . . . (Hard by the jock-itch sand-trap that skirts the asparagus patch of algolagnic *nuits blanches*)" (HBD 32, ellipsis added). As a character lifted from an early symbolist play by Maeterlinck observes, "It's all bits and pieces, spangles, patches, really; nothing / Stands alone" (HBD 33). The characters, both contemporary and antique, are uncomfortable with this hodgepodge. According to Daffy, all the junk that is currently being heaved in his direction – "a mint-condition can / Of Rumford's Baking Powder, a celluloid earring, Speedy / Gonzales, the latest from Helen Topping Miller's [a writer of pulp fiction] fertile / Escritoire, a sheaf of suggestive pix on greige, deckle-edged / Stock . . ." – indicates that "everything is getting choked to the point of / Silence" (HBD 31). He regards the flow of Los Angeles traffic as a "wide, tepidly meandering, / Civilized Lethe" leading to an earthly Tophet. Similarly, the characters from the past lament today's philistinism, the absence of evidence of creative evolution; they find contemporary creations a "disappointing sequel to ourselves" (HBD 33).

Yet the poet who controls these figures and uses them for his amusement is ready to accept the motley collage which comprises the culture surrounding these characters and ourselves:

>                 why not
> Accept it as it pleases to reveal itself? As when
> Low skyscrapers from lower-hanging clouds reveal
> A turret there, an art-deco escarpment here, and last perhaps
> The pattern that may carry the sense, but
> Stays hidden in the mysteries of pagination.
> Not what we see but how we see it matters;
>
>                                    (HBD 34)

He urges us to adventure into the present, which includes all today's junk epitomized by Hollywood, as well as the flotsam and jetsam left by the receding tide of the past. In doing so we are not violating tradition; we are remaining true to its only venerable aspect − a spirit of daring. In fact, most of the old works alluded to in this poem were avant-garde in their time. For example, the *Princesse de Clèves* was a precursor to the psychological novel, and *Aglavaine et Sélysette* was an early experiment in modern nonrealistic drama. As Ashbery sees it, "to be ambling on's / The tradition more than the safekeeping of it" (HBD 34), and therefore his breaking with tradition is paradoxically carrying on the tradition. Ashbery does not deny or disguise the crudity, tackiness, even the "disingenuous[ness]" of our Hollywood-dominated culture. But he is ready to engage himself in it nonetheless, for this is the time that's given to him − "Morning is / Impermanent. Grab sex things, swing up / Over the horizon like a boy / On a fishing expedition" (HBD 34).

By perpetually embarking into the present, Ashbery intentionally places himself on the edge of the future: "The time suits us / Just as it fancies itself, but just so far / As we not give up that inch, breath / Of becoming before becoming may be seen" (HBD 66). In *Houseboat Days* and the succeeding volumes Ashbery emphasizes more than he had previously that remembering the past, both personal and cultural, is essential in our procedure into the future. A number of the poems − "Wooden Buildings," "Two Deaths," "The Other Tradition," "The Thief of Poetry," "Pyrography" − are occasioned by events that engage memory, but their import is not merely elegiac or nostalgic. "Pyrography," for example, a poem commissioned for the American bicentennial, examines the patterns of the nation's history − cycles of westward searches and disappointed returns − in order to learn "To be able to write the history of our time, starting with today" (HBD 9). "The Thief of Poetry" recounts a more personal look backward, revisiting the street where a friend once walked; again the present reenactment and remembering serve to "insure the second / beginning / of that day seen against the street" (HBD 58). Ashbery counsels, "Conceive of your plight // more integrally" (though the stanza break humorously suggests the difficulty of so doing) (HBD 55) and therefore approaches each phenomenon not in isolation but as "the event combined with / Beams leading up to it" (HBD 29–30). He now seems to view history as a spiraling movement in which we are propelled into the future by contact with the past. In "Blue Sonata," whose dry and abstract analysis of the relation of time past to time present and future is reminiscent of the opening of Eliot's "Burnt Norton," Ashbery explains that we cannot leap without temporal continuity into the future:

> It would be tragic to fit
> Into the space created by our not having arrived yet,
> To utter the speech that belongs there,
> For progress occurs through re-inventing
> These words from a dim recollection of them,
> In violating that space in such a way as
> To leave it intact.     (HBD 67)

Even so, as in *Self-Portrait*, Ashbery warily insists on cultivating an awareness of the fundamental ways in which current values and worldview differ from previous ones. In "Business Personals" Ashbery yokes contemporary and traditional materials in order to question the appropriateness of our reliance on inherited authority. To demonstrate that "the tall guardians of yesterday" are encountered "whatever path you take," Ashbery uses archaic terminology, syntax, and allusions that reveal how much current advertising slyly hearkens back to eighteenth-century pastoral and nineteenth-century romantic conceptions of nature. Having questioned whether one could "return / To the idea of nature summed up in these pastoral images," Ashbery shifts to a parable that enacts the proper relation to "leftovers" from the past. Here he presents himself as a twentieth-century Odysseus, thereby acknowledging the validity of appropriating the traditional spirit of quest and wily heroism. In order to get home to the "now," he must confront his Cyclops, a giant whose stature identifies him as one of the "tall guardians of yesterday." Ashbery/Odysseus can escape only if he boldly addresses himself to that danger. The point seems to be that if the past is "properly acknowledged," what is threatening about it "will dissipate" into the surrounding environment while remaining, in non-dangerous form, "still here."

Most of the leftovers from the past must be thoroughly revised if they are to be meaningful in the present, because

> The old poems
> In the book have changed value once again. Their black letter
> Fools only themselves into ignoring their stiff, formal quali-
> ties, and they move
> Insatiably out of reach of bathos and the bad line
> Into a weird ether of forgotten dismemberments.   (HBD 5–6)

Among these "leftovers," the most primitive mythical visions require
the least revision, since they most directly project fundamental human
dreams and longings, which remain largely unchanged. Thus fairy tale
figures and images of ancient quest are easily assimilated into poems of
the present. For instance, in "On the Towpath" contemporary travelers
who turn off the road to "Fred Muffin's Antiques" are motivated by the
same spiritual thirst – a longing to escape the relentless passage of time
so that "the insipid chiming of the seconds / [may give] way to an arc of
silence" – which over the centuries has upheld "a many-colored tower
of longing." This structure is perenially inhabited by characters from
Perrault's fairy tales. But Ashbery points to the limitations of such castles
in the sky by invoking the immediate twilight; this emblem of passing
time and approaching death is "a warning to those desperate / For easy
solutions" (HBD 23).

Many old myths do need to be radically reinterpreted if their contemporary relevance is to be apparent. Thus in "Syringa" Ashbery provides
a new explanation of why the poet Orpheus lost his Eurydice:

> it is the nature of things to be seen only once,
> As they happen along, bumping into other things, getting
> along
> Somehow. That's where Orpheus made his mistake.
> Of course Eurydice vanished into the shade;
> She would have even if he hadn't turned around.
>
> (HBD 69)

The myth teaches not only that art is as ephemeral as Eurydice, but that
transience is the secret of its power: In Ashbery's revision, the Bac-
chantes tore Orpheus apart because they were driven mad by the agonizing authenticity of his art – "The way music passes, emblematic / Of life
and how you cannot isolate a note of it / And say it is good or bad"
(HBD 70). According to Ashbery, art should not aspire to treasure stalled
moments as "tableau"; "It too is flowing, fleeting; / It is a picture of
flowing." Therefore Orpheus's "turning around" is, in this new critique,
the proper behavior for an artist: "the singer . . . builds up his chant in
progressive stages / Like a skyscraper, but at the last minute turns away.

/ The song is engulfed in an instant in blackness" (HBD 71). The artist should not be concerned with cozening death or clutching for immortality. The afterlife for an ordinary artist ("Stellification / Is for the few") is determined by chance; although totally forgotten, an artist's works may happen one day to be resuscitated, thoroughly transformed:

> they lie
> Frozen and out of touch until an arbitrary chorus
> Speaks of a totally different incident with a similar name
> In whose tale are hidden syllables
> Of what happened so long before that
> In some small town, one indifferent summer.    (HBD 71)

Still other "forgotten dismemberments" undergo complete metamorphoses in Ashbery's hands. For him antiquity does not constitute sanctity, and he has no Poundian sense of there being luminous historical moments that should be recovered to guide us. Old artifacts may happen to be useful if they involve us in attention, for "attention . . . evolve[s] into curiosity, which is its own reward."[59] Thus, Ashbery's handing of the early ballad, "The Nut Brown Maid," in his "Fantasia on 'The Nut-Brown Maid' " is no more reverent than his treatment of *Beryl of the Bi-Plane* in his early poem "Europe." Both literary sources are simply objects that caught his attention, useful because, by turning to each regularly as he writes, Ashbery finds them "push[ing] his mind in unexpected directions." Ashbery's poem in thirty sections, usually alternating he and she, does adopt a modified form of the ballad's structure; and many of Ashbery's verse paragraphs contain fragments from the parallel verse in the original. Yet they are such odd selections, often giving no hint of the narrative line ("all the pain and fear" or "all day it is writ and said"), and so thoroughly assimilated, that they remain unidentifiable without a copy of the old text. Moreover, Ashbery's "Fantasia," despite its layout, is not a dramatic dialogue. The "give and take, push–pull" of dialogue is maintained, but in Ashbery's typical polyphonic chorus of different points of view reflecting facets of his own mind. The usefulness of "The Nut-Brown Maid" has little to do with the ballad's technique, subject, or themes, but rather with Ashbery's self-conscious reflections on using it. The relation of the present to the past – "Can one advance one step further without sinking equally / Far back into the past?" (HBD 86) – is a recurring concern as the poem comments on its own method:

> It is revisionism in that you are
> Always trying to put some part of the past back in,

And although it fits it doesn't belong in the
Dark blue glass ocean of having been remembered again.
(HBD 80)

The "moated past" is used in the poem because it offers "something to see, something going on," but the poet stands firmly on this side of the trench. The world of which he sings "alway" is one of lights and cars, urban parks and department stores; "I have chosen this environment and it is handsome" (HBD 88).

Indeed, discussing the inherited sources in *Houseboat Days* one risks distortion. Certainly, Ashbery in this collection seems more at ease incorporating traditional materials and conventions into his work, not fearing that by adopting them he will lose his grasp on immediate experience. But this is preeminently poetry of the mundane present, and Ashbery clearly establishes his role as that of "street musician":

So I cradle this average violin that knows
Only forgotten showtunes, but argues
The possibility of free declamation anchored
To a dull refrain.   (HBD 1)

The "dull refrain" of our daily routines forms the core of this book, and that dullness is usually left intact in flat language and drab scenes.

Ashbery relies on ironic reflexivity, as he had in *Self Portrait*, to keep his readers aware that his imaginative embellishments are "merely stage machinery":

Yes, friends, these clouds pulled along on invisible ropes
Are, as you have guessed, merely stage machinery,
And the funny thing is it knows we know
About it and still wants us to go on believing
In what it so unskillfully imitates, and wants
To be loved not for that but for itself:
. . . . . . . . . . . . . . . . . . . . . . . . . . . . . . . . . . . . . . . .
. . . so we may know
We too are somehow impossible, formed of so many differ-
ent things,
Too many to make sense to anybody.   (HBD 50)

Given this detached and sophisticated perspective (with marked affinities to that we will observe in James Merrill's work), one can adopt the spirit of make-believe as a tool for coping with "vague and dimensionless," dull everyday phenomena. Thus, in "Melodic Trains" the speaker equates the little girl's toy wristwatch, which she wears "for fun," with the briar pipe and tweed coat that give firm outline to his own identity. Such costumes – though they may in fact only be "right twice a day" – and the playfulness with which one dons them are essential supports in a world that works "haphazardly."

Ashbery's juggling of perspectives and weaving of the fantastic into unidealized mundane events reflect his complex understanding of what constitutes accurate mimesis:

> How is it
> With us, we are asked, and the voice
> On the old Edison cylinder tells it: obliquity,
> The condition of straightness of these tutorials,
> Firm when it is held in the hand.   (HBD 37)

The obliquity and bizarreness of this volume's title poem (HBD 38–40) express Ashbery's quintessential vision of the texture of our lives. From our settled yet unstable situations (represented by the houseboat) we send out garbled messages to others, foolishly attempting to argue with them about our sincere convictions, as if certainties could be established. But little order can be ascribed to the mad jumble of inner and outer events:

> I don't set much stock in things
> Beyond the weather and the certainties of living and dying:
> The rest is optional. To praise this, blame that,
> Leads one subtly away from the beginning, where
> We must stay, in motion.

Even hope is "something concrete / You can't have." The only control one can exercise is to adopt the attitude that "Life is beautiful," for then whatever occurs will be, in a sense, what one wants. The rare instant of clarity and full attention – the moment when "the place in the slipcover is noticed / For the first and last time" (and that may even be in the moment of dying) – will occur only if we manage to keep up with "this passage, this movement."

In each volume he has produced since *Houseboat Days*, Ashbery has moved on to new versions of "the recalcitrant thing"; naturally, the success of these experiments varies. In 1979 *As We Know* appeared, containing a poem nearly seventy pages long in two columns of text "meant to be read as simultaneous but independent monologues" (Author's Note). "Litany," as this reckless experiment is called, is a logical extension of the polyvocality that has long been Ashbery's hallmark, though I find the poem more interesting as concept than successful as literature.[60] Each column is itself polyvocal, containing Ashbery's usual collage of inflec-

tions and manners of speaking; but since "Litany" is freed from the limitations of entirely serial presentation, its "long sweetness of simultane-
ity" (ShTn 18) comes closer than Ashbery's other poems to imitating the
intense overlapping of our thoughts and perceptions. In fact, however,
one cannot read two texts simultaneously; this is poetry in the form of
paradox, since both voices are in a sense true, but the reader trying to
assimilate them at the same time finds they cancel each other out.[61] The
other obvious formal innovation in *As We Know* – the very short, playful
poems that combine large and small typeface – also dramatizes the interaction of several voices. In each poem, the first voice shouts, and the
second whispers, but that whisper is a whopping surprise as Ashbery
highlights and subverts our expectations: "THE CATHEDRAL IS / slated
for demolition" (AWK 93).

In *Shadow Train* (1981), Ashbery tries out a new consistency – and
calm elegance – of form: fifty sixteen-line poems, each in four-line verse
paragraphs. The challenge he sets himself here is to create variety independent of structure, and humor proves a great resource, as does the
contrast between flat telegraphic statements – "Poor Warren. He wasn't
a bad egg, / Just weak. He loved women and Ohio." (ShTn 13) – and
long sinuous sentences:

> And when you say, come on let's
> Be individuals reveling in our separateness, yet twined
> Together at the top by our hair, like branches, then it's OK
> To go down into the garden at night and smoke cigarettes,
>
> Except that nothing cares about the obstacles, the gravity
> You had to overcome to reach this admittedly unimpressive
> Stage in the chain of delusions leading to your freedom,
> Or is that just one more delusion?   (ShTn 29)

The strategies in themselves are not new for Ashbery, but with each
volume he stretches their powers in new directions. Despite Ashbery's
ingenuity in creating variety within narrow parameters, *Shadow Train* is
not a particularly strong volume; ultimately the sonnet-like form is too
constraining for such a discursive and meditative poet.

Ashbery's most recent collection – and one of his finest – *A Wave*, is
distinguished by its formal variety. *A Wave* contains several prose pieces,
including a celebratory masque and an essay-like reminiscence about the
movies; a poem after Baudelaire; a popular song in quatrains rhymed
aabb; a pantoum; various one- or two-page lyrics in Ashbery's customary range of irregular and regular length verse paragraphs; thirty-seven
single-line haiku; six haibun (the poetic prose of a haiku artist, Vendler

tells us),[62] each closing with a one-line haiku; and the long meditative title poem. Yet those who speak of the greatness of *A Wave* are likely to have in mind not Ashbery's formal agility but his compelling response to the pressures of life-threatening illness; the volume is much concerned with death, or more accurately, life in the face of possibly imminent death.[63] A tenderly beseeching tone now comes to the fore:

> And now that the end is near
>
> The segments of the trip swing open like an orange.
> There is light in there, and mystery and food.
> Come see it. Come not for me but it.
> But if I am still there, grant that we may see each other.
>
> (W 8)

Though specific biography is no more apparent than before, we share in Ashbery's moving struggle to balance his desire to extend and savor life's sweetness or its strangeness against his courageous wish to accept the approaching end: "That we may live now with some / Curiosity and hope / Like pools that soon become part of the tide" (W 10). Ashbery is now preoccupied with the curious and wonderful fact that despite it all, we desire to go on living: "not that anything prevented us from leaving the theater, but there was no alternative to our interest in finding out what would happen next" (W 27). Without denying his fears and the world's horrors, Ashbery caresses more gently than in any preceding volume what he has come to love: "I believe that the rain never drowned sweeter, more prosaic things than those we have here, now, and I believe this is going to have to be enough" (W 44). Yet if the distinctive character of *A Wave*, like that of each recent volume, seems determined by Ashbery's personal and intellectual development, it is only by bravely reaching always for new forms that he has been able to bring those changes into his verse.

The avant-garde poets of the early twentieth century were hopeful that accuracy of attention and fresh uses of language would bring them in contact with the distinct edges and patterns of reality. The hopes of the contemporary poet are more limited, as coherence, meaning, and knowledge remain largely inaccessible. Sweeping statements, even proclamations of fundamental uncertainty, are tempered by ironic awareness of human limitation. The flux that Stevens sought to render Ashbery sees as swirling tumult, and the process of mind he sought to capture is for Ashbery a disjunctive series of confrontations in a tortuous maze.

The essential differences between the two generations derive from their divergent ideas of order and time. In Ashbery's perspective, no systematic order can satisfactorily be imposed upon or discovered in our experience. He sees life as a "series of accidents" (TP 24), or more positively as "a haphazard field of potentiality" (TP 60). Therefore he allows chance to play a large role in the creation of his flagrantly unsystematic poetry. Since life's moments of meaning or happiness occur randomly, one cannot anticipate them; one can only strive to be there in the present to receive them if they should appear. Ashbery's poetry is obsessed with presentness, with the struggle to keep up with the speeding succession of elusive "nows." Formally this results in extreme disjunctiveness as the poet leaps madly from moment to moment, voice to voice, capturing only fragments of usually banal language and mundane events.

While coherence and a leisurely flow are, in Ashbery's view, unavailable to art that mirrors our actual condition, a certain wholeness is nonetheless possible ("Conceive of your plight // more integrally"). Ashbery's poetry pushes always toward new levels of inclusiveness – admitting subconscious elements, chance discoveries, all kinds of diction, a range of sources both traditional and contemporary, private and public. Our experience is the sum of these heterogeneous "hard-to-combine ingredients" (HBD 50). Ashbery's determination to face the uncertainties and unintelligibilities of our world involves him in thorough dismantling of traditional poetics, which paradoxically frees him to employ traditional methods of coherence at will, without losing sight of the arbitrariness of the ways in which we order our experience.

Ashbery will not offer the neat structures of traditional verse – "No sonnet / On this furthest strip of land" (HBD 48); nor does he claim, as Stevens would and as he himself once did, that art's function is to help us "resemble a taller // Impression of ourselves" (ST 49). Art is not to project a larger-than-life image of "major man." Yet in its multifaceted mirroring surface, we may come close to seeing ourselves wholly and as we really are.

Elizabeth Bishop, whose work Ashbery greatly admires, does employ traditional verse structures. Yet while her poetry might seem far removed from the avant-garde discontinuities of Ashbery's, Chapter 4 will trace in her divergence from modernism – as later chapters will in Creeley's and Merrill's – versions of these same tendencies: a distrust of coherent orders, even of the evanescent ones poets keep weaving from words; an insistence that poetry participate in the processive character of human perception and conception; an interest in worn, ordinary, and even debased diction as the language of the ongoing present; an eclectic ransack-

ing of tradition, including movements or periods the rebelling modernists felt compelled to eschew. Before considering that divergence, however,
I shall examine the affinities between Bishop's poetics and those of her
primary modernist model, Marianne Moore.

# 3 "Piercing glances into the life of things": the continuity between Moore and Bishop

## I

In 1935, the year following Elizabeth Bishop's graduation from Vassar College, several of her poems appeared in an anthology of young poets, each introduced by an established writer. Were it not for Marianne Moore's presence as the commentator for Bishop's selections, a reader of the anthology *Trial Balances* probably would not have guessed that Bishop was an admirer of Moore's poetry. Grouped under the heading "Archaically New," Bishop's pieces rely heavily on conventional conceits, archaic personifications, insistent rhymes, and traditionally "poetic" diction and inversions; for instance, from "Three Valentines":

> Love with his gilded bow and crystal arrows
> 　　Has slain us all,
> Has pierced the English sparrows
> Who languish for each other in the dust,
> While from their bosoms, puffed with hopeless lust,
> 　　The red drops fall.

or

> Now a conundrum Love propounds
> 　　My heart;
> You with himself my Love confounds
> 　　With perfect art,
> Until I swear I cannot tell you two apart.[1]

While the poems in "Archaically New" reveal (as Moore noted) Bishop's esteem for the works of Gerard Manley Hopkins and John Donne, they contrast dramatically with Moore's revolutionary defiance of inherited

79

conventions of poetic form and meter, subject matter and language. Not surprisingly, Moore's masterfully elusive comments, while emphasizing Bishop's poetic promise, tactfully suggest substantial criticisms as well:

> It is difficult . . . not to allow vigilance to fluctuate; an adjective or an "and" easily eludes one, and a mere shadow of the unintentionally mechanical deflects interest. Some phrases in these pieces of Miss Bishop's work are less live than others.[2]

By 1946, however, when Bishop's first book appeared – containing only one of the poems published in *Trial Balances*, "The Map" – both Bishop's poetry and Moore's response to it had changed considerably. With clean economy of phrasing Bishop now employs the diction and syntax of contemporary speech; her images derive largely from ordinary experience; the explicit subjects of her poems tend to be less grandly abstract. Abstractions like "love" or "grief," which previously figured as her subjects, she now approaches obliquely through descriptions of tangible objects or through precise renderings of particular experiences. No longer disguised by the exhausted poeticisms of earlier centuries, Bishop's gift for sparkling fantasy and her skill at remarkably observant and accurate description emerge clearly in *North & South*. Moore's praise of this volume, in a review entitled "A Modest Expert," is unequivocal: "At last," she proclaims, "we have someone who knows, who is not didactic." Moore now extols Bishop's descriptive skills, and instead of faulting her for occasionally lapsing into mechanical word choice, commends her for finding "always the accurate word."[3] The shift in Moore's attitude indicates the extent to which the maturing Bishop aligned her poetry with modernism, and more particularly, the extent to which Bishop's evolution during the middle and late thirties was influenced by the poetic principles and practices of Moore herself.

Bishop and Moore had become personally acquainted in March 1934, only a few months before the preparation of *Trial Balances*. The Vassar College librarian was an old friend of the Moore family; when she learned of Bishop's interest in Moore's work, she arranged for them to meet. The two were immediately taken with one another, promptly began exchanging letters and books to read, and soon were taking joint outings to circuses, museums, and natural history films.[4] Though initially shy about showing her work to the older poet, between September 1936 and October 1940 Bishop was regularly sending Moore new poems and short stories, receiving detailed praise as well as very particular criticism in response. After 1940 she rarely showed Moore her unpublished work, though she continued to read and reread Moore's poems and essays and, until Moore's death in 1972, to practice her descriptive skills in lively letters to her friend.

Bishop's descriptions of natural phenomena, at once rigorously objective and imaginatively associative, are responsible for critics' having linked her poetry with Moore's ever since the publication of *North & South* (1946). Since description is the most obvious link between their work, my examination of their poetic affinities will begin with comparisons between the descriptive techniques of Bishop's first volume and those Moore customarily employs. Many of the descriptive techniques Bishop appears to have adopted from Moore are among the stylistic traits that Marie Borroff, in her fine analysis of Moore's language, has linked to promotional prose (that is, the descriptive prose of feature articles and documentary advertisements); Borroff's work has therefore greatly facilitated my comparison.[5] After placing those descriptive affinities and others – particularly in the poets' approaches to moralizing and to poetic form and language – in the context of modernist aims, I shall determine from *A Cold Spring* (1955) the extent to which Moore's impact remains evident in Bishop's mature style.

As descriptive poets, both Moore and Bishop, like the authors of promotional prose, look for "the eye-catching or mind-boggling detail, for strong colors and color contrasts, for the unexpected, the anachronistic, and the incongruous." In their works "the world . . . is not so much idealized and exalted as it is brightened and heightened, with a kind of 'Believe-It-or-Not' vividness surpassing the qualities of everyday experience."[6] Their aims in descriptive writing are similar to those of promotional prose writers: They intensify visual experience in order to attune their readers to the remarkableness of the small things of this world. Thus, responding to Bishop's information about the appearance of bright Cuban tree snails "with the green leaves as backgrounds for these flaming colors," Moore once exclaimed, "And how careless people are to not broadcast the fact of such exciting things" (6 December 1943).[7]

In order to "broadcast" in poetry the wondrousness of ordinary phenomena, Bishop, like Moore, employs figures that reveal surprising visual congruities between apparently incongruous realms. Moore describes a swan's "flamingo-colored, maple- / leaflike feet" (CPM 38)[8] or "hounds with waists diminishing like the waist of the hour-glass" (CPM 48); Bishop, with comparable precision, writes of a fish's "pink swim-bladder / like a big peony" or of its "brown skin [which] hung in strips / like ancient wallpaper" (CP 42).[9] Both poets' figures frequently involve unexpected juxtapositions of different size-scales or realms – the natural with the man-made, the sentient with the insentient, the minute with the grand. For example, Moore describes "the blades of the oars / moving together like the feet of water spiders" (CPM 49) or a mussel "opening and shutting itself like // an / injured fan" (CPM 32); and Bishop sees "the boulevard and the little palm trees / all stuck in rows, suddenly revealed / as fistfuls of limp fish-skeletons" (CP 41). Such incongruous links – wondrously apt yet the products of a giddy imaginative freedom – are intentionally defamiliarizing: Unsettled, readers must scrutinize the commonplace with new care. These two women share a belief that the vitality of a poem – or of any perception – depends on its freshness and its precision; "we are precisionists, / not citizens of Pompeii arrested in action" (CPM 59).

Bishop's precise "word pictures," like Moore's, "are literally 'color-ful.' "[10] In Bishop's poems the colors tend to be bright and eye-catching; for example, in "Jerónimo's House" she depicts "one fried fish / spattered with burning / scarlet sauce, / a little dish / of hominy grits / and four pink tissue- / paper roses" on a blue table (CP 34). Such lines bring to mind the strong color contrasts prevalent in Moore's poems, e.g., "black butterflies with blue half circles on their wings / tan goats with onyx ears" (CPM 56). More idiosyncratically characteristic of Moore's poetry is her tendency to refine through figurative comparisons the subtle gradations of color. For instance, she writes of "frog grays, / duck-egg greens, and egg-plant blues" (CPM 12), of "the crimson, the copper, and the Chinese vermilion of the poincianas" (CPM 56), and of "the sprinkled blush / of puce-American-Beauty pink / applied to bees-wax gray" (CPM 29) of nectarines painted on a plate. Though generally less elaborate, Bishop sometimes uses similar techniques to discriminate hues. In "Roosters," she describes "glass-headed pins, / oil-golds and copper greens, / anthracite blues, alizarins" (CP 36); elsewhere in *North & South* she speaks of "egg-white" skies (CP 46), of a "pea-green back-pasture" (CP 40), and of "bright green leaves edged neatly with bird-droppings / like illumination in silver" (CP 40).

Bishop does not necessarily compress her descriptive phrases to the extent that Moore does; she often employs lists of common adjectives – "the monotonous, endless, sagging coast-line" (CP 32) or "overhanging pale blue cliffs" (CP 11). But she sometimes adopts Moore's information-compacting device, common also in advertisements, of condensing into adjectival phrases what others might present in explicit similes or dependent clauses. Nouns appear frequently in such modifying compounds, lending a modernist concreteness and concision to the description. For instance, Bishop uses the phrases "gun-metal blue dark," "dropping-plastered henhouse floor" (CP 35), "tide-looped strings of fading shells" (CP 32), "weed-deflected stream" (CP 21), and "star-splintered hearts of ice" (CP 26). Even if atypical, these experiments demonstrate that she was evolving her own descriptive methods by examining and imitating Moore's.

Nowhere is Bishop's imitation of Moore more obvious than in "Florida" – as Randall Jarrell noted in 1946.[11] Depicting a geological region by describing characteristic flora and fauna, "Florida" is comparable in subject to a feature article or to a characteristic early Moore poem such as "An Octopus" (lastingly one of Bishop's favorites). Like journalists, the speakers of "Florida" and "An Octopus" do not reflect upon themselves or their relation to the landscape, but focus on providing information – not the comprehensive or "useful" knowledge one might acquire from an encyclopedia, but those remarkable facts likely to awaken in readers a sense of wonder. In both poems the narrator is present as a lively but impersonal reporting voice.

Nonetheless, the poems' opening lines also hint of significant differences between the two artists' sensibilities. In "Florida" (CP 32–3) Bishop immediately draws attention to the aesthetic character of her subject and suggests a personal attachment; it is "the state with the prettiest name." Moore's fascination with the glacier that is her subject in "An Octopus" derives from a more intellectual interest in its physical characteristics; in her opening lines she notes the remarkable thickness of the ice fields and the anomalous flexibility of that ice. As is her common practice, Moore emphasizes the prosaic character of her subject by employing scientific jargon and quoting from unlyrical "business documents and // school-books" (CPM 267) – in this case, the "Department of Interior Rules and Regulations" and "The National Parks Portfolio." In "Florida" Bishop follows Moore's example of including facts or statistics, informing us that enormous turtles leave "large white skulls with round eye-sockets / twice the size of a man's" and that the alligator "has five distinct calls: / friendliness, love, mating, war, and a warning." She thereby achieves a Moore-like impression of reportorial accuracy and specificity, but both the facts and the manner in which she presents them are more conventionally poetic and more emotionally suggestive than Moore's. Humans are ominously dwarfed in Bishop's fierce and death-littered landscape.

In order to impress upon us that they are reliable witnesses and guides, Bishop and Moore in their descriptive passages insist on careful discriminations. For example, the opening lines of "Florida" record the distinction between the appearance of mangrove roots when living and their appearance when dead:

> The state with the prettiest name,
> the state that floats in brackish water,
> held together by mangrove roots
> that bear while living oysters in clusters,
> and when dead strew white swamps with skeletons,
> dotted as if bombarded, with green hummocks
> like ancient cannon-balls sprouting grass.    (CP 32)

The technical result of such fastidiousness, in this passage as in much of Moore's work, is that descriptive phrases tend to accumulate at length until the thread of the syntax almost breaks under the stress of great extension. Like Moore's images, Bishop's surprising simile comparing hummocks and cannon-balls jars the reader while delighting with its visual exactitude. Moore, however, would be unlikely to use as vehicle a fantastic metaphor-within-a-metaphor such as cannon-balls sprouting grass, and she probably would not describe a state as floating in brackish water unless it were literally afloat. Bishop is less committed to the "relentless accuracy" of "fact," more interested in the dreamier truths of the imagination.

As is typical of Moore's poems (and of the feature article), the point of view in "Florida" could not realistically represent the experience of any single observer. Instead, it shifts freely between sweeping overviews and minute close-ups, noting intriguing pieces of information or describing picturesque sights. The time evoked is a generalized, seemingly eternal present (whether day or night), since the poem, like so many of Moore's, presents features and events that are characteristic and recurrent. Like "An Octopus," Bishop's poem follows an apparently random course, moving from descriptions of birds, to turtles, to trees and rain, to coastal shells, to swamp life. The poem shares the easy inclusiveness of Moore's work; there is room for information about weather, geology, plants, animals, and traditional lore. As in "An Octopus," no obvious transitions are provided; the poem's unity derives from the large subject within which all these phenomena exist.

In both poems general facts are scattered among particular poised moments or vignettes, and detailed descriptions of single objects are interspersed with more comprehensive lists. In these catalogues both Moore and Bishop demonstrate simultaneously the naturalist's delight in factual accuracy and the poet's pleasure in remarkable names. For example, Bishop lists "fading shells":

> Job's Tear, the Chinese Alphabet, the scarce Junonia,
> parti-colored pectins and Ladies' Ears,

arranged as on a gray rag of rotted calico,
the buried Indian Princess's skirt;   (CP 32)

and Moore describes little spotted horses as

hard to discern among the birch-trees, ferns, and lily-pads,
avalanche lilies, Indian paint-brushes,
bear's ears and kittentails,
and miniature cavalcades of chlorophylless fungi
magnified in profile on the moss-beds like moonstones in
        the water;
the cavalcade of calico competing
with the original American menagerie of styles.   (CPM 74)

Both catalogues emphasize the poetic and metaphorical character of America's botanical names, but again, Bishop's more aestheticizing sensibility is evident in her avoidance of markedly technical terminology and her selection of more precious names.

While their shared methods of acute observation and painstaking reporting impress upon the reader their reliability as neutral witnesses, both Bishop and Moore in fact slide easily from detached observations into more subjective and fanciful interpretations. For example, Moore first presents an antelope by noting objectively its "black feet, eyes, nose, and horns" but then moves into more figurative description – "engraved on dazzling ice-fields, / the ermine body on the crystal peak; / the sun kindling its shoulders to maximum heat like acetylene, dyeing them white – / upon this antique pedestal" (CPM 73). Similarly, Bishop notes first the "S-shaped birds, blue and white" but then more imaginatively describes "unseen hysterical birds who rush up the scale / every time in a tantrum." Sometimes Bishop's imposition of her subjectivity is less subtle than Moore's, as when she attributes embarrassment and a desire for "fun" to her tanager and pelican. (I shall return to this distinction later.)

In the works of both poets, subjective interpretations and imaginative additions, whether obvious or not, are essential to poetic meaning; both women present nonhuman nature in ways inviting comparison with human situations and behavior. Thus, Bishop's cannon-ball simile assumes new significance when one reaches the conclusion of "Florida." There, after having presented the most ornamental characteristics of Florida seen by daylight, Bishop uncovers the corruption, the primeval energy of Florida "after dark." The simile provides a preparatory suggestion of violence in nature that is absent from Bishop's descriptions of clowning pelicans, mild turtles, and decorative shells. Moreover, as a reminder of human ferocity, the cannon-balls link the violence in the landscape to that in human nature. Similarly, the terms by which Moore conveys her approbation of the energy and intricate variety of all that the "deceptively reserved and flat" glacier encompasses prepare for the concluding section of "An Octopus." There the glacier becomes an implicit model for the kind of poetry Moore admires – "unegoistic" work characterized by "restraint," "a love of doing hard things," and an apparently limitless "capacity for fact." While the older poet's moral is more explicit, both poets employ the descriptive mode to move toward ethical evaluations that carry implications beyond their immediate subjects.

## II

The Moore-like descriptive techniques that Bishop adopts in *North & South* – accurate depiction of concrete phenomena, heightening of visual experience, avoidance of stock comparisons, impersonal reporting – serve modernist ends. The modernists' attention to visible objects, evident in movements such as imagism and objectivism, arose from a distrust of the abstract nature of language and an awareness of a gap between the reflective act of speech or consciousness and the immediate character of experience. Dissatisfied with concepts and terms that could be detached from sensory reality, the modernists tried to attach their poetry to particular objects and instants. *North & South* demonstrates that by 1946 Bishop would have concurred with Moore's approval of T. E. Hulme's declaration "that language 'should endeavor to arrest you, and to make you continuously see a physical thing, and prevent your gliding through an abstract process' " (MMR 148). The energy Moore and Bishop devote to making their readers see physical things implies a shared faith in the meaningfulness of visible surfaces. As Pinsky has pointed out, poets who appear to develop meaning primarily through descriptive precision wish to "[create] the illusion . . . that sensory perception *is* meaning."[12]

Moore's minutely descriptive method presumes that in scrutinizing appearances one perceives spiritual and intellectual qualities. In "People's Surroundings" she states that the visible character of people's homes answers one's questions about the inhabitants; "with X-ray-like inquisitive intensity upon it, the surfaces go back" so that "we see the exterior and the fundamental structure" (CPM 57). She believes that the surfaces of an artwork can and should be " 'lit with piercing glances into the life of things,' " and that it will thereby "acknowledge the spiritual forces which have made it" (CPM 48).

Bishop's detailed descriptions, too, reflect a belief that "The power of the visible / is the invisible" (CPM 100). Thus, in "Jerónimo's House"

(CP 34), merely by describing a poor Cuban's home, Bishop conveys a sense of his entire existence and his strength of character. Of course, the first-person narration helps the reader enter sympathetically into Jeróni-mo's being; the reader appreciates the imaginative resourcefulness of one who can cheerfully think of his flimsy shack as a "fairy palace" or as a "wasps' nest / of chewed-up paper / glued with spit." But most of the poem's insights are conveyed simply through a list of observable details, usually linked by childlike "and"s. The visible scene suggests the limited pleasures of a life highlighted by participation in an annual parade and by "the voices of / my radio // singing flamencos / in between / the lottery numbers." Bishop's simple description of the man's few possessions cap-tures, too, the loving care with which they are arranged and brightened to create an enclave of domestic warmth in a fragile "shelter from / the hurricane."

Again in "Cirque d'Hiver" the "surfaces go back," first under the scrutiny of Bishop's keen eye and then through the probings of her com-passionate imagination. The first two stanzas are essentially objective visual description in which Bishop notes the fine points of the small toy's ap-pearance with the same care that Moore devotes to, say, the design on a porcelain plate in "Nine Nectarines." Thereafter Bishop intermingles re-alistic details with more imaginative explorations of the miniature circus horse's feelings and his "melancholy" soul. Like Moore, Bishop finds that even the smallest objects or creatures can express or address the hu-man condition and that careful attention often uncovers heroic attributes in the most unassuming subjects. But while Moore's manner remains impersonal even when she explains the significance an object holds for her – "one perceives no flaws / in this emblematic group of nine" or "It was a Chinese / who imagined this masterpiece" (CPM 30) – Bishop, sometimes edging toward the sentimental, expresses a more personal identification with what she describes (the sort of identification we shall see developed more fully yet less heavy-handedly in later poems). While the posing, empty-headed ballerina whirls about, the little horse looks directly at the speaker to mirror her own understanding of human limi-tations and of the tremendous difficulty of small accomplishments; like mechanical toys, people may make a show of gaiety but advance only a few awkward steps before running down.

In their careful attention to the surfaces of small curious objects, both Bishop and Moore "dramatize a meaning / always missed by the exter-nalist" (CPM 100). Moore, however, does not always rest with drama-tizations and often provides explicit moral interpretations. Her tendency to employ moral propositions is in large part responsible for the wide-spread critical notion that "if her technique was Modernist, her temper-

ament was not."[13] Moore's critics have, however, been too quick to isolate the aphoristic morals in her poems, cutting them off from the poetic
contexts in which they arise. It can be misleading to approach Moore as
an epigrammatist, particularly in her earlier books, since her propositions are modified by the descriptive lines and exempla that accompany
them. Very rarely does she present a generalization without the particulars from which it was imaginatively induced; terms such as "truth" or
"complexity" acquire more specific meanings in her poems than in common usage.

For example, "In the Days of Prismatic Color" (CPM 41–2) contains
the neatly quotable propositions that "complexity is not a crime, but
carry / it to the point of murkiness / and nothing is plain," that "sophistication is as it al- // ways has been – at the antipodes from the init- / ial
great truths," and that "Truth is no Apollo / Belvedere, no formal thing."
But in the opening lines "complexity" emerges as a kind of perception –
a mode of seeing in which underlying unities are not appreciated or existing distinctions are blurred – not as an inherent condition. The abstract
term has been molded by the poem's context into a specialized one with
an idiosyncratic definition. Moreover, the poem actually deals not with
"truth," but with the narrower subject of truth in art. Feet, which are
introduced by playing with the etymology of "antipodes," implicitly
identify the subject as poetry itself; a poem not written in poetic feet is
denouncing this traditional formal complexity. Reference to the statue of
the patron god of music and poetry reinforces the reflexive character of
the poem's subject. When Moore declares that "Truth is . . . no formal
thing," she wittily abandons her own formal syllabic construction, moving into free verse for the poem's conclusion. Thus the "imaginary garden" of this poem – and many others – turns out to be more self-
referential and less sweepingly moralistic (that is, more typically modernist) than it might seem.

The descriptive details – those "real toads" – that almost always accompany Moore's moralizing abstractions prevent the poems' neat conceptual formulations from reducing the gray shades of reality to stark
black and white. For example, in "Those Various Scalpels," Moore's
antipathy toward the woman depicted and the sophistication she represents is tempered by her appreciation of the magnificent detail of that
refinement. Moore's careful attention to the woman's ornamental elegance compels her finally to admit that "these things are rich instruments
with which to experiment," though she maintains her strong objection
to "dissect[ing] destiny with instruments / more highly specialized than
components of destiny itself" (CPM 52). Here, as frequently in Moore's
works, precise attention to details gives rise to perceptions that discour-

age oversimplification. Moore's refusal to exclude material that might support another point of view lends a provisional character to her moralizing.

Bishop, too, can be a moralizing poet, particularly in her earlier collections. But, following Moore's example, she develops her morals from the context of a precisely observed particular subject. Like Moore's poetry, hers seems to rest on the principle that, in Kenner's words, "optical experience must be carefully anatomized before we can too readily allow it to be psychic. For the supreme insult . . . to that which is other than we . . . is to have, on too little acquaintance, something to say 'about' it."[14] A poem such as "The Fish" (CP 42–4) demonstrates (the moral is enacted rather than announced) that the proper psychic or moral response to otherness arises only in the process of careful observation.

When the narrator first catches the fish, her attention to it is cursory, noting only the facts that reflect on her skill at fishing – that the animal is "tremendous" but that it "hadn't fought at all." More careful attention, however, leads to an appreciation of the fish as a distinct being, deserving less self-centered consideration. First an examination of the fish's skin, associatively calling to mind old wallpaper, leads to an acknowledgment of the long life he has led. Looking next at his gills, an organ humans do not possess, the narrator begins to empathize with the experience of this alien creature, imagining how it feels to be "breathing in / the terrible oxygen." His strange eyes that will not return her stare impel further attention to the fish's remarkable otherness so that she examines him still more carefully, admiring, as Moore would, the "mechanism of his jaw." Only at this point – "and then I saw" – does the speaker notice the five old pieces of fish line which, as evidence of struggles against previous fishermen, are crucial in determining her final exemplary response.

Not until she has fully assimilated the fish's nonhuman individuality does she permit herself to draw an analogy between the fish and an old man, seeing the fishlines as "a five-haired beard of wisdom / trailing from his aching jaw." She continues to stare, presumably perceiving the creature in all its fishness as well as the parallels between its struggles and a person's battles for survival. From this attention, accurate as well as imaginatively sympathetic, arises a vision in which the fish's past victories merge with the human triumph of achieving wisdom through experience; this is the source of her final victory, the release of her catch.

"The Fish" indicates that the young Bishop shares Moore's awareness that people too easily behave as if a human being were "made / to see and not to see; to hear and not to hear; // . . . accustomed to shout / its own thoughts to itself like a shell" ("Melancthon").[15] In fact, Bishop in

1948 singled out for praise Moore's ability to approach other creatures uncondescendingly and without preconceived notions: "There are morals a'plenty in animal life," Bishop wrote in a tribute for her friend, "but they have to be studied out by devotedly and minutely observing the animal, not by regarding the deer as a man imprisoned in a 'leathern coat.' "[16] Participating in Moore's modernist wariness of mistaking projection for perception, Bishop follows the older poet's example by carefully attaching her poetry to observable surfaces before adopting a particular moral stance.

Though the animals in Moore's poems generally exemplify characteristics relevant to human behavior, Moore does not rely on stereotypical personifications (for example, the sly fox). Instead, she uses animals' observable attributes – the jerboa's ability to live without water, the plumet basilisk's amphibious nature, the snail's "compression" and "contractility" – as the bases for her moral interpretations. Her extended naturalistic description of a creature's appearance and characteristic behavior gives an impression of objective recording. She reinforces the air of neutrality and detachment by using academic and scientific diction, by alluding to esoteric lore, and by quoting from documents. She presents her morals in flat, even pedantic, language, avoiding both rhetorical flourishes and displays of emotion.

Bishop's "The Fish," though it enacts a moral lesson, contains no explicit morals or aphorisms, and in that it differs from most of Moore's poems. "Roosters" (CP 35–9) shows Bishop experimenting with a Moore-like approach to articulated moralizing (though ironically, disagreement between the two women about the construction of this piece prompted Bishop to cease consulting Moore about her unpublished poems). Bishop does use the stereotypical image of the fighting cock, and her presentation is more emotionally heated than Moore's usually is, but in significant ways the poem follows Moore's approach. Description establishes a naturalistic base before the appearance of personifying touches such as "rustling wives" and "cruel feet." By the eighth stanza it is clear that roosters represent martial men; their "traditional" cries proceed "from protruding chests / in green-gold medals dressed, / planned to command and terrorize the rest."[17] Yet despite their obvious symbolic function, roosters in this poem remain roosters, presented as they realistically figure in human lives, either as live creatures or as images in weather vanes and art objects.

After building her descriptive foundation, the speaker asks what the human uses of roosters "project" about humankind. To answer that question, she turns to lore about roosters, employing documentation in a singularly Moore-like fashion – "you whom [the Greeks] labeled //

'very combative . . .' " She characterizes the cock's red comb in academic diction far more typical of Moore's work than her own – "that
excresence" which "makes a most virile presence." Both the quotation
and the objectively formal diction provide seemingly neutral support for
her point of view (though her academic manner may intend, too, a
mockery of such stereotypically male pretension). When the poem moves
into more intellectual discourse, Bishop gives abstract issues visual concreteness – as Moore might – by reference to a particular "old holy
sculpture." The "heart-sick" tears visibly link sculptured Peter and "our
chanticleer" to justify the speaker's assertion that " 'Deny deny deny' / is
not all the roosters cry."

Perhaps, as Anne Stevenson has suggested, if Moore had written this
poem, she would have ended it with that tidy epigram. Certainly, that
was Moore's strategy in "The Steeple-Jack," which concludes with "the
solid- / pointed star, which on a steeple / stands for hope" (CPM 7). But
even if the poem had ended with such neatness, it would nonetheless
invite us to question the adequacy of that message which the sculptured
cock was intended to convey to the Pope and the people, just as the
message of hope in "The Steeple-Jack" must be balanced against the poem's
warning of danger. While Moore's endings tend to be aphoristic, her
poems usually contain something to temper the force of that message
and its air of certainty. Bishop's conclusion of "Roosters" further develops the qualifying tendency latent in Moore's work (just as Ashbery extended the qualifying tendency in Stevens' writing), bringing uncertainty
more to the fore. Bishop returns at the close to a description of dawn far
less threatening than that of the poem's opening, but this hopeful perspective is darkened by the question "how could the night have come to
grief?", recalling the horrified disbelief Peter felt the morning after his
betrayals. The poem ends on a very tentative, heavily qualified upbeat:
Though the "horrible insistence" of the roosters' cries fades as the sun
rises, the sun, like the rooster, is an ambivalent symbol (particularly if
one recalls that Peter was Christ's friend), "faithful as enemy, or friend."

Recognizing that "The passion for setting people right is in itself an
afflicting disease" (CPM 58), Moore often sought ways of conveying her
judgments without appearing to preach. Humor particularly helped her
maintain an air of greater detachment. *Observations* contains a number of
brilliantly satirical portraits – "The Monkeys," "Novices," "To a Steam
Roller," "He Wrote the History Book," to name but a few – in which
Moore lightens her animosity and distaste through wit. She knew
humor's power to provoke insight and effect change: "Among animals,
*one* has a sense of humor. / Humor saves a few steps, it saves years"
(CPM 119).

In prose tributes Bishop has praised Moore's gift of humor, manifest in whimsy or in witty irony (CPr 129, 144); her early poem "Seascape" (CP 40) demonstrates that she, too, prefers mockery to preaching as a way of conveying her opinions. In technique, as well as attitude, the poem is heavily indebted to Moore. The first thirteen lines comprise a single sentence in which the syntax has been stretched, as Moore's often is, by descriptive elaboration and digression. The description itself is very like Moore's in comparing natural phenomena to precious man-made ornaments and using metaphorical vehicles that draw upon specialized knowledge of various subjects. Figurative references to illuminated manuscripts, Gothic arches, and cartoons by Raphael create an effect of collage which Moore frequently achieves. The shifts from colloquial expression – herons "got up as" angels – to more elegant diction – "tiers and tiers of immaculate reflections" – and the punning wordplay – "a fish jumps, like a wild-flower / in an ornamental spray of spray" – are also reminiscent of Moore. Such writing demands from the reader the same intellectual agility that the modernist's "antholog[ies] of transit" do.[18]

Having convinced her readers in the first half of the poem that "this celestial seascape . . . does look like heaven," Bishop then fancifully presents the contrary view of one who "thinks he knows better," the personified lighthouse. For this "clerical" figure, the concept of heaven is so tied up with that of hell that he cannot appreciate the paradisal aspects of his environment; he even assumes that the fires of hell warm the water at his feet. His ridiculously lugubrious determination to "remember something / strongly worded to say on the subject" makes him the object of Bishop's mockery. By having him associate heaven with what is implicitly his own light shining through the night, Bishop ridicules the egotism of the preacher's perspective. With an ironic twist, she makes the lighthouse a "skeletal" figure of death rather than a light of salvation. The poem does not deny the presence of invisible threats, but clearly life is far richer for those swimming and flying – and laughing – than for the fixed figure preoccupied with stern warnings about hellfire and danger.

Generally, Bishop's humor is less severely mocking than in "Seascape"; characteristically she relies on more whimsical wit for attaining a modernist coolness of surface. "The Gentleman of Shalott" (CP 9–10) exemplifies her more typical tone of amused detachment. Her fantastic gentleman, presuming that a mirror is responsible for the symmetry of the human body, is confused about which half of him is "in or out / of the mirror," perhaps a confusion about what is nature and what is art. Bishop's offhand manner of presentation – "This arrangement / of leg and leg and / arm and so on," "only a leg, etc." – implies that her readers, too, are familiar with this dilemma. She touches briefly on the potentially serious consequences of not knowing where one ends and where one's projected vision begins: "There is little margin for error, / but there's no proof, either. / And if half his head's reflected, / thought, he thinks, might be affected." Yet she maintains her lighthearted and journalistic manner, concluding with the deadpan report that "he wishes to be quoted as saying at present: / 'Half is enough.' "

Bishop learned from Moore that in poetry saying "half" is often "enough." She regarded Moore's poems as "nearly all understatement,"[19] and followed the older poet's example of using understatement for attaining a balance between emotional or moral conviction and objective detachment. In Bishop's later, less sentimental works she more consistently imitates this quality she admires, but even in *North & South* she recognizes that, as Moore says, "only rudimentary behavior is necessary to put us on the scent" (CPM 45). For instance, in "Large Bad Picture" Bishop puts her readers on the scent with her title and thereafter refrains from using loaded or evaluative terms. There is nothing obviously objectionable about the painting she describes, and since it is realistic enough to convince the viewer that she can hear its birds crying, the quality of representation, at least, must be quite good. Only from the subtly disquieting accumulation of words like "still," "motionless," "quiet," "perfect," "perpetual" does the reader sense an absence of vitality. Only by the repetition of "crying," "rolling," "round and round" does Bishop hint that the painting is too general and predictable to seem true or interesting. The poem's final lines appear entirely noncommital: "Apparently they have reached their destination. / It would be hard to say what brought them there, / commerce or contemplation" (CP 12). The reader has to infer that Bishop regards as seriously flawed any artwork that does not communicate the distinct and particular impulses leading to the moment depicted. In its inhibition of emotional display "Large Bad Picture" enacts a moral and aesthetic virtue essential to both Bishop and Moore.

Bishop sometimes achieves emotional restraint by constructing fantasies – more often in her early volumes than in her late ones. Her fabulous subjects, like Moore's animals, provide vehicles through which her judgments of human folly can be indirectly and entertainingly expressed. For example, a passionate complaint about the modern urban environment and its effects on human sensibilities underlies her poem about an invented creature, "The Man-Moth" (CP 14–15). The poem contrasts ordinary Man, who is so attached to rational scientific data that "He does not see the moon; he observes only her vast properties," with the highly imaginative Man-Moth, who "thinks the moon is a small hole at the top of the sky." The Man-Moth's vision propels him to push to the limits of what he can discover and achieve. His quest, however, is unsuccessful, and he falls to the ground, where he is dwarfed by huge buildings, trapped in "pale subways of cement," and terrified by trains moving "at terrible speed." It seems that city dwellers are doomed to dull conformity or, if their imaginations are intact, to living in nervously exaggerated pain and fear. Yet the poem is never as heavy-handed as this synopsis. Bishop diverts us from her serious "message" by lively depictions of the Man-Moth's exploits and bizarre habits; since he is ludicrous and grotesque as well as sympathetic, and since he is after all "only make-believe," she does not force our identification with his plight.

Bishop's and Moore's tendencies to temper, qualify, or disguise statements proclaiming significance indicate their desire to recognize the limits of their perceptions and understanding. Moore's often-noted predilection for armored animals is further evidence of her sense that we must approach the world warily, never overestimating our powers. A desire to acknowledge and accept limits is reflected also in the disciplined formal character of their poetry, and in their frequently stylized manners of speaking.

## III

Both Bishop and Moore often adopt strictly regulated poetic forms, and in so doing acknowledge that the gap between consciously shaped human art and the unconscious world of nature is in some senses unbridgeable. Through the blatant artifice of their poetic structures, Moore and Bishop suggest that poems, like the subjects they describe, are to be respected as "other," as objects operating according to strict laws governing their own natures. Thus Bishop's "imaginary iceberg," emblem of the creations of the artistic imagination, "cuts its facets from within" and "adorns / only itself" (CP 4). The two women differ, however, in the forms they use to underline the firmly governed otherness of a poem. Bishop generally did not adopt the major formal innovations for which Moore is known, such as her elaborate syllabic patterns or her method of miscellaneous quotation. It seems that the younger poet, benefiting from the upheaval the modernists had already accomplished in the preceding twenty years, did not need to assert so dramatically her break with traditional poetics and traditional iambic norms in order to feel that her work could be taken seriously.

Like the narrator of her early story "In Prison," Bishop is "unconventional, rebellious perhaps, but in shades and shadows" (CPr 189); she strives to "make it new" largely within traditional restrictions. While adhering to an iambic base, Bishop – like Moore (and Donne and Herbert) – more often invents her own stanza forms than she adopts inherited ones such as the sestina or sonnet. When she does write a sestina, such as "Miracle for Breakfast," she innovatively includes the homely end-words "coffee" and "crumb" (this innovation has been widely imitated since). She takes great liberty with rhyme, frequently employing off rhymes or repeating end words. Often she exhibits Moore's preference for inconspicuous rhyme by using light and feminine rhyme, by rhyming only a few lines in a long stanza, or by varying the rhyme scheme for different stanzas of a poem. Bishop's line and stanza breaks, however, tend to respect syntactic units – and therefore the cadences of speech – far more than do Moore's "intricate grids of visual symmetry"[20] also, Bishop's poems maintain a more discursive and narrative continuity. One cannot say of Bishop, as Kenner does of Moore, that she conceives of the poem as "a system, not an utterance."[21]

While Bishop's poetry remains considerably closer to utterance than Moore's – a difference to be considered at some length in Chapter 4 – the younger poet uses traditional poetic devices in ways that call attention to the artifice of all poetic structures. For instance, her unfashionably frequent recourse to the simile, like Moore's, underlines the distinction between the natural world poems depict and the human constructions that poems are. In "Quai d'Orléans," for example, Bishop highlights the artifice of poetic figures by alternating description of small floating "real" leaves with portrayal of the gigantic figurative leaf of the barge's wake. Both real and figurative leaves "[drift] by / to disappear," yet the indelible "fossils" they imprint in the mind result not only from observation but also from the transformation of what is observed into figurative terms. "The Monument" explicitly announces that the value of art is linked to its obvious unnaturalness. In the artwork's apparent artifice lies the strongest evidence of its origin in the human spirit, and of the human desire to lend cohesive form to ephemeral yearnings or experiences:

> Wood holds together better
> than sea or cloud or sand could by itself,
> much better than real sea or sand or cloud.
> It chose that way to grow and not to move.
> The monument's an object, yet those decorations,
> carelessly nailed, looking like nothing at all,
> give it away as having life, and wishing;
> wanting to be a monument, to cherish something.
> The crudest scroll-work says "commemorate."  (CP 24)

Bishop's rhymes and regular rhythms, her strings of adjectives, and her similes are the "decorations" by which her art, in Moore's words, "acknowledge[s] the spiritual forces which have made it."

In diction, too, Bishop's and Moore's motivating principles are more similar than their apparently divergent practices might suggest. Like many of the modernists, Moore was striving to eliminate the notion of a special kind of diction reserved for poetry and to revitalize the meanings of common words. As W. C. Williams wrote admiringly in 1925, "Miss Moore gets great pleasure from wiping soiled words or cutting them clean out, removing the aureoles that have been pasted about them or taking them bodily from greasy contexts."[22] Similarly, T. S. Eliot praised her for "carrying on that struggle for the maintenance of a living language."[23] To refresh poetic language, Moore embraced an extraordinary range of diction, including the terminology of the natural and social sciences as well as the formal diction and slack syntax of academic prose. Reading, say, the opening of "Marriage,"

> This institution,
> perhaps one should say enterprise
> out of respect for which
> one says one need not change one's mind
> about a thing one has believed in,
> requiring public promises
> of one's intention
> to fulfil a private obligation    (CPM 62)

one sees why early reviewers complained that her eccentricities of spacing were merely "tricks" by which she "tries to give an adventitious effect" to what is in fact "a clumsy prose."[24] Moore's interest in prosaic language was shared by other modernists; though she disapproved of low colloquial expressions and avoided even the verbal contractions that other modernists used to bring art closer to life, her diction, like theirs, is a return to real speech. Eliot aptly characterized her language as

> the curious jargon produced in America by universal university education – that jargon which makes it impossible for Americans to talk for half an hour without using the terms of psychoanalysis, and which has introduced "moron" as more forcible than "idiot."[25]

Even Moore's strangest linguistic mannerisms are commonplace in her private correspondence, suggesting that where her poetic language diverges from most American speech, it does not diverge from her own.

Though the diction of Bishop's poetry is less often technical and less obtrusively educated than Moore's, her language too is heterogeneous, and she too heightens linguistic energy by shifting among varied manners of speaking. For example, in the following four lines she moves from a colloquially figurative to a flatly prosaic mannner, then introduces more elevated "poetic" diction before shifting suddenly to dry scientific phrasing:

> This is a scene a sailor'd give his eyes for.
> The ship's ignored. The iceberg rises
> and sinks again; its glassy pinnacles
> correct elliptics in the sky.   (CP 4)

Like her modernist mentor, Bishop provides a series of linguistic jolts. At times she seems to imitate Moore's adoption of the awkward wordiness of academic writing; "The Man–Moth," for instance, contains such phrases as "of a temperature impossible to record in thermometers," "he regards it as a disease / he has inherited the susceptibility to," "his rare, although occasional, visits to the surface." In general, however, Bishop prefers less stilted language, often trying to convey the impression of an individual speaking. In so doing she sometimes sounds as antilyrical as Moore:

> Now can you see the monument? It is of wood
> built somewhat like a box. No. Built
> like several boxes in descending sizes
> one above the other.
> Each is turned half-way round so that
> its corners point toward the sides
> of the one below and the angles alternate.
> Then on the topmost cube is set
> a sort of fleur-de-lys of weathered wood.   (CP 23)

More typically she achieves an impression of graceful yet casual speech, incorporating quite refined or "poetic" terms into a colloquial foundation. Particularly in this early volume she is less wary of the beauties of traditional lyricism than Moore, more enamored of the music of assonance and alliteration. Nonetheless, she contains her aestheticizing embellishments enough to give the illusion of ordinary speech, demonstrating a modernist desire to avoid inflated rhetoric, romantic gushing, and (in Pound's words) "emotional slither."

## IV

Most of the poems in *North & South* were written between 1933 and 1941, the years when Moore was most directly involved in Bishop's work. In 1955 Bishop published her second collection, *A Cold Spring*; the title poem provides ample evidence that Bishop in her mature and independent work retained many of the modernist methods and principles she derived from Moore.

Still interested in depicting nature's oddities, Bishop now favors landscape poems, describing in "A Cold Spring" (CP 55–6) the stages of spring's arrival in rural Maryland. Like Moore, Bishop pauses deliberately over each detail she presents, making her reader attend to familiar seasonal events as if witnessing them for the first time. For example, she traces the movement of fireflies which "begin to rise: / up, then down, then up again: / lit on the ascending flight, / drifting simultaneously to the same height, / – exactly like the bubbles in champagne." Obviously, Bishop has retained her commitment to discovering images that are as precisely apt as they are witty and unexpected. And as before, these comparisons often juxtapose objects from divergent realms, presenting a calf's afterbirth as "a wretched flag" and bullfrogs' croaking as "slack strings plucked by heavy thumbs." In Moore-like fashion (think, for example, of the jerboa with its "pillar body erect / on a three-cornered smooth-working Chippendale / claw"), Bishop compares natural creatures to finely worked human crafts, again devoting meticulous attention to the colors she sees: "the smallest moths, like Chinese fans, / flatten themselves, silver and silver-gilt / over pale yellow, orange, or gray." (When Moore saw the poem in the *New Yorker*, she raved about this passage so reminiscent of her own work, telling Bishop it was "one of the most beautiful things you have ever done, – as color and as words" [4 June 1952].) As is so consistently true in Moore's work, Bishop's narrator is present more as an eye than as an "I." Though "A Cold Spring" is addressed to a friend, Jane Dewey, she is present only as a pronoun connected with the land – "your big and aimless hills," "your white front door," "your shadowy pastures." Continuing in the tradition of imagism and objectivism, Bishop relegates humanity to the background and focuses on concrete objects and sensations. Like much of Moore's work, "A Cold Spring" often sounds flatly prosy – "The next day / was much warmer" or "the blurred redbud stood / beside it, motionless, but almost more / like movement than any placeable color." And while the poem is carefully crafted, its internal and end rhymes are, in modernist fashion, unobtrusive, occurring irregularly, often linking distant lines or lines of quite different lengths.

Bishop differs from Moore, however, in her relation to the landscapes and creatures she portrays. Moore's acquaintance with her subjects was often wholly or predominantly secondhand. She examined her animals in museum cases, viewed them on naturalists' films, and investigated their habits and habitats from her seat in the library; she found her landscapes in photographs and sometimes in artists' prints.[26] She never in person saw the monkey puzzle tree growing in southern Chile, nor watched the Costa Rican basilisk "basking on a // horizontal branch / from which sour-grass and orchids sprout," nor heard Ireland's "guille-mot / so neat and the hen / of the heath and the / linnet spinet-sweet." Her descriptions are realistic in accuracy, but far more detailed and in-formation-packed than the perceptions one would attain visiting these places and encountering their wildlife.[27] When Moore describes the pan-golin as

> a true ant-eater,
> not cockroach-eater, who endures
>    exhausting solitary trips through unfamiliar ground at
>                                                  night,
>    returning before sunrise; stepping in the moonlight,
>       on the moonlight peculiarly, that the outside
>          edges of his hands may bear the weight and
>                                         save the claws
> for digging, (CPM 117)

she is not pretending to be a naturalist who has spent nights awake in the jungle. Rather, she selects her subjects because, having learned about them from others, she is attracted by certain of their characteristics – in this case, the pangolin's armor and its grace – or simply by the distinc-tiveness of their behavior. Her descriptions reflect this impersonalized admiration or intellectual curiosity rather than direct personal involve-ment.

Bishop's landscapes, by contrast, tend to be places where she has lived or at least visited, and her personal relation to them and to the creatures living there is apparent. In her early poem about Florida (where she lived for some time), Bishop did demonstrate Moore's interest in presenting information-packed overviews and recounting little-known bits of my-thology, history, or zoology. In *A Cold Spring*, however, Bishop re-stricts herself to lore that any villager could recount, for example, that sheep on the "bird islands" of Cape Breton "Sometimes, frightened by aeroplanes . . . stampede / and fall over into the sea or onto the rocks." Sometimes, as in the preceding example, the facts she presents are as surprising as Moore's, but they are included because they reflect the speaker's peculiar views or interests – here, her fearful sense of life's precariousness – rather than a general preference for the most arresting bits of information one might cull from arcane sources. Since Bishop's speaker does not seem unusually well-informed, we understand that emotional rather than intellectual engagement compels her to describe a particular place and the animals and plants seen there. In Moore's work the object described is the genuine focus of interest; in Bishop's work the interest lies less in the object itself than in the narrator's relation to what she describes and in what this relation reveals about her. Bishop appears to be trying, in modernist fashion, to see external things truly, while in fact what she scrutinizes is herself.

Because Moore tends to use her natural subjects as moral illustrations, she can as easily describe a place she has never seen – Ireland – as one she has seen – Virginia. The extent of her first-hand experience is not discernible from either the kind or quantity of information she provides. Bishop, who traveled widely and led a less sheltered life, insists on the clear distinction between the vicarious experience books provide and the immediate experience of personal encounter. This distinction is the subject of "Over 2,000 Illustrations and a Complete Concordance" (CP 57–9). Here Bishop contrasts the "serious, engravable" illustrations of exotic and holy lands which she perused as a child with scenes she observed firsthand as an adult traveler. The illustrations support an ordered view of the cosmos and of human history; the images, "when dwelt upon . . . all resolve themselves." In her voyaging, however, she has encountered a far less tidy world where jukebox music plays while bodies lie in state, where beautiful poppies are inseparable from revoting old men making eyes. In her unmediated experience, holy graves do not look particularly holy and no recognizable pointers – no "one apart, with outstretched arm and hand / [who] points to the Tomb, the Pit, the Sepulcher" – reveal the underlying significance of what she witnesses. (Nor did Bishop's orphaned childhood provide anything approximating the Nativity's image of a cozily secure "family with pets.") What the traveler encounters provides no evidence of a logical or moral system of cause and effect governing human lives. This disquieting randomness – the fact that everything seems "only connected by 'and' and 'and' " – which Moore seems never to have encountered, is central to the experience Bishop's mature poetry conveys, just as it is central to Ashbery's work.[28]

Of course, Moore was not so naive as necessarily to accept another's illustrations of ordered truth as accurate renditions of reality. In "Smooth Gnarled Crape Myrtle" (CPM 103–4), for example, she contrasts the romanticized pairing of birds that "artifice saw" with the loveless solitude of the "Rosalindless / redbird" she observes. But she nonetheless has faith that some underlying order is operating. Thus she discerns a regulated rightness in the bird's singleness, regarding his situation as rationally justifiable: "without / loneliness I should be more / lonely, so I keep it." Although she wishes to correct those who sentimentalize nature, she trusts that more scientific and rational authorities can be relied upon to uncover meaningful structures beneath observed surfaces. Without denying that nature's power can be awesome or even terrifying, Moore generally perceives nature as a moral force. In "Virginia Brittania" she proclaims that natural phenomena constructively "dwarf" people's "arrogance" and "assertiveness"; study of nature gives a balanced perspective on humankind's power and importance while still providing, as it did for the nineteenth-century Romantics, intimations of the divine glory of which humans are part.

This is not to say that Moore pretends to possess anything more than intimations. Like Bishop, she is conscious that for "the defenseless human thing" cradled by potentially overwhelming natural powers, "it is all ifs; we are at / much unease" (CPM 128). Her claims are therefore modest; "the wisest is he who's not sure that he knows" (CPM 130). Nonetheless, Moore discovers in nature guidelines or models for human behavior. Bishop's nature, so often a world of mists, is far less penetrable by human investigations, scientific or otherwise. Its vast inhumanity dwarfs us, but not necessarily in a way that works for our moral improvement. The little we are able to comprehend in this immense nonhuman realm is solipsistically limited to what corresponds to our own inner natures; what is seen reveals more about the perceiver than the perceived. Therefore Bishop writes only about those aspects of nature she has personally encountered, using what she has perceived as a map for exploring her own interior.

Returning to "A Cold Spring," one can detect the increasing personalness of Bishop's approach in her descriptive method. From the start the poem invokes the pathetic fallacy – "the trees hesitated; / the little leaves waited." Human behavior is immediately projected upon the landscape, and the poem's images continue to remind us of human conduct: Obviously deer do not need to practice fence leaping, young oak leaves do not swing though trees, dogwoods do not "infiltrate" or smoke cigarettes, and cardinals do not crack whips. What the description conveys is the speaker's transformation as much as the landscape's – her gradual relaxation in the presence of her friend's warmth, her initially hesitant progress toward an exuberant presence and toward romantic, perhaps erotic, celebration (suggested by reference to guitar music, wavering fans, and glasses of champagne).

Moore's startling images usually seem to have been chosen for their sensory accuracy alone.[29] With them, as Kenner has pointed out, she builds collages by finding visual analogies ("optical puns," he calls them) for each part of a scene or object; when assembled together on the page, these imitate the experience of the perceiving eye. There is no thematic or connotative unity imposed on her figures, since the reality she seeks to create is one of surfaces observed in many separate acts of attention.[30]

Even in *North & South*, Bishop, who was always more traditional and less insistently denotative than Moore, rarely went to Moore's extremes of assembling many incongruous figures; now in her mature work Bishop's tendency to select figures that have their own unity and build a subplot of their own is more pronounced. "The Bight" (CP 60–1), another landscape poem, demonstrates the connotative importance of Bishop's descriptive figures. The poem's subtitle, "On my birthday," is a between-the-lines indication that the poet will be taking stock of her life and its passage as she examines the scene before her. Once again, in Moore-like fashion, the description is precise, the images are unconventional, and the speaker is effaced behind an impersonal "one" who acts as a remarkably acute but seemingly detached observer. Yet the reference to Baudelaire in the seventh line suggests an unmodernist twist in Bishop's use of metaphor. Having noted that the bight's water is "the color of the gas flame turned as low as possible" – an apparently factual observation – Bishop adds, "one can smell it turning to gas; if one were Baudelaire / one could probably hear it turning to marimba music." She is alluding to the symbolist's concept of *correspondances*, according to which "les parfums, les couleurs, et les sons se répondent" and material things or physical sensations correspond to a unified spiritual reality; Baudelaire believed that images are more suggestive than descriptive and that the symbols discovered by the poet in nature reveal the patterns of inner experience.[31] Bishop does go on to detect in the noise of a dredge the "perfectly off-beat claves" of marimba rhythm, but "one" is not in fact Baudelaire. She has only concurred with his theory that nature may be read by the poet so as to suggest the structure of his or her inner life. Unlike Baudelaire, she does not see around her things "ayant l'expansion des choses infinies . . . Qui chantent les transports de l'esprit et des sens." What she sees brings to mind images of human labor – pelicans crashing like "pickaxes," shark tails "glinting like . . . plowshares," birds' tails working like "scissors," stove boats lying like "torn-open, unanswered letters." In the human activities invoked, energy seems expended to disproportionately little effect, and one is more conscious of dreary finitude than of any infinite expansion. Crashing "unnecessarily" hard into the water, the pelicans come up with no fish; the hard-earned hauls of the sponge fishermen appear mere "bobbles"; and storm-battered boats are "not yet salvaged, if they ever will be." That Bishop regards her own life as a similarly inefficient and disordered expenditure of energy in which she has "rarely [come] up with anything to show for it," is the point of her punning announcement, "The bight is littered with old correspondences." Considering "all the untidy activity" of her own life, Bishop cannot salvage Baudelaire's sense of the universe as an animated, sensuous unity. When she digs for correspondences, she comes up with a jawful of marl – a mouthful of dust suggesting entropy and mortality. She stoically pursues her "awful but cheerful" activity, without expecting either to discover Baudelaire's mystical wholeness or to perceive with Moore's clear objectivity.

In the earlier poems of *North & South*, for Bishop – as for Moore – full appreciation of otherness involved simultaneously attending to what can be observed and acknowledging the limitations of the eye's penetration. Both women regard seeing surfaces exactly and sensing depths accurately as interdependent activities: "Will / depth be depth, thick skin be thick, to one who can see no / beautiful element of unreason under it?" ("Melancthon"). However, the more obviously subjective and thematic descriptive method Bishop employs in her later volumes implies that she has reevaluated the extent to which one can determine fundamental structures by examining surfaces; poems in *A Cold Spring* suggest that the human ability to appreciate invisible depths while adhering to surfaces is more restricted than Bishop had previously thought.

In "Cape Breton" (CP 67–8), Bishop uses very Moore-like description to emphasize the limitations of that kind of carefully objective approach. In depicting the Nova Scotian landscape, she notes, as Moore would, its eye-catching yet typical characteristics, identifies species of birds and trees, names particular islands, draws careful visual distinctions and employs striking similes. She even uses Moore's hallmark, the complex noun phrase – "the cliff's brown grass-frayed edge." From this kind of painstaking observation Moore would deduce timeless laws of being, and for her these – along with the wonder experienced in observing – would have comprised the scene's meaning. But Bishop's description leads her to the assertion that "Whatever the landscape had of meaning appears to have been abandoned, / unless the road is holding it back, in the interior, / where we cannot see." What is meaningful remains invisible, though the songs of unseen sparrows hint of that hidden reality and Bishop's imagination allows her to paint its desolate mountains and acres of burnt forest. The poem then takes another un–Moore-like tack, shifting out of a timeless present to a particular Sunday's occurence involving human figures; a bus arrives and discharges a man carrying a baby. Crossing a meadow, he descends out of sight "to his invisible house beside the water." Nature is unaffected by his passing; the mists continue to drift like primeval "ghosts of glaciers" and an "ancient" chill ripples the brook. Yet the speaker has experienced an understated revelation: Hidden where she cannot see them are not only disused trails and stark forests but also homes – and, always magical for Bishop, families with parents. Discovering such meanings inaccessible to the physical eye depends on releasing herself from tangible or rational surfaces and permitting her imagination to project what cannot be seen. As she wrote to Anne Stevenson, "works of art . . . catch a peripheral vision of whatever it is one can never really see full-face but that seems enormously important."[32]

Increasingly, Bishop's attention to surfaces acknowledges the immensity and the fascination of all that does not meet the eye. In her treatment of human subjects as well as natural scenes, Bishop highlights what is mysterious and impenetrable. In "Faustina, or Rock Roses" (CP 72–4), for instance, she probes the curious intimacy between mistress and servant, white woman and black. The "visitor" can see in the servant's "sinister kind face" an unresolvable conundrum; she cannot discern whether Faustina offers the ailing white woman genuine protection and care or manipulative oppression. "There is no way of telling. / The eyes [of observer or observed] say only either." Similarly, in her double sonnet "The Prodigal," Bishop can capture with terrifying verisimilitude the physical horror of the man's life – the stench of the pig sty he lives in, the texture of its dung-plastered walls and flooring; she can describe his responses, drunk or sober, to visible phenomena such as the pigs' stares or the reflection of sunrise in barnyard puddles. But she cannot unveil the "shuddering insights, beyond his control" that would explain the prodigal's exile; nor is it clear that for the man himself those "insights" are anything more definite than the "uncertain" paths of bats swooping through the dark. While Bishop's speakers might like to penetrate to fundamental depths with X-ray like vision, they find instead that the depths of otherness are murky or impenetrable.

In general, then, the maturing Bishop adapts to more personal, psychological materials, and to a more skeptical view of what such observations can reveal, a descriptive method heavily indebted to Moore. The older poet was confident that the scientist and the poet are allied, that rational dissection and objective examination will uncover the knowledge we crave. She regarded the human being as one animal among many in a world governed according to predictable laws; human behavior is "consistent with the / formula – warm blood, no gills, two pairs of hands and a few hairs – that / is a mammal" (CPM 120). As components of a natural system as regulated as her syllabic structures, human beings, though fallen, can make themselves at home in the world. For Bishop, however, human beings remain alien in a world whose strangeness cannot be alleviated by human intellect. The world she encounters – threatening her with electrical storms, hurricanes, and all sorts of unforeseeable losses – is like her jagged iceberg; far more of it is submerged than visible, so one must remain cautious in trusting to what one can see. In regarding herself as adrift in an unpredictable and unknowable universe, Bishop seems closer to Stevens (and to Ashbery) than to Moore:

> From this the poem springs: that we live in a place
> That is not our own and, much more, not ourselves
> And hard it is in spite of blazoned days.[33]

As Borroff has skillfully elaborated, Moore's highly stative language indicates that "hers is an imagination that sees more meaning in fixity than in flux";[34] in this her modernism differs from that of Stevens or Williams. By the late forties and early fifties, when Bishop composed the poems in *A Cold Spring*, such a faith in graspable truths was inaccessible to her, as it was to many poets of the early twentieth century, and as it has been to most artists of recent decades. "At the Fishhouses" (CP 64–6) provides a particularly explicit statement of this attitude that distinguishes Bishop's approach to nature from Moore's.

"At the Fishhouses" begins, as a poem by Moore might, with a description of a scene that seems eternally suspended. The verbs in the opening section are stative – "the five fishhouses have steeply peaked roofs," "all is silver," "the big fish tubs are completely lined," "on the slope . . . is an ancient wooden capstan," etc. Yet what Bishop chooses to describe differs from what Moore would present. When Moore tells us, for instance, that "eight green / bands are painted on / the [plumet basilisk's] tail – as piano keys are barred / by five black stripes across the white" (CPM 22), we know that both lizards and pianos have always looked like that and will continue to do so in the future. But Bishop's description insists that the scene she observes is the product of continual changes caused by both people and nature: The man's shuttle is "worn and polished," the ironwork on the capstan "has rusted," the buildings have "an emerald moss growing on their shoreward walls." Such details make us aware that a future visitor would find a different scene in which these processes of erosion, decay, and growth were further advanced.

The fixity of the scene at the fishhouses is further undercut as the speaker becomes an active participant, offering the old man a Lucky Strike and engaging him in conversation. Reminders of historical process now become more overt; "he was a friend of my grandfather" implies her grandfather's death, and "the decline of the population" tells of broader changes. Moreover, Bishop's enchantment with this place emerges as a fascination not so much with the visible world people inhabit as with the unknowable sea it borders. She is attracted to this silvered village because it bears so much evidence of the sea's touch, while her real desire – like that of her "Riverman" or of Lucy in "The Baptism" – is for "total immersion," though she admits that would be "bearable to no mortal." Drawing a message from the scene very different from any Moore would offer, Bishop presents the sea as a symbol of "what we imagine knowledge to be: . . . drawn from the cold hard mouth / of the world, derived from the rocky breasts / forever, flowing and drawn, and since / our knowledge is historical, flowing, and flown." In suggesting that our knowing anything is itself imaginary, in adhering to a vision of unending process, in believing revelations in this harsh world fleeting and costly, Bishop stands firmly in the mainstream of contemporary art.

The affinities between Bishop's poetry and Moore's are deep, specific, and also limited. That Bishop herself recognized both the profundity of her debt and its boundaries is clear from the poem she wrote about Moore, first published in 1948 but begun in 1940, just about the time when she stopped showing Moore her work in progress.[35] After rejecting in October of that year the older woman's revisions of "Roosters" as "your" poem and not her own, Bishop could see clearly how her aesthetics differed from Moore's, while appreciating all that drew her to Moore's poetry. Bishop's "Invitation to Miss Marianne Moore" (CP 82–3), a playful expression of Bishop's strong affection for her friend and for the bright clarity of her vision, simultaneously imitates and characterizes Moore's poetry. Masterfully capturing much that is essential to the older woman's writing, this poem also defines Moore's poetic territory as distinct from that Bishop claims as her own.

Like many of Moore's works, the "Invitation" accumulates a clutter of concrete images and relies on these to convey abstract qualities. To entice Moore to fly to her, Bishop names precisely those small colorful objects one would expect to catch Moore's eye; and Bishop describes them as Moore would, with figures mingling the beauties of nature and of art, employing technical and specialized vocabularies:

> The ships
> are signaling cordially with multitudes of flags
> rising and falling like birds all over the harbor.
> Enter: two rivers, gracefully bearing
> countless little pellucid jellies
> in cut-glass epergnes dragging with silver chains.

Knowing well the stuff from which Moore derives her poems, Bishop offers her friend facts, statues, skyscrapers, museums, library reading rooms, and morals. Besides celebrating the "natural heroism" of Moore's moral sense and her striking taste in dress, Bishop celebrates all the eccentricities of Moore's poetic style: her syllabic "musical inaudible

abacus," her unexpected grammatical "turns," her "priceless vocabularies," and her "dynasties of negative constructions" (lovingly imitated in
Bishop's "long unnebulous train of words").

All this highlights the uniqueness of Moore's vision and her technique;
indeed, the distinctiveness of Moore and her work has been a consistent
refrain in Bishop's prose statements about her friend. For instance, in a
1977 talk on influences, she declared, "Marianne Moore was so unique –
absolutely unique. There was nobody quite comparable. Auden was very
much influenced by her. He was one of the few people who had a powerful enough gift to absorb her."[36] Bishop's own gift was "powerful
enough" as well; yet she recognized that absorbing too much of such a
peculiar voice would only yield – as she intended in her "Invitation" –
obvious imitation. Bishop learned a great deal from Moore's predilection
for unassuming natural subjects, from her ironies, from her extraordinarily attentive way of observing, and from her relentless insistence on
accuracy, but the younger poet differed from the older in both tempera-
ment and outlook. She had to incorporate into her writing additional
techniques to accommodate the kind of introspective emotional resonance that suited her and to convey her perspective as a member of a
generation uncomfortable with assertions of ordered stability in language
or perception.

# 4 "Resolved, dissolved . . . in that watery, dazzling dialectic": Bishop's divergence from Moore and modernism

## I

From the first poem in her first volume, "The Map," through her last poem, "Sonnet," one can trace Elizabeth Bishop's preoccupation with divisions and boundaries. Equally persistent is her hope that all artworks, like her map and her sonnet, might permit transcendence or erasure of boundaries and release from dichotomies, even while they lend form and order to experience. In "The Map" Bishop prefers maps to histories in part because maps leave so much that is indeterminate, open to interrogation and to the embellishment of fantasy; shadows might or might not be shallows, one can imagine that either the land or the sea actively draws the other close. Looking at maps, one can entertain greater possibilities of freedom; a country's color might be determined by choice and suitability, not, say, by the imposition of colonial rule. It is the words printed on the map that most emphatically defy the historian's boundaries (or the rationalist's delineations of excess):

> The names of seashore towns run out to sea,
> the names of cities cross the neighboring mountains
> – the printer here experiencing the same excitement
> as when emotion too far exceeds its cause. (CP 3)

In "Sonnet" that excitement recurs as the gaity of release from an imprisoning mechanism that divides a creature into dichotomous body and spirit.[1] Appropriately, Bishop invokes the organizing form of the traditional sonnet only to break its constraints in short lines and an idiosyncratic rhyme scheme.

The boundaries and schisms that preoccupy Bishop – such as those between self and world, between conscious and unconscious mind, between art's fixity and time's flux, between language and experience – function differently than the polarizations Moore explores. Moore's oppositions between critics and connoisseurs or between conscious and unconscious fastidiousness, for example, are analytical distinctions that do not threaten her faith in the world's order – a fixed and moral order that includes humankind and which humans can, for the most part, both apprehend and describe.[2] Bishop posits no such order in the world; nor does she pursue Eliot's more typically modernist vision of fragmentation. Unable to approach art, in Moore's fashion, as a means of revealing the wondrous tidiness of an existent order and uninterested in mourning over "a heap of broken images," Bishop attempts to bridge gaps and mediate between opposed poles so that some sense of genuine freedom and wholeness may be achieved. True to her situation as a contemporary artist (and true to her heritage as a "nice watery" Baptist [CPr 215]), she opts for immersion and merging in fluid solutions.

Particularly in her later volumes *Questions of Travel* (1965) and *Geography III* (1976) Bishop seeks that mediation in an approach like Wallace Stevens', that is, in focusing on "the mind in the act of finding." The models who provide the foundation for her portrayal of mental process, however, are as much Romantic as modernist.[3] The nineteenth-century Romantics, responding to the dissolution of societally shared concepts of meaningful order, initiated a poetics of personal discovery. They sought to uncover general truths by tracing in poetry the dynamic evolution of the individual's thoughts, feelings, and beliefs, capturing the moments of insight that occur within immediate experience. Bishop makes use of many of the techniques they developed to insure that the personal experience and emotions portrayed would seem authentic. At the same time, she adapts to a contemporary world view the Romantic emphasis on meanings to be discovered within unfolding internal process. She finds in her own mental processes – of observing, of questioning, of changing her mind, of inventing verbal forms – resolutions for troubling schisms and disjunctions. Maintaining a modernist skepticism and detachment, she does not attempt to derive lofty, sweeping truths from her momentary apprehensions. She focuses on the fluidity of psychological experience as something valuable in itself, without sharing the Romantic hope of its either leading to revelations of general spiritual significance in the universe or providing evidence that the human mind is part of the nature it perceives.

Bishop's divergence from Moore in her sense of threatening divisions is clearly illustrated by comparing the two poets' animal poems, since Bishop's sense of alienation – her belief that, in Stevens' words, "we live in a place / That is not our own, and, much more, not ourselves" – shapes her treatment of animal subjects in her later volumes. While Moore tends to stress the marvelous adaptation of creatures to their environment, Bishop often emphasizes the agonizing separation between living beings and the natural world to which they seem in fundamental ways ill-adapted. For instance, by grouping together the three animal soliloquies of "Rainy Season; Sub-Tropics" (CP 139–42) Bishop stresses each creature's inescapable isolation. Though located in the same place at the same moment, these animals, each preoccupied with its own defenses and unique capabilities, are incapable of communication. The crab taps the snail's shell encouragingly, but assumes the snail will not even know he has done so. In fact, the snail does perceive a tapping on his shell, but he cannot determine its source, much less interpret its condescendingly encouraging tone. Similarly, the snail recognizes that he and the toad share the misery of being "too big" so that "our proportions horrify our neighbors," yet he cries out from an isolated self – not "pity us," but "pity me." The sense organs of each animal register only a tiny portion of what goes on in the environment, and these three have few common perceptions. Moreover, none of the creatures can function comfortably in such threatening surroundings. The toad's eyes hurt, the rain chills him; the crab, in a shell that is "not my home," has strayed too far from the water into a place "too hard" and dry; the snail is too heavy. For all three, survival, even locomotion, is a grim contest.

When Moore describes animal life, she generally presents examples for emulation. Simply by acting according to their natural dispositions, her creatures behave admirably and live in wise harmony with their environment. Moore implies that human suffering derives from failing to follow the dictates of our own best nature; we blunder and stray as animals do not. Her goal is ethical and spiritual reform: If we would face adversity with the invincible spirit of the ostrich, the patient accommodation of the imprisoned elephant, the frugality of the jerboa, the gay civility of the frigate pelican, and the careful self-protectedness of all her armored menagerie, our lives would possess the grace of theirs.

Only occasionally in Bishop's later poetry do animals exist in graceful harmony with nature. In such cases – as with her "grand" and "other-worldly" moose or with the shameless dog and contented bird in "Five Flights Up" – Bishop depicts a gap between the human speaker and the animal, emphasizing the non-humanness of the observed natural order. Whether these creatures inspire joyous awe or envying sadness, they remain glimpsed emblems of an inaccessible state of being. When Bishop's animals more closely approximate human characteristics, they cope no more successfully with the world than we do; they simply reflect our own limitations.

In "Electrical Storm" (CP 100), for example, people and animals equally are victims of natural forces that seem at best strange and "unsympathetic," at worst intentionally malicious. The homely images with which Bishop describes nature's powerful and threatening phenomena only extend the impression of a hostile world; when she describes lightning striking her house with a sound "like a dropped tumbler," thunder banging "spiteful as a neighbor's child," and hailstones falling "dead-white, wax-white, cold – / diplomats' wives' favors / from an old moon party," she makes the small common things appear as strange and forbidding as the obviously alien cosmic energies to which they are figuratively linked. Humans lack control even over human inventions; a single lightning bolt obliterates the electrical power, lights, and telephone upon which we depend. Similarly, in "The Armadillo" (CP 103–4), winds suddenly transform lovely man-made lanterns into deadly apocalyptic flames. People's homes are as vulnerable as owls' nests, humans as helpless as fleeing armadillos; our very hearts, like fire-balloons, beat, expire, or explode at nature's whim. (That nature's power is murderous is similarly suggested in "Electrical Storm" by the appearance three times of the word "dead.") The armor that Moore so often admires seems in Bishop's poem anachronistic; it effectively protects neither armadillos nor humans, who can only cry out and stand with "a weak mailed fist / clenched ignorant against the sky."

Ignorance and powerlessness also characterize Bishop's sandpiper (CP 131), who serves as an emblem of the poet. Struggling in a world of waves, changing weather, and shifting tides, the bird is panicked by the flux of his universe. Bishop treats his predicament with the same combination of wry humor and gravity with which she regards her own. Her portrayal of the "finical, awkward" bird obsessively focusing downward while scurrying on "brittle feet" makes him a ludicrous spectacle; by identifying him as a "student of Blake" (aspiring, as in the "Auguries of Innocence," "to see the world in a grain of sand") Bishop indicates that she mocks herself as well. Nonetheless, since the sandpiper cannot attain a broadly coherent vision, his focusing on tiny details provides a positive model for human behavior. The sandpiper's world, like ours, shifts among disconnected states: "The world is a mist. And then the world is / minute and vast and clear." (Here syntactic severence emphasizes the disjunction, while contrasting terms "only connected by 'and' and 'and' " stress the absence of comprehensible relations.) Organizing systems, if they do exist, are unperceived by the bird, who can't even tell whether "the tide

/ is higher or lower." If this anxiously hurrying creature finds any solace, it will be in the beauty of a few colorful sand grains among the millions of drab ones beneath him. Like Ashbery, Bishop would have us appreciate the consolation available in distinct flashes of loveliness, without lending to them the myth of some larger order. In believing "no detail too small," she remains a student of Moore as well as of the Romantic Blake, but in emphasizing the isolation of each meaningful detail and the absence of a regulating system she speaks for a later time.

Bishop has acknowledged that the sandpiper's constant running mirrors her own peripatetic life: "All my life I have lived and behaved very much like that sandpiper – just running along the edges of different countries and continents, 'looking for something.' "[4] As critics have often noted, travel is a central metaphor in her later works, and as "Questions of Travel" (CP 93–4) explains, the need to travel manifests human deracination in this world. Overwhelmed by the excess of motion and change in the Brazilian landscape, the voyager in "Questions of Travel" ponders whether there isn't too much movement in her own life as well. While criticizing the voyeuristic aspects of travel and the superficiality of the tourist's collection of spectacles and souvenirs – "And have we room / for one more folded sunset, still quite warm?" – Bishop nonetheless concludes that "it would have been a pity to miss" these varied experiences. The traveler's consolations, like the sandpiper's, might appear trivial – randomly discovered curiosities integral to the lives of the country's common folk, such as the sound of clogs on a gas station floor, the construction of a pet bird's bamboo cage, or the beauty of flowering trees along a particular road. Yet these mundane phenomena, rather than the magnificent sights supposed to entice tourists, increase the voyager's understanding, however "blurr'dly and inconclusively," of people and history. (And perhaps blurred and inconclusive thoughts best stimulate further thinking.) Bishop's ultimate justification for traveling, however, is simply that she knows no home.[5] One who acknowledges that "home" signifies something not yet found, or lost and not yet rediscovered, or simply nonexistent is most at home in the process of searching, acting out physically a quest that is metaphysical and spiritual.

Bishop's amusing portrait of herself as disgruntled tourist in "Arrival at Santos" cautions that travel will offer no rewards unless one commits oneself to this difficult quest. The original motive for travel is all too likely the self-indulgent and self-deceptive hope of discovering "a different world, / and a better life, and complete comprehension / of both at last, and immediately" (CP 89). Naturally, the foolish tourist is disappointed; even supposedly exotic ports turn out to be dependent on such familiar practicalities as national flags, commerce, and currency. Morever, the adjectives with which she describes the harbor scene – "self-pitying," "sad and harsh," "uncertain," "feeble" – reflect her own state of mind and suggest that the tourist's own psychological and perceptual limitations determine her disappointment. Discovery of a genuinely "different world" requires that the tourist undertake a more risky expedition. Pushing into the unknown, forbidding territory within herself as well as the unexplored areas of South America, she must "[drive] to the interior."

How few resources individuals usually possess or develop for exploring these alien frontiers is suggested by Bishop's important late poem "Crusoe in England" (CP 162–6), in which Crusoe's bleak situation is a stylized version of the general human situation. The natural environment of Crusoe's island is entirely strange and hostile – "volcanoes dead as ash heaps," hissing turtles, sooty trees offering no shade, goats whose eyes "expressed nothing, or a little malice." The only "sacerdotal beings," whose conventional function would be to mediate between people and the forces governing the universe, are "far out . . . advancing and retreating . . . Beautiful, yes, but not much company."

Crusoe's "miserable philosophy," drawn from thinkers of the past, is inadequate to sustain him: "I didn't know enough." His memories of the books he'd read, even the books themselves, "were full of blanks"; their supposed wisdom proves useless. Crusoe's inability to complete Wordsworth's line "which is the bliss [of]. . ." with the word "solitude" indicates that, tested against his own experience, the Romantic ideal of solitary communion with nature turns out to be a falsified glorification. Far truer to Crusoe's own life, and to Bishop's, is his grimly humorous nightmare of "infinities of islands": "I had to live / on each and every one, eventually, / for ages, registering their flora, their fauna, their geography." The castaway's revision of Auden's line "The more they love, the more they feel alone," (from "Alone") in "the more / pity I felt, the more I felt at home" also suggests the inadequacy of inherited "truths." The interlude when Friday brings love – poignantly understated – to Crusoe's life is the only time when he does not feel alone.

Even when settled back in populous England, Crusoe is still marooned on an island, another "cloud-dump" that doesn't feel like home. With Friday dead, he has lost the sense of connection generated by human intimacy. Released from the struggles for survival on his "poor old island," Crusoe finds himself deprived of the meaning with which the stressful circumstances had imbued his small possessions and accomplishments. The loss of meaning reflects devastating internal changes;

"The living soul has dribbled away" as much from Crusoe as from his knife, for he has lost the creative power to generate adventure and frontiers within:

> My blood was full of [islands]; my brain
> bred islands. But that archipelago
> has petered out. I'm old.
> I'm bored, too.    (CP 166)

For life to "reek" with meaning, new frontiers must be perpetually erupting – and continually investigated – within each individual.


## II

From *North & South* on, Bishop explored through her poetry the enigmatic internal realms of dream and the unconscious, thereby clearly distinguishing her poetics from Marianne Moore's. Moore's poetry is rarely introspective. In accordance with T. E. Hulme's prescriptions, her art focuses on the hard, dry particulars of concrete physical phenomena; she associates clear poetic vision with the objective and rational methods of scientific observation. Despite her genuine appreciation of "the beautiful element of unreason under it" ("Melancthon"), Moore concerned herself primarily with physical and moral laws. She acknowledged the mysterious, but didn't attempt to penetrate it – "we prove, we do not explain our birth" (CPM 80).

Moore admired the achievements of selected surrealist artists, claiming, for instance, in a review entitled "Concerning the Marvelous," that "the fictitiously architectural verisimilitudes of de Chirico, in his enamelled perspective period particularly, and Max Ernst's voracity for a definiteness that cannot defeat mystery, are effects of lasting value for poetry."[6] But she blamed surrealism, which brought to the fore the "element of unreason," for contributing to the lack of clarity in much modern writing. She linked surrealism to the tendency of recent writers "to forget that [writing] is an expedient for making one's self understood" (MMR 171) and declared that "structural infirmity truly has, under surrealism, become a kind of horticultural verbal blight threatening firmness at the core" (MMR 171).

Coming of age in the heyday of surrealism, Bishop more enthusiastically embraced it. While in college she believed that the way to write poetry was to record all one's dreams; thinking that eating cheese at bedtime prompted interesting dreams, she even kept a pot of Roquefort in the bottom of her Vassar bookcase.[7] In 1935 and again in 1937, she lived in the heartland of surrealism, Paris, where she "read a lot of surrealist poetry and prose."[8] Her poem "The Monument" was inspired by the frottages of Max Ernst,[9] and even George Herbert's "Love Unknown," which helped inspire "The Weed," she admires as "almost surrealistic" in "convey[ing] the most fantastic thoughts in the most correct and natural language."[10] Though Bishop's adoption of surrealist techniques was limited, her assimilation of the surrealists' desire to penetrate the unconscious by articulating fantasies and dreams was thorough and enduring.[11] As Moore herself remarked, praising "The Weed" and "Paris, 7 A.M.," Bishop's "exteriorizing of the interior, and the aliveness all through . . . are the essential sincerity that unsatisfactory surrealism struggles toward. Yet the sobriety and weight and impact of the past are also there" (20 September 1936, Vassar).

Though Bishop's poems have little in common with the surrealists' automatic writing, some of her images display the bizarre torsion of surrealist associationalism. For example: "The short, half-tone scale of winter weathers / is a spread pigeon's wing" (CP 26); "the little moons fall down like tears / from between the pages of the almanac" (CP 124); "Arthur's coffin was / a little frosted cake" (CP 125); "the wires, at the moon's // magnetic instances, take off / to snarl in distant nebulae" (CP 151). Such images, which supplement Bishop's Moore-like images of exact optical resemblance, invoke a nonrational way of knowing largely absent from Moore's work.

Using the associational techniques of surrealism, Bishop explores some of the fearful and gruesome aspects of experience which Moore's more decorous poetry rarely touched. In "Paris, 7 A.M.," for example, grotesque surrealistic images confuse inner and outer wintry landscapes to convey the speaker's deadening sense of life's dissolution in time. Similarly, "Love Lies Sleeping" (CP 16–17) presents a partially surrealistic vision of the city awakening. Bishop's depiction of "what presses on the brain" at night merges inner and outer horrors; the "twitching signs" and "neon shapes / that float and swell and glare // down the gray avenue between the eyes" are city lights transformed by a disturbed, perhaps hung over, perceiver. The "love" that does not lie sleeping is that of the "queer cupids of all persons" who prepare all day to dine cannibalistically on each other's hearts. The alternative to such perversion is almost equally appalling: the deathlike trance of one "whose head has fallen over the edge of his bed"

> so that the image of

> the city grows down into his open eyes
> inverted and distorted. No. I mean

> distorted and revealed,
> if he sees it at all.   (CP 17)

Moore would distinguish inversion and distortion from revelation, while Bishop insists on undermining such rational divisions.[12]

"I use dream–material whenever I am lucky enough to have any," Bishop told Anne Stevenson.[13] An early pair of poems about dreaming, "Sleeping on the Ceiling" and "Sleeping Standing Up," convey both the seduction and the terror of dreams' inversions of ordinary consciousness. "Sleeping on the Ceiling" playfully suggests that an absolute inversion of ordinary perception, which I take to mean a complete immersion in the dream world of the unconscious, might bring a longed for peacefulness of spirit. The limited access to that realm offered by our nightly dreams, however, presents a horrifying challenge: "We must go under the wallpaper / to meet the insect-gladiator, / to battle with a net and trident" (CP 29). Again in "Sleeping Standing Up" (CP 30) Bishop describes both the enormous potential of dreams and the inevitable frustration of that potential. In the transposed landscape of sleep our dreams serve as "armored cars . . . contrived to let us do / so many a dangerous thing." Traveling in them we might regain access to the imaginative world of childhood, here presented as our lost home. Yet because of "how stupidly we steered / until the night was past," we fail to locate that imagined place of innocence and comfort. The quest Bishop undertakes as dreamer, then, is the same one she undertakes as world traveler; in both roles she pursues the sense of belonging, of loving and being loved, of understanding one's self and one's surroundings which constitute being "at home."

In several of her Brazil poems, Bishop pays tribute to more wholehearted dreamers who are less bound to the world of rationality than she.[14] The irrational Manuelzinho, "half-squatter, half-tenant," feels entirely at home on what the speaker regards as "my property." He is exasperatingly (and for the reader, hilariously) improvident, impractical, unpredictable, even manipulative. Yet this ludicrously cursed man who produces weirdly shaped vegetables and seems to attract inexplicable blights and disasters, is also unquestionably an artist: "your gardens / ravish my eyes. You edge / the beds of silver cabbages / with red carnations, and lettuces / mix with allyssum" (CP 96). His painted hat rim is evidence of his idiosyncratic imagination, as are his account books, more accurately termed "Dream Books." Beneath the speaker's aggravation with her odd gardener runs a current of admiration for his thoroughly irrational approach to survival, so different from her own: "I take off my hat, unpainted / and figurative, to you" (CP 99).

The Amazonian native who speaks in "The Riverman" is another dreamer, and another of Bishop's protagonists desiring complete immersion in a fluid world. Upon glimpsing supernatural powers, he dares to encounter them naked, dares to journey beneath the surface of ordinary life. Another quester who longs not just for a different world but for "complete comprehension," the Riverman has gained enough wisdom to pass through the boundary between air and water that constrains most mammals. He is convinced that everything we need is right there "in that magic mud" – "one just has to know how to find it" (CP 108).

For most of us, however, integration of unconscious and conscious knowledge is more difficult than for the Riverman; the dark mysteries of our dreams "are all inscrutable by eight or nine" in the morning (CP 146). If we are to absorb the revelations of the unconscious, we need some counterbalancing familiarity amid strangeness; for Bishop the act of observing concrete details furnishes this steadying keel. While Moore's details support a vision of a universe whose parts exemplify the design of the whole, Bishop's provide something upon which one can focus in a vertiginous world of flux, the way the sandpiper watches the grains of sand between his toes. As provisional points of orientation, they yield a needed, if limited, security and clarity.[15] For Bishop, the small objects one encounters provide distraction from one's personal troubles; at the same time, faithfully recording one's perceptions of them, like relating one's dreams, permits an indirect form of self-examination.[16]

Though Bishop's poems are never "confessional," the autobiographical content of her poetry grows more apparent as her career progresses. Kalstone has argued that in this regard Bishop's career follows a pattern typical of her generation, in which autobiographical energies play an increasing role as the poet matures.[17] This general trend toward more autobiographical poetry may reflect widespread skepticism about sweeping patterns; distrusting attempts at generalized understanding and suspecting the prevalence of solipsism, the artist focuses on what is closest at hand, what he or she may best hope to know and understand – his or her self. Certainly, Bishop adapts Moore's techniques of observing and recording external details to introspective explorations of private psychology, although Moore, as is clear from her criticisms of Bishop's early fiction, believed her protegée should aspire to a larger scale of message. After reading "The Labors of Hannibal," Moore warned Bishop that "a thing should make one feel after reading it, that one's life has been altered or added to . . . I am sure good treatment is a handicap unless along with it, significant values come out with an essential baldness" (7 March 1937, Vassar and Rosenbach). She responded to "In Prison," "I can't help wishing you would sometime in some way, risk some unprotected profundity of experience; or since no one admits profundity of experience, some characteristic private defiance of the significantly detestable . . . I do feel that tentativeness and interiorizing are your danger as well as your strength" (1 May 1938, Rosenbach). Though sobered by Moore's remarks, Bishop held to that tentativeness and interiorizing so essential to the integrity of her vision.

In several apparently autobiographical poems about memorable moments of her childhood, Bishop recreates the curious blend of reasoning and imagination, observation and projection, by which we cope in a world where change – and therefore loss – is the only certainty. Her somewhat surrealistic "Sestina" convincingly portrays the oblique ways in which a child's mind confronts suffering. (I assume the poem is autobiographical because Bishop when a small child was cared for by her maternal grandparents in rural Nova Scotia after her father died and after her mother was permanently placed in a mental institution.) Unable to acknowledge directly the source of the pain within and around her – presumably, the loss of her parents – the child, as Vendler has noted, senses unshed tears and displaces them everywhere.[18] Both the woman and the child cling to the mooring of banal details, such as the teakettle and the almanac, lest they drown in emotion. At the same time, the child's imaginative transcription of her environment in a drawing allows her to bring into the open her awareness of emotional repression (represented by the rigidity of her house), her grief (the button-tears), and her longing for the adults (the man she "puts in") missing from it.

Again in "First Death in Nova Scotia" domestic details contribute a concrete anchor to which the inexplicable can be tied, as well as materials for a fantasy that lends some recognizable shape to the utter strangeness of death. The white and red complexion of Arthur's corpse permits the living child to associate Arthur's state with those of two familiar objects – the stuffed loon with the white breast and red eyes who "kept his counsel" in the parlor and the portraits of royal couples "warm in red and ermine." By imagining that Arthur has been invited to leave the loon's chilly parlor and enter the warmth of the king's court, the child is able to formulate a question that expresses her bewilderment and terror before the spectacle of death: "But how could Arthur go, / clutching his tiny lily, / with his eyes shut up so tight / and the roads deep in snow?" (CP 126)

In such poems (as in the stories and prose reminiscences about her childhood) Bishop blurs traditional distinctions between reason and imagination, between the conscious and the unconscious. Contemplating the works of Darwin, the supreme rationalist, she once asserted that "there is no split":

> one admires the beautiful solid case being built up out of his endless, heroic *observations* . . . – and then comes a sudden relaxation, a forgetful phrase, and one *feels* that strangeness of his undertaking, sees the lonely young man, his eyes fixed on facts and minute details, sinking or sliding giddily off into the unknown.[19]

Bishop does not deny that the rational and the irrational are different, but she asserts that within the mind's workings there are unexpected interpenetrations or bridges between them.

Vendler has already identified

> the continuing vibration of [Bishop's] work between two frequencies – the domestic and the strange. In another poet the alternation might seem a debate, but Bishop drifts rather than divides, gazes rather than chooses.[20]

As a corollary to Vendler's insight, I would suggest that Bishop impresses upon her readers the value of that drift, the importance of abandoning an exclusively rational perspective if we are to cope with the strangeness that looms within the familiar. In her wonderful poem "In the Waiting Room" (CP 159–61) Bishop shows that, while a certain attachment to the concrete and rational provides a necessary security, a too-rigid attachment that resists the inscrutable or mysterious results in a short-circuiting of consciousness.

The poem reenacts a rite of passage which is essentially a fall from innocence. In it we witness Bishop's initiation into the illogic, the ultimate strangeness, of personal identity. Hearing the *"oh!"* of pain "from inside" as both her own cry and her aunt's, the perplexed child suddenly recognizes her connection to the whole human species.[21] She has to face that she is one with primitive, even cannibalistic, tribes, one with all women whose breasts she finds so "horrifying," one with her immediate family which includes "foolish, timid" Aunt Consuelo. Yet she also recognizes in the same moment that she is her own singular "I," distinct from them all.

Struggling to maintain her composure before these logically incompatible truths of an identity both unique and common, the child does what Bishop's speakers and protagonists so often do: she attaches her eyes to immediate concrete details – "trousers and skirts and boots / and different pairs of hands / lying under the lamps" – and focuses on indis-

putable facts – "three days and you'll be seven years old." On this occasion "Elizabeth" 's efforts not to sink under the "big black wave[s]"
are ineffective because she still innocently holds on to expectations of
purely rational understanding: "Why," she asks, "should I be my aunt,
/ or me, or anyone? / What similarities . . . held us all together / or made
us all just one?" Overwhelmed by the incongruity between the logical
and the mysterious, she loses consciousness.

The child's "sensation of falling off / the round, turning world / into
cold blue-black space" – so reminiscent of Darwin's giddy sliding off
into the unknown – represents more than simply fainting. Awareness of
one's identity brings with it awareness of all that is other than one's self;
the space into which "Elizabeth" sinks is the immense not-me of our
inexplicable and alien universe. When she regains consciousness, she has
been initiated into the adult's awareness of the world as a place where
order and reason may only be veneers. Having encountered a vast in-
comprehensible dimension underlying the little that we understand, she
no longer asks the world to be thoroughly rational. She can orient herself
by noting that "The War is on," without peering beneath the surface to
question the reasonableness of war's violating the bonds that "held us all
together." She accepts that her immediate surroundings – the wintry
night in Worchester, Massachusetts – are as cold, dark, and strange as
the blue-black void into which she had fallen.

## III

Words are clumsy vehicles with which to communicate such
complex intellectual and emotional experiences. At age seven Bishop knew
no word to characterize her new awareness, and as an adult she settles
for the lame " 'unlikely'." Bishop's use of quotation marks here calls
attention to the problematic nature of language, seeming to question
whether any verbal expression can accurately delineate her sentiments.
In Bishop's mature poetry, her diction and descriptive manner manifest
a significant divergence from Moore's conception of linguistic precision.
The contemporary poet's techniques place greater emphasis on the limitations of art and language than do her modernist mentor's. Bishop, like
Ashbery, attempts to keep her reader conscious of the gulf between things
and the linguistic rendition of them, while trying at the same time to
minimize the gap by bringing her language as close as possible to the
texture and process of consciousness.

Moore believed that "the poet and scientist work analogously"; "each
is attentive to clues, each must narrow the choice, must strive for precision" (MMR 273). Having once trained to be a biologist, Moore af-

firmed the value of scientific study as preparation for her poetic career: "Precision, economy, drawing and identifying, liberate – at least have some bearing on – the imagination" (MMR 255). Consistent with that statement, her poetry testifies that she has exactly drawn and identified the specimens before her. For example, here is her opening description of the cat Peter:

> Strong and slippery,
> built for the midnight grass-party
> confronted by four cats, he sleeps his time away –
> the detached first claw on the foreleg corresponding
> to the thumb, retracted to its tip; the small tuft of fronds
> or katydid-legs above each eye numbering all units
> in each group; the shadbones regularly set about the mouth
> to droop or rise in unison like porcupine-quills.    (CPM 43)

Moore's poems enact, as Kenner has said, "a minute obligation to fact";[22] her meticulous descriptions reflect a faith that, if the poet applies sufficient effort and attention, her language can convey information, can analyze, measure, characterize, as precisely as the scientist's. In Moore's opinion, the only legitimate excuse for the absence of clarity is "one's natural reticence" (MMR 171). Unlike some of her contemporaries such as T. S. Eliot, she never seems to suggest that language itself may be inadequate to depict experience precisely.

The confident sharpness of Moore's description of Peter contrasts with the description that opens Bishop's "Poem":

> About the size of an old-style dollar bill,
> American or Canadian,
> mostly the same whites, gray greens, and steel grays
> – this little painting (a sketch for a larger one?)
> has never earned any money in its life.    (CP 176)

Here the poet's expressions of approximation (besides suggesting the carelessness of her initial examination of the painting) imply a reluctance to approach description as if language could neatly encapsulate her perceptions. Bishop's characterization of her "proto-dream-house" in "The End of March" as "a sort of artichoke of a house, but greener / (boiled with bicarbonate of soda?)" – again approximating and guessing – conveys a similarly modest impression. Employing qualifications and equivocations, Bishop, unlike Moore, suggests that the poet's tropes are only tentative, provisional advances toward an object, requiring continual amendment. Jane Shore has identified several techniques with which Bishop "seems to call into question the accuracy of her images as she writes them," including using adverbs that qualify the degree to which two things are alike, piling up appositive or alternative images, placing images within parentheses, and asking a question as if indicating a change of mind.[23] Such mannerisms imply that a completed description may fall short of accurately rendering objective reality, and that Bishop consequently takes more interest in description as an activity than as an achievement.

In this she differs from Moore, who would seem not to put pen to paper until, for instance, she has examined a pansy long enough to arrive at a formulation for its exact coloring: "grey-blue-Andalusian-cock-feather pale . . . / ink-lined on the edge, fur- / eyed, with ochre / on the cheek" (CPM 108). Bishop's methods are far more similar to the "tricks of phrasing" Wordsworth uses to give the impression of spontaneous utterance. According to David Perkins,

> [Wordsworth] often appears to be revising as he writes, and a word or phrase that he professes to find inexact is not struck out but corrected in the course of the poem. . . . He talks to himself . . . comments on his own sentiments . . . rallies his wandering impulses to the task at hand . . . and changes his mind as he writes. These and similar gestures . . . show an attempt in verse to render or yield to impulsive processes of mind.[24]

Extending Wordsworth's strategies, Bishop makes the process rather than the product of observation the focus of her poems. Instead of excising from her writing all evidence of imprecise, habituated verbal formulae, Bishop often leaves pat phrases which (one imagines) automatically occurred to her, adding a correction that aligns her words closely with the particular phenomena at hand. A few examples:

> She sits and watches TV.
> No, she watches zigzags.   (CP 148)

> and stands there, looms, rather,
> in the middle of the road   (CP 172)

> up in the air – up, rather, in the leaves –   (CP 91)

> Once up against the sky it's hard
> to tell them from the stars –
> planets, that is – the tinted ones:   (CP 103)

> Some comic books provide
> the only note of color –
> of certain color.   (CP 127)

Our visions coincided – "visions" is
too serious a word – our looks, two looks:  (CP 177)

This technique does more than lend an air of casual immediacy to the speaker's mental activity; it also reminds us how easily the calcified forms of language can distort our perceptions and how easily we can attach falsifying labels to what we encounter.

Linguistic formulations are human projections that, as Bishop's translation of Paz's "January First" states, "invent . . . the reality of this world." Thus, the ironical Crusoe can punningly christen his volcano "*Mont d'Espoir* or *Mount Despair*" so that the name of what he observes will reflect his vacillating moods. Because linguistic signs are abstracted from or imposed upon experience, words have a lamentable tendency to fix inaccurately what they supposedly identify.[25] Parodoxically, those who are most adept with words must guard most carefully against the self-serving exploitation of words' inventive power. The temptation to be witty and clever can overpower the desire to be truthful; hence Bishop's speaker chastises herself for reductively and "unkindly" tagging Manuelzinho "Klorophyll Kid." The skillful poet, who can so easily play sleight-of-hand tricks with language, needs to apply special restraint to insure that her language does not, while pretending to represent appearances exactly, become a detached superstructure substituting for those appearances that time invents "with no help from us" (CP 273).

Bishop makes this point in "Going to the Bakery" (CP 151–2), a poem largely about the transforming effects of language. Just as the moonlight alters the ordinary sights of the Avenida Copacabana, the poet's words metamorphose round cakes into creatures "about to faint – / each turns up a glazed white eye," tarts into festering wounds, and bread loaves into "yellow-fever victims / laid out in a crowded ward." Yet even after having formulated images that so powerfully convey the sickness of the times, the poet, confronted by actual suffering in a real villager, fails to respond adequately. Her failure, which has broad social implications, is manifest in her language: A bandaged beggar addresses her "in perfect gibberish," and she replies " 'Good night' / from force of habit." Then with penetrating self-mockery she adds, "Oh, mean habit! Not one word more apt or bright?" (CP 152). An earlier published version substituted "poor" for "mean," suggesting that one whose words fall so far short is impoverished, however "terrific" her money. The final version provides a stronger condemnation of the speaker, and a more politicized perspective, suggesting at once the cruelty, pettiness, and contemptible stinginess of North American liberalism.

"Going to the Bakery" implies that if poetry is to be relevant to common life and emotional (or political) reality, some linguistic middle ground between the extremes of empty automatic formulas and overly refined poetic figures must be discovered. In order to locate this middle way, Bishop turns increasingly in her later volumes to homely or colloquial diction and to a conversational manner. Instead of imitating the density and "vivider-than-life definition" of Moore's descriptions,[26] Bishop now tries to give the illusion of relaxedly inclusive, ordinary speech.

Moore believed that in order to "make one's self understood" "one must have clarity, and clarity depends on precision" (MMR 171). To attain that precision Moore removed words from the "greasy contexts" of familiar usage and "treated [them] with acid to remove the smudges."[27] Bishop's descriptive manner, as I have already noted, seems to question whether the cleanly finished, exact signification to which Moore aspired is attainable. Nonetheless, Bishop does not despair of making herself understood; instead, like Ashbery, she believes that communication depends on much besides precision. A comparison of Moore's and Bishop's approaches to the vernacular will illuminate their divergent conceptions of how language communicates most effectively.

Moore was entranced by "the accuracy of the vernacular" (MMR 254). She collected particularly apt phrases from conversations or newspapers, evidence of the "unconscious fastidiousness" she so valued, and incorporated them into her poetry. For example, she picked the phrase "charming tadpole notes" (used in "The Labors of Hercules") from *The London Spectator*, and "spider fashion," "ghostly pallor," "creeping slowly," "creepy to behold" (in "An Octopus") from the *Illustrated London News*. In "Virginia Brittania" she makes use of the lively accuracy of "the Black / idiom – from 'advancin' back- / wards in a circle.' " Often she places such snippets in quotes, and usually she uses them in contexts quite different from those in which the phrases were discovered. Moore can assimilate vernacular bits into her poems, but her poetry remains essentially formal and distinct from spoken utterance.[28] She has admitted that while she is "much interested in dialects and intonations . . . scarcely . . .[any] comes into my so-called poems at all" (MMR 254).

Occasionally Bishop, like Moore, calls attention to idiomatic accuracy by inserting idiomatic expressions as treasured found objects; for example, she admires the Portuguese name for scaling-ladder vines which translates " 'one leaf yes and one leaf no' " (CP 91) or the name "god-mother" given to the lead donkey "who wears a fringe of orange wool / with wooly balls above her eyes, and bells" (CP 154). (Similarly, her letters to Moore from Brazil and Florida frequently report colorful local expressions and names.) Far more often, however, she incorporates colloquial idiom into her own speaking voice, treating vernacular expressions not as curiosities but as the forms in which experience most naturally becomes utterance. In Bishop's later poems vernacular expressions abound: "get the idea through your brain" (CP 96), "the whole thing's ruined again" (CP 96), "drops dead on the spot" (CP 97), "fumes . . . knock me over" (CP 152), "beat-up enamel" (CP 169), "read it right straight through" (CP 159), "quite comfy" (CP 127), "what on earth have we done?" (CP 149). To a considerable extent, Bishop tries to make the language of her poetry appear indistinguishable from informal speech. Therefore her descriptions often employ the vague adjectives that predominate in casual conversations: "painted that awful shade of brown" (CP 176), "with beautiful bright blue eyes and a kind expression" (CP 89), "really a very nice old man" (CP 187). Her words gain expressive power not as distinct cleansed crystals, but as components of our well-smudged everyday discourse.

Of course, many of Bishop's later images are as breathtakingly exact and as unconventional as ever, while her poetry's diction and syntax are in fact far more varied and controlled than those of spoken discourse. She has supplemented, not abandoned, the exactitude and refinement that educated and literary language permits. Like the Romantics and a number of the modernists, she attempts to refresh her perceptions and formulations by making use of less sophisticated ways of seeing and expressing which seem closely bound to fundamental realities. In order to combine the advantages of both formal and colloquial linguistic modes, in her mature work Bishop often disguises the sophistication and artfulness of her poetic idiom. She provides a linguistic foundation in which short, common words predominate. She intersperses simple, heavily monosyllabic sentences among her long sinuous ones. When her syntax is complex, the phrases still tend to be brief and to flow without Moore-like disjunction. Without losing an aura of informality and naturalness, Bishop manages to weave into this fabric occasional Latinate polysyllables such as "divagation," "ambulating," "attenuated," "incandescent"; technical terms such as "silicate," "variegated," "collaterally"; and poeticized phrases such as "throbbing roses" and "burning rivulets." Like her Romantic predecessors, she seeks the *appearance* of artless spontaneity, wanting to convince her readers that they are hearing the Wordsworthian "simple effusion of the moment." Bishop's companionable narrative voice and her strategic uses of colloquial diction and informal syntax make her seem "one of the folks" and endow her work with a chatty immediacy.

At the same time, it would be a mistake to regard Bishop's assimilation of common language as merely a mask or a trick. Unlike Moore, Bishop treasures the aromas and the grime attached to words, believing that social and emotional connotations are essential in what makes language a viable means of human communication. Like Wittgenstein and the ordinary language philosophers, Bishop regards the meaning of a word as inseparable from its ordinary linguistic, social, and historical contexts. Her uses of colloquial language imply that the familiar emotional contexts for common expressions enable them, at least on some occasions, to convey the poet's meaning more fully than would more explicit and ostensibly precise formulations.

Spoken language has the additional value of being, by definition, communal: it is spoken together with others. As the ordinary language philosophers have emphasized, language is only one element in the complex pattern of human interactions. Its use is governed by intricate conventions which, though not always consciously recognized, are the shared understanding of its speakers. Thus ordinary language is more than a vehicle for transmitting information; it is an active bond between human beings (which may explain Bishop's desire to write "some really 'popular songs', not 'art' songs").[29] Just as Bishop places greater emphasis on the process of seaching for accurate words than on actually locating them, she often sees more significance in the process of linguistic exchange than in its denotative precision.

In "Under the Window: Ouro Prêto" Bishop points to the kind of language that best maintains and expresses human community, suggesting that the most meaningful human contact occurs within ordinary language and mundane events. From her window in this Brazilian mountain town Bishop overhears conversations that are "simple," both in subject and style. They pertain to mundane acts, common troubles, elemental sensations – matters about which "all have agreed" for centuries. What she hears is a common language, shared by those of all ages, of different genders, of varied walks of life and social standing, and of different eras. The interchange of such simple remarks affirms those characteristics that "made us all just one" (CP 161): "The seven ages of man are talkative / and soiled and thirsty" (CP 154). Therefore these speech fragments are as beautiful as the flashes of oil glinting in the ditch; in fact, the simile with which the poem closes – "like tatters of the *Morpho* butterfly" – brings to mind "morpheme" and "morphe" (the smallest meaningful linguistic unit and the ancient Greek word meaning *form*) to underline the affinity between simple verbalization and the perception of intense beauty.

Again in "The Moose" (CP 169–73; a poem begun early in her career, but not completed for twenty years), Bishop demonstrates the communicative efficacy of banal statements which are denotatively vague or flat, but tonally resonant. Traveling in a bus, she overhears fragments of a "recognizable" conversation, a reenactment of her grandparents' dialogues that she heard as a child. The unseen couple recount elemental events, and their manner of discourse is, again, simple:

> the year he remarried;
> the year (something) happened.
> She died in childbirth.
> That was the son lost
> when the schooner foundered.
>
> He took to drink. Yes.
> She went to the bad.

What the man and woman communicate goes far beyond the factual content of their statements; to emphasize the wealth of nuance conveyed by their ordinary language Bishop draws out the implications of a single word in its context:

> "Yes . . . " that peculiar
> affirmative. "Yes . . ."
> A sharp, indrawn breath,
> half groan, half acceptance,
> that means "Life's like that.
> We know *it* (also death)."    (poet's ellipses)

Their interchange is an instance of an eternal human process by which life's events are set in order in the human psyche – of "things [being] cleared up finally." The old couple communicate to Bishop their peaceful acquiescence so that she can feel "it's all right now / even to fall asleep."

The travelers' verbal responses to the moose when it appears also are not, in Moore's sense, precise. Removed from its context, "Look at that, would you" could indicate fondness or amusement; "it's awful plain" could reflect disgust; "curious creatures" could imply an academic detachment. Yet here these remarks so unmistakably register wonder and awe that Bishop is convinced her own sentiments are shared by all those present: "Why, why do we feel / (we all feel) this sweet / sensation of joy?"

Moore's language attempts to convey information rather than to communicate "sensation." This is not to say that she takes no interest in emotions, but that in her poetry she seeks to establish objective or permanent validations for the heart's predilections. She detaches her "real toads" from personalized and temporal contexts so that they might be examined objectively, appreciated intellectually. Her interrupted syntax, her idiosyncratic conglomerate diction, her line breaks that counteract speech intonation lend a cool crispness to her work. Bishop's more fluid syntax, her narrative discursiveness and more colloquial diction, while maintaining an understated manner somewhat like Moore's, attempt to bring poetry closer to the immediate process of living. One might say that Bishop strives to create the illusion of real toads in non-imaginary gardens – that is, gardens where emotions are constantly evolving as events unfold, where language can capture only ephemeral clarities in the muddle of living.

## IV

Moore's poetic language, as noted in the preceding chapter, tends to evoke a timeless present. Marie Borroff has demonstrated that the infrequency of finite verbs and the frequency of nouns (whose meanings "are not 'time located' by tense-inflection") in Moore's poetry " 'abstract[s]' " the content of her poetic statements "by removing it from temporal process." Her language "attempts to hold its subject matter constant."[30] Thus, from the opening of "The Frigate Pelican" – "Rapidly cruising or lying on the air there is a bird / that realizes Rasselas's friend's project / of wings uniting levity with strength" (CPM 25) – it is immediately clear that the bird is exemplary as the fixed sum of its characteristic actions. The species, moreover, was the same "marvel of grace" in Rasselas's time that it is in ours. Moore's use of quotations from others is equally ahistorical. Statements overheard at the circus are treated no differently than words of Xenophon or Isaac Walton. Reading "Novices" without the poet's notes, one would not guess that the phrase " 'split like a glass against a wall' " comes from the *Decameron*, written in the 1350s, while " 'that tinge of sadness about it which the reflective mind always feels . . .' " comes from the *Illustrated London News* of February 26, 1921. Even when a quotation unmistakably derives from an antique source, as with "He 'Digesteth Harde Yron,' " Moore employs the phrase not for its historical resonance, but for its admirably concrete depiction of, in this case, the ability to endure and triumph over hardships. While the phrasing and spelling are archaic, the characteristic identified is timeless.

Moore, like Pound, seems to regard art itself as immune to the effects of time. She believes that an artistic representation can be so finely wrought and true that both the power of the work and the relevance of its message will last. Such an aesthetic assumes that changes which take place over time are essentially irrelevant to art. In "No Swan So Fine," centuries after the death of King Louis XV, for whom the china swan was created, the bird remains perched on "polished sculptured / flowers – at ease and tall" (CPM 19). The figure still seems lifelike and is still unequalled as an artistic representation of its subject. In her own art, Moore aspires to a comparable exactness of replication, so true as to transcend the workings of time. As Borroff says, "Moore works toward an apprehension of her subject that, once achieved, need not change."[31]

Bishop's poetry, and particularly her later poems, bear a very different relation to time; she creates not timeless replicas but dramatic reenactments of particular moments. It is instructive that Bishop does not share Moore's interest in discussing the relationship of the artist and the scientist, but in several poems she defines the artist by reference to history or the historian. In "Objects & Apparitions" Bishop and Octavio Paz pay tribute to the artist Joseph Cornell as "the opposite of History, creator of ruins, / out of your ruins you have made creations" (CP 275). In "The Map" Bishop aligns the poet with the map-maker as distinguished from the historian, whose imaginative freedom is more restricted. Nonetheless, cartographers are implicitly responsive to historical processes because they record new discoveries, changing national borders, and so on. In both poems Bishop portrays the artist working in some sense in opposition to history, yet very much within the context of history and passing time. (Indeed, in poems such as the "The Burglar of Babylon" or even "Pink Dog" Bishop herself acts as rueful historian for the poor of Brazil.) Bishop conceives of the poet as simultaneously entangled in the process of time's passage and trying to compensate for the losses imposed by that process.

In her later poems Bishop rarely portrays a Moore-like timeless present, and when she does, she subsequently undercuts its fixity by hinting of the processive action of time. "Song for a Rainy Season" opens with a generalized and static present tense, but in the last two stanzas the speaker looks to the future, revealing that the ferns, the fog, the waterfalls, and virtually everything she has described will vanish shortly. Approaching Stevens' sense of change as the source of value and of death as "the mother of beauty," she tells us that these phenomena are to be cherished precisely because they are ephemeral: She urges her damp, "maculate" house to "rejoice!" in its current condition, "For a later / era will differ. / (O difference that kills, / or intimidates, much / of all our small shadowy / life!)" (CP 102).

More often in Bishop's later works, her use of the present tense is obviously processive. She said in an interview that she admires in Hopkins' poetry the attempt "to dramatize the mind in action rather than in repose," adding that in her own work "the use of the present tense helps to convey this sense of the mind in action."[32] Often she narrates events as if she were writing while they were happening, like an on-the-spot reporter speaking into a microphone at the very moment incidents are taking place.

"Arrival at Santos" (CP 89–90) uses this sort of narration. The present tense declarations with which the poem opens – "here is . . . here is . . . here . . . is" – seem at first to depict a Moore-like present, one achieved with the cessation of movement. But Bishop immediately places them in the context of past and future – "is this how this country is going to answer you . . . after eighteen days of suspension?" Time presses on the speaker too rapidly for her to ponder detachedly: "Finish your breakfast. The tender is coming." Disembarking, she is caught up even more breathlessly in immediate events: "And gingerly now we climb down the ladder backward. . . . Watch out! Oh! It has caught Miss Breen's // skirt!" In attaching her poem to ongoing time, Bishop suggests that emotional resolution must be discovered within the flow of progressing events. Rather than resting passively with what seems to be given by "here is," the speaker triumphs over the frustration of her expectations by leaving behind both stative verbs and a static stance. As Ashbery does so insistently, she willfully engages herself in moving her own present into the future: "We leave Santos at once; / We are driving to the interior."

Many of the events narrated in Bishop's later volumes took place in her past, yet even her retrospective narratives recreate the perspective of immediate experience. In relating remembered events, Bishop recaptures the action of her mind in an earlier time; I have already shown, for example, that Bishop reclaims the child's perspective in "First Death" and "In the Waiting Room." Like the nineteenth-century Romantics, Bishop uses the action of memory to establish the self's continuity over time. Her portrayals of past events differ from those of the Romantics, however, in the extent to which she appears to be not so much recollecting in tranquility as participating in something currently taking place. Bishop's preference for verb forms that lend a sense of immediacy is apparent in "In the Waiting Room"; she often avoids the past perfect tense, using instead the past progressive so that the actions or sensations seem ongoing: "I – we – were falling, falling," "I was saying it to stop / the sensation of falling off," "[the waiting room] was sliding / beneath a big black wave, / another, and another." She also phrases some of the child's questions so as to make them indistinguishable from those she might still be asking: "Why should I be my aunt, / or me, or anyone?", or "How had I come to be here, / like them, and overhear / a cry of pain . . .?" Such techniques blend the past into the present, bridging the gap between them.

Artworks, in seeming to merge and bind the past with the present, can help people reconcile themselves to continual flux. "Poem" (CP 176–7) reenacts Bishop's discovery of this wondrous capacity in an apparently insignificant painting by the same great-uncle who painted the "Large Bad Picture." (The title, "Poem," establishes that her thoughts about painting apply also to poetry.) Bishop's initial description immediately fixes the painting in historical time: "it has spent seventy years / as a minor family relic." Yet she subsequently discovers that, despite the painting's age, she can identify the region depicted: "It must be Nova Scotia; only there / does one see . . ." Attending more closely, Bishop suddenly recognizes the particular landscape; though "those particular geese and cows / are naturally before my time," and though her memory of the farmer's name has faded, the scene matches the mental image retained from her own childhood. The painter's fidelity to details – the proper placement of the church steeple, the accurate recording of flora and fauna – are what make this recognition possible. These details have a different effect than Moore's; they trigger associations that bring to life a particular season – "early spring" – and the sensations that accompany immediate experience – "the air is fresh and cold."

In tones of wonder the concluding verse paragraph explores how the painting has brought into communion individuals of different eras, how art can link those separated by time. Bishop feels a powerful bond with the great-uncle she never knew because he, like herself, loved the place enough to memorize – that is, to learn by heart – and memorialize its exact appearance. Bishop explains this miraculous power of art in terms of a blurring of boundaries:

> art "copying from life" and life itself,
> life and the memory of it so compressed
> they've turned into each other. Which is which?
> Life and the memory of it cramped,
> dim, on a piece of Bristol board,
> dim, but how live, how touching in detail.   (CP 177)

While the dollar-sized sketch may never have earned any money, as a catalyst for an epiphany, part of "the little that we get for free," it proves of inestimable value. With a characteristic blend of apparently incongruous scales, Bishop establishes the tiny work as "about the size of our abidance."

In the concluding lines Bishop dramatizes art's power to counteract the divisive effects of passing time by merging the three temporal perspectives of the long-deceased painter, of Bishop as a child, and of Bishop in the 1970s. The cows of seventy years past are now actively "munching," the iris "crisp and shivering," and the water "still standing from spring freshets." Yet she does not deny the inexorable motion of time. With the phrase "yet-to-be-dismantled elms" Bishop superimposes the inevitable triumph of ongoing time and death on art's momentary ability to revivify the past in the present.

Bishop's art appears neither to stop time nor to remove itself from the flow of time. In "Poem" both memory and attention are processes; we witness the speaker's evolution from relative uninterest in the painting to deep personal involvment in both the scene and the artist who depicted it. Similarly, a poem such as "Filling Station" traces the speaker's transition from a dismissive stance to an appreciative one as increasingly careful attention brings her to acknowledge that even the grimiest spot may be a well-loved home. Nonetheless, any artistic representation finally stands apart from the forces of change and dissolution that govern our lives. Whether art portrays specimens representing entire species and generalized moral characteristics, as Moore's poetry does, or particular moments and ephemeral revelations, as Bishop's does, art fixes its subject.

In Bishop's thinking, art's fixity defines its limitations. In "North Haven" (CP 188–9), written in memory of her close friend Robert Lowell, Bishop sadly juxtaposes nature's ability to change and constantly renew itself against the human being's limited ability to accommodate flux. In nature, death and loss are balanced by rebirth, since collective identity overrides individual identity. Each summer the birds and flowers appear the same – "The Goldfinches are back, or others like them. . . . Nature repeats herself, or almost does." A person's changes, in contrast, are nonrenewable and ultimately run toward loss. Nonetheless, human flexibility is in some ways greater; while living, one can "pretend," "learn," "discover," and "float" geographically as islands cannot. Each moment of human experience may be distinct from all others – Lowell's "classic summer" of 1932 remains unique. But his death will not be followed by rebirth, and no matter how hard he tries, his creations cannot keep up with the progressing present. Addressing a dead poet whose revisions were more public but hardly more insistent than her own, Bishop mourns, "you can't derange, or rearrange / your poems again. (But the Sparrows can their song.) / The words won't change again."[33] For Bishop, as for Ashbery, the life of an artwork is in the moment and process of creation.

Yet on the other hand, art's fixity – the reliability of unchanging words – can be of tremendous value as we try to cope with flux. It is telling that Bishop, who uses art as a means of exploring what is shifting and disorderly, often relies on the traditional regularities of predictable rhymes, strong iambs, and inherited poetic forms, while Moore feels no need for such traditional patterns. For each of her poems Moore invents a system that lasts only for the duration of that piece. Her rules, however, derive from the atemporal unchanging symmetry of numbers; they testify to her faith in an ordered cosmos. Bishop can give shape to experience only by turning to the "home-made" orders that people have improvised. From her darker perspective, poetry, like Crusoe's scruffy parasol, is a precarious human contrivance, another "island industry."

In "One Art" (CP 178) Bishop takes up one of the most regulated and predictable poetic forms, the villanelle, as a means of giving form to life's unpredictable (though agonizingly inevitable) losses. A container for her bitterness and self-pity, the rigidly ordered poetic structure permits the speaker to step back from the loss of an intimate and beloved companion to view the ludicrous spectacle of humankind fumbling through a world where "things seem filled with the intent / to be lost." "The real expression of tragedy, or just horror and pathos," Bishop told Anne Stevenson, "lies exactly in man's ability to construct, to use form";[34] form does allow one to "master" "disaster," but that mastery is necessitated by excruciatingly painful events beyond one's control. Similarly, the regular incremental form of "Visits to St. Elizabeth's," gradually accumulating one change after another, allows the poet to come to terms with her multiple and ambivalent responses to Pound's complex character, his achievements and failures, his tragic fate.

As an artist who attempts to mediate between the flux of experience and the fixity of language, Bishop particularly values the preservation in poetry of those ephemeral moments in which an individual experiences a sudden revelation of clarity or harmony. In this she bears an obvious affinity to the Romantics, though she does not share the Romantic tendency to locate in these "spots of time" general truths linking the human spirit to the supernatural. The isolated epiphany of "The Moose" is as close as the skeptical contemporary poet can come to a Wordsworthian religion of nature. Once again, Bishop's narration incorporates the passage of time, recording a succession of presents. The leisurely flow of time in this rural Canadian province is imitated by the long opening sentence (36 lines) whose periodic structure – "where . . . where . . . where . . ." – mimics the gentle tidal rhythms of the Bay of Fundy. The westward journeying bus is assimilated into nature so that its sides are "flanks," its movement "patient." To the travelers, at peace with this easy progression, evening itself is a "commence[ment]," not simply an ending. Yet within the flow of nature's cycles, the journey, like the life of an individual, is composed of a collection of unrepeated, distinct phenomena. Bishop depicts these in short sentences or sentence fragments so that each event is momentarily present and then past: "A pale flickering. Gone. / . . . Two rubber boots show, / illuminated, solemn. / A dog gives one bark." Then suddenly "A moose has come out of / the impenetrable wood." As in Ashbery's works, a tremendously meaningful perception occurs apparently by chance in the course of ordinary events and within the motion of time. (In an interview, Bishop went so far as to claim that "it all just happens without your thinking about it. . . . I'm afraid in my life everything has just *happened*.")[35] For a few moments the travelers take comfort from seeing this emissary from the impenetrable realms. "High as a church, / homely as a house / (or safe as houses)," the moose reassuringly combines the security of female domesticity with the awesome magnitude of the "otherworldly." The bus moves on, but Bishop's poem, like the "dim smell of moose" that wafts through the accelerating vehicle, is a trace testifying to the authenticity of that ephemeral vision.

"The End of March" (CP 179–80) describes a similar visionary moment, this time explicitly juxtaposed against the desire for a lasting condition of tranquility. The poem's events take place on a particular day of a season when nature is especially harsh, hostile, forbidding. In this chilly scene, "Everything was withdrawn as far as possible, / indrawn." Fortunately, neither Bishop's wit nor her imagination is numbed by the fierce winds. Her witty play with the colloquialism "giving up the ghost" tempers the morbidity of her vision of snarled string like a corpse awash on the sand. And she can divert herself by imagining that the shack she approaches is the "proto-dream-house" to which she would like to escape: "I'd like to retire there and do *nothing*, / or nothing much, forever." The activities she envisions – "[I'd] look through binoculars, read boring books, / old, long, long books, and write down useless notes, / talk to myself, and, foggy days, / watch the droplets slipping" – are flat and drab, as well as cozy, and that is precisely their appeal.[36] No dramatic disruptions, no emotional turmoil; simply an uneventful monotony – with plenty of opportunity for the imagination to play – in which the passage of time would hardly be noticed. Yet as soon as Bishop has refined her fantasy to perfection, she yanks herself back into reality: "But – impossible. / And that day the wind was much too cold / even to get that far." Nonetheless, on the way back she experiences the kind of satisfaction that *is* possible, a more fully developed version of the sandpiper's solace:

> The sun came out for just a minute.
> For just a minute, set in their bezels of sand,
> The drab, damp, scattered stones
> were multi-colored.   (CP 180)

That flash of beauty is enough to lift her spirits and take the dark edge from her perceptions. Now when the stones' shadows are "withdrawn, indrawn," she thinks this may be nature's form of lighthearted teasing. Phenomena which earlier seemed ominous – unnaturally large dog prints and the "man-size" kite string without a kite – are no longer threatening. Instead, they seeem traces left by a majestic yet personable sun "who perhaps had batted a kite out of the sky to play with." A momentary illumination is so comforting that, at least for a little while, the universe does not seem alien.

The content and techniques of Bishop's later works establish reconciliation and mediation as the artist's most significant activities. If the contemporary poet is to point us toward value discoverable in all the "untidy activity" of our lives, he or she must draw together the resources of reason and imagination, of the conscious and the unconscious. She must accommodate language to flux and ongoing process and must erase the distinction between the language of poetry and that of ordinary live speakers. She must reconcile the human desire for secure understanding with the world's "unlikely" ways, revealing the interpenetration of chaos and order, of the ordinary and the otherworldly.

In one of her last poems, "Santarém" (CP 185–7), Bishop discloses that one of her deepest desires has been to liberate herself and others from the tyranny of rigid categories. ("Exchanging Hats" suggests a similar desire in calling attention to widespread "perversities" and to the commonness of "a slight transvestite twist" [CP 200].) Santarém, like Bishop's dream house, is a place where she would like to remain. But the appeal of this city is not that it is removed from disruptive events. Rather, as the place where two great rivers come together, this lively spot embodies flux without "derangement." Santarém is a locus of "conflux," which Bishop emphatically distinguishes from flowing apart. She emphasizes, too, that the *idea* of flowing together is as appealing to her as the actual place because it represents the dissolution of dualism:[37]

> Even if one were tempted
> to literary interpretations
> such as: life/death, right/wrong, male/female
> – such notions would have resolved, dissolved, straight off
> in that watery, dazzling dialectic.

This spot, then, is an external equivalent to the point the surrealists aspired to reach; as Breton wrote in the "Second Manifesto of Surrealism":

> Everything tends to make us believe that there exists a certain point of the mind at which life and death, the real and the imagined, past and future, the communicable and the incommunicable, high and low, cease to be perceived as contradictions.[38]

Breton, like Bishop, does not deny that the dominant mode of experience is one of polarities, but believes we can find or search toward a point where dichotomies are resolved.

This blue and gold city is the closest thing to paradise the earth offers. Nature is still dangerous and unpredictable; lightning can unexpectedly crack man-made structures in two. Time's destruction is still at work; the belvedere is about to fall into the river. And life is still chaotic: "Two rivers full of crazy shipping – people / all apparently changing their minds, embarking, / disembarking, rowing clumsy dories." Yet changing one's mind is a vital freedom, and this is a place of uniquely bright beauty and cheer. Disparate things are perceived in their individuality, yet all appear unified by the golden light as day merges into night.

Reluctantly responding to the summons of her boat's whistle, Bishop returns on board taking with her the pharmacist's wasps' nest she so admires. Back in the ordinary world of divisive categories, a fellow passenger labels this treasure "an ugly thing." Since we have seen the wasps' nest through Bishop's eyes, appreciating its spare aesthetic, Mr. Swan's judgment seems almost shockingly insensitive. (Perhaps Bishop achieves a humorous retaliation by using the name Swan; responses just like his led others to mistake the swan for an ugly duckling.) Yet we feel more pity than outrage toward the old man who "wanted to see the Amazon" but remained unseeing; his experience is diminished by his not perceiving the interpenetration of beauty and ugliness. Mr. Swan's dualistic orientation – in which smallness, hardness, and bareness apparently align with ugliness, not with beauty – severs him from the consolation of this world's small wonders.

The image of the artist retrieving a "small, exquisite" object from a briefly glimpsed, half-fantastic place ("I may be remembering it all wrong / after, after – how many years?") aptly summarizes Bishop's achievement. The wasps' nest, like the poems she retrieved from her life of travel, is simultaneously a presence – the physical object, "hard as stucco" – and an absence – the empty nest, an abandoned home. Bishop strives to resolve dichotomies of presence and absence, loss and possession; though she herself finds no permanent resolutions ("I couldn't stay"), only more journeying and more questions, Bishop's poems offer her readers places of conflux. Rendering her life's events in immaculate yet modest and ordinary terms, they provide, like Cornell's boxes, "tales of the time" and also "cages for infinity." In them the oppositions of our disjunctive world – between order and chaos, past and present, internal and external, language and experience – are momentarily resolved; our apparitional longings and dreams "become visible for a moment" (CP 276).

# 5 "A small (or large) machine made of words": the continuity between Williams and Creeley

Just as World War I contributed to the young modernists' break with the past, so World War II, and the subsequent upheavals of the cold war and Vietnam years, fostered an iconoclastic impulse in members of the generation that came of age in the 1940s. Robert Creeley, who served as an ambulance driver at the Burma-India front in 1945, was among the young artists seeking alternatives to the models and strategies of the establishment in the postwar years:

> Many of us had been involved in this huge global nightmare, and we came back to our specific personal lives, situations, feeling a great confusion and at times a great resentment about what had been given us as a rationale for all this. So we had that reason to move upon something – upon a clarity that could confront these dilemmas more adequately than the generalities we had been given. (CP 9–10)[1]

American colleges and universities, insisting upon "the *idea* of form extrinsic to the given instance," offered only further generalities. Creeley has often recalled the exhilaration he therefore felt upon discovering an alternative to the academies' "assumption of a *mold*" in William Carlos Williams' introduction to *The Wedge* (1944):

> Therefore each speech having its own character the poetry it engenders will be peculiar to that speech also in its own intrinsic form. . . . When a man makes a poem, makes it, mind you, he takes words as he finds them interrelated about him and composes them – without distortion which would mar their exact significances – into an intense expression of his perceptions and

137

> ardors that they may constitute a revelation in the speech that he
> uses. (CLP 4–5, as quoted in QG 44)

Williams was also calling for "a direct expression of the turmoils of today
in the arts. Not *about* today in classical forms but in forms generated,
invented, today direct from the turmoil itself."[2] So in 1945 – when Creeley was eighteen and Williams, at sixty-seven, was considered only a
minor writer – the young man "put [him]self to school with [Williams']
work."[3] After five years, a few published lyrics, and much scrutiny of
Williams' poetry and polemical prose, Creeley summoned the courage
to contact the master by mail (the occasion: soliciting contributions to a
little magazine Creeley was planning). Williams then directly assumed
the role of mentor, offering Creeley encouragement, answering his questions, commenting on his style, and putting him in touch with like-minded
young writers – among them Charles Olson.

During the early 1950s Creeley and Olson carried on an intense and
frequent correspondence, exchanging views on the literary scene, developing their intentions for its new directions, working out their understanding of how one makes things with words.[4] It is not surprising, then,
that Creeley's poetry of this period should be more obviously imitative
of Olson – and Olson's master, Pound[5] – than Williams. The poems in
Creeley's first collection, *Le Fou* (composed 1950–52) tend to look like
Olson's projective compositions. (In some instances, Creeley even allowed Olson to alter their lineation.)[6] The lines are grouped in irregular
units, spaced and indented to indicate the conceptual relations among the
poems' parts; Olson-like mannerisms abound (shorthand "&" and "sd,"
open or closed parentheses), and the conventions of syntax are broken
open in Olson's fashion. Many of these poems, like Olson's, move by
intellectual analysis or rational argument; abstract propositions are stated
and then elaborated, demonstrated, or qualified in an impersonal manner:

*Love*

Not enough. The question: what is.
Given: grace
            the time of this moment
which I do not see as time.
The particulars: oak, the grain of, oak.    (Coll 26)

or

Relative to cost, the high figures
of production:

> you, sweetness & light
> are destructive only in your
> inveterate tendencies.
>
> The poor are poor. The statement
> the little people would not
> I think
> accept is
>
> that there is any refuge    (Coll 28)

Yet several allusions to Williams' work in this volume indicate that the New Jersey poet continued to define and embody Creeley's artistic ideal. In "Hélas" Creeley's lines "(nothing else but / to bite home! there, where / the head could take hold . . . )" (Coll 21) echo Williams' definition of the poet in "The Wind Increases" (CEP 68–9):

> a man
> whose words will
>      bite
>           their way
> home – being actual
>
> having the form
>           of motion

In Williams' poem the wind tossing the spring flowers is procreative; it is also the poet's breath, his words. These words, the exhalation of love, bring something "new // upon the tortured / body of thought," offering the mind relief by connecting it with the earth's generative forces. Hence, in the windswept world of Williams' poem, objects are sharply defined: "tulip's bright / tips," "twigtip," "leaftip." Creeley longs for such contact, such clarity. He invokes Williams' lyric as a foil for his own alienation from sensual particularity and from the keen defining power of language. For Creeley, "The day is the indefinite," and the wind merely pushes his head in circles, leaving his senses of sight and hearing "vague." By denying two of Williams' most positive terms – "no edge / or delight" – the contemporary poet defines his dispirited condition as antithetical to the modernist's. He upholds the older poet as a model, both for what Williams does with words and for how that doing brings him into emotional and sensual contact with his world.

Again in "Love" Creeley uses Williams to represent states of mind he would like to attain. Disappointed that love is "Not enough," Creeley pleads, "speak to me, of love . . . "; the response – ". . . *the stain of love is upon the world!*" – is an exclamation from Williams' "Love Song" (CEP

174). In Williams' poem, love transforms the entire world; because his beloved is absent he finds the "honey-thick" yellow of desire "spoiling the colors / of the whole world." This all-consuming passion leaves no room for anxious questions like Creeley's "what is [enough?]"

In these early years, when Creeley was most unhappy and uncertain, Williams seems to have been more important as a personal than as a prosodic example. The young man looked to the older as one who shared his own doubts and handicaps and succeeded as an artist despite or even because of them. Thus Creeley's early poem "For W.C.W." (Coll 126) pays tribute to Williams' ability to transform private pain into creative energy that sustains him during anguished periods. Having noted that the times of happiness in Williams' life were "not the periods in which his most intensive writing took place,"[7] Creeley could hope that he too might compensate for "trouble" with the "wild exultation" of creativity.

Creeley admired Williams as a man who originally shared his own "Puritanically deprived senses of speech and sensuality" (QG 61) yet had managed to free himself from those fetters. The young man was "shy of the word 'poet' and all its associations" (QG 61), so he found comfort in Williams' awkwardness with that designation: "I *am* a poet! I / am. I am. I am a poet, I reaffirmed, ashamed" (PB 120; see QG 59–60). Coming from a moralistic background, Creeley needed a moral justification for poetry, and Williams provided it. In a letter he reassured Creeley that art which served in "cleansing the language of all fixations upon dead, stinking dead, usages of the past" was assisting the state "since the government can never be more than the government of the words."[8] Creeley recognized in Williams a sense of ignorance that in Creeley's case fostered a tentativeness with words: "I know that he did share with me a tacit fear of the well-trained, academically secure *good English* he felt the comfortable equipment of various of his contemporaries" (WTRP 102). Even Williams' attitudes toward women were confirmation for his own.[9]

However idiosyncratic these personal identifications may have been, they constituted a crucial permission for Creeley to write the kind of poems "given" him. He could not look to Olson or Pound to dignify the presentation of intimate feelings and sexual tensions in poetry; that was not their subject. From Creeley's perspective, one of the greatest values of Williams' works is that they articulate a "complex and intimate and modulated quality of feeling" (CP 81) which Olson's more intellectual constructs do not:

> I think the most significant encounter for me as a young man
> trying to write was that found in the work of William Carlos
> Williams. He engaged language at a level both familiar and ac-

tive to my own senses, and made of his poems an intensively *emotional* perception, however evident his intelligence. (QG 61–2)

Creeley has credited Williams with reassuring him "that my emotions were not insignificant, that their articulation was really what I was given to be involved with" (CP 122).

The intimate and modulated emotional quality Creeley admires in Williams' work derives in part from intraphrasal line breaks. As Robert Duncan has pointed out, one of the most important resources Williams offers his imitators is "the juncture that could raise the pitch on a preposition or an article at the end of a line and increase the stress on a noun at the return to give something like the shifts in meaning and tone that one heard in common speech."[10] Though Williams is not yet Creeley's dominant prosodic model, in the more personal, emotionally charged poems of *Le Fou* Creeley follows the modernist's example of using line breaks within phrases to chart emotionally telling pauses and shifts in intonation. Adapted to Creeley's voice, the tense pauses register moments of almost desperate searching for the appropriate words or of painful hesitation to express what is in his mind.[11]

"For Rainer Gerhardt" (Coll 114) is such a poem, recording Creeley's anguish at being unable to enact a friendship in accordance with the affection he feels. He wants to "be of use" to Gerhardt, but the two men "(this night)" have found communication difficult; a "petulance" in both comes between them. The poem's hesitating movement reflects the vulnerability Creeley feels as he tentatively reaches out to his friend in the face of that mutual irritation:

> Impossible, rightly, to define these
> conditions of
> friendship, the wandering & inexhaustible wish to
> be of use, somehow
> to be helpful
>
> when it isn't simple, – wish
> otherwise, convulsed, and leading
> nowhere I can go.

We feel the poet groping for the exactly right words: "these what?" he asks himself. "The wish to what, precisely?" The answer to the first implied question unfolds over two lines so that the word "friendship," coming at the stressed initial position, takes on double force; no doubts about the underlying bond remain. The words Creeley locates to answer the second question are less satisfactory – "somehow" is appended.

Reading on, however, one finds that the poet has intentionally placed "somehow" in a position of syntactic ambiguity so that it can be part of the phrases both preceding and following it. This, too, is a technique derived from Williams, as in Williams' lines "to make a man aware of nothing / that he knows" (CEP 433). In the second line of the second strophe Creeley conveys the "convulsed" wrenching of frustrated desire through twisted and broken syntax. Here syntactic energy enforces the sense of "leading"; eager for resolution of both the phrase and the poet's discomfort, the reader pushes on – only to encounter the emphatic disappointment of "nowhere." Creeley's lineation, which so exactly articulates the progress of his emotions, enables his audience to follow and participate in the most minute shifts of feeling accompanying the process of utterance.

Like Williams, young Creeley does not employ intraphrasal junctures where the subject or emotion does not warrant such hesitant suspension. Thus the heated opening of "The Crisis," using the speech idiom Williams cherished, moves rapidly, unhindered by intraphrasal pauses:

> Let me say (in anger) that since the day we were married
> we have never had a towel
> where anyone could find it,
> the fact.    (Coll 113)

The restrained celebration, "A Song," contains both delicate pauses like "A murmur of some lost / thrush" and the graceful resolution, "A song. // Which one sings, if he sings it, / with care" (Coll 112).

## II

During the next few years following *Le Fou*, Creeley published several small collections in quick succession.[12] Olson remains an important example – for instance, in the propositional mode of "The Kind of Act Of." However, the irregular line-groupings and shifting margins of projective layout appear with diminishing frequency, and Creeley turns to more visually regular stanzaic forms, especially to free-verse couplets. The chronologically arranged selection from these volumes in *The Whip* (1957, later the first section of *For Love: Poems 1950–1960*)[13] reveals a progression toward more obvious and profound imitation of Williams' "machine[s] made of words" (CLP 4).

This is not to say that Creeley's poetry assumes the concretely sensual quality of his model's. Being a more anxiously introspective person, Creeley lacks Williams' ability to lose himself in the myriad objects of a fertile world; the world he portrays is that within his consciousness.

Moreover, Creeley's poetry contains few images. As Pinsky has noted, "the 'thing itself' . . . appear[s] as a kind of ghost. The modernist reservations about ornament, and indeed about words themselves, persist; while the image, the technique inspired by that mistrust, is itself spurned as one more form of ornamental verbiage."[14] But while Creeley – recording every tremor of his affections, fears, doubts – presents material that is more obviously subjective than the people and visible objects Williams usually describes, the younger poet is no less involved in the imagists' "direct treatment of the thing." Insisting that "the thing" need not be palpable matter, Creeley has identified "the kind of literalness that really is consistently useful in Williams' writing" as being "involved with the substance of an emotion, with a very distinct content of feeling. . . . I feel that feeling is substantial and is literal and can be articulated" (CP 99). An emotion, exactly depicted, is no more abstract than a woman munching plums.

Creeley could not attain that substantiality when relying on the thoroughly abstract and impersonal language with which he had often masked his feelings in his early poems – e.g., "Loss exists not as perpetual but, exact, when the attentions / are cajoled, / are flattered by their purport or what they purport / to attend" (Coll 33). Gradually, as he grew more comfortable presenting his immediate emotions in poems, Creeley moved toward a more direct, conversational manner of speaking, as in "The Whip" (1955):

> I spent a night turning in bed,
> my love was a feather, a flat
>
> sleeping thing. She was
> very white
>
> and quiet, and above us on
> the roof, there was another woman I
>
> also loved.    (Coll 146)

Largely from Williams' example (supplemented by Olson's example and encouragement),[15] Creeley was learning to use the speech that was naturally his.

Creeley understood that in championing the "American idiom" Williams was not simply encouraging the use of common diction in poetry:

> if one reads Williams carefully, he finds that the words are *not* largely common. What is common is the *mode* of address, the way of speaking that's commonly met with in conversations. . . . I think what really was gained from that sense of source in

common speech was the recognition that the intimate knowing
of a way of speaking . . . offers the kind of intensity that poetry
peculiarly admits. (CP 75)

Indeed, Williams' verbs tend to be more forceful and his modifiers more
vivid than those generally used in familiar speech; and his syntax, often
accumulating modifying phrases, is far more elaborate. Creeley's language is comparably un-"common" in that, while his vocabulary is much
sparer and his syntax simpler than Williams', he continues throughout
his career to employ abstract and academic terms that rarely appear in
casual talk. Yet by cultivating his sensitivity to the cadences of the vernacular, and by mixing colloquial phrases with his more disembodied
ones, Creeley, too, learned to create a more pervasive effect of common
idiom than his diction might seem to warrant.

Strategic uses of banal colloquial expressions lend an idiomatic character to the poems of both Williams and the maturing Creeley:

> Williams:   In a case like this I know
> quick action is the main thing.   (CLP 57)
>
> That's what you get out of
> it. But put it down in your memory that this
> is the kind of stuff that they can't get away
> with.   (CEP 317)

> Creeley:        And
> why not, I thought to
>
> myself, why
> not.   (Coll 144)
>
> Were
> proud? Of what? To buy
>
> a thing like that.   (Coll 135)

Because vernacular terms imply an informal context and an unpreten-
tious attitude, they diminish the gap between poet and reader; they also
contribute to an impression of sincerity and frankness essential to the
appeal of both poets' work. Williams is prominent among those from
whom Creeley learned that "To borrow the language of other times and
places when it is not intimate is to risk faking . . ." (CP 93). Hence:

> Williams:   I, a writer, at one time hipped on
> painting, did not consider . . .   (CLP 99)

I make really very little money.
What of it?   (CEP 311)

Creeley:   I would tear up all the checks
made out to me,
not giving a good goddamn
what the hell happened.   (Coll 142)

A poem that begins with a discursive confession may achieve a similar effect of confidential intimacy:

Williams:   Sometimes I envy others, fear them
a little too, if they write well.   (CLP 23)

Creeley:   When I know what people think of me
I am plunged into my loneliness.   (Coll 133)

By relying more on flat prosaic statement than on lyrical eloquence, both poets attain a distinct and familiar voice, not distanced by the lofty formality of the "poetic."

In addition to helping establish their personal voices, the vernacular proved useful to Williams and Creeley in creating poems that were "pruned to a perfect economy" (CLP 4). Williams' work showed the younger writer that a few lines of dialogue can convey a dramatic situation as fully as a descriptive explication, and with far more immediacy and compression. For example, in the following lines Williams registers not only the nature of his patient's complaint but also her tone of defiance defensively covering embarrassment: " – Wore my bathing suit / wet / four hours after sundown. / That's how" (CEP 309). Similarly, bottled-up anger, condescension, and flirtation are captured in Creeley's "She says, / if I thought it would get any better I // would shoot you, you / nut, you" (Coll 143).

Williams, believing that all verse "must be governed by some measure" (SE 339), used the pronounced rhythms of vernacular utterance to create rhythmical patterns in his nonmetrical verse. Creeley does the same, but – perhaps because of his passionate interest in jazz (especially Charlie Parker's timing) – more often than Williams he plays the marked rhythms of speech against the beats enforced by his lineation.[16] Thus, without depending on a background of regular syllable-stress meter, he creates something comparable to counterpoint in a metrical poem; the interplay is between the expected phrasal rhythm determined by syntax and the line as a rhythmic unit.

In Creeley's best idiomatic poems this rhythmic tension is emotionally expressive. For example, most of the line breaks in "I Know a Man," coming midphrase, create hesitations one would not find in relaxed conversation:

> As I sd to my
> friend, because I am
> always talking, – John, I
>
> sd, which was not his
> name, the darkness sur-
> rounds us, what
>
> can we do against
> it,    (Coll 132)

Because of the asyntactic line breaks, the first syllable of each line receives extra emphasis. The crowding of stresses and the unnatural pauses communicate both the speaker's anxious restraint and his need for release, well before he mentions the threatening darkness or the car in which he might escape it. The unexpected break in "the darkness sur- / rounds us" – sounding as if the speaker were almost suffocating or breathless with fear and forced to inhale midword – conveys his heightened panic. When the speaker hits upon a possible solution, the poem's rhythms reflect his momentary confidence and sense of liberation; "buy a goddamn big car" is the poem's only phrase of any length that flows unimpeded. In "John" 's cautionary rejoinder, Creeley returns to midphrase junctures that interrupt ordinary speech rhythms; the abrupt, heavy stresses of this lineation register the urgency of "John" 's warning – "for / christ's sake, look / out where yr going."[17]

By the late 1950s, when he was composing the poems in *A Form of Women*, Creeley had established his own distinctive blend of colloquial and flatly abstract diction and had learned to manipulate the rhythmic possibilities of the vernacular. At the same time he had settled into a characteristic mode, one – as Duncan has pointed out – defined by Williams: "the common-speech song with a persisting convention of two, three, or four-line stanzas, highly articulated to provide close interplay and variation" (B2 234). That deft articulation involves manipulating not only the speech patterns and line junctures I have already examined, but also the broad range of sound patterns that Creeley, following Pound as well as Williams, includes within the category of "rhyme."

In his earliest, most passionate revolt against the constraints of rhyme and meter, Williams had wanted to escape all patterning in his free verse. He soon discovered, however, that however "sick of rime" he might be,

      yet there is
the rime of her white teeth

the rime of glasses
at my plate, the ripple time
the rime her fingers make –

and we thought to escape rime
by imitation of the senseless
unarrangement of wild things –

the stupidest rime of all –    (CEP 330)

In that poem, "This Florida: 1924," he went on to distinguish the "varying shades" of the color orange in his immediate surroundings, thereby revealing a subtle pattern organizing his environment. Following Williams' recognition that good free verse is not a matter of "senseless / unarrangement," Creeley has defined the poem as "a structure of sounds and rhythms which cohere to inform the reader with a recognition of their order." He considers rhyme to be any "recurrence of a sound sufficiently similar to one preceding it to catch in the ear and mind as being the 'same' " (WTRP 68), a definition that encompasses not only conventional end-rhymes and internal rhyme, but also word repetition, alliteration, assonance, parallel syntactic structures, and echoing cadences. Like Williams, Creeley relies on such sound patterns to give to his free verse the shapeliness which end-rhymes and regular stresses provide in traditional metrical forms. Having assimilated Williams' notion that any formal characteristic of a poem must be an "essential of the work, one of its words" (IM 102), Creeley believes that the modifications and modulations of sound "[can] carry the emotional content of the poem as ably as anything 'said' " (CP 76).

"A Form of Women" (Coll 152–3) can illustrate how Creeley, by arranging his words and phrases so that they echo and recall one another, weaves into his prosody both an organizing pattern and an expressive melody. Some of the techniques he uses are obvious and simple – occasional end-rhymes, frequent repetitions of end-words, pounding recurrence of key monosyllabic nouns and verbs (face, hands, moon, know, fear, touch, love, see). Others are more sophisticated and subtle. For example, in the first stanza Creeley presents four consecutive instances of an iamb following an anapest:

      I have come far enough
from where I was not before
to have seen the things
looking in at me through the open door.

To prevent this regularity from being tedious, he precedes the first of these with an additional iamb, "from where," and eliminates the pause of the line juncture between the last two. At the same time, he provides additional coherence by repeating the *f*-sound in "far," "enough," "from," and "before," and by reinforcing the end-rhyme "before/door" with the slant rhymes of "far" and "where."

The first line of the next stanza repeats the same anapest–iamb pattern – "and have walked tonight" – but then that is abandoned and Creeley turns instead to alliteration, consonance, and assonance: "by myself / to see the moonlight / and see it as trees." Assonance operates not only within single stanzas, but as a means of linking stanzas to one another. For example, the long *o* which occurs twice in the repeated "know" of the third stanza reappears in the first line of the next: "My face is my own, I thought." Creeley later adopts "My _____ is my own" as the pattern for the seventh stanza and, using a less elementary technique, echoes the close of the fifth stanza, "but could not," in the stanza that breaks the pattern, "but I am not." In the following (eighth) stanza, the long *o* of "own" recurs for the last time, in the end-word "alone." The sound similarity between these two words reinforces the link between selfhood and isolation that is the thematic center of the poem.

The first twelve lines compose a single sentence – unusually long for Creeley – and the lines break between phrases and clauses. Because no junctures occur within phrases until the eighteenth line, the unexpectedness of an intraphrasal break heightens its expressive power:

> I could not touch you.
> I wanted very much to
> touch you
> but could not.

Without verse lineation these two sentences would sound flat. But Creeley's arrangement, which brings out the rhyme and trochaic patterns linking "touch you" / "much to" / "touch you," effectively underlines the intensity of his desire to make contact. Even more resonant is the aching pause after "to," which makes audible the poet's painful constraint; the depth of his emotion sounds in his voice breaking.

Creeley could have discovered virtually all the "rhyming" techniques of "A Form of Woman" in Williams' poetry – for example, in the opening of "Burning the Christmas Greens":

> Their time past, pulled down
> cracked and flung to the fire
> – go up in a roar

All recognition lost, burnt clean
clean in the flame, the green
dispersed, a living red,
flame red, red as blood wakes
on the ash –

and ebbs to a steady burning
the rekindled bed become
a landscape of flame    (CLP 16)

Williams repeats the monosyllabic words "clean," "flame," "red" (in his more adjectival and less verbal style, the repeated words are adjectives and nouns, not verbs). While he uses more alliteration than Creeley, the two men play upon the melodies of their vowels in much the same way. Here the *a* of "past" recurs in "cracked" and "ash"; the *a* of "flame" in "wakes"; both *a*'s in "landscape"; the *e* of "clean" in "green"; the *e* of "red" in the rhyming "bed" as well as in "ebbs" and "steady." Spondaic patterns recur throughout – "pulled down," "burnt clean," "flame red." The phrases "flung to the fire," "up in a roar" and "clean in the flame," near syntactic parallels, provide additional rhythmic patterning. These repetitions do more than lend formal coherence; since the theme of Williams' poem is the interdependence of destruction and creation, many of the connections established by sound – for example, between "flame" and "wakes" or "clean" (from the fire) and "green" – reinforce the poem's sense.

Like most successful free-verse poets, Williams and Creeley establish only enough aural patterning to create what Barbara Herrnstein Smith terms a "limit of variability" within which their irregularities can be effective.[18] Thus in Williams' poems of the thirties and forties – those with the greatest impact on Creeley's prosody[19] – the number of syllables and stresses in the lines of a given poem usually varies within a narrow range. The lines tend to be brief so that individual words and syllables gain weight and definition. Yet because such short lines could easily result in a monotonous pounding of unrelieved stresses, Williams and Creeley vary their rhythms. Sometimes they do so by altering the lineation of successive syntactic parallels or of recurrent phrases; sometimes they add a syllable or two so that the pattern is slightly modified. They avoid consistently ending their lines on either a rising or falling cadence; this varies the tempo because a reader tends to move more rapidly to the next line after a line ending on an upbeat.[20]

Their skill at achieving such variety is perhaps best demonstrated by examining poems in which repetition is particularly prominent. Here is Williams' "To a Poor Old Woman":

munching a plum on
the street a paper bag
of them in her hand

They taste good to her
They taste good
to her. They taste
good to her

You can see it by
the way she gives herself
to the one half
sucked out in her hand

Comforted
a solace of ripe plums
seeming to fill the air
They taste good to her    (CEP 99)

The closing lines of the first and third stanzas parallel one another in sharing the same number of syllables and the same final three words, but the initial iamb of the former and the spondee of the latter distinguish their cadences. Similarly, "good to her" and "Comforted" narrowly avoid exact mirroring because three words demand more distinct articulation than three syllables of a single word. Although "seeming to fill" (which echoes "munching a plum") seems about to repeat the accentual pattern of "solace of ripe plums," Williams replaces the single accented syllable "plums" with the iambic phrase "the air."

Of course, the most obvious repetition in the poem is the restatement of "They taste good to her." By shifting his line breaks, Williams significantly alters the cadence and thus the semantic emphasis. As Denise Levertov explains, "we have first the general recognition of well-being, then the intensification of that sensation, then its voluptuous location in the sense of taste. And all this is presented through indicated pitches, that is, by melody, not by rhythm alone."[21]

Creeley uses markedly similar techniques in "Goodbye":

She stood at the window. There was
a sound, a light.
She stood at the window. A face.

Was it that she was looking for,
he thought. Was it that
she was looking for. He said,

turn from it, turn
from it. The pain is
not unpainful. Turn from it.

The act of her anger, of
the anger she felt then,
not turning to him.   (Coll 159)

Repetition could hardly be more insistent (and at times Creeley carries it
too far; we could do without tautologies like "The pain is / not unpainful"). Because verbal material is so minimal, the slight shifts in pitch and
emphasis become the poem's most significant means of expression.

The third line is not rhythmically or melodically identical to the first
because "A face." is a complete statement – what she sees reflected in the
window – while "There was" is a fragment leading us more quickly to
the following line. In the second stanza Creeley repeats a sentence much
as Williams did above, first stating it as a complete unit, then shifting the
emphasis with a different line juncture. By raising the pitch on "that,"
Creeley conveys the intensity with which the man tries to probe the
woman's thoughts, hinting of despair or anger as well as bewilderment.
Though "he thought" and "He said" are parallel in syntax and follow
the same statement, they receive different intonation because "said" comes
at the end of a line and leads into the words following it. The repetition
of "turn from it" enacts the insistence of the man's desire; the emphasis
on "turn" in the second statement stresses the importance of that action,
so that in the poem's concluding line the reader feels the full significance
of the woman's refusal to perform it.

In Williams' manipulation of syntax Creeley discovered additional ways
free-verse forms could serve as "an extension of content."[22] Williams,
whose constant desire was to awaken his readers to the vital energy in
the things he depicted, characteristically used syntax as what Kenner has
termed a "suspension system."[23] His short poems, for example, are often
a single sentence in which the verb is deferred while details accumulate
in modifying phrases; consequently, "we are drawn past unit after unit
of attention by the promise of a verb."[24] Though the poet must momentarily arrest his subject from the flux, the energy he gains from playing
upon grammatical expectations parallels that which infuses the objects he
observes. As Kenner has pointed out, Williams creates patterns of syntax
analogous to the inherent energy of his subject.[25] Creeley often does the
same. For example, in the closing lines of "Goodbye," Creeley could
have smoothed out his syntax to indicate first that she did not turn and
then to explain that this resulted from her anger. Had he done so, the
poem's force would have dissipated anticlimactically, since we would

have witnessed the crucial act before the poem's end. The last line would have lacked the ring of finality which convinces the reader that this is indeed a moment of decisive schism, a real "goodbye."

Similarly, in the closing stanza of "The Door" (Coll 201) Creeley uses syntax to enact the tensions within the events he renders. Here the two prepositional phrases "before me across the floor" create a sense of reaching forward so that the word "beckon" confirms an impulse we are already experiencing:

> In my mind I see the door,
> I see the sunlight before me across the floor
> beckon to me, as the Lady's skirt
> moves small beyond it.

In the last line, the separation of the verb and the adverbial phrase by the adjective "small" creates a syntactic analogue to the aching distance the poet feels between himself and the muse he pursues.

Because most stanzas in *A Form of Women* are end-stopped, the manipulation of syntax is less pronounced than in Williams' more extended sentences. In the third section of *For Love* (1959–1960), however, Creeley loosens his forms so that the ends of his stanzas and of his sentences less consistently coincide. There several poems imitate Williams' method of using a single sentence as a frame on which to weave the poem. The strategy of offering a sentence as a complete poem suits well an aesthetic which holds that "so much depends upon" a single object, a single event, or a single moment's thinking approached "without forethought or afterthought but with great intensity of perception" (IM 8). Challenging traditional notions of what makes a poem meaningful, such works substitute for inherited conceptions of developed profundity the value of representing directly "what is here to be seen, right now."[26] The single sentence poem, because grammatically self-sufficient, forces the reader to contemplate the sufficiency of whatever it contains.

Yet Williams' sentences are not necessarily complete in the usual sense; he approaches the construction of a sentence as a process of discovery often leading in unexpected directions. For example, he may develop a dependent clause so far that it takes over the central focus while the main verb is left dangling without an object. As Kenner has pointed out, using "Young Sycamore" as paradigm, "the sentence offered, left not really finished, becomes a prime Williams strategy."[27] In discussing what he learned from Williams, Creeley has said, "I didn't realize before reading Williams that many circumstances of statement had no appropriate conclusion."[28] Williams' poems in which sentences do not in fact conclude exemplify the "provocative" quality which "goes on generating" and "which you have to resolve endlessly" that so impressed Creeley.

Creeley achieves a comparable effect of ongoing, unresolved energies in some of his own single-sentence poems, such as "Out of Sight" and "Lady in Black." The first five lines of "Out of Sight" (Coll 220) form an enigmatic but complete independent clause: "He thinks / always things / will be simpler, / with face // of a clown." Twisted syntax provocatively allows "always" to refer to both "will be simpler" and "thinks." The referent of "with face // of a clown" is also ambiguous: Is the clown's face intended to simplify things in general, or does it accompany thinking that things will be simpler? To answer, the reader looks to the dependent clause that occupies the remaining lines. Here Creeley describes the clown-like contraction of his physiognomy, presenting closing his eye (Creeley has only one) and compressing his lips as a literalized attempt to prevent the loss of patience. The poem reaches a resounding termination ("to hold patience, / patience, / in the locked mind"), yet the reader must refer back to the ambiguities of the opening lines and ponder the word "simpler" to understand its implications: that one can retain a faith that life will grow simpler only by withdrawing inward and cutting oneself off from the world. By defying grammatical conventions of subordination and concentrating so much of his poem's interest in the dependent clause, Creeley has created a charged conflict of syntactic energies. The final period actually sends the reader circling back to the poem's beginning.

The syntax of "Lady in Black" is far more tangled, so that to follow it is to experience the "perplexing" aspect of the "mental picture" the poet sketches:

> The mental picture which the
> lady in black if she be
> coming, or going,
> offered by the occasion
>
> to the church, behind the
> black car, lately
> stepped out of, and
> her dress
>
> falls, lets
> all eyes as if
> people were
> looking
>
> see
> her still
> an attitude
> perplexing.   (Coll 211)

The opening line seems to promise a statement about the significance of this mental picture, but instead one finds only the development of the image. That the speaker cannot define the significance is conveyed as much through syntactic complication and deviation as it is through the summary adjective. The sight is sufficiently important to prompt a poem, yet all the accompanying feelings – sexual interest, curiosity, sober awe, and an ambiguous wonder at the woman's self-conscious poise (is he repulsed by her vanity? envying her confidence?) – jostle without resolution. The poem enacts a version of the psychological complexity Creeley admired in Williams' work:

> a poem can be an instance of all the complexity of a way of thinking. Williams makes us aware of all the emotional conflicts involved in the act of thinking, so that you get apparent juxtapositions of feeling in a Williams poem that would not be understandable unless one were to take it literally as the context in which the mind has shifted to another point of contact in the very writing. (CP 16–17)

Presumably, it is because syntactic disruptions seem so natural to the thought process that Creeley is unaware of his own propensity for inverted syntax, recognizing only that his syntax necessarily "jumps and moves" with his emotions.[29]

While the sentence provides a recognizable unit that can be disrupted to highlight the mind's shifts, neither Williams nor Creeley restricted himself to this minimal syntactic unit in explorations of mental process. Creeley often quotes Williams' statement that "the poet thinks with his poem, in that lies his thought, and that in itself is the profundity" (e.g., WTRP 100). Again and again he has remarked that in writing he discovers what he did not know beforehand: "writing has always been the way of finding what I was feeling about what so engaged me as 'subject'. . . . I could find the articulation of emotions in the actual writing" (CP 96). "The Figures" (Coll 245) provides a particularly lovely example of this process being captured in the syntax of a poem several sentences long.

In the opening line Creeley identifies the essential quality of the wooden figures that makes them so compelling, their "stillness." But that word is apparently too general, for the next fourteen lines attempt to define more precisely where that stillness originates and how it is communicated:

> The stillness
> of the wood,
> the figures formed

by hands so still
they touched it
to be one

hand holding one
hand, faces
without eyes,

bodies of wooden
stone, so still
they will not move

from that quiet
action ever
again.

Pursuing syntactic tangents without regard to grammatical completion, the poet is able to establish that the stillness must have been in the hands of the artist, and that, while the figures are eyeless and their bodies like stone, their fixity nonetheless contains a kind of energy; they are permanently engaged in the "quiet / action" of holding hands. The Williams-like juncture between the adjective "quiet" and the noun "action," emphasizing both terms, insists on that almost paradoxical balance between stasis and kinesis. In addition, the poet links the figures' stillness with careful distinction of forms, a distinction mirrored in his line breaks: "one // hand holding one / hand." The extreme simplicity of Creeley's diction throughout the passage implies that the sculpture's stillness derives also from the simplicity of its forms.

Having explored that stillness, Creeley discovers a question of particular concern to him as an artist: "Did the man // who made them find / a like quiet?" The lines break between phrases, and hereafter a smoother flow and more conventional syntax allow the reader to feel how the poet's initially tentative and grammatically flexible examination opened the way for more confident understanding:

In
the act of making them

it must have been
so still he heard the wood
and felt it with his hands

moving into
the forms
he has given to them,

> one by singular
> one, so quiet,
> so still.

"The Figures," written in September 1960, was one of the latest poems included in *For Love*. By the time Creeley composed it, he had already received a letter from Williams acknowledging how well the younger poet had learned the fundamental lessons of his master. The letter, dated 18 January 1960, begins with remarks upon the importance of "appreciation of the measure" – a measure founded on "the local idiom and the variable foot." Williams complains of the apparent deafness of most contemporary poets, but adds:

> I don't know why I go on in this way because of all people writing about you need it the least. You have the subtlest feeling for the measure that I encounter anywhere except in the verses of Ezra Pound whom I cannot equal. At your best, rarely, you perhaps surpass me with a passage that leaves me flat on my back but there is never much of that. As you yourself say it is mostly unconscious when something of that sort appears on the page.[30]

The grudging tone here only underlines the authenticity of the tribute; its author, after all, had publicly admitted years before, in lines I have already quoted, "Sometimes I envy others, fear them / a little too, if they write well" (CLP 23).

At the bottom of the same letter is a postscript, "THE ROSE is good." It is no wonder that Williams approved of that poem, since it provides such clear evidence of all that Creeley had assimilated from him in the first decade of his career. A brief description of "The Rose" (Coll 246–7) summarizes the essential continuities between the two poets. Like Williams' lyrics, this poem proceeds from immediate, particular, and commonplace events: Two lovers are in a room; the woman feels restless, goes for a walk; the man follows and is able to soothe her, reestablishing the closeness between them. No great truths are proclaimed or generalizations offered; instead, the poem's meaning derives from careful recording of individual experience.

Following Williams' advice, Creeley makes his poem from "words as he finds them interrelated about him" and favors denotative over symbolic usage. Thus, while the rose has been a central symbol in love poetry for centuries, Creeley's focus is on the literal flowers that Bobbie grows. In its heterogeneity, his diction is comparable to Williams'; Creeley's predominantly simple and prosaic language gains texture and interest from a sprinkling of formal terms ("monstrous," "discloses") and from occasional surprising turns of phrase ("a movement / quietly misled," "a cloud had / broken at last / open").

Following Williams' example, Creeley adjusts his syntax, line junctures, rhythms, and pace to accord with the most minute changes in emotion. The straining pauses and abrupt sentences of the opening stanzas enact the tension between the lovers, while the poem's resolution sounds in wavelike repetitions of gradually unfolding syntax. Line breaks occur within phrases when the poet reaches most tentatively and painstakingly toward understanding of the other and the evolving situation: "flowers, a pose of / nature, her / nature has disclosed to him." Creeley's enjambments, like the modernist's, capitalize on the directed energy inherent in syntax; at the same time, the short lines and frequent stresses created by his junctures slow the momentum enough to highlight the boundaries of each word, each emotional nuance.

What distinguishes "The Rose" from most of the poems in *For Love* is its slightly more relaxed cadence, and this too can be traced to Williams. In "A Character For Love," his 1954 review of Williams' *The Desert Music* (Williams would seem to be linked even to Creeley's selection of a title for his first volume), Creeley had written, "What the poem is – beyond his sense of this service as 'capsule for punishable secrets' or including it – comes again and again to the fact of women" (QG 113–14). Creeley had identified the force behind Williams' work as a "hammering at the final edge of contact" with the female principle. This persistent hammering is perhaps even more characteristic of Creeley than of Williams, but in the last poems of *For Love* it assumes a new form very close to the modernist's. With the bitterness of his first unhappy marriage behind him and the possibilities of fulfilling love and contact renewed in his marriage to Bobbie Hawkins, Creeley gained access to the mellower cadences of Williams' late love lyrics. Thus, the halting grace of Williams' tercets in "Asphodel, That Greeny Flower" echoes in "The Rose":

> You understand
> I had to meet you
> after the event
> and have still to meet you.
> Love
> to which you too shall bow
> along with me –
> a flower
> a weakest flower
> shall be our trust   (PB 161)

And as if,
as if a cloud had
broken at last
open

and all the rain
from that,
from that had fallen
on them,

on them there is a mark
of her nature, her flowers,
and his room, his nature,
to come home to.   (Coll 247)

This is not to deny the differences between the two passages: Creeley's repetitions still seem to stutter when placed next to Williams', his lines progress more cautiously than the modernist's, and his work remains more context-bound. Nonetheless, we hear in Creeley's writing a lessening of constraint on which he commented in 1961: "Now, as I begin to relax, as I not so much grow older, but more settled, more at ease in my world, the line can not so much grow softer, but can become . . . more lyrical, less afraid of concluding" (CP 7). It is Williams' line that provides Creeley's model as he reaches toward a more relaxed and confident lyricism.

## III

The reverence Creeley felt for Williams and his writing in 1950 did not diminish in later years. Writing to Williams in 1962 about his review of *Pictures from Breughel and Other Poems*, Creeley declared, "it was a great honor to have the occasion, to make clear even so quickly why I value every damn thing you've done," adding at the bottom of the letter, "And/or: you're like they say great!"[31] Nor has that admiration decreased since Williams' death in 1963. Nonetheless, Creeley (along with Olson) had long recognized that his generation had new work to do, however helpful the example of older innovators ("love the Dr [Williams], love the Master [Pound], still, even they, are in the way" Olson had written Creeley in May 1950).[32] Not surprisingly, Creeley's second major volume, *Words* (1967) demonstrates not only the consolidation of what he had adopted from the modernist, but also a transition toward new modes and concerns more typical of postmodern than of modernist poetry.

Creeley's prosodic debt to Williams remains as strong as before, but it is clear that the imitative phase of his career is over. In a 1965 interview he explained:

> [Imitation] is the way one learns, by having the intimate possibility of some master like Williams or Pound. Writing poems in those modes was a great instruction to me insofar as I began to "feel" what Williams was doing as well as "understand" it. And so I found possibility for my own acts. (CP 124)

Thus, this volume's poem "For W.C.W." (Coll 273) takes as its subject poetic devices Creeley originally learned from Williams, but which the younger poet has further developed until they are unmistakably his own. It was Williams who taught Creeley that any "repeated / insistence" – related ideas, parallel constructions, recurrent sounds, or repeated words – constitutes "rhyme." He also showed Creeley the effectiveness of tiny variations within this patterning: "There, you say, and / there, and there, / and *and* becomes // just so." But because Creeley's style is more reductive – images less frequent, lines shorter, words fewer – such manipulation has come to be more central to his poetry than to Williams'. In "For W.C.W." Creeley points to the important semantic differences determined by whether or not the "and" between two "there' "s comes at the end of a line, or whether a phrase like "I want" is followed by a dash or a period. He pays tribute to the modernist for having led him to these discoveries, but feels no need to imitate Williams as he had done, for example, when he modeled "Wait for Me" (1954, Coll 137) on the older poet's "The Testament of Perpetual Change" (CLP 103).

Creeley's thematic concerns in *Words* have shifted somewhat from those of *For Love*, bringing into focus interests of Williams' which were not so essential to Creeley earlier. Among these new preoccupations is a reaction against mind/body dualism:

> I wanted to get out of that awful assumption that thinking is the world. . . . [It wasn't] until the sixties that people [began] to, as Allen Ginsberg would say, come back into the experience of their own bodies as primary, and to realize that the mind is physiological. . . . I was thinking of that sense of Williams' of the interest in the mind and body as one. (CP 166–7)

Some of the poems in *Words* directly express Creeley's desire for release from the mind's dominance:

> Tonight let me go
> at last out of whatever

mind I thought to have,
and all the habits of it.    (Coll 269)

There is nothing
but what thinking makes
it less tangible. The mind,
fast as it goes, loses

pace, puts in place of it
like rocks simple markers,
for a way only to
hopefully come back to

where it cannot.    (Coll 297)

Often, a sense of futility accompanies the poet's desperate longing to escape from his imprisoning consciousness, to break through to any experience unmediated by self-conscious intellect.

As part of this struggle to ground his thinking in the body, Creeley's descriptions take on a new physicality that brings to his work more of the muscular and sensuous force of Williams'. The younger poet strives especially to lend concreteness to concepts generally considered abstract. For example, in "The Window," Creeley presents position as something established by the perceiver's effort, place as a consequence of physical action (fall, drop, lift, put), and his attitudes as physiological sensations: "My // face is heavy / with the sight. I can / feel my eye breaking" (Coll 284). Even more graphic is his grotesque literalizing of the expression "to catch someone's eye":

With a quick
jump he caught
the edge of

her eye and
it tore, down,
ripping.    (Coll 286)

or the following depiction of emotional vulnerability:

    It
hurts
to live

like this,
meat
sliced
walking.    (Coll 342)

In *Words* Creeley gives more attention to the tangible details of his surroundings; for example,

> the way of feeling
> secured by walls and books,
> a picture hanging down,
>
> a center shifted, dust
> on all he puts his hand on,
> disorder, papers and letters
>
> and accumulations of clothing,
> and bedclothes, and under his
> feet the rug bunches.   (Coll 302–3)

Such concreteness brings an echo of Williams' "Fine Work with Pitch and Copper" ("One still chewing / picks up a copper strip / and runs his eye along it" [CEP 368]) to "For Helen":

> a huge encrusted
> sense of grooved trunk,
> I can
> slide my finger along
> each edge.   (Coll 320)

For the first time, the women Creeley writes about become particular physical presences, not just the metaphysical other or the generic sexual object:

> Always your
> tits, not breasts, but
> harsh sudden rises
> of impatient flesh   (Coll 291)
>
> Squatting, her
>
> head reflected in the mirror,
> the hair dark there, the
> full of her face, the shoulders,
>
> sat spread-legged, turned on
> one faucet and shyly pissed.   (Coll 281)

Yet Creeley's efforts to unite thought and sensation seem only to have increased his consciousness of the void within and around him. Words, as objects formed by the teeth, tongue, mouth, and breath, become things with which one fills that emptiness (though words are themselves "full // of holes" and speech as "a mouth" is empty hole as well as substance):

then what
is emptiness
for. To

fill, fill.
I heard words
and words full

of holes
aching. Speech
is a mouth.    (Coll 283)

The sexual act is analogous – the filling of a hole – and several poems in *Words* slide between the act of speech and that of sexual penetration, blurring the distinction between them. "The Hole" (Coll 344–5), for instance, begins "There is / a silence / to fill" and moves quickly to thoughts of an asshole filled with toilet paper and a vagina stuffed with a coke bottle. Fantasies of penises and pleasure, some involving violent dominance, lead to "I want / to, now I / can't wait any / longer." This seems an expression of sexual craving, but the lines immediately following reveal that the longing is equally for language and linguistic connection: "Talk // to me, fill / emptiness with / you, empty / hole."

Neither sex nor words, however urgently desired, truly fill the void; in fact they bring it closer. In "The Pattern" (Coll 294) Creeley presents verbalizing as a ludicrous act which reifies a self that might otherwise prove nonexistent – "I // speak to / hear myself / speak" – while the self generated is inevitably other, distanced to third person: "As soon as / I speak, I / speaks." In "A Sight" (Coll 340–1) sex is a similarly paradoxical descent into a vacuum; physical contact in love-making gives Creeley "the feeling of / falling into no // matter. . . . The sudden / thing of being / no one." He describes the experience of orgasm as a loss of contact with the sensory world and with his own senses; his own cry is a

roar-

ing unheard,
like stark sight
sees itself
inverted

into dark
turned[,]

while both the poem and the couple's intercourse end with his "onanistic" gesture (Coll 292). The "sexual shock" (Williams' phrase in the epi-

graph to *Words*) makes Creeley all the more aware that the mind's confines define him; when momentarily released from individual
consciousness, he finds himself nowhere, threatened with nonexistence.

In Williams' work there is no such void. His erotic approach to the
world enables him to merge with and possess it; when his personality is
obliterated in overpowering emotion or sensation, his mind adheres to
external things. Even when orgasmic experience "[goes] over" to nothing, as in "Queen Anne's Lace," that nothing is the flowers' whiteness,
not a pit's blackness. For Williams neither words, nor people, nor objects
fill a void; rather, they are forms whose common source is the earth.
That ground is formless, chaotic, but teeming and fertile – never vac-
uous.[33] Despite his proclamation that "only the imagination is real,"
Williams was nothing of a solipsist. As Kenner has said, for Williams
"The given world is *there*. It is neither a blank for our talk to fill, an
amorphism for our words to shape, nor a disappointment for 'noble imagery' to transfigure."[34] As Williams himself stated, "Nature is the hint
to composition . . . because it possesses the quality of independent existence, of reality which we feel in ourselves" (IM 121). The imagination
provides witness to the richness of the present moment: "The only means
[one] has to give value to life is to recognize it with the imagination and
name it" (IM 115).

By contrast, Creeley displays an increasingly tenuous sense of things
existing outside the mind that names them. Rather than recognizing the
world, one perhaps creates it: "for me it *is* true that this complex piece
of meat, *me*, is factually the author of that 'world' the also present 'I' has
as experience" (WTRP 130). Creeley's assumption that the mind creates
the world (and even the self) is a source of terror and loneliness, but it
also enhances "the delight of thought as a possibility of forms" (CP 169).
He gives the title "Joy" to a poem in which he celebrates the "infinite
emptiness" of the world previous to the mind's engagement, declaring,
"I could look at / an empty hole for hours / thinking it will / get something in it" (Coll 350). Though Creeley has always been a poet of "lo-
gopoeia – head trips,"[35] his later poems (following a progression that
parallels Ashbery's and Bishop's development) demonstrate an increasing fascination with the process of thought. In them he explores not only
how the thinking process locates a person in the world, but also how it
locates the world within the individual. Creeley's poetry is evolving in
directions far more epistemological, and more solipsistic, than Williams'
poetry did.

Creeley's movement toward philosophic solipsism has important consequences for his poetic forms. If words are one's only means of reifica-
tion, their substantiality must be reinforced as much as possible. Hence,

Creeley's lines contract still further until they are often only two to four syllables long. They force us to pause over and savor each syllable, and also to feel the tangible weight of the silences between them. Creeley's belief that we live largely within the world our words create compels him to give verbal form to as much of his daily experience as possible. He therefore began in 1963 deliberately to loosen his writing habits (writing in various situations or when "high," using different sizes of paper, and using pen or pencil instead of his familiar typewriter) so they would be better adapted to capturing the flow of immediate events. Trying to be more "open to the casual, the commonplace" (WTRP 104), he focused on poetry as a "tracking process as opposed to a record of distilled thoughts"[36] and avoided "any immediate decision as to whether or not the effects of such writing were 'good' " (CP 41). Creeley was particularly pleased by those poems toward the ends of *Words*, such as "A Piece" ("One and / One, two, / three.") and "The Farm" ("Tips of celery, / clouds of // grass – one / day I'll go away."), which opened for him "the possibility of *scribbling*, of writing for the immediacy of the pleasure and without having to pay attention to some final code of significance" (CP 42).

Creeley inherited from Williams a dual desire – for spontaneity and for precision. In Williams' work the urge to define was predominant, since the poet (typical of his generation in longing for order) felt he had always to resist the pull toward formlessness exerted by the "unfathomable ground." In Creeley's later works, immediacy begins to take precedence over formal definition, since he is threatened not by formless chaos, but by a silent void.

# 6 "Let / go, let go of it": Creeley's divergence from Williams and modernism

## I

Contemporary developments in the nonverbal arts, including abstract expressionism, as profoundly affected Robert Creeley's development as they did John Ashbery's.[1] Creeley has recalled that before going to Black Mountain College in the spring of 1954, he had not realized

> that a number of American painters had made the shift I was myself so anxious to accomplish, that they had, in fact, already begun to move away from the insistently *pictorial*, whether figurative or non-figurative, to a manifest directly of the *energy* inherent in the materials, literally, and their physical manipulation in the act of painting itself. *Process*. . . was clearly much on their minds. (WTRP 77)[2]

At Black Mountain Creeley encountered major abstract expressionist painters – Kline, Motherwell, de Kooning, Vincente, Guston – who were just then beginning to get public recognition. Excited to see the vitality art gained when the painters "[rid] painting of having to be pictures . . . of some otherwise present reality" and "forced the sense of limiting edge [i.e., the frame] to give place to what was happening in the painting itself" (QG 348), Creeley moved closer to that "shift" in his own writing.

Williams' focus on process, energy, immediacy, as well as his concern with the material quality of words, had prepared Creeley to respond sympathetically to the principles of abstract expressionism (just as Stevens' orientation had helped prepare Ashbery). The painters, however, were more radical than Williams in exploiting the possibilities of whatever happens to occur in the act of creation. Williams did say, "write carelessly so that nothing that is not green will survive,"[3] but he stopped far short of the younger painters' abdication of control in their cultivation of the accidental. Creeley himself took more than a decade to assimilate into his art the painters' extreme experiments with randomness.

The turning point seems to have been the summer of 1967, when Creeley toured several universities with six other artists, including John Cage and Merce Cunningham, whose ideas aligned closely with the aesthetics of abstract expressionism. These men were concerned with "*perception and the arousing of it*" rather than "*conceptions and their communication*" (QG 359); consequently, instead of presenting lectures and performances, they staged a series of mixed-media "happenings." One evening while Cunningham danced, the others were placed on separate sections of the stage which were raised and lowered with a "lovely randomness" by a stage manager who could not see them; each had a microphone "either to note senses of dance or to say whatever we wished" (QG 358). On another occasion they presented a "TV dinner" at which they prepared and consumed a meal on stage. Though the sometimes hostile audience response to the nine evenings indicated that many spectators felt cheated, Creeley found "the world of my own head, selfishly enough, was changing significantly" (QG 358). In an interview conducted the following fall he declared,

> even the most sophisticated intelligences of our time, I should say, are premising all their activites on the so-called *chance* factors, or on whatever provides the possibility of chance environment. Not trying to gain information from, but trying constantly to situate something in . . . evidently or experientially random occasion. Because once you enter purpose, you're stuck with that kind of circumstance that Heisenberg implies, that observation impedes function. . . . To me life is interesting insofar as it lacks intentional "control," and finds a situation of its own making. (CP 130–1)

By 1969 Creeley would identify the appreciation of chance as one of the attitudes distinguishing contemporary from modernist sensibilities. The following passage is worth quoting at length because the continuities and divergences he points to (including, but not limited to, interest in chance) correspond with those already observed between Ashbery and Stevens, Bishop and Moore:

> Supposing "modern" to define the primary consciousness of a decisive shift in the conception of *reality*, which becomes in-

creasingly clear toward the end of the nineteenth century, then one may feel that that consciousness is now a general condition in human experience. The world cannot be "known" entirely. . . . In all disciplines of human attention and act, the possibilities inherent in the previous conception of a Newtonian universe – with its containment, and thus the possibility of being known – have been yielded. . . . Reality is continuous, not separable, and cannot be objectified. . . .

Writing, and all of the arts as well, have entered the altered consciousness of men's situation in the world. One might speak, possibly, of "the modern" as the first impact of that realization in the arts. . . .

Much that the modern writers got said seems to me still of great relevance. . . . However, what is at first feared as a loss of coherence . . . starts to become less that as other situations of experience occur. High and low art begin to melt as historical valuations blur. All being *now*, all that *is* there has possibility. The ego's authority tends to relax, and conceptions involved with proposals of "good, better, best" also lose ground. Most interesting to me is the insistent presence of what has been called the *chance factor* in the activity of all the arts of the past several years. (CP 185–6).

Creeley's burgeoning interest in randomness and his willingness to embrace an apparent loss of coherence made him bored with his previous poetic practice – the "tidy containment" of single lyrics about specific events on single sheets of paper. If his life was a "continuance," his writing should be so as well (WTRP 103). The result: a decisive shift in his 1969 volume, *Pieces*, toward open-ended work, hospitable to chance associations and effects, in which poetic statements are discovered in the process of making – that is, an alignment of Creeley's poetics with the principles of abstract expressionism.

In *Pieces* Creeley no longer arranges poems as isolated statements, one per page, and he often dispenses with the framing device of titles. Having composed the volume in a journal as daily writing, for publication he simply lets three dots mark the end of a day's accumulation and a single dot divisions occurring within a day's composition (CP 192–3). The result is a sometimes disjunctive, but essentially continuous movement; the units of writing are pieces of a single if undefined whole. Preoccupations recur; images and ideas in one day's work are frequently picked up in the next. Individual entries are often only a few lines recording "small facts" either in prose or free verse – jottings of Creeley's thoughts, depictions of immediate sensations or observed scenes, transcriptions of his dreams, or notes from conversations. Creeley also includes verbal found objects, such as a lengthy quotation describing the fool card of the tarot deck, words overheard on a Canadian radio broadcast, a quote from John Muir, a line from a popular song, and a commercial slogan, "*When holes taste good / we'll put them in our bread*" (Coll 406). Creeley has explained that he "wanted a mode that could include, say, what people understandably might feel are instances of trivia," and he has related this sense that there is a place for everything in the poem to Williams' statement, "The total province of the poem is the world" (CP 192).

Yet Creeley's approach to the trivial differs significantly from Williams', as one can see by comparing *Pieces* with Williams' most journal-like volume, *The Descent of Winter*. This series of lyrics written during the fall of 1927 uses dates rather than titles and, like *Pieces*, records a scattering of the poet's immediate impressions – descriptions of autumn weeds or the passing of a freight train, casual thoughts about his likes and dislikes, bits of others' speech. Yet Williams describes common sights and ordinary people with such detailed care that the very particularity of his attention implies the significance of these humble subjects. Williams' imagery as well as his use of simile and metaphor give grand resonance to "trivia." A canna becomes the "darkly crimson heart / of this poor yard" (CEP 299); the town idiot is a figure of all aging men (CEP 310); a label above the poet's berth and the two nails fastening it are "like stars / beside / the moon" (CEP 297–8); and a sunlit beech tree glows "with a soft stript light / of love / over the brittle / grass" (CEP 301). Mundane sights call to Williams' mind the most sweeping human problems: A pile of rubbish burning in a field of dead weeds prompts him to comment upon the suffering of the aged; a poor organ grinder forcing his tunes on passersby brings to mind "the meanness of love." Williams often suggests psychological, sociological, and historical patterns within which bits of local color can be understood; even the tiniest actions and objects have a place in cosmic patterns of descent and ascent, destruction and rebirth. Beneath the unassuming and fragmented surfaces of these poems lies a moralistic exhortation to the reader to search out underlying coherence: Williams is more than half serious that "someone should summarize these things / in the interest of local government" (CEP 309–10).

For Creeley the "trivial" takes on importance in a far more inward, and more abstractly philosophical way. He less frequently transforms its scale or generalizes its meaning, since his intention is not, like Williams', to proclaim the dignity of the poor and commonplace or to correct conventional misconceptions about the unimportance of what is small and familiar. Creeley's descriptions, like Ashbery's, do not give sharper definition to what appears blurred or drab in ordinary living. Instead, he

**imm**erses himself in domestic and linguistic banality – "our businesses **of** the / evening, eating supper, talking, / watching television, then / going to bed, making love" (Coll 394) – because this is the stuff of his life in which he can locate his own here and now. The whole volume addresses – and attempts to redress – the problem that " 'Here' as a habit is what we are lacking *here*" (Coll 424). "Grease / on the hands – " (Coll 437) is a complete poetic unit simply because in the moment of writing it, Creeley is present experiencing his own body; that is its significance. While Williams, securely located in the present, demonstrates for his readers acts of attention or social perspectives within which "trivia" can be recognized as untrivial, Creeley pushes anxiously moment by moment and syllable by syllable to make contact with his "now," the material and linguistic contents of which happen most often to be "trivial."

Individual poems in *The Descent of Winter* are often unified by a propositional declaration that appears in either the opening or closing lines – e.g., "The justice of poverty / its shame its dirt / are one with the meanness / of love" (CEP 302); "What an image in the face of Almighty God is she" (CEP 311); "That river will be clean / before ever you will be" (CEP 309). The presence of such summary statements reveals a "will to closure" that Creeley regards as "the whole pattern of intention in the Moderns" – "the ability to *see* beyond the world as given to some not idealization . . . but [a] very hopeful sense of resolution and [a will to] bring it to a coherence" (B2 15).[4] According to Creeley, the world now "has become immensely larger or immensely more diverse and immensely more present" (B2 16) so that contemporary artists honestly engaged with "the *real*" have had to abandon aspirations for coherence (B2 16). The poems in *Pieces* lack the concentration, the emotional particularity, and the finished quality of Creeley's earlier works and of Williams' poetry, for, as the first entry makes clear, they are intended as open-ended gestures tracking unfolding possibilities:

> As real as thinking
> wonders created
> by the possibility –
>
> forms. A period
> at the end of a sentence
> which
>
> began *it was*
> into a present,
> a presence
>
> saying something
> as it goes.   (Coll 379)

Not "saying something," but "saying something as it goes" – for Creeley, " 'subject' as a conceptual focus or order has given place to the literal activity of the writing itself" (QG 48). His generation, he claims, is particularly wary of poetic subjects (which themselves may seem to call for closure) "because it came of age at a time when a man's writing was either admitted or denied in point of its agreement with the then fashionable concerns of 'poetic' comment. Williams Carlos Williams was . . . as much criticized for the things he said as for the way he said them" (WTRP 13). Williams himself insisted that "it isn't what [a writer] says that counts as a work of art, it's what he makes" (CLP 5), but he did regard the words which were his materials as attached to the signified things outside the poem and outside the mind. Therefore his desire to maintain the autonomy of the imagination's creations and to respect the processes of apprehension did not impinge upon his ability to examine a subject. For Creeley, however, reference to the external world may drain the immediacy from a poem: "it was never what [poems] said *about* things that interested me. I wanted the poem itself to exist and that could never be possible so long as some subject significantly elsewhere was involved" (QG 54). This attitude accounts for his avoidance of descriptive figures like similes; any comparison is "always a displacement of what *is* happening" (Coll 419). What is not significantly elsewhere is the working of one's mind and the working of words; these cannot be productively talked about, only tracked and enacted.

The contemporary shift in focus from either what one says or what one makes to one's *making* reflects a modification of the artist's sense of the poem's function. Creeley's orientation is far more self-referential and epistemological than Williams' because the later poet needs writing in order to experience his own reality. For Creeley, one's mind can be known or reified only through evidence of its activity, and poems are such evidence:

> it must be that this factual person, *me*, is familiar, so like so many, in fact, his hair, teeth, pants, etc. But the *I*, as Wittgenstein put it, is what is "deeply mysterious." In a world of objects, *mes*, this is the one manifestation of existence that cannot so see itself as literal *thing*. . . . [W]hat I feel to be the creative has location in this place of personal identity. (WTRP 30)[5]

As a revelation of his thinking, Creeley's art is to "give witness not to the thought of myself – that specious concept of identity – but, rather, to what I am as simple agency, a thing evidently alive by virtue of such activity" (WTRP 15). In *Pieces* he tries to approach his mind's reality as "a taking, finding place."

Complications arise, however, in attempting to capture the immediate workings of consciousness free from self-consciousness and intentionality because "it is very difficult to think of thinking apart from functions of language" (WTRP 121), and language is bound up with the human propensity to abstract and symbolize, being itself "that most powerful, possibly, of human abstractions" (WTRP 33). The problematic circularity of the poet's task is demonstrated in one of Creeley's pieces: "You want // the fact // of things // in words // of words" (Coll 429). That is, one wants a reality experienced and known as substantial "fact," but one's only means of knowing is through the abstract system of language, itself self-contained and ultimately self-referential. Creeley's aims, then, are philosophically or conceptually complex – and indeed, critics like Stephen Fredman have illuminated them by reference to the ideas of Nietzsche, Heidegger, and Wittgenstein[6] – but his means of returning abstract words to an elemental presentness is an apparently primitive simplification: e.g., "Here I / am. There / you are" (Coll 389). Only at this minimal level can language for Creeley find transparency, clearly demonstrating its double character as an abstract man-made system that nonetheless carries possibilities for particular, personal use. For each speaker, the general abstractions "I," "you," "here," "there" designate unique and meaningful locations in time, space, existence itself. In using such generalized terminology, Creeley permits his reader to enter into the same mental activity as the poet but within the context of the reader's immediate situation – something that would not be possible if Creeley used specifically referential expressions such as Paterson, Bolinas, or November 11. Creeley hopes that language at this level of flat simplicity may not only enable one to be more fully "here" in the present, but also, as a created system with its own rules and energies, may push the one using it (writer or reader) into new presents, new awareness.

Consider, for instance, the four line piece, "Cup. / Bowl. / Saucer. / Full." (Coll 382) Presumably, the three dishes are within sight as Creeley writes; he locates himself "here" by attending to what is around him. The fourth term, "full," may describe the immediate condition of all three pieces of concave dishware. Yet even if that is so, in adding the adjective Creeley opens out further possibilities in his immediate environment by seeing familiar objects as forms – shaped spaces that are or might be filled. At the same time, placing the adjective "full" after three nouns sets in motion observations of how language systems work: The adjective might modify only the last noun, or all three nouns that precede it. Or, as complete statement set off by a period, it might apply to none of them; instead, "Full." might describe the observer's sensation at the moment when he is fully "in" the experience of recognizing the three objects, each round and complete. Alternatively, the word might not function descriptively at all; rather, as an item followed by a period and located in the series, "Full." may suggest that a signifier for a person, place, or thing has no more or less substance and autonomy than other sorts of words.

Taking pleasure in the sounds and shapes of words and in the systematic organization of grammar can momentarily lift one out of isolating self-absorption into a realm where isolates may be connected. Often in *Pieces* Creeley permits language itself to generate the movement of his poems; for example, "Forms face / facts find" (Coll 415) takes shape from the patterns (forms) of alliteration and cliché (face facts). Giving himself over to the energies within language, Creeley is at his most exuberantly playful: "Count down, count / Orlovsky, count up – / in the air, you filthy / window washer. Why // not clean up the world" (Coll 413). Writing such pieces is for Creeley (as reading them is for an engaged reader) an act that generates possibilities, all of them immediately present in the poem's language yet all possessing personal immediacy.

Creeley's fascination with abstract man-made systems and their personalized application is most evident in the series "Numbers."[7] In these poems he explores the range of perceptions and associations that accumulate for him around the numerals one through nine and zero. He approaches the numerals as distinct entities and as parts of a series within a mathematical system, as words to be sounded and as figures to be drawn, as quantities to be arranged, as quantifiers that order our experience, and as loci for personal, often metaphorical associations. For instance, in "Six" he refers to the "twisting" shape of the arabic numeral, to the number's biblical significance as a day in the creation, to the earth's relation to the sun in the sixth month, to the special character of the mathematical factors of six, to its symbolic combination of the male and female sex organs, and to a geometrical form made by lines connecting that number of points. Under "Seven" Creeley presents several associations with seven involving responsibility for him as poet (through allusion to Wordsworth), as working man, and as husband; then a sentence of seven words arranged in seven lines; seven as the hour of Creeley's birth; a proverbial (metaphorical) phrase including that number; and some questions growing out of the entire exercise: "Are all // numbers one? / Is counting forever / beginning again?" (Coll 401–2). Numerals have no concrete place in nature; yet, reading these poems one is made aware of the variety of contexts – historical, religious, superstitious, literary, scientific, temporal, private, and communal – in which they assume meaning.

For Creeley, nothing in human use can remain purely abstract: "I want to say almost didactically that there is no information that does not have an affective content even if it's blinking lights or numbers in random series" (B2 27). At the same time, it is the unemotional abstractness of an artificial system that allows it to be orderly – eight is invariably twice four which is twice two, nine remains a "triad of triads," and after nine the sequence returns to its origin in a fertile nothing, thereby forming the most perfect of forms, the circle. This order is useful. Like so many twentieth-century artists, Creeley does not believe any governing order is inherent in the universe; and he wishes to avoid the fate of artists like "Delmore Schwartz or Randall Jarrell or John Berryman or Roethke" who, in attempting to imitate the response of the early modernists, were "*broken* on that painful wheel of trying to sustain a continuing cohering imagination of the world. . . . not only won't it cohere but it literally breaks in the process" (B2 17). Instead, like Ashbery and many other of his contemporaries, Creeley provisionally entertains arbitrary orders (keeping in clear view both the arbitrariness and the provisionality) which are momentarily useful as measures of his experience.

In *Pieces* Creeley so consistently exploits these orders that the volume as a whole creates a well unifed, even tidy effect. Thematically, as I have suggested, the book revolves around Creeley's effort to attain " 'here,' as a habit." Focusing on ways of saying and perceiving, he explores the obstacles – imposed by language either in its nature or in its current corrupt state, by the limits to what one can know, and by the nature of thinking itself – hindering this accomplishment. While some of the individual pieces remain open possibilities – "Oh no you / don't, do you?" (Coll 413) – or circle endlessly – "The head / of a / pin on. . . " (Coll 389) – Creeley seems nonetheless drawn toward certain forms of closure. Often his lines have an epigrammatic ring, his verse paragraphs an apparent symmetry. At the volume's conclusion, he turns to his readers and invites then to continue the exploratory processes he has enacted in the preceding pages: "What do you do, / what do you say, / what do you think, / what do you know" (Coll 446) – four lines, each four words long, providing a neatly "open" close. Though Creeley may well be "tired of purposes," he has not been able to resist the habit of imposing shapeliness. Within the book Creeley once catches himself expressing a shaping intention and confesses his frustration with that tendency:

> My plan is
> these little boxes
> make sequences. . .
>
> Lift me
> from such I
> makes such declaration.    (Coll 440)

Certainly, as Denise Levertov has remarked, the "sprawl" and the "absence of perfectionism" of this volume show Creeley "letting his hair down." Compared to his earlier works, *Pieces* is indeed "a breaking open."[8] Nonetheless, a strong desire to control remains in evidence. Looking back in 1977 Creeley admitted that while he used to "*insist* upon trusting things" his actual ability to trust things was very limited. "I tended in Pound's phrase to 'overprepare the event' " (B2 56). By the time he published his next major volume, *A Day Book* (1974), Creeley had relaxed more thoroughly into unplanned process. Unfortunately, Creeley's successful alignment of poetic practice with poetic principle has neither fostered his continued growth as a poet nor produced exciting literature; I will briefly characterize this recent work before addressing the evaluative issues it raises.

## II

*In London*, the poetic section of *A Day Book* (a journal written between November 1968 and June 1971), derives its wholeness simply from temporal sequence. Creeley's deracination and the temporariness of his settlement in England seem to have heightened his consciousness of flux – "This world of such changes, / nothing stable but in that motion" (Coll 457). Preoccupied with time's passage and with mortality, Creeley is increasingly aware that his life's only inevitable ordering is as a succession of moments. Prefabricated patterns such as those provided by numbers, even page numbers, he discards as extraneous. In their place, temporal progression: "We resolve to think of ourselves, / . . . as involved with / a necessary system, of age and its // factors" (Coll 477). Fleeting days gain solidity and more intense presence for Creeley when rendered as a succession of poetic jottings; their "Linkage: // the system, the / one after another" (Coll 468).

The volume, then, carries further some of the developments of *Pieces*. Radically extending Williams' interest in rendering the minute particulars of experience in order to enrich one's appreciation of immediate events, Creeley continues to take greater risks than Williams in "depend[ing] on such a low level of 'significant' statement . . . seeing how close you can get to the casual and still have the grit of a poetic."[9] He pushes to even greater extremes of triviality than in *Pieces*:

12:30   (*Read as Twelve Thirty*)

(Berrigan
Sleeps on)                    (Coll 460)

or "Hair is a / long thing / hanging off" (Coll 455) or "ALL AROUND / the town / he walked" (Coll 457) or "Sitting – / shitting" (Coll 455). These "Little bits / of it" (Coll 454) are one way Creeley tracks his mind's motion.

An alternative mode, also exploited in *In London*, is the fluidly meandering meditation that follows for an extended period the associative movement of Creeley's consciousness. In desultory ramblings like "An Illness" or "Bolinas and Me" Creeley admits into the poetic fabric memories of the past and speculations about the future, as well as observations and idle musings on the present situation, for all these are present in his thoughts. These discursive poems are more emotional in texture than the short notations, many conveying an urgent care for particular memories, a cherishing of what is close – familiar places, old friends, wife and family. Both the short discontinuous poetic forms and the longer more continuous ones represent for Creeley a divergence from the modernists' "optative" method, which is "involved with particularized, determined choice among possibilities" rather than an acceptance of "what comes of the moment of possibility."[10]

Again extending the interests of *Pieces*, Creeley is also tracking the possibilities inherent in words – sometimes playing with "the way words can tell a story – or what a story is and what that has as affect" (either tiny epigrams or loose ramblings may be narratives), sometimes exploring "the disposition of words as activities or as 'things in themselves.' "[11] To these ends he experiments with temporal signs ("Waked to past now dream / of previous place was about to / get all the confusions at last / resolved when he then woke up" [Coll 449]); with permutations of syntax ("Small dreams of home. / Small of home dreams. / Dreams of small home. / Home small dreams of." [Coll 460]); and with associational and aural progressions ("Walking down a / walk, a stone / sees, *assizes*, sizes, // taxes, form / forms" [Coll 509]). Even the verbal transformations of chance typing errors he accepts as creative forms:

> That tidy habit of sound
> relations – must be in the
> very works,★ like.
>
> ──────────────
>
> ★Words work
> the author of many pieces     (Coll 463)

The tricks language plays with the mind and the tricks the mind plays with language are, for Creeley, worth pondering not only as they bring him to presentness but also as evidence of what it is to be human. For Creeley the arts give us the "most specific, intensive information" we can obtain about being human (WTRP 118). Where words and language (human creations) posit things that may not exist outside the mind, they reveal a great deal about humanity. Thus any use of language may prove a vehicle for self-knowledge or an autobiographical record, even when the user knows no such intention. For example, Creeley has pointed out that "because" is "only, dearly, *language* . . . there is no 'because' other than in the mind" (WTRP 122). Clearly then, people need to invent the possibility of causality, and whether or not such order is externally operative, language gives it actuality: "in language, what *is* said is always the case" (WTRP 122). Similarly, language posits a plural of "I," and though Creeley finds that "we" in one sense "unimaginable" (WTRP 53), its possibility is an essential human hope. Even presenting a thought using the second person pronoun is an act of linguistic fabrication that brings into being the possibility of communication, of some responsive person's being there to receive one's messages:

> YOU WILL never be here
> again, you will never
>
> see again what you now see –
> you, the euphemistic
>
> I speaks always, always
> wanting a you to be *here*.    (Coll 472)

"The *you* imagined locates / the response" (Coll 496); without such words, one would be overwhelmed by discontinuity and condemned to agonizing isolation. *In London* includes more than a dozen poems Creeley lovingly dedicates to specific friends, making particular language's general – and treasured – reaching out for stablizing connection with others.

Creeley's short volumes written during the next few years – *Thirty Things* (1974), *Away* (1976), and *Hello: A Journal* (1976) – offer only slight variations on the developments of *In London*. Creeley now attempts to find a sense of satisfying wholeness in moments that remain stubbornly discrete and small. He abandons the search for fluid continuity evident in *A Day Book* and approaches life's relentless flux as if it worked on the same principle as the moving picture – "a sequence of rapidly changing single, static images" (WTRP 125). By restricting his focus to one frame at a time, Creeley avoids preoccupation with what is absent.

To insist formally on exclusive presentness, Creeley in *Thirty Things* essentially abandons discursiveness for epigrammatic and aphoristic statement, almost always in the present tense. Yet despite the conclusive ring of poems like "One day after another – / perfect. / They all fit"

(Coll 564), Creeley intends these not as didactic pronouncements but as provocative points around which the mind may linger; "the terminals are like handholds at best."[12] A maxim such as "Friends make / the most of it / the more of it / quite enough" (Coll 556) is simply evidence of a moment's consciousness in exactly the same way as a description, or a twisted cliché – "The apple in / her eye" (Coll 561), or a catalog of relations – "Patsy's / brother / Bill – // Meg's mother – / Father's // home. / Sweet / home" (Coll 563). As Creeley's equalizing one-thing-per-page, one-illustration-per-thing arrangement implies, the meaning of one is no more profound or lastingly alive than another.[13] Creeley presents his material so as to demonstrate his concurrence with Olson's sense of art as "the only true twin life has – it 'means nothing,' it doesn't have a point" (WTRP 42) – or perhaps it would be equally accurate to say it has an infinite number of points.

The plainness of Creeley's "things" – in every way so minimal – represents a purposeful avoidance of all transforming embellishment. Unlike Williams, he has become wary even of the imagination as something that may draw him away from immediate and elemental existence. Creeley in the seventies aligns himself with the painter Jasper Johns (whose work falls somewhere between abstract expressionism and pop art), who instead of regarding the imagination as useful, finds it "a great distraction." Creeley comments,

> You could never imagine a Modernist . . . saying that[,] whereas the Postmoderns you can absolutely understand why that's said that imagination constantly posits not possibilities but distracting images as against the initial apprehension. (B2 18)

The same refusal to enliven sensory details imaginatively, to heighten meaning, or to intensify emotions – that is, the same commitment to keeping art directly and accurately responsive to life in process – shapes *Away* and *Hello: A Journal*. These collections may offer somewhat greater formal variety than *Thirty Things*, but one familiar with Creeley's work since *Pieces* is likely to find that the flatly matter-of-fact mode of presentation has grown tiresome. One understands why Creeley should treasure moments like "Sitting at table – good talk / with good people" (*Hello*), but such generic articulations are not sustaining material for those who have no specific memories of the event. The lesson of presentness, and of its difficulty, is quickly apprehended while one's interest in the casual minutiae of Creeley's life flags.

Tiresome repetitiveness is a problem built into Creeley's mature aesthetic, since he refuses discriminations of "good, better, best" (CP 186) while he insists on the necessity of giving verbal form to as much experience as possible. Without words, many thoughts and feelings remain for Creeley abstract, insubstantial; we speak and write because "we . . . want our lives to be known to us, we don't want it all a seeming dream" (WTRP 53). He is therefore compelled to record as many moments as he can. Collecting the resulting poems in books produces a "sense of increment, of accumulation" that Creeley treasures. Selecting for publication only the "best" would permit the reader "to miss the factual life they [all the poems] had either made manifest or engendered" (Coll ix). It is as if keeping out of print one poem, no matter how slight, risks erasure of a moment's living. Unfortunately, many of Creeley's multitudinous poems *are* slight.

Modifying the modernists' sense of one's craft as a test of one's sincerity, Creeley in his forties and fifties seems to have believed that sincerity in itself will guarantee craft. In his poems since *Pieces*, his line breaks, which in *For Love* and *Words* so painstakingly sounded emotions, appear haphazard or automatic:

> Here
>
> is a street, and
> now a car seems
> to be coming,
> the lights
>
> signal approach at
> an intersection when
> a locked group
> beats upon the
>
> locked door an
> inextricable tenderness
> of one man's
> desire to be there.    (Coll 516)

Why the tense pauses between "and" and "now," between "at" and "an intersection," between "the" and "locked door," between "an" and "inextricable"? Perhaps these are intended to register "one man's / desire," but when intraphrasal breaks repeat so predictably, instead of the forward urge of longing one hears only an irritating hiccup.

Readers like myself who were intrigued by *Pieces'* explorations of the ways in which thinking both constitutes and interferes with experience, of the ways words "form / forms," of the struggle to both observe and experience the flux of successive moments, will find nothing new in subsequent collections and therefore are likely to find the work considerably less exciting. The moment Creeley's reader ceases to participate in the poems' repeated movement into presence, he or she will find Creeley's statements either too obscure and elliptical to be meaningful or, more often, too obvious, trivial, or naive to command much interest.

In his most recent collections, *Later* (1979) and *Mirrors* (1983), Creeley has retreated somewhat from the careless openness of the previous decade's work, returning to more varied subject matter, greater emotional complexity, and, at least intermittently, more attention to craft. Creeley's fascination with the usefulness of communally shared and arbitrary orders – those of mathematics, of linguistic systems, or of the clock and the calendar – now recedes as he becomes increasingly involved in the patterns that the individual mind, aided by memory, constructs from experiences accumulated over time: "It's man-made // endurance I'm after, / it's love for the wear // and the tear here, / goes under, gets broken, but stays" (L 78). Though troubled by the signs of his own mortality and age, Creeley finds in these volumes new tones of acquiescence, more embracing gestures that suggest a greater ease with living and with himself. In *Later* he has even found a muse to replace the oppressively demanding, perfect Lady who appeared in his early works. This is Hermes, "god / of crossed sticks, / crossed existence" (L 119), a figure of human weakness and duality, patron of thieves and trickery but also patron of the arts and inventor of the lyre. This "brother spirit" allows Creeley to expose his own frailty and inconsistency without having to denigrate himself for his imperfections. Creeley finds comfort in imagining that Hermes understands his "persistent pain, the scarifying / openness he makes do with" (L 121) and that the divinity supports his impulse to tell it all.

But while the older and mellower Creeley discovers in Hermes possibilities for bridging difficult rifts within himself, this figure of mediation between polarities has not led to the same aesthetic enrichment Elizabeth Bishop found in the dissolution of dichotomies or Ashbery in a fence-sitting stance. Unlike Ashbery and Bishop, Creeley has relinquished his powers of discrimination and analysis. In "Thinking of Walter Benjamin," for instance, Creeley raises a genuinely interesting question – "what to say / these days / of crashing disjunct, / whine, of separation" (L 22) – but he fails to engage himself in its terms. His answer is platitudinous: anything and everything so long as it is not abstract, so long as it is grounded in hand and mind and heart together. Equally unenlightening is the answer Creeley presents in "For Rene Ricard" when he asks himself what life is "all about" – a potentially endless list beginning:

It's garbage
dumped in street,
a friend's quick care,

someone who hates you
and won't go way,
a breeze

blowing past Neil's
malfunctioning dear ears,
a blown-out dusty room.    (L 82)

As already suggested, Creeley's determination to write "of whatever *is* the instant" puts excessive demands on the reader's empathetic powers as well as on his or her sustained intellectual interest in the conceptual frame behind Creeley's minimalist work. Granted, Creeley's solipsistic orientation has, since *Words*, necessitated his enlarging the areas of internal experience that poetry can map. Because words are "tangible," even "voluptuous," "they tell / the reassurances, / the comforts, / of being human" (L 18); without them one has only the most precarious sense of identity and location. Yet even an artist who places such importance on unselectivity and inclusiveness must keep his audience in mind and provide a context rich enough or statement intriguing enough for readers to become engaged in his experience. This is Ashbery's achievement. While rendering a "one-size-fits-all" mental experience, Ashbery involves his readers in varied textures of language and intellection that are both challenging and interesting to follow. Creeley, however, tends to reduce and, at least on the surface, to simplify. Believing that "Happiness [or any emotion] / finds itself / in one or many / the same – " (L 32), Creeley imagines that he has only to record at the moment of his happiness the fact that he is happy for a reader to find the experience meaningful. Thus, in "For Rene Ricard," Creeley notes that he is walking with his friends, "talking, gossiping, / thank god – the useful news – // what's presently the word / of X and Y and Z / in NYC" (L 80). Presumably Creeley recalls what that news was and who those people were, but recognizing that does not make the lines "useful" to his audience. Applying Roland Barthes' terms, Creeley "prattles"; his is an "undifferentiated orality" that does not take the audience into account.[14] In allowing himself to sketch whatever passes through his mind without attempting to make its sound or image either fresh or distinctive, Creeley is not making something out of banality, as Williams does; his work is itself a wearisome repetition of the humdrum.

Because Creeley in his late work is concerned only with authenticity, he opens himself to a number of stylistic corruptions, among them the mannered line breaks already noted. In addition, many lines in *Later* and *Mirrors* sound "like / an old song"; his formulations are truistic and clichéd, his tone often pompous or sentimental; his predominantly monosyllabic vocabulary dull. Creeley's images now tend to be conventional, his metaphors dead or dying:

> it's got to be luck
> keeps the world going round
> myself moving on
> on that train going by    (L 63)

The straight use of such tired figures, without the variation and ironic play that Ashbery would provide, often results in a tone simultaneously saccharine and grandiose. Here, for example, Creeley describes the elation he felt upon learning that his last name is Irish:

> and the heavens opened, birds sang,
> and the trees and the ladies spoke
> with wondrous voices. The power of the glory
> of poetry – was at last mine.    (L 70)

Furthermore, the trite formulation of Creeley's questions – e.g., "What then / is this life all about" (L 82) – virtually guarantees that the answers will be equally insipid.

These limitations – intellectual indolence, banality, and a hackneyed style – are evident throughout Creeley's works since the late sixties. They are somewhat alleviated in *Later* and *Mirrors*, where occasional poems have all the poignancy and nervous clarity that his best early works possess. (Among the strongest poems in *Later* I would list the ten–part title sequence, "Waiting for a Bus 'En Frente de la Iglesia,' " "If I Had My Way," and "This Day"; in *Mirrors*, "Prospect," "Mother's Voice," and "Bresson's Movies.") But the successes of Creeley's recent volumes are his past successes almost regained, earlier strengths sometimes relocated, rather than new triumphs achieved. Where Ashbery and Bishop in moving beyond their central modernist models found a freeing eclecticism that fostered their poetic growth, Creeley, so devotedly a son of Pound and Williams, took a few steps away from their work only to stop developing. Although his late works allude to or quote from a broad range of writers – including Dyer, Shelley, Flaubert, Yeats, Wyatt, Dickinson, Hardy, Stevens, Zukofsky – they actually draw upon the resources of a very limited tradition: a narrowed modernism combined with some aesthetic notions initially associated with abstract expressionism and then popularized in the 1960s.

Creeley's poetic strengths were fostered by the example of the modernists, especially Williams, in their care for particularity of voice, of image (whether subjective or objective), and of musical phrase. In Creeley's work of the fifties and early sixties, the anguished hesitancy and the almost reverent delicacy with which he rendered intimate emotions attained such an "intense expression of his perceptions and ardors" that a number of his poems did "constitute a revelation" in his own distinctive speech (CLP 5). Creeley's anxious yet candid voice, modulated through careful and innovative prosody, did invite readers to "meet" him.

While Creeley is at his best when he stays close to Williams' manner in personal lyrics of particular emotion, he seems to have been handicapped by his strict allegiance to certain modernist principles. As Pinsky has noted, Creeley has carried the modernist reservation about ornament to such extremes that his idiom seems "worn down rather than sculpted."[15] Exaggerating Williams' wariness of "the beautiful illusion" and insisting on honest mimesis, Creeley turned away from invention as Williams himself did not. (Williams' lines come to mind: "All that which makes the pear ripen / or the poet's line / come true! / Invention is the heart of it" [PB 95].) In addition, Creeley has extended the self-conscious, reflexive character of modernism to the point where meaningful statement or intelligent evaluation of experience are frequently impossible. Perhaps Creeley's passionate admiration for Pound and Williams, those dogmatic spokesmen for making it new, even contributed to the programmatic tendency that stalled his development amid the (previously avant-garde) orthodoxies of the 1960s.

Creeley's most dramatic divergence from modernism – his relaxation in the late sixties into the pleasures and possibilities of immediate experience and of the fundamental structures of language – was at first a liberating expansion. But Creeley's urge to "*Let / go, let go of it*" (Coll 524) soon solidified into a restrictive poetic program of necessarily verifying random moments of living and thinking using whatever language comes most immediately to mind. Having lost interest in the modernist's careful selection of fresh images and particular formulations, Creeley does not intend to provide a dramatic or imagistic focus for the reader's feelings. Yet his language games, unlike Ashbery's or Bishop's explorations of the possibilites of worn and ordinary speech, fail to provide a rich enough substitute to sustain the reader's imaginative, intellectual, or emotional engagement in the poet's discoveries.

Creeley, then, provides an instructive example of an ultimately unsuccessful response to the polarized impulses of the modernist inheritance. His work deteriorates as he pursues a purified form of certain modernist tenets, while he remains uncomfortable experimenting with the resources of earlier traditions outside those authorized by Williams' particularly homemade version of modernism. As a young poet Creeley was supported by modernist inventions which he skillfully adapted to his own reduced scale of statement. Later, in seeking alternatives to the modernist impulse to "make it cohere" – something Bishop and Ashbery also did in their own ways – he left behind technical resources that had served him well and failed to locate others equally powerful.

# 7 "Those who love illusion / And know it": the continuity between Auden and Merrill

On October 18, 1983, more than a dozen distinguished poets gathered at the Guggenheim Museum to read their own choices from W. H. Auden's work in commemoration of the tenth anniversary of his death. It was a moving event, eerily concluded with Auden's voice reading his villanelle "If I Could Tell You" as if speaking from the dead: "Will Time say nothing but I told you so? / If I could tell you I would let you know." The poets' tribute, powerful testimony to their admiration for Auden and his work, brought into focus several issues of twentieth-century literary periodization. For one thing, the physical presence of Auden's contemporaries, Christopher Isherwood and Stephen Spender, provided a vivid reminder that Auden was of a younger generation than the high modernists, none of whom survived into the 1980s despite their remarkable longevity. Stevens was born in 1879, Williams in 1883, Moore in 1887; Auden was born a good twenty years later, in 1907. Why, then, does Auden stand beside Stevens, Williams and Moore in this study? To what extent is Auden a modernist, and to what extent can a recent poet's relation to Auden's work reflect his or her relation to modernism?

A second, related issue highlighted that evening at the Guggenheim is that Auden's work changed dramatically over his career, and the nature of his influence on other writers has varied accordingly. No two writers will ever make use of exactly the same aspects of a forerunner's work, but the apparently distinct stages in Auden's career make his impact especially diverse. On that October evening, Ashbery, having announced his interest in Auden as lyric poet and as a poet of words rather than ideas, read some of Auden's earliest works, "As I walked out one evening," "At last the secret is out," and "As well as can be expected" [i.e., "Taller to-day"]; Joseph Brodsky, focusing on Auden's ideas and political conscience, proclaimed from memory the oracular "September 1,

1939"; and Amy Clampitt celebrated Auden's subverting the grown-ups by reading "Voltaire at Ferney." Richard Howard singled out Auden's late poems, Anthony Hecht and John Hollander midcareer works from the late forties; James Merrill read from part IV of "Letter to Lord Byron," one of the most straightforwardly autobiographical passages – as well as one of the lightest and most eighteenth-century – in all Auden's work. Different sides of Auden's achievement and of his influence were revealed by each different reader. To what extent, then, can Merrill's poetry represent Auden's impact on the next generation?

First, to consider Auden's place among poetic generations: Literary generations cannot be identified simply according to birth dates, by grouping, say, those born between 1900 and 1920 in one category, and those born between 1920 and 1940 in another. Certainly, poets born about the same time are responding to many of the same political and cultural pressures, and reacting to the same artistic fashions and dominant figures. Yet a poet's impact on his or her own generation and on younger artists depends on his or her publishing history as well. Although Auden was more than twenty-five years Stevens' junior, Auden's first book (*Poems*, accepted for Faber & Faber by T. S. Eliot) appeared in 1930, only seven years after Stevens' first book; and the younger poet was almost immediately acclaimed as a leading experimental figure, a spokesperson for the thirties generation.[1] Consequently, there is not a quarter century's – or a full generation's – gap between Stevens and Auden in their canonical impact. On the other hand, some important writers born only a few years later than Auden had no real impact on the literary scene until the 1950s. Charles Olson, for instance, was born in 1910, but did not publish his first volume until 1947, and his influential projective verse essay appeared still later, in 1950. Similarly, Elizabeth Bishop was born in 1911, only four years after Auden, yet she and her contemporaries, Roethke (b. 1908), Jarrell (b. 1914), Berryman (b. 1914), Lowell (b. 1917), and Schwartz (b. 1913) began writing in the shadow of Auden's precocious achievement. (Bishop's first volume appeared only a few years before those of Merrill, Creeley, and Ashbery, who were born in 1926 and 1927.) Auden and Bishop are treated here as members of different generations, despite the proximity of their births, largely because Auden came into prominence extraordinarily early. For America's young writers in the late forties and early fifties who were confronting the hegemony of Eliot and his Agrarian and New Critical followers, Auden (like the less canonical older modernists, Stevens, Moore, and Williams) provided an alternative model.

Auden's earliest works, while responding directly to the immediate political climate, have much in common with modernist works of the preceding decades. Auden's poems of the late twenties and early thirties follow Eliot's and Hulme's prescriptions that writing should be hard, austere, impersonal, "classical." That compressed, elliptical, and obviously modernist work lastingly affected some younger poets, including John Ashbery. One can easily detect models for Ashbery's methods in these early lines of Auden, read by the younger poet at the Guggenheim:

> Taller to-day, we remember similar evenings,
> Walking together in a windless orchard
> Where the brook runs over the gravel, far from the glacier.
>
> Nights come bringing the snow, and the dead howl
> Under headlands in their windy dwelling
> Because the Adversary put too easy questions
> On lonely roads.    (CP 39)[2]

Yet Auden reacted against modernism as well as participating in it, and he emigrated to the United States in 1939 partly to avoid conforming to the comfortable literary establishment Eliot then fostered in England. For James Merrill, Auden's early poems were of minimal interest, while his less obscure American works using traditional poetic forms and a conversational, discursive manner were of tremendous importance. The same is largely true for Howard, Hacker, Hollander, and Hecht; Merrill's poetry demonstrates one important strain of Auden's influence, though certainly not the only one.

Auden's American work was not markedly modernist, either in prosody or attitude: not formally innovative, not compressed and economical, not taking the impersonal hawk's eye view. While he worked to avoid repeating himself or standing still, Auden was not driven by a desire to "make it new" as, say, Pound and Williams were. He felt an easy continuity with the inherited literary tradition. While not pretending that traditional writing could any longer be understood as repeating the methods of one's immediate forebears with slight modification, and while recognizing, too, that the twentieth-century writer must glean useful techniques from a range of earlier periods, the American Auden nonetheless did not share the early modernists' sense that the tradition desperately needed renewing. As a critic he cast himself in a moderating role, pointing out a middle way that would recognize the real novelty of the present while revealing which modern tasks and achievements were in fact analogous to those of the past (see FA 215).

At times he seems to have envied the generation of artists that came of age before 1914, "the founders of 'modern' art," because "the need they all felt to make a radical break with the immediate past was an artistic, not a historical, imperative, and therefore unique for each one of them" (FA 434). Auden imagines each of them thinking, " 'It is only by creating something "new" that I can hope to produce a work which in due time will take its permanent place in the tradition of my art.' " The temptation in subsequent eras – "times of rapid social change and political crisis" – is to respond to an apparent historical imperative (for example, the sixties' concern with "relevance") and thereby "to reduce art to an endless series of momentary and arbitrary 'happenings,' and to produce in artists and public alike a conformism to the tyranny of the passing moment which is far more enslaving, far more destructive of integrity and originality, than any thoughtless copying of the past" (FA 435). Eager to avoid this, the mature Auden did not aspire to lead an avant-garde; he deemphasized the value of originality and stressed the importance of authenticity instead. He was wary of false identification of the genuine with the novel. Make it true, make it you, he might have said, but not "make it new."

Merrill shares Auden's lack of interest in innovation for its own sake. He cherishes *not* feeling that he has to "think of something new every year": "I've yet to see a poem that I can't relate to something at least fifty years old if not two hundred." He also denies having felt the need to resist or to compete with the two generations of modernists preceding him (Eliot, Stevens, Auden, etc.). While one need not take him completely at his word on that always touchy subject, it is certainly true that Merrill aspires to no avant-garde.

Just as Merrill's affinities with Auden do not necessarily align with modernism, so his divergence from Auden's poetics does not always represent a divergence from modernism. Nor does it always parallel the development of the other three contemporary figures already discussed. Instead of an early absorption and imitation followed by increasing divergence from Auden's example, as has been the pattern in the preceding pairs, in Merrill's work the polarized impulses toward continuity and discontinuity are more simultaneously and continuously balanced. Merrill's affinities with Auden are at least as pronounced in the seventies as they were in the fifties.

Auden and Merrill remain in some ways apart from the mainstream in modernist or contemporary writing, without being in any way peripheral to the development of twentieth-century poetry. The avant-garde movements of the fifties and sixties, represented here by the work of Ashbery and Creeley, tell only part of the story of American poetry's development since World War II. Other, less radical changes have been taking place quietly, almost covertly. Bishop and Merrill demonstrate some of these more conservative developments. Precisely because Merrill's divergence from Auden does not entirely fit the paradigm that has been emerging with the preceding pairs – he does not, for instance, approach poetic form as an unfolding process of discovery, nor seem to restrict himself to scales of statement and ambitions more modest than his predecessor's – this fourth pair provides a particularly good test of the general applicability of the patterns so far observed.

# I

Early in the second volume of James Merrill's massive trilogy, *The Changing Light at Sandover* (1982), the spirit of the recently dead W. H. Auden begs to join the seminars in which Merrill and David Jackson are, via Ouija board, learning about the cosmos. Because Merrill is eager to have Auden there, the higher powers acquiesce. Thereafter, Auden is a main character who plays Virgil to Merrill's Dante; his wisdom and common sense, his inquisitive intellect, as well as his sense of humor, help reduce the burden and the terror of Merrill's task. The human participants in the seminars form a loving family, with Maria Mitsotáki assuming the maternal role and Auden the paternal one for the two earthly "enfants." Not surprisingly, Auden's fathering is largely poetic: he is the "senior scribe" and the "father of forms." That Merrill sees himself as carrying on the work of his adopted father is evident from an interchange in *Mirabell* concerning Auden's talents being "mined out" to living writers. Describing the "ODD SENSATION" of being deprived of some of his poetic "densities," Auden says he feels as if he's missing his "SPECS" (as well as his phallic "STUBBY PENCIL"). Only a page later he announces, "U JM HAVE GOT MY SPECS ON" (M 95–6).[3] The implication is clear: Merrill has inherited part of Auden's poetic vision, a portion of his poetic power.

While Auden's singular importance for Merrill is more obviously dramatized in *Sandover* than in his earlier collections, in fact Auden's influence extends back to the early years of Merrill's career. Merrill's first collections were marred by a stiff insistent impersonality, by a cold preciosity; throughout the fifties and early sixties, however, he was developing a more personal, contemporary manner, though he differed from many contemporary poets in not abandoning traditional poetic forms. Auden's example was instrumental in this development, partly because Auden's own writing had followed a similar course, moving from a detached modernism to a more personal, conversational formalism. Sometimes Merrill's poems reveal Auden's direct influence; more often, while one cannot establish with certainty that Merrill was drawing specifically from Auden rather than from a number of other poets, Auden's work nonetheless provides the best context for understanding the extravagant artifice of Merrill's witty yet humane fabrications.

Merrill began writing poetry in prep school (circa 1940), from the start favoring traditional verse forms. His earliest efforts were sonnets written "as much with French models as with English – the melodic, empty-headed fin de siècle sort of thing."[4] *Jim's Book*, privately printed in 1942, contains four such sonnets, along with two translations of Baudelaire, an essay on Elinor Wylie (Merrill's "first twentieth-century passion"[5]), and a good deal of verse in regular rhymed quatrains. Merrill then had little acquaintance with twentieth-century poets other than Wylie and Frost. The poems collected in *The Black Swan*, however, written in 1945 and 1946, "bubbled up" in excited response to Merrill's discovery of modernist poetry:

> Each [poem] took an afternoon, a day or two at most. Their author had been recently dazzled by all kinds of things whose existence he'd never suspected, poets he'd never read before, like Stevens or Crane; techniques and forms that could be recovered or reinvented from the past without their having to sound old-fashioned, thanks to any number of stylish "modern" touches like slant rhyme or surrealist imagery or some tentative approach to the conversational.[6]

Among those poets whose work so stimulated Merrill was Auden: "Auden's poems I had begun reading while I was in the Army and *The Sea and the Mirror* came out [published in America in the late summer of 1944]. That and the Christmas oratorio *For the Time Being* absolutely captivated me."[7] Auden's earlier poems – the clinically impersonal, elliptical, politically engaged works that had made him "Court Poet of the Left"[8] – did not have this appeal for Merrill, seeming instead "to belong to another part of history." Merrill recalls that what meant most to him about *The Sea and the Mirror* at that time was the work's "range of forms" (a sonnet, a villanelle, a ballade, terza rima, and so forth): "I was inspired to try some of these things myself."[9] Initially, then, Auden's greatest impact on Merrill was as an exemplar of poetic craft who helped legitimize the young man's formalism within a modern context.

When Merrill's earliest commercial volume, *First Poems*, appeared in 1951 (winner of the Harriet Monroe Prize), he was already a remarkably skilled craftsman, but refinement of craft was not yet matched by depth of feeling. Nor, despite distinct echoes of Crane, late Yeats, and especially Stevens, did his writing seem more than superficially modern. While the volume does contain "stylish 'modern' touches," no amount of slant rhyme can lend contemporaneity or emotional immediacy to the poems' fountain statuary, elegant gardens, gilt and crystal objects. The anguish announced in these decorative "roulades of relinquishment" (FP 25) seems unreal, being distanced not only by static emblematic subjects but also by archaic and eupheuistic language and opulent images. In "Foliage of Vision," for example, the luxurious sound patterns of the opening lines – "As landscapes richen after rain, the eye / Atones, turns fresh after a fit of tears" – have such a narcotic effect that they blur the thematic statement: that sorrow-enriched vision attunes one joyfully to all parts of life's cycle, even loss, calamity, death. The poem's archaic diction and inverted syntax – "the sun / Dragging with it a scarlet palace down," "creatures / Of air and earth noble among much leafage" – by suggesting some distant chivalric age, remove the reader further from the poem's claims. Instead of exploring the problem of loss and time's passage through some compelling human experience, Merrill's speaker proceeds to ex- amine a ripe fruit, emblem of life in its prime, being destroyed by the "lean wasp" of time. Because he discovers a marvelous beauty in the spectacle of the plum "all brocaded with corruption," he sententiously proclaims, "The eye attunes, pastoral warbler, always." But how easy for the speaker to assert that human vision can transcend suffering when he has wept only for his symbolic plum!

Oracular – and unpersuasive – claims for the powers of the imagina- tive eye are characteristic of *First Poems* and point to the volume's Ro- mantic orientation; we find here Keats' sensuousness and Wordsworth's nostalgia for childhood's innocent perception, combined with Shelley's grandiose claims for the imagination's transcendent value. Yet while Merrill in *First Poems* repeatedly insists on the power of imaginative vision to compensate for or transform pain, dissolution, loss, he vacillates in tone and stance, sometimes adopting a world-weary, self-consciously cynical irony that echoes Laforgue and early Eliot. For instance, in the following lines, not-so-innocent children take the place of Eliot's singing mer- maids: "I have loitered by the wall, being somewhat taller, / Wanting to die, but that life was a flattery, / And seen the children pose in their vanity" (FP 25). "Wryness is all" one speaker tells his "dear wastrel" (FP 24).

We may detect in this guarded worldliness, as in the volume's sweep- ing idealistic claims, evidence of extreme vulnerability. Anxious self- protection combined with a strong sense of decorum apparently compel Merrill in his early poems to withhold from his readers the lived sources of genuine feelings. Thus, the artist he portrays in "Dancing, Joyously Dancing" (FP 19) is characterized by a neurasthenic hypersensitivity to the world's ordinary discomforts. The poem's depiction of the art- ist/fiddler imitates Stevens' "Man With a Blue Guitar" ("Fiddler, the dancers cried, / Addressing perhaps the sun, teach us this joy"), with Brueghel's painterly model substituted for Picasso's. But while Stevens' artist insists that the imagination must not withdraw from reality, Merrill's does withdraw from "a morning's imperfections" – from "too many elbows in the dance / And too much pity in the cobblestones / And flowers shriveling." To evade crowding reminders of mortality, young Merrill's artist converts the throbbing scene to cool artifact: "And daring to be gracious the fiddler grew / Unmoved by all but his most private music," with the result that the cold pulses of his instrument freeze the dancers, each locked in solitude. The speaker asserts that "in this stillness there was a kind of joy," but the limitations of that "frosted" joy are the equally obvious limitations of Merrill's earliest published verse.

Merrill's awareness of these limits is suggested by "Willow" (FP 69–70), a poem in rhyming triplets placed very near the close of *First Poems*; he has since singled out this poem as one of two in which he felt "humanly more involved" than in the rest of the volume.[10] It begins by exposing the anthropocentrism of our ways of thinking and speaking: "invoking in our imagery not much of willows," we project human emotions upon the trees we designate as "weeping." This projection is generated by a desire to lend grace and beauty to human pains that, unadorned, would be unbearable. But unfortunately, it results in our rehearsing the "eloquent charade / Of willows," thereby blurring our awareness of "What we *did* bear." (Merrill has commented that the popularity of "we" in poetry at this time, his own and others', "probably started with Auden" who in turn probably found it in Rilke.)[11] Metaphor, and poems that use it, threaten to remove us from reality: "At times we thought, Gesture is all that grieves." That line encapsulates the complaints early critics leveled against Merrill. Yet the poet's own discomfort with artifice that distances emotion is evident in the closing lines, where a gesturing hand alone, and not the person it is attached to, responds to another's death:

> The hand has slanted (like the willow's leaves)
> From touching faces it alone conceives
>
> Downward to drop its pennies on shut eyes
> Before the habit fades of their surprise
> Past blood and tissue where remembrance lies.   (FP 70)

Because of his dissatisfaction with his poems in which figures are frozen and elegant gestures replace feelings, Merrill as he matured through the next few volumes strove for an art less evasive about its autobiographical emotional roots, less cool in manner and matter. The example of Au-

den's casually conversational and humorous verse assisted him in this
process.

In *Short Stories* (1954; most of it reprinted in *The Country of a Thousand
Years of Peace*, 1959) he was reaching toward more genuine human interest by experimenting with blank verse narratives that employ a more
discursive, prosaic manner deemphasizing the formal intricacy of the work.
Auden's poetry of the same period provides one model for these developments. In "The Octopus" and "The Greenhouse," Merrill adopts a
rhyme pattern Auden introduced in several poems published in magazines in the late 1940s and collected in *Nones* in 1951.[12] Here couplets
rhyme a penultimate syllable with an ultimate one, alternating masculine
and feminine endings:

> What there is as a surround to our figures
>     Is very old, very big,
> Very formidable indeed; the ocean
>     Stares right past us as though
> No one here was worth drowning, and the eye, true
>     Blue all summer, of the sky
> Would not miss a huddle of huts related
>     By planks, a dock, a state
> Of undress and improvised abandon
>     Upon unshadowed sand.   ("Pleasure Island," CP 265)

This formal pattern is unobtrusive, particularly when syntax is extended
to minimize end-stopped lines and when rhymed lines are of unequal
length, as in "Pleasure Island." Merrill imitates these strategies, but while
Auden's layout calls attention to the couplet unit, Merrill makes the formal organization less apparent by standardizing the left-hand margin:

> There are many monsters that a glassen surface
> Restrains. And none more sinister
> Than vision asleep in the eye's tight translucence.
> Rarely it seeks now to unloose
> Its diamonds.

In these opening lines of "The Octopus" (CTY 3), syntactic breaks are
purposefully at odds with rhyming units, and when the end of a sentence
does correspond with the end of a line, it does not mark the end of a
couplet. The poem's diction and syntax remain obviously literary – "a
glassen surface," for instance – but the rigors of its form are largely
disguised.

"The Octopus" is similar to many of Merrill's *First Poems* in being
based on a conceit – this one comparing the sea creature lured from the

gloom of its aquarium tank to vision coaxed from the drab prison of mortal flesh by "lusters / Extraordinary." In its subject, then, the poem continues *First Poems'* Romantic preoccupation with visionary imagination and the awakened dreamer. But in contrast to the earlier volume, vision here is presented as a "sinister" "writher," and the dreamer is ironically undercut. Vision's awakening is not an uplifting experience, though the dreamer fumbles to make it so. Vision generates first an atavistic possession – or is it merely a headache? – "Percussive pulses, drum or gong, / Build in his skull their loud entrancement." Believing himself in the presence of some Shiva-like deity with "many fleshlike arms," the dreamer, rendered slightly ridiculous, tries to imitate the "Volutions of a Hindu dance." Since Shiva is both destroyer and creator, allusion to him underlines Merrill's ambivalence, as does the list of contradictory verbs, "destroy, adore, evolve, reject." The poem's last two lines suggest that the dreamer's clumsy attempt at worship becomes a grotesque fit, punningly a "seizure" of the octopus's arms, that ends in horrifying catatonia: "Till on glass rigid with his own seizure / At length the sucking jewels freeze." That is a far cry from "The eye attunes, pastoral warbler, always."

"The Octopus" is characteristic of *Short Stories* and *Country* in that Merrill seems to be struggling against the lofty exaggeration of *First Poems'* Romantic claims for the imagination. By this time, irony provides a primary means for Merrill to counteract and temper his early oracular pretensions. In *Short Stories* and subsequent volumes, Auden's good-humored and less cynical ironies increasingly replace Eliot's and Laforgue's as models for Merrill's work.[13] Auden's exuberant ironic manner serves particularly in Merrill's humanizing deflation of the Romanticism he now wishes to disavow.

In "Midas Among Goldenrod" (*Short Stories*, CTY 30), Merrill dissociates himself from Romanticism by reducing to a buffoon the Romantic artist who "invariably . . . shows up" in spots of "divine uncultivation." Merrill's solitary quester is, ludicrously, a butterfly collector with hay fever, seeking not eternal truths but "some flighty flattering thing." The tears streaming from his eyes, seeming to flow in suffering from the mind's Shelleyan "chasms," are merely symptoms of his allergy. Deflating transcendental pretensions by focusing on the limits of the human body – corns, for example – is typical of Auden's writing, since he insists on our recognizing the partnership of body and spirit in humanity's mixed nature. That is the message of much of Caliban's discourse in *The Sea and the Mirror*, in which considerable humor derives from attempts by artists and audiences to deny the body. Throughout his career, when Auden wishes to underline human limitations, he calls attention to the

unruly Caliban in each of us. Thus in one of his "Shorts" he says of the
ordinary person: "Large and paramount the State / That will not coop-
erate / With the Duchy of his mind: / All his lifetime he will find /
Swollen knee or aching tooth / Hostile to his quest for truth" (CP 231–
2). Merrill's depiction of the artist Midas rests on the same assumptions:
"Damp, flushed, his eyes are streaming, his mouth / Shuts and opens
like a ventriloquist's dummy / Eloquent with opinions it does not really
believe."

In "Midas," the young Merrill distances himself more completely from
the target of satire than the mature Auden usually does. However, Merrill sounds less smugly superior and more self-mocking in "A Narrow
Escape" (CTY 28–9), another "short story" in which he uses irony to
undermine nineteenth-century aesthetics. His target here is Romanticism's self-aggrandizing earnestness about "the inner / Adventure." In
this narrative a "vampire" at a dinner party "frankly / Confess[es]" herself a symbol of that adventure, calling up in the speaker an "old anxiousness." The anxiousness is linked with the Romantic period both by
the characterization of her tone – that of an 1830 pianoforte – and by the
images, half-Keats and half-Coleridge, she calls to mind: "Crags and
grottos, an olive dark that lured / Casements to loosen gleamings onto
the Rhine." Her dinner companions escape the lure of this exotic inner
landscape by taking an ironic, urbane perspective. The speaker, in a gos-
sip's tones, reduces the vampire's dangers to "ghastly scenes over letters
and at meals / Not to speak of positive evil," and that is followed by
Charles's knowing deflation: "It was then Charles thought to wonder,
peering over / The rests of venison, what on earth a vampire / Means by
the inner adventure." Such worldly and humorous questioning is characteristic of Auden, e.g., "What right have I to swear / Even at one a.m.
/ To love you till I die?" (CP 214). For both poets, comic diminution
triumphs over the Romantic's anxious seriousness.

While the voice of "A Narrow Escape" has a camp edge, it remains
distinctly upper-class.[14] Merrill's sensibility has always been, and continues to be, class-bound; the "laquered screen[s]" of *Jim's Book* evoke the
same milieu as the "jonquil lawns" of *First Poems* and the "venison rests"
of *Short Stories* or *Country*. In his earliest work, however, Merrill communicated that sensibility of the wealthy, cultured cosmopolitan largely
through scenes and objects depicted rather than through personal voice,
as he does in "A Narrow Escape." As he learned to use the conversational manner of "our particular circle," cultivating his own lightly ironic,
witty speech as if addressing his equally urbane acquaintances, his work
gained considerable appeal from its more human scale.

Merrill's poetic maturation involves a growing interest in what Auden called "the human clay." Though that development was in fact gradual, Merrill dramatized it three quarters of the way through *The Country of a Thousand Years of Peace* as if it were a sudden reversal. On the sixty-sixth page of that volume he placed one of his previously published "short stories," "About the Phoenix" (CTY 66–8), whose abrupt opening line seems a rejection of all Merrill's preceding work: "But in the end one tires of the high-flown." The "high-flown," associated with the "giant jeweled bird" of the title, is a poetry of extremes characterized by "flights between ardor and ashes" and trafficking in "strong prescriptions, 'live' and 'die'!" Swinging back and forth between such extremes proves monotonous; more dangerously, the brilliant light cast by the flames of this phoenix-art so outshines ordinary daylight that it devalues human experience and mundane relations:

> Caught in whose talons any proof of grace,
> Even your face, particularly your face
> Fades, featureless in flame, or wan, a fading
> Tintype of some cooling love, according
> To the creature's whim.

Rejecting this distortion, Merrill reinterprets the phoenix myth, suggesting that its "point" is not "agony or resurrection, rather / A mortal lull that followed either." In the faint dawn light of that lull, he can see his lover's face, described in the poem's plainest language, "for that moment neither / Alive nor dead, but turned in sleep / Away from whatever waited to be endured."

The problem Merrill now wishes his art to confront is not how to attain immortality or capture life's most blazing sensations, but how to carry on in one's daily living. This is the same realm of experience that Auden sought to redeem in his American work, what he called "the time being." Both Merrill's expressed goal and the conversational manner in which he approaches it suggest that he is no longer content merely with modern "touches." His art by the mid-fifties was aiming to be fully modern as W. H. Auden (writing in 1962) defined modernity:

> The characteristic style of 'Modern' poetry is an intimate tone of voice, the speech of one person addressing one person, not a large audience; whenever a modern poet raises his voice he sounds phony. And its characteristic hero is neither the 'Great Man' nor the romantic rebel, both doers of extraordinary deeds, but the man or woman in any walk of life who, despite all the impersonal pressures of modern society, manages to acquire and preserve a face of his own. (DH 84)

Merrill enters this modern mode very much in Auden's conservative way: For both poets, as we shall see, the "intimate tone" has little to do with confession, and the "speech of one person" (its intonations registered with sound patterns of traditional metrics) depends on, rather than precludes, formalism.

## II

In the late fifties and sixties, Merrill continued to loosen his forms and began to break the formal continuity of longer poems by mixing sections of differing patterns of rhyme and meter. Nonetheless, his experiments took place largely within traditional formal conventions: "It's simply the way that I know how to write. Even when I sort of slyly thought of changing to irregular line lengths I always found some way to justify them, by secret scanning and rhyme."[15] Of course, Merrill's formalism is not simply a habit; he has always believed that formal constraints are valuable, and in the sixties he saw metrical regularity as providing essential resources for exploring the range of voices and tones that lie between the extremes of "ardor and ashes." He has insisted that the full vocal range, "not just bel canto or passionate speech," "would be utterly unattainable without meter and rhyme."[16] Frost and Auden are the modern masters whose work best supports such a claim.

Auden was for Merrill a more lastingly useful model than Frost because Auden's development anticipated the pattern of Merrill's progression from impersonal, oracular extremes toward more modest conversational tones. Because of temperamental affinities, the two men had to fight some of the same artistic temptations. Like Merrill, Auden felt the lure of lofty, earnest proclamation and therefore had his own reasons for being wary of "the grand old manner . . . sung from a resonant heart" (CP 472). By the mid-thirties Auden had recognized the need to temper his own sweeping didacticism and announced his desire to "disown, / The preacher's loose immodest tone" (CP 165). By 1940 he particularly needed to purge Yeats' oracular voice from his writing, since it led him into dishonesty.[17] Politically, too, the highflown came to be suspect. In its Romantic form as a resounding glorification of art and the artist, the highflown had alarming affinities with fascism. The poet, Auden came to believe, should remind himself and his audience of the limits of art's powers. Moreover, since the fanaticism dominant in the modern political climate had debased "All sane affirmative speech / . . . To a horrid mechanical screech," the poet's responsibility was to set a counterexample to hysteria and obfuscation through flat, quiet talk – "The wry, the sotto-voce / Ironic and monochrome" (CP 472). Auden's conversion to the religion whose "Lord Jesus Christ was made the Most Insignificant of All the Elephants" provided yet another confirmation for his sense of "something fishy about a High Style / and the character it suits" (CP 607–8).

So Auden made himself into a master of unemphatic conversation, using shifts away from regular metrical or rhyming norms to help register subtle variations in speech tones. He began in the mid-thirties with the flamboyant talk of "Letter to Lord Byron," written in rhyme royal, progressed to the more sober but wittily aphoristic mode of the "New Year Letter" octosyllabic couplets, and thereafter explored the conversational possibilities of less tightly closed forms, including syllabic stanzas modeled on Marianne Moore's. Auden believed that the formal restrictions, whether apparent to the reader or not, helped prevent the poet from falling back on easy formulas dictated by subjectivism or by didactic righteousness: "Blessed be all metrical rules that forbid automatic responses, / force us to have second thoughts, free from the fetters of Self" (CP 642).

From the thirties on, Auden's poetic talk is almost invariably lightened by humor. Sometimes he introduces comedy through zeugma-like incongruities in his lists (e.g., his praise of music "which can be made anywhere, is invisible / And does not smell" [CP 415]), sometimes through unexpected deflating realism ("So my embodied love / Which, like most feeling, is / Half humbug and half true, / Asks neighborhood of you" [CP 215]), sometimes through play with clichés ("ready, / Though, to take on the rest / Of the world at the drop of a hat or the mildest / Nudge of the impossible"), sometimes through cutting observations, bits of bawdry, puns, unlikely rhymes, or touches of sheer superciliousness. Auden's humor and irony are typically infused into serious material, enabling effects that have figured importantly in his legacy to Merrill. Auden often means most seriously precisely what he presents most amusingly. His mockery and buffoonery occasionally qualify but rarely undercut his statements. Paradoxically, Auden's ironies permit him sincere access to highflown touches, along with other outmoded styles of diction or rhetoric. He can preach and teach without seeming to do so, while ironic comments and comic exuberance draw the reader closer by implying shared tastes and judgments. Auden's dependable sense of humor strengthens his poetry's aura of personal speech.

In his talky works, particularly the long rambling letters, Auden introduced more autobiographical material than previously, and in a more direct manner. In the twenties he had frequently disguised private references through dense riddling and code terminology (his spies, borders, etc.) so that the reader could discern only generalized political or psychological allegory. Such strategies are comparable to the young Merrill's holding his reader at arm's length through an emblemizing generality of context and through impeccably polished language. Twenty years apart, the two poets developing from precocious but chillingly impersonal beginnings came to see the advantages of establishing closer connections and warmer relations with their audiences. For both, this entailed diminished reticence, yet both felt that good manners precluded revelations that might embarrass either the reader or the author. As we shall see, Auden and Merrill achieve this mannerly restraint by shared or similar methods – methods that often distinguish their aesthetics from those of the mid-twentieth-century mainstream.

Auden has identified "good manners or good breeding" as "a style of behavior and speech which is no less precious in art than in life,"[18] adding:

> To be well-bred means to have respect for the solitude of others, whether they be mere acquaintances or, and this is much more difficult, persons we love; to be ill-bred is to importune attention and intimacy, to come too close, to ask indiscreet questions and make indiscreet revelations, to lecture, to bore. (FA 394)

Without manners, he claims, we would all be unbearably selfish and serious; manners infuse into our behavior valuable frivolity and insincerity that assist us in being less serious about ourselves and more serious about others.[19] Confessional writing emerges, then, as the nadir of bad manners; "Literary confessors are contemptible" (DH 99).

Merrill, too, has emphasized the importance of manners, using the term in two senses. First, he himself writes poems or novels of manners – that is, works that portray a particular social world, registering its nuances of gesture and intonation. Merrill claims that the author of such works can "provide a framework all the nicer for being more fallible, more hospitable to irony, self-expression, self-contradiction, than many a philosophical or sociological system." "Manners for me are the touch of nature, an artifice in the very bloodstream," he adds, shifting to the second meaning of the term, as proper behavior.[20] Like Auden, Merrill discriminates between works of art demonstrating good and bad manners; if the manners are inferior, he claims, the poem will seem unreal or allegorical.[21] His own sense of decorum, like Auden's, prohibits unmediated confession. Merrill's feelings are discreetly implied, rather than stated, in his poems. He makes only sparing use of the first person singular in combination with present indicative verbs; when he speaks in the first person, good manners require temporal distancing through the use of other tenses and some "veil[ing]" or "ritual effacement of the ego."[22]

Formalism helps these poets live up to their own standards of good breeding. The challenges imposed by given formal constraints emphasize the game-playing aspect of creation, and this both helps prevent the artist from "importuning attention" as a suffering individual and helps restrain him from "indiscreet revelations." Focusing on the traditional requirements of poetic craft reduces the likelihood of an artist egotistically regarding himself as an inspired genius whose every thought, twitch, or yearning is noteworthy. Conversely, the absence of rules and restrictions in free verse, according to Auden, often results in "a repetitious and self indulgent 'show-off' of the writer's personality and stylistic mannerisms" (FA 396). Formalism can also provide what Adrienne Rich terms "asbestos gloves," enabling a writer to handle powerful emotional material without scorching either self or audience.[23] Thus, discussing Shakespeare's sonnets, Auden declared that "without the restraint and distancing which the rhetorical devices provide, the intensity and immediacy of the emotion might have produced, not a poem, but an embarrassing 'human document' " (FA 99). Merrill too, though more cognizant of the limits of form's control of feelings, advocates feeding "the drug of Form" to our nightmares, our passions, our hungers, in order to render them at least momentarily tame and harmless ("The Cruise," CTY).

Merrill in the sixties and seventies, following the course of Auden in the forties and fifties, approaches his readers cordially and respectfully, using a voice that charms and invites, that makes no indiscreet revelations, that does not preach or take itself too seriously – and that manages to *sound* personal. Though several poems in *Country* straightforwardly present autobiographical material – most notably "Dream (Escape from the Sculpture Museum) and Waking" – Merrill does not fully locate this mannerly personal voice until the opening poem of *Water Street* (1962), "An Urban Convalescence" (WS 3–6).

This is the first of Merrill's lyrics to employ what was to become one of his most characteristic and effective patterns: A present experience recalls some past event(s), and the overlay of several temporal frames, like transparencies that build a single image, brings new insight as well as resolution of some internal conflict. Here the immediate event is the speaker's discovery, during a walk after a week's illness, that a building is being torn down on the block where he has lived for ten years. He struggles to recall that building but can envision only a stone garland over its lintel. Wondering "When did the garland become part of me?" he remembers a cheap engraving of garlands purchased in Paris a decade before. In his mind's eye it is held by the "small red-nailed hand / of no one I can place." His inability to remember the woman forces him to see that he, like New York, has "torn down" his past without allowing "time to care for it"; the structure of his past life "soundlessly collapses" before he can appreciate and learn from it.

Already, in the first half of the poem, Merrill has in several ways departed from his preceding works. For the first time we are made to feel that Merrill lives in contemporary urban reality rather than the Europe of Henry James. Merrill's depiction of grit, filth, rubble, and shabby stone has more in common with the industrial landscapes of Auden's thirties work than with the "sculpture garden" of his own earlier poems. More striking than the shift to the contemporary and unglamorized setting is the change in Merrill's manner of speaking. Avoiding the stasis of his early emblematic works, Merrill works to convey psychological action. The primary model for his rendition of mental process seems to be Elizabeth Bishop, whose work he has so often praised, particularly for its refusal of "oracular amplification."[24] The informal talking to oneself and wondering aloud – "Was there a building at all?" "Wait. Yes." – the self-deprecating and approximating manner – "Vaguely a presence rises / Some five floors high, of shabby stone / – Or am I confusing it with another one / In another part of town, or of the world?" – the questions, as well as the explanatory parentheses – "(my eyes are shut)" – are surely inspired by Bishop. The deliberate flattening and slackening, however, can be traced to Auden, from whom Bishop also learned: "I have lived on this same street for a decade," "It is not even as though the new / Buildings did very much for architecture," "Well, that is what life does."

In speaking of this poem as a turning point, Merrill has singled out not the developments mentioned so far, but rather his hitting upon "the self-reflexive side of the poem – that you can break up the argument in a very fruitful way."[25] He has specified the point "when I felt I was on the right track: when I thought to use the phrase 'the sickness of our time.' I loathe that phrase and tried to put it into perspective."[26] Four lines after using that phrase in all seriousness, Merrill wrote:

> There are certain phrases which to use in a poem
> Is like rubbing silver with quicksilver. Bright
> But facile, the glamour deadens overnight.
> For instance, how 'the sickness of our time'
>
> Enhances, then debases, what I feel.

Auden (himself renowned for poetic diagnoses of the modern era's sicknesses) provides precedents for this sort of commentary. In "Letter to

Lord Byron," for instance, he comments on his choice of rhyme royal instead of Byron's ottava rima and calls attention to its potentially ridiculous repetitions: "Et cetera, et cetera. O curse, / That is the flattest line in English verse." A few stanzas later, after lines ending with "point" and "joint," he inserts "(There is no other rhyme except anoint)" (CP 80). Of course, such light verse remains tonally distinct from "An Urban Convalescence." Yet in both poems self-conscious commentary serves the same purpose as Auden's serio–comic mode does generally: it allows the poet to mean and use what he would also mockingly stand apart from. Furthermore, this calling attention to poetic artifice (anticipated earlier in "An Urban Convalescence" by the phrase "as it were" – "So that I am already on the stair, / As it were, of where I lived") is one of several anti-Romantic strategies both poets use to underline the separation between art and life.[27] In a variety of ways, the mature works of both Auden and Merrill continually remind us that the world of art is subject to ordering frames and figures not so easily imposed upon life.

Equally significant among the developments signalled by "An Urban Convalescence" is the transformation it records in the speaker's attitude. The poem portrays a conversion experience of sorts; religious allusions – the crowd's "meek attitudes," the old man like a vengeful God directing the crane's demolition, the speaker's posture of prayer with "head bowed, at the shrine of noise" – prepare for the speaker's confrontation with his own failures, or, one might say, his sins. With a humility new to Merrill's verse, his speaker swears upon the world as his Bible:

> To abide by what it teaches:
> Gospels of ugliness and waste,
> Of towering voids, of soiled gusts,
> Of a shrieking to be faced
> Full into, eyes astream with cold –
>
> With cold?
> All right then. With self-knowledge.

By the poem's close, he no longer rationalizes his behavior with "that is what life does" and instead determines to care for whomever and whatever he encounters. Refusing to fantasize about a lost world of Jamesian elegance – "that honey-slow descent / Of the Champs-Elysées, her hand in his" – he focuses on another destination: "the dull need to make some kind of house / Out of the life lived, out of the love spent." Auden's Christmas oratorio, *For the Time Being*, the work that (along with *The Sea and the Mirror*) so captivated Merrill in the mid-forties, helped Merrill identify that destination. Auden's poem celebrates Mary and Joseph as people who might "Redeem for the dull the / Average way" (CP 284) and insists that moments of revelation have little to do with life's real challenge: "In the meantime / There are bills to be paid, machines to keep in repair, / Irregular verbs to learn, the Time Being to redeem / From insignificance" (CP 308).

## III

In his later trilogy Merrill singled out as one of his "touchstone stanzas" (M 70) the Third Wise Man's speech from *For the Time Being*:

> Observing how myopic
>   Is the Venus of the Soma,
> The concept Ought would make, I thought,
>   Our passions philanthropic,
> And rectify in the sensual eye
>   Both lens-flare and lens-coma:
> But arriving at the Greatest Good by introspection
> And counting the Greatest Number, left not time for affec-
>     tion,
>   Laughter, kisses, squeezing, smiles:
> And I learned why the learned are as despised as they are.
>   To discover how to be loving now
>   Is the reason I follow this star.    (CP 286)

Much of Merrill's best poetry from *Water Street* on explores problems of "how to be loving," often by describing and evaluating personal experiences of "love spent" (in both senses, as given and used up). Here again, temperamental affinities between Auden and Merrill as well as their parallel courses of literary development encouraged Merrill in the 1960s to look to Auden for exemplary poetic strategies for making this private material public.

The early love poems of both men suggest unhappy isolation and failure to establish genuine intimacy within sexual relationships. Mendelson has pointed out that Auden during the thirties repeatedly "addresses a lover, but does so to express his inability to love."[28] Merrill similarly acknowledges the coldness of his behavior and the barriers he tends to erect between himself and his lover. In "Dream (Escape from the Sculpture Museum) and Waking," a poem that comes unusually close to what Auden might consider "an embarrassing 'human document,' " he recalls a quarrel: "You called me cold, I said you were a child. / I said we must respect / Each other's solitude. You smiled" (CTY 75). In the speaker's dream the clear link between himself and a snowman (he breaks into a cold sweat when the snowman melts) confirms his lover's claim. More subtly, the later poem "Between Us" suggests that what comes between the two lovers is imposed by the speaker. The shrunken head he sees on the pillow between them turns out not to be some third person, a dreaded rival. Instead it is "A hand, seen queerly. Mine. / Deliver me, I breathe / Watching it unclench with a soft moan / And reach for you" (ND 18). He prays for deliverance from himself and rescue from his own distancing impulses.

Both Merrill and Auden seem to have been initially uncomfortable with their homosexuality, and both were profoundly troubled by the gap they discovered between sexual satisfaction and emotional fulfillment.[29] In Merrill's first novel, *The Seraglio* (1957), the protagonist, whose social background and family situation closely resemble the author's, is so disturbed by the "myopia of the soma" that he castrates himself. He would rather be a eunuch than again find himself unwillingly carried away by sexual desire. (The precipitating sexual experiences were with women; his desperation results partly from confusion about sexual preference.) Merrill in his youth, more than Auden in his, feared the uncontrollable power of the id. Thus the animals he imagines having broken away from the restraining "Charioteer of Delphi" become "the killing horses" who have equally violent twins within us:

> Broken from his mild reprimand
> In fire and fury hard upon the taste
> Of a sweet license, even these have raced
>
> Uncurbed in us, where fires are fanned.   (CTY 26)

Apparently, the damage inflicted by uncontrolled lust is of two kinds. First there is the libertine's guilt-ridden loss of self-respect suggested in "Amsterdam." In that city where "desire is freed from the body's prison," the speaker pleads "Once, once only to have laid absolute claim / Upon that love long held in readiness, / Not by the flesh in any stale undress . . . so to have taken hold / Of certain volumes violent yet controlled / As to leave nothing for regret" (CTY 40–1). Second, there is the pain of rejection that one risks in passionate involvement. Merrill's "Fire Poem" in *Country* revives the proverb "once burned, twice shy" in that context:

> Yet fire thereafter was the burnt child's name
> For fear, and many ardent things became
> Such that their fire would have, could fire take fear,
> Forgot the blissful nester [phoenix/lover] in its flame.
>
> (CTY 4)

"I lay me down in love in fear," intones an ardent but wary adult in "A Vision of the Garden" (WS 8).

Yet Merrill, like Auden before him, did find a lasting love (and one more rewardingly mutual than Auden's relationship with Kallman). By the time *Water Street* appeared, Merrill could already describe in "Poem of Summer's End" (WS 9–11) a love relationship that had endured for ten years, depicting its dull habituations and diminished romance – "these weeks . . . we touch / By accident" – as well as its wonders – the lovers' mutual understanding and the days "When lover and beloved know / That love is what they are and where they go." Since then, Merrill has continued to produce love lyrics prompted either by his ongoing relationship with David Jackson or by affairs with others. In addition, like Auden, who often philosophized about love as Eros and Agape, Merrill has broadened his poetic concern with love in more extended, more philosophical meditations on the nature of love and on the relationship between eros and psyche, body and soul. Two such long poems comprise nearly half of Merrill's 1966 collection, *Nights and Days*. Because Auden's aesthetic practices and principles provide models for these works, it will be useful to examine Auden's approach to poetic philosophizing before discussing the long poems "From the Cupola" and "The Thousand and Second Night."

Auden, always interested in communicating abstract ideas, and always striving to bring together public and private significance, developed during his career multiple strategies for giving life and dramatic flourish to concepts. For example, in the late thirties his specialty – widely imitated – was the apparently incongruous simile linking the abstract with the concrete, e.g., "Anxiety / Receives them like a grand hotel" (CP 155). He typically modified abstract nouns with concrete adjectives or attached abstract modifiers to concrete nouns, and fleshed out abstractions with detailed lists of examples. Merrill sometimes experimented with these strategies. In the early poem "Wintering Weeds" (CTY 20) he used such Auden-like phrases as "deprived dusk," "cold dazzle," "slender hungers" (comparable to Auden's "dozing afternoon" and "lenient amusing shore" in "Pleasure Island" or to "warm enigma" and "ignorant shadow" in "At the Grave of Henry James"). However, since Merrill was a more sensuous writer to begin with, tending to provide luxuriously detailed description, he has had less need for such techniques designed to ground the abstract in the material. More lastingly useful to Merrill has been Auden's manner of personifying abstractions so that conflicts between faculties, points of view, or moral qualities can be dramatized in parables or allegories. In "The Octopus," for instance, where "vision" is figured in the octopus, the abstraction almost begs for the allegorizing capital V Auden would have given it. Personification becomes an essential strategy in Merrill's recent trilogy, where even elements of the vegetable and mineral realms are animated with souls and voices.

Auden's reliance on personification and on many other techniques that lend dramatic flare and physical costume to the abstract ideas his poems propose reflects his belief in the essentially theatrical nature of human behavior (and of human art). This notion preoccupied him during the forties and the early fifties, when World War II had made him particularly aware of the danger of the Romantic view of the goodness and sincerity of "unaccommodated man." In *The Age of Anxiety* (1947) Auden's narrator asserts,

> Only animals who are below civilization and the angels who are beyond it can be sincere. Human beings are, necessarily, actors who cannot become something before they have first pretended to be it; and they can be divided, not into the hypocritical and the sincere, but into the sane who known [sic] they are acting and the mad who do not. (CP 395–6)

In a conversation with Howard Griffin in the late 1940s that was published in *Hudson Review* in 1951, Auden said, "The most dishonest people are those who are unaware they are acting. To be honest with oneself means to know oneself as an actor, not to take oneself too seriously."[30] It is dangerous for a poet to aspire to sincerity or to so-called naturalness. Thus, Auden was quite serious, in his serio-comic way, in his birthday wishes for the seven-year-old son of friends:[31]

> So I wish you first a
> Sense of theatre; only
> Those who love illusion
>     And know it will go far:
> Otherwise we spend our
> Lives in a confusion
> Of what we say and do with
>     Who we really are.
>
> You will any day now
> Have this revelation:
> 'Why, we're all like people
>     Acting in a play.'
> And will suffer, Johnny,
> Man's unique temptation
> Precisely at the moment
>     You utter this cliché.   (CP 249–50)

The temptation Auden refers to involves forgetting the human creature's "proper station," imagining that we really do own the earth, that we really are gods, instead of recognizing that we merely act that way. Birthday celebrations and the arts, the poem goes on to argue, are justified because their deliberate pageantry reminds us that our ordinary lives are equally forms of pageantry and fiction.

Certain kinds of art and certain styles of writing are better suited than others to this double task of reminding us of the distinction between illusion and reality while celebrating the value of consciously invoked illusion. The more theatrical the art – that is, the more it proclaims and delights in its own artifice – the better. The "theatrical" aesthetic principles behind Auden's American work diverge radically from many basic modernist tenets. Unlike Pound or Williams, Auden does not regard craft as a test of sincerity; rather, it is a manifestation of the unique human ability to play. He appreciates the image's ornamental function. He does not strive for more sophisticatedly modern forms of mimesis to capture human perception, to mirror the action of human thought, or even to fix on the page "the thing itself." He proclaims:

> Be subtle, various, ornamental, clever,
> And do not listen to those critics ever
> Whose crude provincial gullets crave in books
> Plain cooking made still plainer by plain cooks,
> As though the Muse preferred her half-wit sons;
> Good poets have a weakness for bad puns.    (CP 470)

This does not mean that art is untruthful, only that the truths it unveils or the philosophical ideas it develops must be approached indirectly and fancifully – through jokes, and through structural, formal, and verbal extravagance. The passage just quoted, written probably in September 1953, comes from "The Truest Poetry is the Most Feigning," which concludes:

> For given Man, by birth, by education,
> Imago Dei who forgot his station,
> The self-made creature who himself unmakes,
> The only creature ever made who fakes,
> With no more nature in his loving smile
> Than in his theories of a natural style,
> What but tall tales, the luck of verbal playing,
> Can trick his lying nature into saying
> That love, or truth in any serious sense,
> Like orthodoxy, is a reticence.    (CP 471)

In the context of these beliefs, Auden's multiple styles and shifting tones – his refusal to rest with a single personal style; his eclectic diction that mixes archaic poeticisms, tired sayings, esoteric polysyllables, kennings, specialized scientific terminology, and current slang; his shameless use of heightened and hortatory rhetoric as well as quieter conversational tones; his combination of terse epigrammatic statement with baroque syntax; his delight in elaborate personification; his word games and fancy rhetorical figures; the demands he places upon himself to be constantly humorous and to meet formal challenges – all come together into a whole whose unifying purpose is to keep us aware of life-as-performance. Auden's dramatic and semidramatic long poems that first attracted Merrill – *The Sea and the Mirror, For the Time Being,* "The Age of Anxiety," and the long epistles – embody this theatricality more fully than any of his other works, except perhaps the opera librettos.

Auden's largest legacies to Merrill concern the theory and practice of poetry as theater. While Merrill's styles are not as various as Auden's, he too has come to insist on poetry as play, as tall tale, and as performance, and in this he too stands apart from the dominant poetic fashions of his time. Despite contemporary trends, he does not eschew "poetic" words or elegant periodic syntax; he loves conceits, flaunts his puns and joking rhymes ("Eliot / so what" [ND 7]), and is a master of shifting ironies and varied tones. Merrill does not speak of this in terms of acting, but, as many critics have noted, he makes extensive use of the related theatrical concept of masking. By *Water Street*, Merrill thought of art as a form of masking; by *Nights and Days*, the volume Auden helped select for the National Book Award, he thought of life that way and believed that love, our necessary fiction, could be sustained only by masks. These volumes, then, demonstrate Merrill's adoption and adaptation of Auden's theatrical aesthetic and its techniques.

# IV

*Water Street*'s "For Proust" depicts the exemplary writer as a maker of exquisite masks. Merrill dramatizes a moment when the dying novelist finds he again needs to leave his hotel room and "go into the world," where he meets his conjured beloved and then reexperiences the pain of losing her. Having "drained" the "bitter stimulants" of this venture, he returns to his writing; in the fiction he produces, "The world will have put on a thin gold mask" (WS 19). Proust's art (which Merrill regards as the single most important influence on his work)[32] is not life mirrored, but life delicately embellished with a precious veneer. Like the "artifice in the bloodstream," manners, the artifice of the writer's masking does not diminish the pain he has experienced, but it enables him not to inflict his pain on others and to give them pleasure instead.

Merrill takes his theory of masking further in a long poem from *Nights and Days*, "From the Cupola," suggesting that masks not only benefit those who perceive us from without, but also enrich our inner lives by transforming everyday perception. In the opening section of "From the Cupola" when the poet/narrator (later identified as "James") asks Psyche to tell him about her unseen lover, he announces that the subject of this poem, unlike that of a confessional work, will be masked:

> The point won't be to stage
> One of our torchlit hunts for truth. Truth asks
> Just this once to sleep with fiction, masks
> Of tears and laughter on the moonstruck page.    (ND 38)

In this "staging," veils gradually are lifted enough for us to discern the outlines of at least two superimposed stories: the Greek myth of Eros and Psyche, and the modern tale of a young New Englander who lives with her two sisters in a house with a glass cupola (Merrill's Stonington home has such a cupola) and receives love letters from someone who remains "sheer projection." The poem hints that modern Psyche's admirer was once the little boy she and her sisters used to pass in childhood on the way to the beach in Alexandria, a boy whose water wings link him to Cupid. Though initially alarmed by the attentions of her unknown correspondent, Psyche has come to love him in return; a "rosy veil" now colors the words of his letters she has learned by heart.

Unmasking, in several forms, threatens their love. Merrill uses figures involving light (for example, the "torchlit hunts" above) to stress the danger of destroying love's illusions by beaming the intellect's dispassionate quest for truth directly upon the lover; when Psyche shines her sister's "electric torch" on him, she sees a beast's "tear-streaked muzzle," and the inner light of their love is snuffed out at that moment when all is made "plain." Remembering Auden's objections to "plain cooking," we are not suprised to learn that unmasking by plain words is equally destructive:

> Eros  husband  names distort
>     you who have no name
> Peace upon your neophytes
> Help me when the christenings shall start
>         o my love
> to defend your sleep from them
> and see according to our lights    (ND 45)

(No doubt Merrill, because homosexual relationships are often "christened" or labeled perversions and cannot produce offspring for conventional christenings, is particularly sensitive to such injuries.) Similar grotesque distortions – or revelations of grotesque and unwelcome truths – result from attempts to reveal love directly in a visual image; when Psyche has to suffer through the drive-in movie's portrayal of Venus as Hollywood sexpot blown up to monstrous proportions on the screen, her faith in Venus' son, her lover, is shaken:

> Eros are you like her so false a naked glance
> turns you into that slackjawed fleshproud youth
> driving away  Was he your truth
> Is it too late to study ignorance   (ND 49)

The poet reassures her that it is easy to avoid such penetrating "naked glances." At the close of a "pyrotechnic" tour de force in an elaborate stanza form, he invokes proverbial wisdom in asserting:

> All our pyrotechnic flights
> Miss the sleeper in the pitch-dark breast.
> He is love:
> He is everyone's blind spot.
> We see according to our lights.   (ND 46)

Only at the very beginning and end of this long poem does Merrill hint of his own relation to the plot, explicitly acknowledged in an interview: Merrill himself was the recipient of such mysterious letters.[33] Theatrically embellished with several layers of fiction, this unsettling experience provides a means of dramatizing the mystery of artistic creativity. Within the poem's fiction, when Psyche has finished "dictat[ing]" her story and her pains are as clear as the glass panes she scrubs, another kind of performance is introduced. Now the typewriter becomes an amphitheater in which a crowd, the keys, is waiting. The poet's fingers at the keyboard set them dancing as he begins, "I have received from whom I do not know / These letters." The letters that form the poem's words have been given him by Eros, the sender of love letters, and by Psyche, the teller of the tale. Married, the two compose a single muse.

What Merrill has done here with personal experience and with received fiction or myth involves theatrical strategies markedly similar to Auden's performance in *The Sea and the Mirror*. Both poems operate on several half-masked personal levels simultaneously. Merrill, as already noted, was writing about a curiously intimate correspondence he received from a person he had "never met, who seemed to know everything about [him]."[34] Auden listed "Prospero to Ariel" among the poems alluding to his relation to Kallman;[35] it was written shortly after Kallman's withdrawal from their "marriage" and after Auden had moved away, leaving him behind in Ann Arbor. In addition, Auden in 1942 needed to reassess the function of art in terms of his recent conversion to Christianity. The latter subject is a clear focus of the poem, particularly in the preface and in the last part of Caliban's speech, just as Merrill's personal involvement in the aesthetic issues explored in his poem becomes explicit at its conclusion.

The poems are also alike in adopting a preexistent fiction in order to create further fictions beyond it. Auden takes the given frame of *The Tempest* and produces an epilogue exposing the condition of the characters on their return journey; he extends and revises not only the play's temporal frame but its themes and theses as well. In "Caliban to the Audience" Auden moves a level of artifice further from the Elizabethan drama (as Merrill does with the Eros/Psyche tale when he speaks as "James" in the final section of quatrains); Auden breaks the "fourth wall," as well as conventions of stable characterization, by having Caliban stand before the curtain and address the audience, analyzing the nature of art from multiple points of view. As is true in Merrill's use of his myth, Auden does not invent any new plot elements; the action of his work is psychological and intellectual.

In nearly every possible way Auden's "Commentary" on *The Tempest* calls attention to its own intricate inventedness, its theatricality. Not only are fictions built upon a fiction, but characters speak in a variety of exaggeratedly literary forms, ranging from villanelles to slightly ridiculous Jamesian prose; each shift in form provides a further reminder that all this is art, quite distinct from "reality," a game to be enjoyed for its own sake. (Or, more accurately, a series of games, for Auden took pleasure in regulated poetic forms precisely because they provide "the fun of games.")[36] Caliban's exuberant lists, complicated syntax, and thickly applied adjectives communicate this spirit of play, the sheer fun of pouring out words:

> Had you [the artist's mind], on the other hand, really left me alone to go my whole free-wheeling way to disorder, to be drunk every day before lunch, to jump stark naked from bed to bed, to have a fit every week or a major operation every other year, to forge checks or water the widow's stock, I might, after countless skids and punctures, have come by the bumpy third class road of guilt and remorse smack into that very same truth which you were meanwhile admiring from your distant comfortable veranda but would never point out to me. (CP 333)

Auden even gives lines to the prompter and stage manager, whose labors to create dramatic illusions are usually hidden backstage. Clearly, Auden glories in these illusions, provided they are not mistaken for truth ("those who love illusion / And know it will go far"). Merrill does the same. He, too, shifts from one stanzaic form to another, from one mode of speaking to another (the intensely lyrical, say, to matter-of-fact contemporary idiom), from one level of artifice to another, while manipulating the overlay of different times and places and double meanings. Like Auden, he underlines the gap between truth and illusion. The obvious philosophical difference between the two men is that because Merrill identifies no absolute spiritual Truth, no "real Word which is our only *raison d'être*" (CP 340), he is less interested in disengagement and places less restricted value on illusion.

Thus in the closing poem of *Nights and Days*, "Days of 1964" (ND 54–6; the title alludes to poems by Cavafy, a homosexual writer important to both Merrill and Auden), Merrill admits that all human love may be merely illusion, a facade applied to beautify crude physical need. He celebrates love none the less for that:

> Where I hid my face, your touch, quick, merciful,
> Blindfolded me. A god breathed from my lips.
> If that was illusion, I wanted it to last long.

It does not matter that he cannot see his lover truly (as in "From the Cupola," love is blind), that he himself is not "really" Eros incarnate, or that their relation involves degradation as much as spiritual elevation.

"Days of 1964," like the long poem "The Thousand and Second Night," is actually more typical than "From the Cupola" of Merrill's adaptation of Auden's theatricality, because in these works the autobiographical elements are not disguised. Most of Merrill's mature lyrics do seem to portray personal experiences; whether or not the events are "true," he gives the impression that they are. Merrill's sort of masking only occasionally involves obviously invented personae like his contemporary Psyche. Although Auden's own practices were somewhat different – he invoked more public material and more factual knowledge – he recognized that "All attempts to write about persons or events, however important, to which the poet is not intimately related in a personal way are now doomed to failure" (DH 81). Auden understood that the material to which Americans (especially apolitical ones like Merrill) are "intimately related" is particularly limited:

> Lacking a common mythological past, every American artist has,
> in weaving his pattern, to make use of a personal mythology

which means that, in order to make this intelligible to others, he has to provide many more autobiographical facts than a European would need to. (FA 423).

So "The Thousand and Second Night" (ND 4–15) opens with a first-person diary entry recording a strange ailment: Awakening in Istanbul, a tourist finds that half his face is an apparently lifeless mask, "though sentient, stupified." Merrill uses this intimate yet bizarre experience as a theatrical occasion for developing his meditation on the human search for a soul and for a love that will unite body and spirit. The poem's first section, "Rigor Vitae," dramatizes the modern alienation of body and soul through three experiences rendered in different verse forms that function as reflectors of the speaker's condition. The decrepit domed mosque of Hagia Sophia represents his mind; the link is explicit, as the speaker addresses the ruin, "You'd let go / Learning and faith as well, you too had wrecked / Your precious sensibility." The steambath in which he is entombed emphasizes the physical aspect of his rigor, while artistic paralysis is stressed by the "memory that promises to uncramp my style." That memory, prompted by associating the silhouette of a mosque with a wen on his grandmother's hand, is one of encircling love and security. Love, then, is what is missing.

With theatrical flourish, Merrill has largely avoided propositional discourse in analyzing the loveless death-in-life that is his subject. Where such statements might clarify, he lets others make them. Among the authorities whose statements Merrill uses to present his ideas, two are apparently fabricated; I have not been able to uncover works by either Germaine Nahman (the name a punning clue, *germane no one*) or A. H. Clarendon. These fictitious authors are dramatically useful, however, as is the caricatured professor in section 4 whose pretentious commentary does illuminate both the structure of the first section and the affirmation implicit in the poem's formal order.

Merrill's ritualized bowing to his predecessors, imaginary or real – "Try, I suppose, we must, as even Valéry said, / And said more grandly than I ever shall" – is just one of the poem's many varieties of highly conscious self-mockery. The speaker's extreme self-consciousness, his detachment from his own malady, is a further symptom of his disease. Even so, we are amused by his urbane humor throughout: "I'm here alone. Not quite – through fog outside / Loom wingéd letters: PAN AMERICAN." In Auden-like serio-comic fashion, the poem's surface is lightened with jokes, with satiric characterizations, with mock-heroic exaggerations ("Great drifts of damask cleaned our lips of grease"), with plays on words and on proverbs.

In Merrill's mature work, jokes, puns, and word games are essential, not ornamental, as the image was essential to the modernists; such play is fundamental to the theatrical aesthetic. In one of his rare pieces of critical writing Merrill has lamented that the pun is generally regarded as "unseemly," "like slipping a hand up the hostess's dress":

> Indeed, the punster has touched, and knows it if only for being so promptly shamed, upon a secret, fecund place in language herself. The pun's *objet trouvé* aspect cheapens it further – why? a Freudian slip is taken seriously: it betrays its maker's hidden wish. The pun (or the rhyme, for that matter) "merely" betrays the hidden wish of words.[37]

Merrill's wordplays (or his curious rhymes, for that matter) identify genuine links between seemingly disparate feelings, experiences, or concepts. Thus, all the punning as well as the metaphorical play that interweaves the process of writing with a sea journey in section 3 of "The Thousand and Second Night" is thematically significant.

Metaphors of sea travel, particularly of the whale hunt, provide the speaker with wittily discreet language for debauchery and promiscuity:

> A thousand and one nights! They were grotesque.
> Stripping the blubber from my catch, I lit
> The oil-soaked wick, then could not see by it.
> Mornings, a black film lay upon my desk.

When the sea voyager becomes the "skimmer of deep blue / Volumes fraught with rhyme and reason," and, through puns, sex and writing merge, the double meanings help us see both activities as part of his groping search for his soul. The thousand and second night is simultaneously the night after Scheherazade has told her last tale and the night when the libertine redirects his course, if only toward the ambiguous carnival figure suggesting both love and death. In the affirmative close of section 3, the soul's quest has survived physical dissolution, and the earth's sensual joys have survived the attenuation of verbal abstraction:

> Voyages, I bless you for sore
> Limbs and mouth kissed, face bronzed and lined,
> An earth held up, a text not wholly undermined
> By fluent passages of metaphor.

In this quatrain Merrill achieves the resonance typical of his multilayered fictions, in which double meanings are taken seriously and developed until vehicles and tenors alternate roles; everything becomes potentially figurative *and* potentially literal, while only belabored explication could delineate the shimmering vibrations of his meanings. The poem's many "charades" – the tourist outings, the pornographic postcards, the literary quotes and allusions, the myths invoked and metaphors elaborated – are not screens erected for Merrill to hide behind. Rather, as in Auden's works, these inventions are theatrical costumes for the otherwise intangible and ineffable.

Merrill's theatricality – his love of artifice and performance, his embrace of illusion, his camp extravagance – has enabled him to create one of the century's most ambitious epics, *The Changing Light at Sandover*. Here, openly turning to Auden for assistance, Merrill dramatizes the debt he already owed to Auden in the development of his own aesthetics. While the epic does not suggest how much Auden's example assisted Merrill in outgrowing the weaknesses of his early work – the icy preciosity and impersonality, the tired Romanticism of his exaggerated claims for the imagination – *The Changing Light at Sandover* gloriously commemorates the ways in which Auden's theatricality, his humor, and his conversational voice have enabled Merrill to handle personal material with a decorum that doesn't sacrifice warmth. And in *Sandover*'s frank dependency on the voices and works of Merrill's literary forebears, we see more clearly than before his affinities with the anti-Romantic stance toward tradition that W. H. Auden has made available to recent American poets.

## V

If Merrill needed an excuse to bring Auden into his long poem in a major speaking role, it was provided by the increasingly intellectual and scientific nature of his epic's subject matter. One of the most distinctive characteristics of Auden's poetry is its consistent forty-year engagement of current intellectual trends and issues. When most poets were accepting the New Critical demands for autonomous art works, Auden was using poems for serious and informed applications of Freudianism, Marxism, existentialism, and Christianity. Having trained in the sciences, Auden also kept abreast of major scientific developments throughout his life, and included terminology and concepts of modern science in his poems, early and late. Until the 1970s, Merrill, chronically shy of ideas and abhoring politics, did not imitate this aspect of Auden's work. While he made considerable use of popularized Freud (both he and Auden are frank about their Oedipal relations to their mothers), he did not seem a serious student of psychology or of other intellectual systems; nor did his poetic lexicon include the scientific terms Auden savored. Naturally, when Merrill wished to expand his poetic range and produce "poems

of science" in the second and third books of *The Changing Light at Sandover*, he looked to Auden as his guide.

"The Book of Ephraim" gives little indication of the prominent role
Auden was to play in the trilogy's subsequent volumes. "Ephraim" records that, when living, Auden (whom Merrill had come to know somewhat in his later years)[38] expressed a predictable disdain for the "fol-
derol" of the Ouija board, considering only *"his* dogma substantial" (DC
131). Nonetheless, Merrill included a passage from "As I Walked Out
One Evening" in "Ephraims'" Q section of pertinent quotes. There, Auden's teacup opening a lane to the dead seems to foreshadow Merrill's and Jackson's use of a willowware teacup as pointer in their com-
munications with the dead. Presented in this context, Auden's lines appear to confirm the authenticity of his young friends' contact with the
spirit world. After his death in the fall of 1973, Auden briefly appears on
the other side of the mirror in the Y section of "Ephraim" before reap-
pearing to assume a major role in 1.9 of *Mirabell*, when Merrill has already begun his struggle to absorb scientific materials and has begun self-
consciously to employ a scientific vocabulary. For example:

> I lolled about one winter afternoon
> In Stonington – rather, a whole precarious
> Vocabulary of each different cell,
> Enzyme, ion, what not, millionfold
> (Down to the last bacterial organelle)
> Particles that "show a tendency"
> To form the person and the moods of me,
> Lolled about. We were not feeling well. (M 16)

Having joined JM and DJ in their seminars, WHA, like the historical
Auden, is the exuberant embodiment of intellectual curiosity – FANCY
NOT / ASKING ABOUT THE UNIVERSE! (M 37) – and thus the counter to
Merrill's ingrained wariness of ideas. In the exhausting and frightening
labor of gathering the material for the last two books, Merrill and Jackson needed what Jackson has called "that cool eager voice of Wystan's":
"Anything experienced was O.K. with Wystan. Not an ounce of fear in
him."[39] "He was a kind of object lesson, because he made us so ashamed
of ourselves for lack of curiosity."[40] Merrill's affectionate gratitude is
everywhere apparent in the poem, e.g., "Dear Wystan, / Dead or alive,
a mine of sense" (M 35), or "See how Wystan's / Intellect begins to light
the way" (M 37).

Merrill's portrayal of WHA provides an opportunity for him to pay
tribute to Auden for other, long-standing lessons besides this newly relevant one of intellectual daring. Consistent with Auden's importance to

Merrill as a teacher of poetic craft and an inventor or popularizer of difficult poetic forms, WHA is designated "father of forms" (M 41). Because Auden was an expert on poetic form, WHA can play the dramatically useful role of commentator, taking up lines that Merrill's own persona uttered self-reflexively in earlier poems such as "An Urban Convalescence." Now it is WHA who sympathetically exposes Merrill's problems of audience:

> WE MY BOY DRAW FROM 2
>
> SORTS OF READER: ONE ON HIS KNEES TO ART
>
> THE OTHER FACEDOWN OVER A COMIC BOOK.
>
> OUR STYLISH HIJINKS WONT AMUSE THE LATTER
>
> AND THE FORMER WILL DISCOUNT OUR URGENT MATTER     (M 53)

or who suggests verse forms appropriate to various beings, explaining their fitness:

> So fourteeners might
> Do for the bats? NOT SKITTERY ENOUGH
> WHY NOT MY BOY SYLLABICS? LET THE CASE
> REPRESENT A FALL FROM METRICAL GRACE.    (M 146)

In giving such lines to WHA, Merrill acknowledges that it is Auden who taught him – as early as his mid-forties encounter with *The Sea and the Mirror* – to select the established forms that will best suit character, situation, and concept. At the same time, such passages also comprise a disarming strategy to protect Merrill against criticism: WHA can take credit or blame for the poem's exceedingly schematic design; WHA can voice excuses or defenses that Merrill wishes to offer his audience in anticipation of their objections; WHA can allow Merrill to maintain an appearance of modesty while calling attention to effects Merrill would have us notice:

> I THOUGHT IT (OVER YR SHOULDER)
> BRILLIANTLY SOLVED RIGHT DOWN THE LINE JM:
> TETRAMETER FOR US, PENTAM FOR THEM
> NEF [Nefertiti] EVOKED BY THE ONE FEMININE
> ENDING, & PLATO BY THE ONE SLANT RHYME
> But it was awful – not the slightest ring
> Of life. DEAR BOY ONE CAN'T HAVE EVERYTHING!    (S 63)

From Auden, Merrill and other contemporary poets inherited a range of forms revived from the traditions of many languages, as well as newly invented forms. (By the end of his life, Auden "liked to boast that he had written a poem in every known metre.")[41] Merrill has carried on Auden's efforts to expand the usefulness of established patterns. His seamless narrative sequences of sonnets, such as "The Broken Home," follow Auden's example of building a sequence with sestinas in "Kairos and Logos." The construction of *The Changing Light at Sandover* demonstrates Merrill's more original extension of Auden's work: smoothly integrating elaborate lyric stanzas into long poems so as to provide formal and tonal variety without the disjuncture of modernist collage. Merrill's magnificent canzone, "Samos," that opens the & section of *Scripts*, is a direct tribute to Auden. Of course, using this form also pays homage to their common ancestor, Dante, but as Rachel Jacoff has pointed out, Merrill employs Auden's modification of Dante's form, Auden's five-line close being particularly appropriate to the numerology of Merrill's trilogy.[42] The sixty-five-line lyric, which uses as end-words "sense" and his version of the four elements, "land," "water," "light," and "fire," is an astonishing tour de force; Merrill and Auden are the only twentieth-century poets who could employ that intricate form with such grace.

Since Auden functions as one of Merrill's poetic fathers, it is not surprising that Auden's own most significant forebears become Merrill's as well. In adopting some "other tradition," to use Ashbery's phrase, that would distinguish his work from the mainstream of tired midcentury modernism, Merrill turned to many of the same writers who were Auden's models. As Mendelson and others have demonstrated, Auden's mature poetics aligned him closely with classic and neoclassic aesthetics. Though Mendelson exaggerates some of the distinctions between Auden's "civic" poetry and modernist work, it is certainly true that Auden stands apart from his important contemporaries by concerning himself with authenticity rather than originality; by revering "Terminus the Mentor," patron of traditional poetic regulations, of "games and grammar and metres" (CP 609); and by using poetry to present not immediate, individual perception but to teach supposedly universal, durable truths. In many ways Auden was a neo-Augustan. Thus, his models for creating a conversational voice within traditional metrical patterns were Pope and Byron:

> if Wordsworth had Pope in mind as the enemy when he advised poets to write 'in the language really used by men,' he was singularly in error. Should one compare Pope at his best with any of the Romantics, including Wordsworth, at their best, it is Pope who writes as men normally speak to each other and the latter who go in for 'poetic' language. . . . To find 'natural speech' in

> the verse of the early 19th century, one must go to the least
> 'Romantic' and most Popean in spirit of the poets – to the Byron
> of *Don Juan*. (FA 119)

Merrill first absorbed Byron through Auden's "Letter";[43] Pope he studied more thoroughly, and in "Ephraim" we learn that Merrill's patron was once an editor of Pope's work. This information supposedly explains the couplets that "bedevil" Merrill (DC 56); certainly it advertises that Merrill's poetics, like Auden's, have deep roots in the eighteenth century. Indeed, what is conventionally regarded as Pope's spirit of reason is reinvigorated in Merrill's trilogy, where the spirits teach that the "new house godlet" is "pure reason," with metaphor providing its rituals and language its rites (M 145).

The Q (quotes) section of "Ephraim" contains a passage from Quennell's biography of Pope, the book Auden reviewed in "A Civilized Voice" (FA 109–24). It may be (to use *Sandover*'s phrase) "no accident" that both Auden and Merrill quote the same passage describing Pope's grotto; perhaps Merrill wishes to stress that his Pope is Auden's. Auden's review, however, does not contain the last sentence Merrill includes: "Pope intended . . . that the visitor, when at length he emerged, should feel that he had been reborn into a new existence" (DC 105). With this quote Merrill does to Pope what he does to Auden in the same section: makes him seem to anticipate the cosmic system of reincarnation that DJ and JM have discovered through the Ouija board.

Dante is another ancestor equally important to Auden and Merrill. Auden made Dante his first judge in his "New Year Letter," read and reread his works in the original,[44] and alluded to Dante's poems frequently in his own. The Dantean precedent for Merrill's trilogy, suggested initially by the title *Divine Comedies*, is obvious.[45] While Merrill's touchstone is the *Paradiso*'s vision of divine light,[46] Auden refers more to the lower regions, especially to the *Inferno*'s portrayal of carnal sinners. That Auden should focus on love and "human unsuccess" while Merrill looks to an abstract perfection indicates their temperamental divergence; Merrill is indeed a "silver" poet, Auden "platinum." They are fundamentally alike, however, in wishing to live up to the standard established by the poet Auden refered to as "the supreme master of the Dream," the greatest exemplar of "the mythopoeic imagination" (FA 268–9).

In his trilogy, Merrill places himself – or manages to have others place him, so the arrogance of his claims will be masked – in an illustrious line of poets who (supposedly) received their poems by dictation, with Dante, Yeats, and Eliot prominent among them. JM is a link in "AN UNBROKEN CHAIN  HOMER DANTE PROUST  EACH WITH HIS SENSE / OF THE MINDS POWER

ITS GENERATIVE USES" (M 27); he continues their earlier efforts through which the other world's powers hope that man will learn to "LOVE HIS MIND AND LANGUAGE" (M 27). In view of the intellectuality of Auden's verse and his passionate belief that every poem should be "a hymn in praise of the English language,"[47] we hardly need to be told that Auden's densities are Homeric (S 232) in order to place him as the chain's link immediately preceding Merrill.

While Merrill takes pride in claiming this ancestry, the character JM nonetheless periodically expresses frustration that so little of his verse seems original. Because so much of *Changing Light* is dictated at the Ouija board, he complains to WHA, "it's all by someone else! / In your voice, Wystan, or in Mirabell's" (M 167). This statement may be read as testifying to the immensity of Auden's impact on Merrill's works; beyond that, the problem of dictation serves as a metaphor for the situation of the modern formalist writer. Defending the use of traditional forms and meters in a recent interview, Merrill remarked:

> Of course they breed echoes. There's always a lurking air of pastiche which, consciously or unconsciously, gets into your diction. That doesn't much bother me. . . . No voice is as individual as the poet would like to think. In the long run I'd rather have what I write remind people of Pope or Yeats or Byron [again, those leaders in Auden's "other tradition"] than of the other students in that year's workshop.[48]

Dictation is one way of dramatizing that "lurking air of pastiche," and the defense Merrill offers in the interview is similar to those Auden offered in his lifetime. When WHA responds to JM's lament, "it's all by someone else," his eloquent defense of tradition is entirely true to life, not only in the claims he makes about the self's minor role in creation, but also in the manner and method of his argument.

WHA's speech opens:

> YR SCRUPLES DEAR BOY ARE INCONSEQUENT
> IF I MAY SAY SO   CAN U STILL BE BENT,
> AFTER OUR COURSE IN HOW TO SEE PAST LONE
> AUTONOMY TO POWERS BEHIND THE THRONE,
> ON DOING YR OWN THING: EACH TEENY BIT
> (PARDON MME) MADE PERSONAL AS SHIT?   (M 168)

One recognizes Auden's heterogeneous diction, mixing formal abstractions – inconsequent, autonomy, scruples – with current American slang – doing your own thing, shit. The syntactic suspension between the second and the fifth lines is also a typical Auden–like flourish, as is the play with folk sayings – time to shit or get off the pot – and the reliance on Freudian theory – obsession with the personal resulting from inadequate toilet training – in subsequent lines. The rest of WHA's lecture applies Auden's allegorizing technique of *paysage moralizé* to the "rosebrick manor" of poetic tradition. (That manor later becomes the Sandover mansion in which the schoolroom is located [S 37].) WHA reminds JM of the estate's idyllic beauties:

> FROM ANTHOLOGIZED
> PERENNIALS TO HERB GARDEN OF CLICHES
> FROM LATIN-LABELED HYBRIDS TO THE FAWN
> 4 LETTER FUNGI THAT ENRICH THE LAWN,
> IS NOT ARCADIA TO DWELL AMONG
> GREENWOOD PERSPECTIVES OF THE MOTHER TONGUE    (M 168)

and of the privilege it is to take even an insignificant place in the illustrious family line.

JM needed this reminder; presumably, Merrill did not. He needed only the opportunity to construct this proclamation, for he already shared Auden's anti-Romantic attitude toward tradition. The very fact that communication with the dead forms the foundation of the entire trilogy asserts the importance of tradition and demonstrates how much Merrill values listening to the dead and giving them voice. Auden in a late interview expressed pity for today's young people who are bored and rootless because "They're not connected with the past."[49] "We must have communication with the past, with the dead. Otherwise our mental life-line is broken," he explained. In late years he was fond of saying, "Art is our chief means of breaking bread with the dead."[50] The structure and method of *Changing Light* demonstrate Merrill's concurrence with these sentiments. Further evidence of Merrill's anti-Romantic allegiance to his literary forebears is provided by the content of the trilogy's revelations of the history and structure of the cosmos. His cosmology, too, is pastiche, constructed from elements of past myths – unicorns, Atlantis, Eden, and so forth. These are not treated as fragments to be shored against his ruins, but as metaphoric approximations of a single truth which his own myth also approaches.

WHA's defense of traditional writing is one of many examples of his importance in illuminating the central values espoused by Merrill's trilogy, many of which were shared by the historical Auden. It is WHA, for instance, who reminds JM of the preciousness of language, the "WHOLLY [and holy] HUMAN INSTRUMENT" that even the gods rely on. As "the laughing poet," WHA demonstrates Auden's life-long "Carnival" solution to the difficult ambiguities of the human situation. (Laughter, he explained, "is simultaneously a protest and an acceptance" [FA 471].) WHA's sustained wit and humor, as well as his enduring sense of wonder are perfect "manners" in the highest sense – grace and generosity that amount to a spiritual triumph.

*The Changing Light at Sandover* is a celebration of all human bonds, especially those strong enough to last through and beyond death. In particular, it celebrates the twenty-five years of love between Merrill and Jackson, whose literal hand-to-hand collaboration at the Ouija board makes the entire work possible. Without the chronicle of their lives that is interwoven through the trilogy, the epic would remain chilly and abstract. Homoerotic love, then, is another of the trilogy's values that WHA defends. The work makes grand claims for homosexuality: "NOW MIND IN ITS PURE FORM IS A NONSEXUAL PASSION / OR A UNISEXUAL ONE PRODUCING ONLY LIGHT" (M 62), according to 741, and consequently most of the world's greatest poets and musicians have been homosexual. (This theory may develop from Auden's notion "that any unmarried person who was a major artist must be homosexual. He was convinced . . . not just of Shakespeare's homosexuality but of Beethoven's.")[51] In this passage, as elsewhere in his *oeuvre*, Merrill confronts the homosexual's guilt over childlessness (see, for instance, *The Seraglio*, "Up and Down," "Childlessness"), but in the trilogy his apologia for the homosexual's fertility being manifest in metrical rather than mortal feet sounds more confident than before. WHA's cheerful and frankly homosexual bawdiness contributes to that positive tone. In fact, his presence provides an excuse for Merrill to loosen up and write more bawdily than he ever has, crudely when using WHA's voice and with greater sophistication when using JM's.[52] WHA's delight in homosexuality slightly modifies Auden's attitudes, at least those publically manifest: though Auden freely acknowledged his sexual preference and pursued his desires without hesitation, he nonetheless spoke of homosexuality as an illness and in print he emphasized the unhappiness of homosexuals' sex lives (see FA 450–8).

This modification is only one of several liberties Merrill takes in creating WHA, who revises a number of the attitudes for which Auden was best known on this side of the grave. Many of these revisions are determined by dramatic necessity. Others are useful indications of what aspects of Auden's work Merrill found least compelling. In the former category is WHA's rescinding Auden's allegiance to the church; his usefulness would certainly have been limited had he remained committed to a Christian understanding of the cosmic order. So before joining the seminars, he revises his creed: "THE CHURCH / MY DEARS THE DREARY DREARY DEAD BANG WRONG / CHURCH & ALL THOSE YEARS I COULD HAVE HELD / HANDS ON TEACUPS" (M 34). (Here, as elsewhere, WHA's clowning provides comic relief amid all the solemnity of the seminars' explication of the universe.) Leaving dogma aside, Auden's religiousness contained a strong mystical streak: He himself experienced a mystical "Vision of Agape" (see FA 69); he even believed that the primary experience behind Shakespeare's sonnets was a mystical "Vision of Eros" (FA 103). This mysticism, retained in WHA, is useful to Merrill in making WHA's acceptance of Ouija board spiritualism more plausible. It is also a quality Merrill has long shared. "I must have some kind of awful religious streak just under the surface," he told one interviewer.[53] His mysticism is detectable as early as *Jim's Book*, where the essay on Wylie, "Angel or Earthly Creature," focuses with obvious fascination on her mystical belief that she was Shelley reincarnate and on her absorption in magic and witchcraft. A "Vision of Eros" forms the core of most of Merrill's mature work; the theme of "Ephraim," for example, is announced in section A as "The incarnation and withdrawal of / A god" (DC 47), and that god is surely Eros. In the trilogy's later books, where JM expresses less skepticism about the Ouija board revelations coming from a source beyond DJ and himself, WHA lends authority to the outrageous mystical framework, encouraging readers willingly to suspend their disbelief.

In several ways WHA's preferences revise Auden's to align him more closely with Merrill. In the afterlife WHA takes an interest in French writers for the first time, having in life focused on the German. Because Merrill had so long been governed by Proust's example and influenced by the French symbolists, this shift vindicates his tastes. Similarly WHA's modification of Auden's explicit preference for truth over beauty (in heaven, we're told, the two are wedded) brings him closer to Merrill's aestheticizing sensibility.

What Merrill does not alter in WHA is Auden's voice, capturing with amazing accuracy his mannerisms, his diction, his cultivated wit.[54] One of the trilogy's delights is simply listening to WHA talk. As Helen Vendler observes, "The Book of Ephraim" takes conversation as "the highest form of human expression": "this espousal of the conversational as the ultimate in linguistic achievement is a moral choice, one which locates value in the human and everyday rather than in the transcendent."[55] The same can be said of the two later volumes, and there WHA emerges as a master of the mannerly art of civilized conversation. Merrill's ability to recreate Auden's voice so effectively (as well as his adoption of Auden's manner in passages not attributed to WHA) proves how carefully he has listened to Auden over the years.

In addition to talking, WHA creates poems in the other world, and reviewers disagree about how much these sound like Auden. Geoffrey Stokes finds *Changing Light* so believable that "one wonders what Auden scholars will make of his posthumous work,"[56] while others like William Harmon criticize Merrill for assigning Auden verses unworthy of the master.[57] Merrill has tried to deflect such criticism by periodically reminding us that WHA's powers are somewhat diminished both by the stripping process that accompanies the lessons and by having his talents mined out to the living. Wisely, Merrill limits WHA's poetic performance largely to brief bits of occasional light verse. Usually WHA produces playful tetrameter, e.g.,

> O LORDS WITH JOY & WHOOP & HOLLER
> YOU GAVE US FOUR THE FIVE
> BUT WHEN (FORGIVE) WILL YOU 4 GIVE
> US THEM IN LIVING COLOR?    (S 63)

though occasionally he produces a pentameter couplet or even a limerick. These passages employ the rhyme schemes – true, slant, and internal – as well as the meters that Auden favored. Their quality is no more uneven than that of Auden's work as a whole; the most offhand bits are comparable to his "Shorts."

Nonetheless, Harmon has some grounds for feeling that first-rank poets like Auden do not in the trilogy write first-rank lines, and I would suggest as explanation Merrill's perhaps unconscious competitive desire to diminish their achievement. Despite his neoclassical sympathies, Merrill is not free from the Romantic tradition and the need it instills for surpassing one's predecessors. Demonstrating the Oedipal drives associated with the anxiety of influence, on at least a few occasions Merrill does, however playfully, trim WHA's "stubby pencil."

Merrill plants in the trilogy a number of criticisms of Auden's work. Via 741 he criticizes Auden's "MISMARRIAGE / OF LYRIC TO BALD FARCE" (M 49); WHA himself says he was wrong in looking for inspiration in "RITUAL & DIFFY MORAL STRICTURES" (M 70); JM objects to one of Auden's favorite genres, "Allegory, in whose gloom the whole / Horror of Pop-think fastens on the soul, / Harder to scrape off than bubblegum" (M 42). (He protests too much, for the trilogy often employs allegorizing techniques.)

More amusingly, Merrill makes fun of WHA's poetic powers. On one occasion, WHA attempts to improve on a couplet of Michael's (the Archangel of Light is an aspiring poet, but drearily affixed to rhymes with "day"): "SO NEXT WE DON THE GLAD ARRAY / OF ALL OUR SENSES TO MEET THE DAY." WHA revises it, varying the pentameter of the first line and smoothing the cadence of the second: "NEXT WE DON OUR SENSES IN GLAD ARRAY / AND MEET HERE AGAIN ON ANOTHER DAY." JM comments, "that too could stand some work, if I may say so," but escapes having to prove himself through the prudently engineered interruption of Michael's un-expected return (S 70). On another occasion WHA tries to compose a verse and cannot find a rhyme:

> READY FOR THE TRAILER?
> AHEM: IF LANGUAGE IS THE POET'S CHURCH
> LET US CONSTRUCT
> A TO Z AN ALTAR LIKE AN ARCH
> GROUNDED ON NUMBERS   DRAT   WHAT RHYMES WITH UCT?
> ON NUMBERS   HMM   I TWITCH IN MY RED GOWN
> LIKE AN OLD CARDINAL WHOSE LATIN'S GONE
> NO DOUBT THE STRIPPING PROCESS    (M 158)

No doubt, but we know who has stripped him of his powers. It is very funny to imagine Wystan Auden without a rhyme, especially for a syl-lable easy to match (*plucked, sucked, deduct* come to mind immediately), but this is also a way for the son to assert his own freedom from and superiority to his father's powers. The trilogy's magical recreation of Auden's voice is an attempt at exorcism as much as an act of powerful love.

That love and Merrill's desire to pay Auden tribute ring in the only serious piece of poetry by WHA that assumes dramatic prominence in the trilogy, the lyric that closes the Yes section of *Scripts*. This is WHA's response to seeing the words that God B sings out into the universe, the "HEARTBREAKING" song of one "ALONE / KEEPING UP HIS NERVE ON A LIFE-RAFT" (that raft being, among other things, language). Auden regarded aloneness as "man's real condition" (CP 190) and often sang of it himself, so WHA is the appropriate character to produce these compassionate verses. In correspondence with the author, Merrill said he composed this lyric with several arias from the Auden/Kallman/Stravinsky opera, *The Rake's Progress*, in mind.[58] Presumably, he was thinking of Rakewell's song calling upon the sacred name of love in the brothel scene (act 1 scene 2) and of Anne's soothing lullaby (act 3 scene 3, a song the chorus hears as "sacred music of the spheres") in which she sings of a boat gliding to the Islands of the Blest. The rhyme scheme is particularly close to that of Rakewell's aria, while the imagery is close to Anne's. In WHA's verse, God B is like Rakewell, a "YOUNG TENOR . . . HOMESICK, HEARTSICK." The term "heartsick" is applied to Rakewell in the opera, and the "green shores" God B longs for are analogues for the orchards that "greenly grace" the islands that Venus' boat approaches. Such echoes of *Rake's Progress* hold particular significance for Merrill because he and Jackson attended the opera's premiere, which took place in Venice, the trilogy's earthly paradise. He recalls how the performance "sparkled" – "All of us present cheering long and loud / While you and Chester and Stravinsky bowed" (S 199) – and his WHA remembers the occasion as a "PEAK AGLISTER / IN THOSE GIDDY ALPS OF LIFE IN LOVE WITH CHESTER" (S 199).

By alluding to *Rake's Progress* numerous times in *Scripts*, Merrill alerts us to themes and formal characterstics shared by the two works, while underlining both poets' affinities for that most unashamedly theatrical of the arts, opera. In theme the opera, like the trilogy, is a celebration of lasting and faithful love – in part, of Auden's love for Kallman – and it, too, is a collaborative work. Merrill's allusions stress the extent to which both poets concern themselves with both the precariousness and the god-like power of love. Moreover, the libretto's poetic style is "largely 18th century pastiche,"[59] appropriate to the Augustan spirit of the trilogy and to its construction as stylistic and intellectual pastiche. Perhaps no work by Auden better portrays the values and aesthetic principles Merrill shared with and derived from him than this colorful pageant that so delightfully joins fantastic comedy and moral seriousness within its Mozartian formal elegance.

# 8 "I knew // That life was fiction in disguise": Merrill's divergence from Auden and modernism

Unlike most modernists, Auden did not strive to reduce the distance between art and life by recreating in his poems the processes of ordinary perception and consciousness. He stressed instead the danger of mistaking the arbitrary rules of poetry, taken up as a game, for the necessary rules of life, which we cannot escape. Once he had rejected the notion that poetry could be politically efficacious, he emphasized the gratuitousness, the frivolity of writing. Even so, Auden's oeuvre – like Eliot's, Pound's, Stevens', Williams' – tells of a continuous effort to make human experience cohere. His was an organizing intellect, fond of ennumerated categories and tidy aphorisms. According to Auden, the best description of the artistic process is Virginia Woolf's:[1]

> There is a square; there is an oblong. The players take the square and place it upon the oblong. They place it very accurately; they make it a perfect dwelling-place. Very little is left outside. The structure is now visible; what is inchoate is here stated; we are not so various or so mean, we have made oblongs and stood them upon squares. This is our triumph; this is our consolation.

This passage leaves little doubt that art is an ordering, and in his later work Auden regards the rules of that order as paralleling the laws of the universe.

Auden's poetic explorations of order reveal a preoccupation with doubleness, and the same is true for Merrill. The younger poet's formalism reveals his own pleasure in the design and symmetry of "squares and oblongs," while his poems are filled not only with double meanings, but with explorations of all sorts of doublings, bifurcations, and polarities. In order to define the significant ways in which Merrill diverges from his "father of forms," this chapter will focus on the differences between the two poets' conceptions of and attitudes toward duality, first in a brief overview, then in a more detailed look at Merrill's recent poems.

# I

According to Auden, "The cogitations of Descartes / Are where all sound semantics start" (CP 169), so it is hardly surprising that one split recurring in his poetry is the Cartesian one between mind and body. Often in his poems one half of his being will address or discuss the other, as in "No, Plato, No," where the speaking mind objects to a disembodied existence, while admitting that the body may well long to be freed from the spirit that animates it. The division between flesh and spirit parallels others that preoccupy Auden either implicitly or explicitly: reason/ feeling, public/private, aesthete/moralist, and so forth. The most fundamental of these contrasting pairs in Auden's mature work is the Christian dichotomy of the worldly and the otherworldly, human and divine.

Although the devil is "the great schismatic who / First split creation into two," the consequences of his fall are not entirely devastating: the positive response of creation has been the "wish to be / Diversity in unity" (CP 171). Auden can therefore glorify the "gift of double focus," believing that simultaneous perception of difference or division on the one hand and wholeness or unity on the other creates a precious balance that prevents complete schism. This double focus is embodied in the Carnival perspective Auden celebrates in his late work: Tension-releasing laughter in which "we laugh simultaneously *with* and *at*" (FA 471) – a gesture Auden defines as "the spirit of Carnival" – accommodates the ambiguity of perceiving "that each great I / Is but a process in a process / Within a field that never closes" (CP 167). True laughter can both accept and protest against the double vision of oneself as a unique individual and as an undifferentiated part of a continuous species. Auden's goal is synthetic vision, not the "either/or" perspective the devil advocates in "New Year Letter." He believes that "human folk" are distinguished from the less conscious creatures in the natural world precisely in "hav[ing] their unity to win" (CP 505) by holding the two sides of their nature (manifest in so many contrasted pairings) in symmetrical balance.

Art, in Auden's view, can assist us in attaining this order, so long as we do not mistake art's order for life's, and instead regard artistic order and balance as models of the harmony we should strive for in our lives. In art's reconciliation of contradictory feelings we see an analogue to the paradisal state (an analogue, Auden emphasizes, not an imitation), which enables us to perceive the possibility of regaining paradise. Order, however, is achieved more easily and more surely in art than in living – that is one source of aesthetic pleasure – for only in art are events *caused by* our will to form felicitous patterns (CP 330).

Art's pleasing patterns, then, have a moral purpose, which Auden spells out at the close of "Caliban to the Audience." (How much and how lastingly Caliban speaks for Auden is suggested by his remark in a 1972 interview identifying this "poem written in prose, a pastiche of the late Henry James" as the single work of which he was proudest.)[2] Having shown us our "estrangement from the truth," the "gap between what you so questionably are and what you are commanded without any question to become" (CP 339), the work of art is to inspire us to bridge that gap. Yet paradoxically, as Caliban argues, the more effectively art portrays either our condition or the truth from which it is estranged, the more easily the audience complacently mistakes awareness of the gap for the bridge over it. So the artist must wish for some unforeseen mishap that will direct the audience to the original "real-life" drama inspiring the artist. The image Auden develops for that "first performance" helps explain his allegiance to the theatrical aesthetic outlined in the preceding chapter. The image is that of "the greatest grandest opera rendered by a very provincial touring company indeed" (CP 340). As the limitations of the company would lead us to expect, their (that is, our) performance is a fiasco, and its conclusion leaves the desolate, exposed performers in a position to see themselves as they are: trapped, hanging over the abyss. At that moment, art's moral purpose may be fulfilled: "for the first time in our lives we hear, not the sounds which, as born actors, we have hitherto condescended to use as an excellent vehicle for displaying our personalities and looks, but the real Word which is our only *raison d'être*." Only then are we "blessed by that Wholly Other Life from which we are separated by an essential emphatic gulf of which our contrived fissures of mirror and proscenium arch – we understand them at last – are feebly figurative signs" (CP 340). Art, and most obviously the theater, should remind us of that all-important split between our flawed mortal existence and the perfect immortal life that should be our goal.

This elaborate theory seems worth quoting and paraphrasing at length because it presents so emphatically Auden's belief in a single "raison d'être," in a single correct understanding one can attain "at last," in one grand stage to which all our theatrics point and an absolute reality in relation to which our performances assume their true meaning. James Merrill's sense of human doubleness does not resolve itself in such a final monism, and his sense of performance has no comparably true referent.

The doubleness that preoccupies Merrill is rooted in language, in its dual powers of literal and figurative reference. He is nervously conscious of his inability to resist the pull of metaphor and symbol. In *Water Street*'s

"To a Butterfly," he interrupts a heavy-handed allegory that presents the insect's metamorphoses as stages of human biblical history (the fall, the flood, etc.) to lament:

> Goodness, how tired one grows
> Just looking through a prism:
> Allegory, symbolism.
> I've tried, Lord knows,
>
> To keep from seeing double,
> Blushed for whenever I did,
> Prayed like a boy my cheek be hid
> By manly stubble.     (WS 43)

Yet he cannot even get through this protestation without slipping in the doubleness of a pun (his cheek), preparing us for subsequent stanzas' acquiescence to the inevitability of such "rigamarole."

Of course Auden shares – even provides models for – Merrill's figurative doublings in allegory and symbolism, as well as his linguistic doublings in puns or etymological wordplay. The important difference between them is that Merrill locates no primal gap that all gulfs between tenor and vehicle signify, no Wholly Other reality where metaphor's buck stops. True, he seems to suggest in *Sandover* that all existent myths are figurative distortions of some ur-truth, but his belief, in that as in all else, proves partial.

The two poets, then, stand in very different relations to the ordering systems they invoke in their poems. Auden's entire career can be seen as a search for the properly fitting ideological system, like a search for the right hat. He was comfortable donning a series of established styles – the Marxist's cap, the existentialist's beret, and so forth; Merrill, by contrast, has refused to try on anything more firmly molded than the wispy veil of manners. Consequently, while the American Auden confidently affirms his belief in God and the Devil,[3] Merrill, when asked whether he believes in the elaborate system spelled out through his Ouija board, can only answer "yes and no." When Helen Vendler asked how real the trilogy's mythology seemed to him, Merrill replied, "Literally, not very – except in recurrent euphoric hours when it's altogether too beautiful not to be true. Imaginatively real? I would hope so. . . . But the point remained, to be always of two minds."[4] When asked a similar question by Ross Labrie, he responded with similar ambivalence: "when you are caught up in it you believe it wholeheartedly; when you cool off you see it as a stylization of various things in your experience or in the world's experience." And when asked whether he believed specifically in reincarnation, a basic tenet in the Ouija board revelations, he answered, "Yes and no. I simply couldn't say. I think it's a very fruitful belief to have. I think it does wonders in a way for the way you live."[5] Beauty and usefulness – and for Merrill the two are almost synonymous, since only the beautiful seems of much use in improving the quality of life – comprise his criteria for acquiescence, not truth in any absolute sense. Happy to entertain orderly systems provisionally, and to be entertained by them, Merrill does not regard the word of his angels as "the real Word."

Thus, when an interviewer remarked upon Merrill's seeming "a bit self-conscious as an 'intellectual' " and inquired about the seemingly "unrelieved meaning" of the trilogy's caps, Merrill cautioned:

> a lot of what we're loosely calling "meaning" turns out, on in-spection, to be metaphor, which leads one back towards lan-guage, wordplay, etymology, the "wholly human instrument" (as Wystan says [from JM's spirit realm]) I'd used and trusted – like every poet, wouldn't you say? – to ground the lightning of ideas. We could say that the uppercase represented a *range* of metaphor, a depth of meaning, that hadn't been available to me in earlier poems.[6]

In composing the trilogy, Merrill seems to have struggled to balance a coherent narrative – something which tends to take on a comfortably nonmetaphorical substance in the reader's mind – against devices (com-parable in aim to Ashbery's typical methods) which interrupt that coher-ence so as to keep us aware of the provisional, purely linguistic nature of its meaning. Periodically, he jars his readers with reminders that the crea-tures whose voices appear in upper case are subatomic particles, or fa-culties of human intelligence, that a crust around the greenhouse earth may also be an outer ring of the atom's structure, an outer orbit of the solar system, a layer of brain matter, and so forth. None of these levels is finally more true than the others; and all, presented as they are through the medium of language, are creations of humankind and of the individ-ual poet (or, in *Sandover*, perhaps of the poet and his double in the form of a same-sex lover).[7]

Although the historical Auden, like his fictive counterpart WHA, would celebrate language as the wholly human instrument, his conceptions of the relation between language and reality nonetheless differ from those Merrill evolved. In discussing language, Auden tends to concentrate on its social validity, on language as a communal possession. The poet, he argues,

> is more protected than [other artists] from another modern peril, that of solipsist subjectivity; however esoteric a poem may be,

the fact that all its words have meanings which can be looked up in a dictionary makes it testify to the existence of other people. . . . a purely private verbal world is not possible. (DH 23)

This is not to suggest that he is naively unaware of the conventional and possibly fictive nature of the "external" reality our words denote. As Mendelson has explained, "In his later poems [Auden] treats the gulf between language and world . . . as a condition that must be accepted but that does not prevent language from being shared, or prevent it from illuminating and affecting a physical and ethical world whose order and events are not only verbal ones."[8] "Ode to Terminus" (CP 608–9), for example, acknowledges how easily the solitary thinker can lose confidence in distinctions betweeen inner and outer, literal and figurative. But language for Auden is the thinker's lifeline, not the web from which his confusions are woven; ordered by grammar – and, in poems, by metrics – language supports sanity by attaching the thinker to the world "where all visibles do have a definite / outline they stick to," where the distinction between figurative and literal is firm enough that one can "see a joke or / distinguish a penis from a pencil." Moreover, that world of conventional distinctions is semantically privileged:

> True seeing is believing
> (What sight can never prove)
> There is a world to see:
> Look outward, eyes, and love
> Those eyes you cannot be.   (CP 449)

Thus, while he never lost his "sense of theatre" (CP 651), as he grew older Auden modified and restricted his attachment to "conscious theatrical exaggeration" and to the poet's various "ways of not calling a spade a spade" (DH 47–8; 1956). Taking a decreasing interest in the poet's role as Ariel, magical creator of "a verbal earthly paradise, a timeless world of pure play" (DH 338), Auden more frequently wore the robes of truth-telling Prospero, striving to "disenchant and disintoxicate" (DH 27). The extent of the shift in Auden's orientation is apparent in this statement made in 1964:

> In so much "serious" poetry – poetry, that is to say, which is neither pure playful song nor comic – I find an element of "theatre," of exaggerated gesture and fuss, of indifference to naked truth, which, as I get older, increasingly revolts me. This element is mercifully absent from what is conventionally called good prose. In reading the latter, one is only conscious of the truth of what is being said, and it is this consciousness which I would like what I write to arouse in a reader *first*. Before he is aware of

> any other qualities it may have, I want his reaction to be: "That's
> true." . . . To secure this effect I am prepared to sacrifice a great
> many poetic pleasures and excitements.[9]

By contrast, Merrill as he grows older seems increasingly willing to acknowledge explicitly that poetic pleasures and excitements are indistinguishable from truth; they *are* truth in its most valuable guise.

In denying absolute truths and accepting fiction as a substitute, Merrill
aligns himself with other modernists such as Stevens. Yet his divergence
from Auden is in subtler ways also a divergence from modernism. Modernist structures, though reflexively acknowledged as fiction, nonetheless attempt to hold at bay the world's disorder and frame "what is in-
choate," while Merrill's often do not. He carries irony and wordplay to
such extremes and so highlights the instability of linguistic signs that the
world's confusion often seems to have penetrated his poetry as it is embraced and mirrored in his kaleidescopic language.

For Merrill the purpose of art's order must remain purely aesthetic,
not moral, since the "truth" upon which systems of morality might be
based dissolves for him into shadowy multiplicity. Art's order does not
reflect laws governing the universe, but rather those governing language,
which is a gorgeously flexible net of humankind's imagining. The artist's
primary delight is in self-conscious manipulation of the linguistic material's shifting and blending layers. Examination of Merrill's volumes since
the late 1960s will reveal in more detail how these attitudes that distinguish his work from Auden's evolved and were embodied in his mature
poetry.

## II

The curious inconsistencies, the experiments and the uneven-
ness, of the two volumes immediately preceding *Divine Comedies* and the
trilogy – *The Fire Screen* (1969) and *Braving the Elements* (1972)[10] – document Merrill's development toward an acceptance that truth does not
exist apart from fiction, in the face of an opposing desire to establish, as
Auden does, a far more straightforward and simple relation between his
poetic language and the actual or the "naked truth."

"Friend of the Fourth Decade" (FS 4–9), the opening poem of *The Fire
Screen* (excepting the brief invocation with which Merrill customarily
opens his collections) announces the more simply referential idea of language that the book will explore, while suggesting, too, its inevitable
inadequacy for Merrill. The speaker's alter ego friend finds himself tired
of the familiar world governed by manners and by masking – weary of

his sophisticated understanding of social nuance, and of all the hypocritical pretense and deception disguised by polite interactions: "knowing // Just what clammy twitchings thrive / Under such cold flat stones // As We-are-profoundly-honored-to-have-with-us / Or This-street-has-been-torn-up-for-your-convenience." Consequently, he has determined to start a new life in foreign countries where verbal nuance will be totally lost on him, where he intends to learn only enough of the language to "ask for food and love." Before embarking, he erases the ink from his collection of postcards, eradicating the messages that bind him to his past. His aim is to establish a relation to the actual material world in which objects, creatures, sensations will be primary, "Rinsed of the word." The narrator is envious of his friend; inspired to attempt the same liberation, he, however, is less successful in cleansing his postcard's scenes either of words (his mother's) or of memories. His attempt and his failure enact on a smaller scale the course of the larger experiment of the volume's writing – an experiment symbolized also in the love affair between Merrill and Strato that is chronicled in a number of the poems.

"To My Greek" (FS 19–21) finds Merrill's speaker not as far east as his friend's "dung-and-emerald oasis," but as far away as Greece, where he and his Greek lover (Strato) avoid learning words for abstractions like "justice, grief, convention." They limit the terms of their interaction to the material (except for the word "Forbidden") and sensual – "Salt Kiss Wardrobe Foot Cloud Peach" – and to the immediate present. This Edenic "way of little knowledge" is new to Merrill, and he prays to sustain it, using figures of nakedness that contrast with his usual images of masking: He implores, "under my skin stay nude," "[let] The barest word be what I say in you." (The same imagery recurs in "More Enterprise"; living in Greece, the speaker discards his "swank" suit and Roman shoes for the "scant wardrobe of gesture.") For Merrill this sort of interaction, so unmediated by the veils and double meanings of cultivated language, is entirely fresh, lending a "rainbow edge" to experience.

Merrill's speakers have frequently suffered from a sense of unreality or estrangement from reality. The protagonists of his novels provide particularly obvious examples. Francis Tanning in *The Seraglio*, for instance, considers his having always had access to money as having deprived him of a sense of either his own or the world's reality; Sandy in *The (Diplos) Notebook*, for whom life and fiction are interchangeable, is paralyzed by a deadly detachment from reality. Strato suffers no such debilitating skepticism or self-consciousness; his sensibility – crude, direct, raucous, even (in "The Envoys") brutal – seems the opposite of Merrill's. Later, in the O section of "Ephraim," Strato's animal nature is underscored as he is revealed to be in his first human incarnation, having previously been a cat. Merrill explains his attachment: "(This being seldom in my line to feel, / I most love those for whom the world is real)" (DC 95). In "To My Greek" we sense Merrill's hope that the liaison with Strato may permit a shift in his own orientation toward the world.

Yet even in the most glorious days of their romance, he fears for their future and recognizes that "the sibyl I turn to // When all else fails me, when you do" remains the "mother tongue" in all her elegant subtlety. Aware that his lover lacks "her blessing" – and aware that she is a virago – he dreams of doing away with her, knowing full well that his ties to her will prove more lasting than those binding him to the "Radiant dumbbell" he now adores. Sure enough, "Flying from Byzantium" (FS 29–31), the poem describing the lovers' parting and the searing pain Merrill experiences as he flies alone back across the Atlantic, ends with him praying to his Mother – that is, to the woman who bore him (and to whom he is so Oedipally attached), to the homeland, and, most of all, to the mother tongue – for help upon his return to her. He prays now to be removed from life, particularly from physical sensation, and retreats from being one who experiences directly to being one who, well distanced, writes about experience: "Far off a young scribe turned a fresh / Page, hesitated, dipped his pen." Again in "Mornings in a New House" (FS 40–1), when the lovers have broken up and the speaker is left "a cold man," he protects himself from further wounds as "Habit arranges the fire screen." Inevitably, he reverts to reliance upon something inherited from his mother – here, an elaborately embroidered design to be placed between him and the flames, preventing direct sensation of passion's heat. He has had to abandon the attempt to remove his masks.

This is not to say that Merrill's love affair with man-as-animal or word-as-thing has simply ended once and for all. He has, however, learned from experience the dangers of oversimplification. In a 1972 review of Francis Ponge's *Things* and *The Voice of Things* Merrill carefully qualified his attraction to experience stripped of the swaddling of ideas, abstractions, and fanciful wordplay.[11] Agreeing with Ponge's expression of disappointment with ideas because they so easily procure consent, "produc[ing] no pleasure in me but rather a kind of queasiness, a nausea," Merrill extends Ponge's logic:

> No thoughts, then, but in things? True enough, so long as the notorious phrase argues not for the suppression of thought but for its oneness with whatever in the world – pine woods, spider, cigarette – gave rise to it. Turn the phrase around, you arrive no less at truth: no things but in thoughts. Was the apricot any more

*real* without a mind to consider it, whether this poet's or that starving goat's? We'll never know.

Later, again elaborating a point of Ponge's, Merrill asserts, "For a thought is after all a thing of sorts. Its density, color, weight, etc., vary according to the thinker, to the symbols at his command, or at whose command he thinks. One would hardly care so much for language if this were not the case." The poet, recreating things in words and using objects to reflect thoughts, must love both. Merrill senses, however, that writers of his historical era are likely to forfeit resources of language to retain the admirable honesty of "the barest word." This he laments: "Even today, how many poets choose the holy poverty of some second-hand diction, pure dull content in translation from a never-to-be-known original. 'There is no wing like meaning,' said Stevens. Two are needed to get off the ground." The other wing, balancing that of mere content (or doubling the content with a second meaning generated by wordplay), is feathered with "fantastic gaiety and invention." Merrill turns his attention to that more decorative means of flight in the closing poems of *The Fire Screen.*

Several of these poems deal with the opera, symbol of a very different relation of language to life than that represented by Strato. Taking now less interest in the denotative power of words than either Auden or Strato would, Merrill focuses on music's "sound of sheer feeling – as opposed to that of sense, of verbal sense."[12] The sonnet sequence "Matinees" (FS 47–51) is a formal twin to "Friend of the Fourth Decade"; both are composed of eight sonnets, though appropriately only "Matinees" follows the sonnet's formal rhyme scheme. The structural parallel alerts us that "Matinees" describes another solution to the tedium the friend described, an alternative to stripping away the "swaddlings" of civilization and the refined rites of language: costume rather than nakedness.

"Matinees" depicts Merrill's introduction to opera at age eleven and opera's effect on his life since, thereby exploring the powers and purposes of an elaborately costumed art. Alluding to Yeats's "Sailing to Byzantium" ("Soul clap its hands and sing, and louder sing"), Merrill sketches his own ideal "artifice of eternity" as a fiery operatic extravaganza:

> Soul will cough blood and sing, and softer sing,
> Drink poison, breathe her joyous last, a waltz
> Rubato from his arms who sobs and stays
>
> Behind, death after death, who fairly melts
> Watching her turn from him, restored, to fling
> Kisses into the furnace roaring praise.

The singing masters of his soul are just that, singers, and unlike Yeats's need not be sages. Adopting their operatic perspective in this world lends the vibrance of passion to ordinary routines, "Tongues flickering up from humdrum incident."

Merrill's attitude toward the theatrical diverges from Auden's here. While Auden would delight as much as Merrill in such enlivening embellishment, he would probably be less comfortable with the (a)moral effects Merrill laughingly flaunts:

> The point thereafter was to arrange for one's
> Own chills and fever, passions and betrayals,
> Chiefly in order to make song of them.

For Auden, it is one thing to embellish with song experiences that would otherwise seem drab or painful; it is another to direct significant events so that they may better serve art's purpose, that is, to make "a religion of the aesthetic."[13] Well aware of his own temptation toward aestheticism, Auden has labeled such religion an "error" (and has identified both Merrill's hero Proust and Baudelaire as men who never got beyond that mistake).

Where Auden would caution us against identifying art with life, Merrill encourages their confusion; after all, the passions of opera, however gratuitously evoked, have "fed his solitary heart" in youth and have left him in later years with a large repertoire of grandly romantic scores, "Old beauties" (referring to both the former lovers and the plots he enacted with them) ready to be replayed in memory. Thus, in the second section of "The Opera Company," Merrill savors a union possible only in art, not in life: In a recording ("low fidelity," he puns) the voices of his two favorite sopranos merge in gorgeous harmony, although their relations in life were characterized only by antipathy and discord. No doubt Auden, too, would have savored the recorded performance, but Merrill differs from the older poet in his refusal to proclaim one version of the singers' relation as more true, more real than the other; similarly, he hedges:

> Dependably for either [soprano], every night
> Tenors had sobbed their hearts out, grates
> Fluttering with strips of red and orange paper.
> Such fires were fiction? Then explain
> These ashes if you please.[14]

For Merrill, opera is perhaps the ideal art because it combines verbal sense with the musical sense of feeling, thereby attaining far greater expressive power than words alone. Recalling in an interview why his first grand opera seemed "the most marvelous thing on earth," Merrill explained, "It was the way it could heighten and stylize the emotions – a kind of absurdity dignified by the music, or transformed by the music. There seemed to be nothing that couldn't be expressed in opera."[15] He was particularly excited by "the sense of a feeling that could be expressed without any particular attention to words."[16] Suggesting the symbolist allegiance he shares with Stevens, but not with Auden, he declared, "Words just aren't that meaningful in themselves. *De la musique avant toute chose.*"[17]

Auden's emphasis contrasts:

> through listening to music I have learned much about how to organize a poem, how to obtain variety and contrast through change of tone, tempo, and rhythm, though I could not say just how. Man is an analogy-drawing animal; that is his great good fortune. His danger is of treating analogies as identities, of saying, for instance, "Poetry should be as much like music as possible." I suspect that the poeple who are most likely to say this are the tone-deaf. (DH 51–2)

He has explained: "One can speak of verbal 'music' [in poetry] so long as one remembers that the sound of words is inseparable from their meaning. The notes in music do not denote anything."[18] One reason Auden valued the experience of translating opera libretti was that the activity "will cure us of the heresy that poetry is a kind of music in which the relations of vowels and consonants have an absolute value, irrespective of the meaning of the words." (DH 499) Merrill would not claim an *absolute* value, but he does believe that poetic music can carry the sound of meaning with little attention to verbal sense.

It is not surprising, then, that Merrill should have taken some different approaches than Auden's to the play of sound in verse; again the difference between the two is that between a poet who wishes to enchant and one who strives to disenchant. While both men are inventive rhymers, exceptionally skillful in controlling rhythm and in weaving elaborate patterns with their vowels, Merrill's sound play is far more obviously lavish and more pronouncedly sensual than Auden's. Even his relatively unlyrical passages ravish us with their music. The opening lines of "In Monument Valley," for instance, serve the prosaic function of locating the poem's action:

> One spring twilight, during a lull in the war,
> At Shoup's farm south of Troy, I last rode horseback.
> Stillnesses were swarming inward from the evening star
> Or outward from the buoyant sorrel mare.   (BE 10)

Yet the lulling balance of motion in and out, of the beginning that is spring and the end that is twilight, is sounded for us in Merrill's balancing reversal of vowels near the quatrain's middle – "swarming inward" – and by the echoing sounds preceding and following – war, were, outward, sorrel, mare. Where Merrill's music is more ostentatious than this, his model often seems to be Stevens' exotic vocabulary and chiming consonants, e.g., "Tones / Jangling whose tuner slept, moon's camphor mist // On the parterre compounding / Chromatic muddles which the limpid trot / Flew to construe" (BE 25). Lines like those make more musical than verbal sense; they communicate with the opera singer's resources rather than the orator's.

They also demonstrate Merrill's appreciation for "clotted poetry" like Mallarmé's. Discussing such poetry Merrill admitted, "I occasionally still work in trying to produce a poem that resists the intelligence almost successfully, as Stevens said."[19] The purpose of this effort is to make the poem more open to the feelings and the subconscious of both writer and reader. Stevens' intoxicating language provides one resource for such resistance of the intellect; near-surrealist privacy of reference provides another:

> Cricket earphones fail us not
> Here in the season of receptions
>
> One prism drips ammonia still
> Penknife-pearl-and-steel ripples
>
> Paring nobody's orchard to the bone.    (BE 40)

A clipped telegraphic mode provides yet another:

> To let:
> Cream paint, brown ivy, brickflush. Eye
> Of the old journalist unwavering
>
> Through gauze. Forty-odd years gone by.
> Toy blocks. Church bells. Original vacancy.
> O deepening spring.    (BE 28)

Of Merrill's volumes, none offers a heavier dose of this hermeticism than *Braving the Elements*, from which all these passages are taken; in that collection more than any other, Merrill seems intent on finding, perhaps extending, the limits of verbal music's expressive power. Reducing the referential meaning carried by words opens up other ways of, in *Sandover*'s phrase, "making sense of it": If the denotative sense of our language seems feeble because of the uncertainty of our grasp on "reality," a strong sensory experience of the sounds of words can provide some very real compensation. One can at least "[Come] to [one's] senses through a work of art" (BE 68).

The patterns of his poems' lush sounds are stylistic evidence of Merrill's sense that what one experiences as most real may be most fabricated. That notion becomes the central theme of one of the finest poems in *Braving the Elements*, "Days of 1935" (BE 11–21). Even the poem's method depends on regarding fable as fact, for this is one of two ballads in which Merrill presents his personal history in fantastic form.[20] (The other is "The Summer People," with which *The Fire Screen* concludes. In that poem the half-mythical character Jack Frost is half-Merrill – a doodling artist in a Greek revival New England town who looks younger than his years, who loves cats, four-hand piano, and bridge, and who enjoys spending money on food and drink and flowers.) "Days of 1935" narrates the fantasies of Merrill's lonely wealthy boyhood, when he would compensate for the absence of parents and playmates by imagining the companionship he longed for. His dreams took the "plausible" form of kidnapping, imitating the capture of the Lindbergh baby; yet he is abducted not merely by the man he imagines, that "masked and crouching form," but by imagination itself:

> Then sheer imagination ride[s]
> Off with us in its old jalopy,
> Trailing bedclothes like a bride
> Timorous but happy.

The world imagined by the boy is less mystifying than the one he actually inhabits; his mind boggles wondering about his parents: "was it true he loved / Others beside her?" "Eerie, speaking likenesses," he says, referring to his parents' imaginary photos in the newspaper, but suggesting too the almost ghostly unreality his parents possess for him. In such an inexplicable, disconcerting world, what becomes most real is precisely what is imagined: "Tingling I hugged my pillow. *Pluck* / Some deep nerve went. I knew // That life was fiction in disguise." By similar logic, the boy's highest moment in the imagined drama occurs when Jean, that "lady out of *Silver Screen*," asks him to tell her stories: "Real stories – but not real, I mean. / Not just dumb things people did." Even his captor recognizes that stories are more real than ordinary life. The little boy who fantasizes for his emotional survival is, like Scheherazade, one who lives by storytelling. As he recounts tale after tale – "Wunspontime, I said and said . . ." – he thinks, "Who knows but that our very lives / Depend on such an hour."

Nor is his dependency on the disguised life of fiction limited to his childhood. The adult who looks back upon the fantasy (in the section beginning "Grown up, he thinks how") finds himself carried away by love as he once was by "sheer imagination." If the adult's romances seem less like fairy tales or glamorous movies ("Tehuantepec," "Belshazzar's Feast"), that is only because their creator takes more care to ground them in "fact" with his "fine / Realistic touch." As a grown lover, once again he is taken in fortunate captivity ("Captivity . . . will set you free"), driven far enough to be liberated from the controlling powers of the superego – embodied especially in his mother's "Grade / A controls" and his father's wealth – far enough "To stitch with delicate kid stuff / His shoddy middle age." Moreover, there is a clear continuity between the homosexuality of the child's erotic fantasies involving Floyd (whose name brings to mind the legendary "Pretty Boy Floyd") and the adult's behavior: "I / Will relive some things he did / Until I die, until I die."

Details of the poem suggest that neither the child who acts out his dreams while sleepwalking nor the man who wills himself captive to myths of love is idiosyncratic in confusing life with fiction. Our entire culture decorates kitchen walls with "board / Painted like board. Its grain // Shiny buff on cinnamon / Mimics the real, the finer grain." What exactly is finer here? The "real" grain of the board hidden under the paint and recreated by it, or the "real" grain of some imagined board thought to be imitated in paint? Such sleight-of-hand decor relies as much on "A golden haze / Past belief, past disbelief" as does any child's, or lover's, "true to life" fantasy.

"Past belief, past disbelief" – we have entered the challenging mode of paradox, a central device in Merrill's work, most obviously in his late volumes. Paradox, of course, was often used by the modernists as they sought to display multiple perspectives, to reveal complexity and not reduce it. Merrill, in using paradox not as a way of containing multifaceted truths but as a way of fostering fluid, open-ended transformations, offers a characteristically contemporary slant on this trope. When asked about his fondness for paradox, Merrill explained, "I suppose that early on I began to understand the relativity, even the reversability of truths." After mentioning some situations in his childhood that might have made him see "there was truth on both sides," Merrill suggests a more fundamental source than biography for his delight in phrases like "Au fond each summit is a cul de sac":

> I believe the secret lies primarily in the nature of poetry – and of science, too, for that matter – and that the ability to see both ways at once isn't merely an idiosyncrasy but corresponds to how the world needs to be seen: cheerful *and* awful [he alludes

to the close of Bishop's "The Bight," "awful but cheerful"],
opaque *and* transparent. The plus and minus signs of a vast
evolving formula.[21]

If science and poetry represent two evolving sides of knowledge, both
are true, and consideration of either leads us to the paradoxically double
nature of reality as something both created and discovered. This idea
recurs often in Merrill's recent works; for instance, it provides the serious
underpinnings beneath all the lighthearted paradoxes – for example, that
Merrill's goddaughter's clothes are "Priced inversely to their tininess,"
that a mere baby should be a weighty burden for him, that his finally
becoming a parent of sorts seems to coincide with the incipience of his
own second childhood – presented with half-genial, half-grudging humor in "Verse for Urania" (DC 30–6). Because his godchild is being
named for a science – one "whose elements cause vertigo / Even, I fancy,
in a specialist" – Merrill can make it clear that mythmaking, like truth-
telling, is as much the province of science as of art. Contemplating primitive astronomy's assignment of names and explanatory tales to the con-
stellations, Merrill suggests (with an almost Wordworthian hint of the
child trailing clouds of glory) that a few of those names reflect some
essential knowledge instinctively the child's:

> From out there notions reach us yet, but few
> And far between as those first names we knew
> Already without having to look up,
> Children that we were, the Chair, the Cup,
> But each night dimmer, children that we are,
> Each night regressing, dumber by a star.
> Still, fiction helps preserve them, those old truths
> Our sleights have turned to fairy tales.

At the same time, those "old truths" we are somehow given to know
are also sheer invention, orders imposed by "our wisest apes" who "Stared
the random starlight into shapes." The same paradox characterizes poetry:

> Take, for that matter, my beanstalk couplet, above,
> Where such considerations as rhyme and meter
> Prevail, it might be felt, at the expense
> Of meaning, but as well create, survive it;
> For the first myth was Measure.

Thus, near the poem's close when Merrill pleads, "help me to conceive
/ That fixed, imaginary, starless pole / Of the ecliptic which this one we

steer by / Circles," the term "conceive" has two very different meanings: He is asking for a more encompassing understanding of what already exists, and he is asking to invent a fiction. What he wishes to conceive, designated by our phrase "true north," is real *and* imaginary.

## III

In differentiating Merrill's sense of doubleness from Auden's, I have suggested that while Auden tries to hold side by side two seemingly contradictory aspects of actuality – e.g., that each person has a body and an intellect, that people are unique individuals and undifferentiated members of a species – Merrill's double focus takes in the fictional and the "actual." Moreover, I have argued that while Auden believes that a single overriding Truth and Order govern our universe, Merrill is skeptical about the reality of the actual or of its apparent orders. More like Stevens than Auden, he therefore embraces the imagined and the beautiful as substitutes for possibly nonexistent truth. A third difference is now emerging, one in which Merrill's stance is characteristically contemporary: that while Auden's doubleness (or other modernists' multiplicity) aims for a stabilizing balance of contradictory views, Merrill's involves dazzlingly fluid movement, constant expansion, contraction, inversion of perspective, simultaneous multiplications and mergings of meanings and identities. "Yánnina" (DC 259), from *Divine Comedies*, will demonstrate further.

According to a revealing interview conducted by David Kalstone, Merrill composed the poem having in mind the theme of "a double life" – that is, the kind of life undertaken by the "Friend of the Fourth Decade," and less dramatically by Merrill, who divided his time between Stonington and Athens.[22] The poem's genesis was, one might say, "operatic" in that things were done, passions induced, just for the sake of having something beautiful to sing about. The poet arrived at Yánnina equipped with some knowledge of its lore and history, and with a hope of finding something to write about: "I didn't spend twenty-four hours on the spot. But the piano had been prepared, and only the notation remained. That whole element – do we dare call it reality? – had to be unforeseeable, accidental, something to fill in then and there." The events of those twenty-odd hours were "experience[d] in the light of a projected emotion, like a beam into which what you encounter will seem to have strayed." In this sort of creation – the notion is by now familiar – "the poem and its occasion will have created one another," with neither one more real nor more an imitation than the other. As we have by now come to expect, Merrill in writing about that occasion tried to let the "succession of scenes convey not meaning so much as a sense of it," hoping to create that deliciously operatic sense "that something both is, and isn't, being said."

As is true, though less obviously, of so much of Merrill's work, an atmosphere of unreality, or half-reality, pervades the scene. The geographically actual city of Yánnina is portrayed also as a realm of dreams where all people are somnambulists. The sun, too, sleepwalks, and the speaker himself seems to doze off in midphrase: "But right now she's asleep, as who is not, as who . . ." Drowsiness spreads even to the reader, who doubles for the speaker's companion, so that the speaker must ask, "Awake?" In this situation the condition of the dead becomes indistinguishable from that of the living: The old Turk by the water, presumably a statue, sleeps too, as does Frossíni, centuries drowned.

Paradoxically, the most active figures are those fixed in works of art. The postcard of "Kyra Frossíni's Drown" seems as immediate as Bishop's depiction of the moment when a boathook catches her travelling companion's skirt. In Merrill's description of the card, "A devil (turban and moustache and sword) / Chucks the pious matron overboard – / Wait – heaven help us – SPLASH!" Art takes on the immediacy of life, and conversely the living are distanced through comparison with artworks; for example, men are selling crayfish scarlet "as the sins in any fin-de-siècle villanelle." In another paradox, historical figures, whether or not depicted in sculpture or painting, seem present (as they do most obviously in *Sandover*) – "It's him, Ali. The end is near," or "Byron has visited. He likes / The luxe." Yet at the same time the poem emphasizes transcience – particularly of its two versions of the feminine, one "brief as a bubble," the other "gone up no less in smoke." We are being forced into seeing "both ways at once," absorbing the notion of "the reversibility of truths."

Byron's presence in the poem – along with the speaker's preoccupation with the oblivion of sleep, death, or love-death – evokes the Romantic poets' reluctant admission of our inability to have it both ways. They acknowledged the impossibility of enjoying both death's permanence and sensation's intensity. Almost smugly, Merrill contemplates the Romantics' dreamy death wish "in full feather." Jokingly extending the figure with several bird images (ravens, pigeons, doves), his passage culminates with an allusion to the questions that conclude "Ode to a Nightingale": "The brave old world sleeps. Are we what it dreams / And is a rude awakening overdue?" But Merrill's fancy, unlike Keats', deceives as well as she is said to, permitting him the comfort of continued sleep and dream. At the end of the poem, Merrill does not plummet to the earth, like the unfortunate Keats; instead he invites his companion, who seems to have been hurt by love or parting, to take his arm and dare with him "the magician's tent" – that is, the space of art. There, what is torn in two heals again (recalling Bishop's desire for the dissolution of dichotomies). "The magician," Merrill explained in the interview, "performs the essential act. He heals what he has divided. A double edged action, like his sword. It's what one comes to feel that life keeps doing."[23] The poem's image for this double-edged action is a constant "scissoring and mending" taking place in the water as Ali's barge and its reflection (which is also its rendering in art's mirror) travel "outward and away." Doubleness, though inescapable, is at the same time continually being eradicated, particularly by art's "mending" magic.

To the extent that Merrill is willing to point to *a truth*, it is the same one that preoccupies the other contemporary poets whose work we have examined: process. Perhaps in Merrill's case, the proper term for his sense of continuous transformation would be the literary one, "translation," that figures so importantly in his great poem, "Lost in Translation." In that lyric Merrill is less concerned with translation as product, an achieved version in another language (Rilke's version of Valéry's text), than with translation as action, as the transformational process described in both poets' versions of that poem about a palm. Even when considering the translated poem, Merrill focuses on the action of its translator, who is imagined making himself forgo "much of the sun-ripe original / Felicity . . . / In order to render its underlying sense" (ellipsis added). Merrill's interest is in the changes made in turning the poem from the "warm Romance" language French into the cool starkness of German. And while most of the poem concerns memories of the distant past – primarily of the summer when his parents divorced – these past events are not fixed, beyond translation. To remember the past is to make it active in the present and to find it changing, just as the speaker's recent experience with a medium and a puzzle piece changes his sense of his boyhood's many puzzles. Thus, as is appropriate for a poem about translation, the poem's conclusion takes the insistently ongoing present tense:

> But nothing's lost. Or else: all is translation
> And every bit of us is lost in it
> (Or found – I wander through the ruin of S
> Now and then, wondering at the peacefulness)
> And in that loss a self-effacing tree,
> Color of context, imperceptibly
> Rustling with its angel, turns the waste
> To shade and fiber, milk and memory.

For Merrill, all art acts as the coconut palm does, translating loss, absence, waste into something substantial and nourishing.

One meaning of the verb "to translate" is "to express one thing in terms of another." That is also a standard definition of the action of metaphor. In Merrill's oeuvre the text most obviously concerned with the process of translation, and with the action of metaphor, is his trilogy, . *The Changing Light at Sandover.*

## IV

Warning against an approach to the trilogy that is "too doggedly literal," Judith Moffett has invoked a useful distinction: "its Message and its meaning are not the same."[24] I would go further and assert that much of the epic's liveliness derives from the radical difference, and the resulting tension, between the two. The message – even though not entirely consistent and though subject to revision – emphasizes determinism, permanent dualisms, rigid hierarchy, and absolutes. The meaning, as I understand it, evolves largely from the poems' metaphorical method and involves "unrelenting fluency," fluidity, relativism, and free play. The differences between message and meaning are essentially those I have been outlining between Auden and Merrill; consequently, if one reads the trilogy with Merrill's divergence from Auden in mind, one can understand the conflicts enacted in the work's structure and method as reflecting the nature and processes of that divergence.

The doses of message administered in the first installment, "The Book of Ephraim," are light, pleasantly sweetened by the skepticism of Merrill and Jackson and by the wit of their familiar spirit. The medicine becomes less palatable early in *Mirabell* when the poet is informed, "ABSOLUTES ARE NOW NEEDED YOU MUST MAKE GOD OF SCIENCE" (M 19). The voices of 40070, 40076, and 741 (later Mirabell) then provide instruction about the nature and history of the universe by translating their mathematical formulas into terms more or less appropriate to their audience. Mirabell, who most successfully learns the manners and affection that ease communication with humans, explains:

> THUS MATH ENCAPSULATES COMPLEX TRUTHS WHICH AS WITH
> OUR 1ST
> MEANINGLESS TO U & THERE4 FRIGHTENING VOICES MUST
> BE RENDERD INTO YR VOCABULARY OF MANNERS    (M 130)

The bats' outline of cosmic history, adapted for JM's and DJ's consumption, evokes many legends of Western tradition, but is proclaimed accurate nonetheless, since "ALL LEGENDS ARE ROOTED IN TRUTH" (M 68). Centaurs, for example, preceded and evolved into dinosaurs; the Faust legend derives from the actual history of Pope Innocent VI; the evil released by the fallen angels of Christian mythology was in fact atomic energy. Similarly, it turns out that "IN THE BEGINNING WAS THE WORD" was one man's response to "THE UNEARTHLY MUSIC OF THE SINGLENOTED ATOM" (M 149), and Dante's glimpse of God as a brilliant point of light surrounded by concentric rings of halos (*Paradiso*, XXVII) was a vision looking "INTO THE ATOM'S EYE" (M 38).[25] Thus, according to the trilogy's message, the truth does exist and, though veiled by the metaphors and images human limitations dictate, is revealed to the extent that humans can benefit from knowing it. Sometimes the Ouija board's metaphors are even translated by those of higher rank and greater understanding so that their truth will be more accessible to JM and DJ. Maria, for instance, interprets:

> THESE MYTHS THAT ANTECEDE ALL MYTH ARE COUCHED
> IN DAUNTING GENERALITIES. FOR MICHAEL/SUN
> READ: GENERATIVE FORCE. FOR GENERATIVE FORCE
> READ: RADIATION TO THE BILLIONTH POWER
> OF EXPLODING ATOMS. FOR EMMANUEL,
> H2O. FOR SEEDS, THAT COSMIC DUST
> LADEN WITH PARTICLES OF INERT MATTER.
> FOR GOD READ: GOD.    (S 106)

She suggests that while God is not a metaphor, most of the lessons' terms are metaphors with identifiable referents.

Knowing that his epic's creatures – unicorns, fallen angels, and so forth – are metaphors standing for atomic formulas, Merrill several times has to be reassured that he need not render them in their true numbers and "MAKE A JOYLESS THING / OF IT THRU SUCH REDUCTIVE REASONING" (S 179–80). Metaphor is the poet's permitted freedom, though his proclaimed discomfort with it persists. JM often appears troubled by the shifting scale of the board's accumulating metaphors. Early in *Mirabell* he begs the voices to "Speak without metaphor. / Help me to drown the double-entry book / I've kept these fifty years" and complains "It's too much to be batwing angels *and* / inside the atom, don't you understand?" (M 28). He questions why, having nearly convinced us that their works "include / Ancient happenings of a magnitude / Such that we still visit their untoppled / Bones in England, Egypt, and Peru," the bats should then

> Imply that we must also read your story
> As a parable of developments
> Remoter yet, at matter's very heart?
> Are we to be of two minds, each nonplussed
> By the other's vast (or tiny) scale?
> Are we to take as metaphor your "crust

World" – for, say, the brain's evolving cortex?
Or for that "froth of electrons" locked within
Whose depths revolve the nuclear Yang and Yin?    (M 31–2)

The answer, an approving "HEAD OF CLASS." JM and DJ are to accept their peacock as "both a subatomic x / *And* a great glaring bugaboo"; no doubt they are better equipped to do so since Merrill had already determined many years and poems earlier "That anything worth having's had both ways" (M 80). To further complicate *Sandover's* doubling of scale, the grand design spelled out by the bats in *Mirabell* and the angels in *Scripts* involves a great many dualisms, among them white and black, matter and antimatter, positive and negative electric charges, God B and the monitor. All these exist in parallel situations of precarious balance. The resistance the paired entities offer one another (their "pressing back," to use Stevens' formulation that Merrill favors) is a universal impulse, operative on all scales. Consequently, when JM asks near the end of *Scripts*

> When we suppose that history's great worm
> Turns and turns as it does because of twin
> Forces balanced and alert within
> Any least atom, are we getting warm?

he is warmly congratulated for having "MADE SENSE OF IT" (S 196). With all its elaborate dualisms, the cosmos, as presented in the trilogy's message, is clearly and firmly ordered. In fact, the primary purpose of the bats' instruction is to warn humankind against the chaos they themselves once worshipped, i.e., the uncontrolled energy of smashed atoms. They insist that the orders, rules, and hierarchies they depict and obey have been established to prevent chaos from slipping in, to protect the inviolability of the atom. One of the most unpalatable but essential lessons they force down the throats of their human pupils is that all things affecting human history are governed by a NO ACCIDENT clause, with even humanity's resistance to that concept having been programmed.

So goes the tidy take-home message, revealing a securely ordered universe, threatened by humankind's predetermined meddling with its primary ordering unit, the atom. But the Auden-like sense of balance and consistency the message precariously achieves is not easily maintained, even on the level of pronouncement, and it is certainly undercut by the poem's method. Examining both the complicating pronouncements and the translational method, we will see that the work's multiplying levels of metaphor often cancel each other out until all that one can hold onto – as is true in much of Ashbery's work – is the process of transformation from one level to another. When Merrill dutifully recites his lessons:

> Bon. We will try to remember that you are not
> A person, not a peacock, not a bat;
> A devil least of all – an impulse only
> Here at the crossroads of our four affections

he has not fully absorbed the dynamics of the bat's meaning. Mirabell gently corrects him, "OR MAKE OF ME THE PROCESS SOMEWHERE / OPERATING BETWEEN TREE & PULP & PAGE & POEM" (M 79).

Of the three installments, "The Book of Ephraim" draws the least attention to, or takes least seriously, the revelations about the systematic makeup of the cosmos. Pronouncements of message here lend themselves to interpretation as metaphorical statements not about any aspects of planetary, atomic, or supernatural reality, but about the process of artistic creation. Ephraim's scheme of reincarnation serves largely as an image for the process by which aspects of the artist's self and experience are reborn, transformed, in his successive works of art.[26] This is the point of the poem's interweaving of events from the poet's past, the lost novel, and the poet's present ongoing experience; all are different versions of the same story. Each character the artist creates is an "old self in a new form" (DC 112) – that is, a way for him to revitalize his existence, escaping once more the dreaded fixity of being "cut and dried," and a way perhaps to attain immortality. Consequently, Wallace Stevens and Carl Jung, who have identified God as the imagination and the unconscious, emerge as the book's authorities on the nature of God. Ephraim himself defines heaven as "the surround of the living" (DC 103), and his admission that heaven will vanish if humankind destroys itself (DC 100) also suggests that the mirror world is purely a human creation. Specifically, this heaven is the creation of two individuals, DJ and JM. Merrill's "Book of a Thousand and One Evenings Spent with David Jackson" celebrates not only the reincarnation of the artist in his imaginative creations, but also the continual rebirth and rejuvenation of the love and "refining passion" (here God is also Eros) between him and his chosen mate.

Keeping in mind these personal and self-reflexive aspects of the drama that sound as muted undertones in the pronounced message, we appreciate the epic's machinery as most essentially a means of self-knowledge – one which eases the erasure of conventional boundaries that limit understanding of oneself and one's mental processes. The Ouija board rituals allow an expanded perception of the self as multiple, ambiguous, fluid. The fundamental mysteries illuminated in the trilogy, then, are human, not superhuman. Thus, Merrill not only admits the possibility that the whole Ouija board rigamarole may be an elaborate "folie à deux" by which the two lovers "sound each other's depths of spirit" (DC 74); he goes further to stress the arbitrariness of the poem's frame:

Hadn't – from books, from living –
The profusion dawned on us, of "languages"
Any one of which, to who could read it,
Lit up the system it conceived? – bird-flight,
Hallucinogen, chorale and horoscope:
Each its own world, hypnotic, many-sided
Facet of the universal gem.
Ephraim's revelations – we had them
For comfort, thrills and chills, "material."
He didn't cavil. *He* was the revelation
(Or if we had created him, then we were).    (DC 75–6)

The parenthetic statement is an important one, echoed several times in Merrill's interviews. "If the spirits aren't external, how astonishing the mediums become!" he remarked to Vendler;[27] and to McClatchy:

> don't you think there comes a time when everyone, not just a poet, wants to get beyond the Self? To reach, if you like, the "god" within you? The board, in however clumsy or absurd a way, allows for precisely that. Or if it's still *yourself* that you're drawing upon, then that self is much stranger and freer and more far-seeing than the one you thought you knew.[28]

By giving voice to heavenly beings, old myths, dead friends, and then by allowing their identities to merge and reflect, to multiply and fuse, Merrill grows beyond a narrow sense of self, since his own sight and experience expand with those of the beings he has brought to fictive life. Although the process of expansion and contraction could – presumably does – go on indefinitely, Merrill shapes his trilogy so that the overall tendency is first to expand the cast and then to reduce it. This enables him at the end to return to the scale of his earlier lyrics, having acquired (and given his readers) a changed awareness of his creative freedom. A typical example of the epic's fluid identities is provided by the four archangels representing the four elements, who expand to twelve beings, since each has three natures, which in turn reduce to six twins. As the cast shrinks toward *Sandover*'s close, we learn that the angels are also the supreme moments of "the five," one of whom is Maria (Plato), and that she in turn is all nine muses. Ephraim turns out to have been an incarnation of the archangel Michael (his only homosexual life to date). Moreover, for all history there is only one Academy (and, by implication, one audience, a select coterie of the living and the dead).

How this play with identities pertains to Merrill's sense of the self is most apparent when *Sandover*'s greatest cosmic powers are unveiled as immense projections of the estranged parental figures who have loomed over Merrill's work for decades. God B and Nature (Queen Mum) are versions of the always puzzling divorcing parents of "Lost in Translation"; as Merrill had written in *Nights and Days*, "Always the same old story – Father Time and Mother Earth, / A marriage on the rocks" (ND 28) (even Eden for him "tells a parable of fission, / Lost world and broken home" [M 98]). The Sandover Ballroom then becomes a magnified version of the one in his first Broken Home, and humankind's uncertain fate the enlargement of one boy's. We return by the trilogy's close essentially to the dramatis personae of Merrill's lyrics – the triangle of estranged parents and contested child, along with a small group of intimate friends. Yet the dynamics of *Sandover* leave us with an altered perspective so that we can regard as neither silly nor presumptuous Merrill's play upon the name of God – ABBA (Aramaic) – as designating his own favorite poetic form, the envelope quatrain.[29] Whether or not God and Merrill's art are forms of one another, they merge in undertaking the same awesome task originally identified by Stevens: pressing back against reality, holding off the darkness. Similarly, after we have for hundreds of pages experienced metaphoric levels that constantly change and identities that fuse and multiply, we do not perceive as reduction the shift into literary terminology that occurs at the climactic moment of the trilogy's plot. This is the epic's most wrenching scene, when JM and DJ must finally let go of their dead friends, Maria, Wystan, George (and soon, Robert), and send them into their new lives by breaking the mirror through which they have communicated. The double-meaning laden language with which the emotional moment is portrayed makes it a literary event:

> JM WILL TAKE THE MARBLE
> STYLUS & GIVING US THE BENEFIT
> OF A WELL AIMED WORD, SEND OUR IMAGINED SELVES
> FALLING IN SHARDS THRU THE ETERNAL WATERS
> (DJ CUPBEARER) & INTO THE GOLDEN BOUGH
> OF MYTH  ON INTO LIFE   (S 234)

But because we have been made to feel the power of the stylus and the substantiality of imagined beings (or the insubstantiality and fluidity of all beings, real and imaginary), Merrill's conflating the grief-filled moment on the terrace with his laborious writing of the poem no longer seems the reduction of scale or the evasion of emotion it might otherwise have seemed.

The epic's locus of power is the human intelligence, particularly as manifest in the many levels of language and meaning it can control. Early in *Scripts*, WHA predicts that "WE SHALL DISCOVER / [the angels'] POWERS

ARE IN US QUITE AS MUCH AS OVER," but the statement turns out fully to apply only to the living. God B's generative light, also associated with the Archangel Michael, can be revealed only to the live humans in the cast because only the humans are capable of imagining its forms: "S/O/L [the abbreviation suggests source of light, source of life, the Latin for sun, and a phonetic spelling of soul] / IS ROOTED IN THE LIVED LIFE ONLY MAN RECEIVES GOD B'S / MAIN MAGIC: IMAGINATIVE POWER." (Elsewhere intelligence is explicitly identified as the source of light [S 14] and imagination as the element fertilizing it [S 11].)

One of the obvious ways in which humanity's divine power is dramatized in *Sandover*'s composition is in Merrill's use of language to bestow appearances on the other world. We are frequently reminded that there are no appearances on the other side of the mirror (a notion JM repeatedly asks to have explained), but Merrill goes to elaborate lengths to smother that world in appearances and sensory stuff so that despite all protestations to the contrary, we retain vivid mental images of a trotting hornless unicorn nibbling green hedges, of Maria and Wystan dressed each day in different specified colors, of bats' eyes glowing with the red of "nuclear fire ache," of bat-winged forms perched around the edge of a lit-up mirror, and so forth. When the incorporeal bat 741 is translated into an equally incorporeal peacock and much is made of his gorgeous plumage, MM (a spirit who has literally neither brain nor heart) explains that he appears only "IN US OUR MINDS (HEARTS) ARE HIS MIRROR" (M 63). The Tinkerbell sentimentality of it all (he is even temporarily demoted to bat again with a moment of human doubt) does nothing to qualify the resulting recognition of the mind's power: We can make anything real, can sustain the life of any being, in our mind's eye and in the reflecting field of verbal intelligence.

The pretense behind the italic sections of word-painting in *Scripts* is that they are descriptions provided by MM and WHA after the events and inserted earlier by Merrill, but the pretense is thin, and intentionally so: The passages are presented as a playwright's stage directions, and the pleasure provided by all the details of gesture, light, color is once again that of sheer invention, e.g.:

> *At a light footstep all profoundly bow.*
>
> *Enter – in a smart white summer dress,*
> *Ca. 1900, discreetly bustled,*
> *Trimmed if at all with a fluttering black bow;*
> *Black ribbon round her throat; a cameo;*
> *Gloved but hatless, almost hurrying*
> *– At last! the chatelaine of Sandover –*
> *A woman instantly adorable.* (S 125)

We know it is all a manner of speaking, but such writing makes us feel in "the theatre of the blood" how language overpowers "naked truth," creating fable that *is* fact.

While Merrill's play with heavenly appearances often seems sheer camp indulgence, the trilogy's involvement with death and loss reminds us of more essential applications of God B's main magic, in coping with death. Thus, in "Ephraim" section R, an elegy for Maya, the poet is to transform the hellish heat of a painful September and "remake it all into slant, weightless gold: / Wreath at funeral games for the illusion / That whatever had been, had been right" (DC 107). Auden's faith that "whatever is, is right" is inaccessible to Merrill, but for him the artist's role is to revise the appearances of our world to bring us moments of such consoling belief. It is immaterial whether art's recouping of losses is, as DJ suggests, just lies (S 53) – the point is to provide "A WAY OF TELLING THAT INSPIRES BELIEF" (M 112).

Given the outrageousness of the trilogy's Ouija board format, the reader's belief can be only momentary inspiration, not lasting credence – and Merrill would have it so, for all his show of didacticism. Belief here, as in the postmodern perspective generally, is necessarily provisional and processive, as Bishop says, "flowing, and flown." It would be an error to read the progressive revisions of message in the trilogy as closer and closer approaches to *the* truth, despite hints to that effect (apologetic dismissals of previous "satellite truths," "partial fictions," "pearlgray lies," "small charades" that were supposedly necessary means of breaking the truth gradually to mere humans).[30] The revised messages, as much as the earlier ones, remain metaphors, enlarging perhaps with the poet's increasing confidence and daring; they ask of us not simple credulity, but "yes & no." DJ and JM enact a model renunciation of fixed certainty in "The Higher Keys" when they determine not to rendezvous with Maria (reincarnate as an Indian scientist-to-be) in 1991, as they had previously arranged:

> Worse yet, my dear, what if in fact
> Two old parties tottering through Bombay
> Should be accosted, on the given day,
> By Plato posing as a teenage guide?
> What if The Whole of It were verified?
>
> No, henceforth we'll be more and more alone.
>
> (CLS 539–40)

The work demands tolerance of uncertainty as well as resistance to outmoded absolutes and firm boundaries. Merrill's "characters, this motley alphabet, / Engagingly evade the cul-de-sac / Of the Whole Point" while remaining nevertheless "drawn by it."

By clownishly signalling many of his epic's metaphors with (m), Merrill heightens our awareness of the provisional, self-created, and mercurial nature of our truths. His parenthetic letter, instead of signalling an anxiety, allows us to anticipate delightful surprises. The wonder of language – humanity's home and highest achievement (or, more metaphorically, "MANS TERMITE PALACE BEEHIVE ANTHILL PYRAMID" as well as his "liferaft") – is its "unrelenting fluency." Despite all the epic's lessons in hierarchy, its energizing principles turn out to be continuity, flux, and synthesis – continuity between anima and animal, between dead and living, real and imaginary, self and other. The entire poem celebrates Merrill's having outgrown his youthful desire for secure distinctions, for "remission of their synthesis" (a nostalgic desire retained by many modernists facing uncertainty and disorder). Our bicameral minds and the poems they generate operate as puns do – simultaneously contracting or imploding several meanings into one statement and expanding or exploding one statement into many; the process in Merrill's hands is a liberating one and also evidence of human liberty. Both the mirror and the Ouija board are fields of reflection, which is to say they dramatize the action of the thinking mind. That dramatization is only possible with metaphor and other figures of speech that point two or more ways at once. It is the final paradox of Merrill's paradox-packed epic that its ostensibly deterministic frame should contain a vast anti-scheme so empowering of humankind: "The setting nothing, but the scope revealed / As infinite, for *Light* is everywhere, / Awaits the words that clothe it – which we wield" (S 201).

# Conclusion:
# "The possibility of free declamation anchored / To a dull refrain": the postmodernist estate

"The squirming facts exceed the squamous mind," Stevens noted.[1] Thus the density of detail in the preceding discussion of four poets' careers is intended to counter the tendency to impose on facts the mind's scaly rigidities. Ideally, one would not generalize about the differences between modernist and contemporary poetry without examining in equal detail numerous other poets. Since the distinctive poetry of Ashbery, Bishop, Creeley, and Merrill naturally "exceeds" neat patterns, one should, perhaps, resist reducing the squirming multitude of contemporary poems to any single paradigm. "And yet relation appears," Stevens added. Thus this book's subtitle, *Contemporary American Poetry and the Modernist Tradition*, points toward general trends. A brief review of the affinities and divergences already observed in the four pairs of poets will provide the basis for clarifying those trends.

Of the contemporary poets, Ashbery most dramatically reenacts the modernist insistence on innovation; he most obviously revels in the freedom for artists to find and define their own tradition attained by the modernist avant-garde. Ashbery's work reveals profound affinities with Stevens' – in poetic aims and principles, in stylistic techniques, and in thematic preoccupations. Following Stevens, Ashbery presents "the mind in the act of finding / What will suffice." That is, he seeks not merely to explore mental acts and the relation between them and external reality (concerns revealing Ashbery's and Stevens' shared Romantic roots), but to convey the process, the continual flux inherent in those activities. The greatest technical resources Ashbery found in Stevens' poetry were syntactic: forms of extended syntax permitting lengthy digression, suspension of conclusion, the suggestion of explanation without its actual assertion, as well as directional shifts that can mirror the fluidity – yet also the disjunctiveness – of mental process. Applying the rhetoric as well as the syntax of Stevens' "qualified assertions," Ashbery uses apparently logical discourse to blur logical distinctions and confound oppositions.

Ashbery's poetic diction is as heterogeneous as Stevens', but far more colloquial – a reflection of Ashbery's greater determination to tie poetry to immediate, ordinary living. Ashbery employs banal and demotic phrases because he especially values the language in which people actually communicate present feeling; he has little of the modernists' faith in the potential exactitude of words or metaphors. Similarly, Ashbery is less positive than Stevens in evaluating our tendency to live according to "necessary fictions" – and far less interested in assuming a hieratic role as provider of such fictions. Instead, he adopts a whimsical yet intensely self-conscious fence-sitting stance: Insisting on the fictionality of linguistic structures, he works to keep his readers aware of their own inevitable collaboration in ordering the randomness of experience.

In experimenting with the ways we generate or find order, in undermining the oppositions between order and chaos, in trying to make available for art whatever appears in the environment, and in exploring the possibilities of chance elements, Ashbery looks to models other than Stevens, especially to radically processive models in the nonverbal arts. With a reflexive irony adapted from the modernists, he continually reminds the reader that no art in fact avoids selection, escapes ordering, or captures immediate experience, even as his art strives to do just that. Yet viewing language and order as inevitably fictional does not prompt in him the modernists' anxious desire for coherence. From his stance of knowing approximation and half-joking acceptance, Ashbery can celebrate prehension of the disorderly, prosaic present as, finally, enough.

The affinities between Bishop and Moore, perhaps less pervasive than those between Ashbery and Stevens, are certainly as specific. Early in her career Bishop developed a descriptive manner heavily indebted to Moore's in its sharp observations, precise yet surprising figures, careful discriminations, understated manner, and detached journalistic stance. Bishop extends a qualifying tendency discernible in Moore's moralizing, bringing uncertainty more to the fore. She is more skeptical than Moore about deriving truths from visible surfaces or finding in the world stable orders that may be reflected in art.

Romantic impulses are as apparent in Bishop's work as in Ashbery's so that in her divergence from Moore's example, Bishop too sought to portray "the mind in the act of finding / What will suffice." Like Ashbery, she locates value in the fluidity of psychological experience; she also shares his interest in surrealism and in liminal mental processes. In her mature work, Bishop's sense of relentless flux causes her to approach description as an endless sequence of temporary approximations, rather than as a product that can, with discipline, be perfected and fixed. While Moore's details are exemplary and stable, Bishop's are only provisional points of orientation in a world governed by randomness (" 'and' and 'and' "). Yet Bishop's attitude toward the power of language is as much a fence-sitting as Ashbery's: At the same time that she puts more emphasis than Moore on the limits of art's accuracy and on the inability of words to capture experience precisely – that is, on the separation of art from life – she nonetheless searches for a language that will bring her poetry close to the process and texture of ordinary consciousness. Like Ashbery, she embraces the colloquial and vague diction of informal speech, believing that communication depends not simply on denotative precision (far more elusive in her eyes than in Moore's), but on the contexts of ordinary language. Bishop attaches her increasingly personal narratives to the movement of ongoing time as she seeks momentary confluences of past and present, familiarity and strangeness, dream and actuality, poetic language and communal speech.

As a young writer, Creeley inherited from the modernists a preoccupation with poetic form and a respect for the technical rigors of even the most experimental writing. Approaching free verse as a disciplined making rather than a casual expressing, Creeley in his early work adopted a number of prosodic techniques from Williams. Adapting to his own inward focus Williams' interest in rendering minute particulars, Creeley used Williams' intraphrasal line breaks and his strategies for playing upon the grammatical expectations of syntax to chart the tiniest shifts in his thoughts and feelings. Creeley learned from Williams techniques for making the diction and rhythms of American speech personally expressive.

In the sixties Creeley became increasingly aware of language as an arbitrary system, of words as markers for absences, and he became increasingly interested in exploring the workings of that abstract system of no-things. He began rejecting the particularized character of modernist work, including Williams' particularity of image, diction, and rhythm. Attributing to the modernists a falsifying desire for coherence and closure, Creeley, like Ashbery, was drawn instead toward the abstract expressionists' exploitation of chance, randomness, and indeterminate process. He has turned toward generalized and minimal terminology and toward fragmentary structures that highlight the provisionality and arbitrariness of all orders. (This should be distinguished from the modernists' efforts to mirror in collage the fragmentation of experience and culture. Creeley, like many postmoderns, does not attempt to represent in imitative form a shattered order; rather, he attempts to reenact a non-order inevitably structured by the action of language itself.) Wary even of the imagination as a distraction from his immediate apprehensions, Creeley rejects all transforming embellishment. Unfortunately, he has not brought to this project the rigorous double focus of Ashbery; too often Creeley seems to lose sight of the very questioning that prompted his efforts, as if believing language might be so pared down as to capture an unmediated "here."

Just as the example of Williams' poetry helped Creeley find and use his own speech, the example of Auden's conversational verse helped Merrill move from the "highflown" manner of his earliest work toward a more individual speech. Since the American Auden did not share the early modernists' suspicion of established poetic forms, he provided for Merrill an example of work that was traditionally formalist and at the same time decidedly modern. Auden's poetry showed Merrill how to employ colloquial language and to present ordinary, domestic events within formalist structures, how to register his own voice through and against regular metrical patterns, how to temper his oracular and exaggeratedly Romantic tendencies with wit, humor, and irony. Auden by the 1940s had developed a range of anti-Romantic techniques with which he could underline the separation of art from life and counter the pretensions of poet as priest or as generator of an organic, "natural" style. Auden's theatrical art remained conscious of its own illusion and always ready to laugh at itself, yet took seriously the need for illusions. In the example of Auden's midcareer work, Merrill found a serious and humanizing context within which he could exploit his sense of style as play, his love of verbal games, extravagant artifice, and masked ways of speaking.

In diverging from Auden, Merrill rejected the ordering hierarchies and the faith in nonfictive truths underlying Auden's poetics. While Merrill's elaborately reflexive art insists, as Auden's does, on the gap between itself and life, at the same time he undermines that distinction and conflates the two by insisting in myriad ways that "life [is] fiction in disguise." While Merrill, like the other three contemporary poets, offers informal conversation as the model for the highest communication (even his supernatural beings resort to it), like the other three he is equally aware that language is an arbitrary, fictional system bound to no fixed truths. Despite the apparent claims to orderly and secure truth made by his trilogy, the epic remains uncomfortable with its own grand scale and with its claims for coherence: its method undercuts that message. The work celebrates and demonstrates the fluid open-endedness that is language's only truth, the endlessly translational process in which any user of language is inevitably engaged. Thus, despite his lack of interest in the avant-garde and his willingness to echo writers of past centuries, Merrill shares the characteristically contemporary emphasis on mental process, and the contemporary acceptance of being "always of two minds" about the fictionality of linguistic structures.

When these eight poets are grouped according to their generations, substantial parallels (also outlined in the Introduction) emerge among the four contemporaries in their relation to the four modernists. These contemporary poets share with their predecessors a desire that poetry not fix the flux of their world. They have extended the modernists' attempts to track the action of the mind in the ongoing present – to portray not the mind finding meaning but the objectless process of finding. Even Merrill's trilogy, which sometimes seems didactically to present a meaning, turns out only to dramatize the action of loving minds playing with the alphabet. The American modernist most concerned with mental process, Stevens – whose work was admired by all four contemporaries – most fully anticipates this trend.

The contemporary poets' interest in assimilating the language of ordinary conversation, even its most banal and cliched forms, dramatically extends and modifies the modernist impulse to expand poetic diction and keep it responsive to living speech. Contemporaries have placed far less faith than the modernists in startling figurative language as a source of fresh accuracy; dubious about the possibility of linguistic precision or of individualized usage, they tend more to immerse themselves in eroded and debased dictions. The contemporary poets value the "dull refrain" of ordinary speech as least distorting present reality and best fostering interpersonal connections. While Merrill's diction is consistently more high-toned than the others', even he invokes a vernacular of sorts (high-class camp); and while the others accept the worn forms of prosaic, hackneyed speech, Merrill accepts having to echo in pastiche the familiar voices of long-established literary tradition.

The Romantic strains within modernism (however strenuously denied by the modernists themselves) have come to the fore among contemporary writers. Each of the contemporary writers is more personal and more autobiographical than the predecessor with whom he or she is paired, for recent writers have been intent on exploring the workings of their psyches, their private imaginations. "Still," Ashbery explains, "it is the personal, / Interior life that gives us something to think about. / The rest is only drama" (*A Wave*, p. 13). Thus, while the brokenness of modernist poetry – particularly of such grand collage works as *The Cantos, Paterson, The Waste Land* – reflects the poets' sense of their cultural and historical situation, the disjunctions of contemporary poetry seem more often to register those of individual psychology. This contemporary inwardness seems in part a retreat from the large sweep of the most dramatic and ambitious modernist works.

Indeed, the most essential differences between the generations involve a more modest stance in the younger generation: They generally favor quieter, more playful, and more personal voices; more limited ambitions, often reflected in smaller-scale works or, when the works are on a grand scale, in less totalizing vision; more modest assessments of the powers of language and of art. Recent poets are particularly diffident in assessing art's ordering role; they question the value of the artist's rage for order. What chaos, their works seem to ask, is not inevitably ordered by the perceiver? What perception is free from the mediation of the conceiving mind? What reality is not at least processed through, if not created by, the illusions of language? Answering "none" to all these questions, the contemporary poets reject the modernists' desire for coherence as yielding only further, perhaps avoidable, distortion. Although contemporary artists recognize their own activity as an ordering one, they do not glorify it as such. Instead, they place particular value on art that accepts the action of chance and the absence of determinate order.

In their efforts to avoid the imposition of false coherence, all four enact paradoxically double strategies – trying to immerse their poems more directly in the processive and contingent present and yet trying to highlight the aspects of writing that inevitably mediate, fix, order, and fictionalize. The contemporary poets strive, on the one hand, to bring art close to life in all its fluid non-order, and on the other, to bring life closer to art by underlining the fictionality of all perceptual, conceptual, and verbal structures. This desire to blend life into art and art into life is one aspect of the characteristically contemporary urge to dissolve boundaries and undermine oppositions. By blurring the distinctions between opposed categories and by inverting the hierarchy implicit in polarities such as order/chaos, percept/concept, reality/illusion, they subvert the traditional basis for ordering structures that falsify the disorder and the flux of immediate experience.

Thus Creeley in his later (less modernist) work tries to bring his poems into immediate presentness by recording disjunctive bits and pieces of his experience in linguistic forms so bare and basic that they will not admit the distancing of self-interrogation; alternatively, he plays with verbal structures so obviously self-generative that there can be no pretense of referentiality. Similarly, Ashbery attempts to track the random or serpentine gestures of consciousness, motion without closure, while also calling attention to the inevitable shapeliness that author and reader impose. Bishop uses exact descriptive techniques to record insistently processive, mysterious experiences; she tries to weave into poetic language the world's fluidity, and yet as a semi-formalist who makes no pretense to organic form, she highlights art's distance from flux. Of the four, Merrill employs the most blatantly ordering poetic structures, yet he constantly plays with words to undermine stability or singleness of reference, and he presents in his trilogy systems of truth that endlessly revise themselves. Different as their poems are, all four poets hope that what emerges from their work is what Ashbery (praising Bishop) has identified as "the one thing that is useful for us: our coming to know ourselves as the necessarily inaccurate transcribers of the life that is always on the point of coming into being."[2]

While individual influence operates within each pair of poets, the common trends among the more recent poets reflect the operation of an entire tradition. Collectively, the works of these contemporaries demonstrate that much recent poetic technique relies on or refers to modernist poetry. In addition, they reveal the complicated dynamics of a tradition that is oxymoronically a tradition of the avant-garde. Because of its inherently revolutionary stance, modernism more than most traditions pushes its inheritors to react against, discard, or violate its practices, while exerting the usual pressure to imitate and extend its achievements.

These dynamics have been further complicated because modernism began functioning as a tradition while it was still evolving. Poetic modernism as encountered by those coming of age in the 1940s was not limited to the practices and principles of the 1910s and 1920s, though the revolutionary works of that era were already awe-inspiring classics. By the late 1940s a narrowed modernist orthodoxy had evolved, based on selected features of the earlier upheavals. This later modernism – dominated by Eliot, upheld by Tate and Ransom, followed at that time by young poets like Wilbur, Lowell, Rich, Merwin, Simpson – advocated not free verse, collage, and open forms, but allusive, well-wrought, impersonal structures shaped by the balanced tensions of paradox and ambiguity. It was the existence of such an orthodoxy that made possible in the fifties a replay of the avant-garde energies of the twenties and the consequent shattering of orthodoxy (by the confessional writers, the Beats, the projectivist poets, the New York School, etc.) into a plurality of styles. In rebelling against the dominant mode of the fifties, the young poets could look to the earlier versions and practitioners of modernism not only as authorities to rebel against but also as models of iconoclasm and even as potential icons in a new tradition alternative to that authorized by Eliot and the New Critics.

Change and renewal are themselves sanctioned by the experimental tradition of modernism; as Ashbery says, "to be ambling on's / The tradition more than the safekeeping of it." This does not mean, however, that the younger artists who inherit avant-garde achievements are necessarily themselves avant-garde. Of the four discussed here, only Ashbery and Creeley have presented themselves in the avant-garde's adversarial relation to the dominant culture while fighting on the front line of poetic innovation. Yet as Hilton Kramer has observed, "the impulse to act as the creative conscience of a usable tradition was as much a part of the avant-garde scenario . . . as the impulse to wage war on the past."[3] All four of the poets I have considered engage in creative renewal of the deepest impulses of their cultural heritage. Bishop and Merrill, who are not concerned with establishing any marked contemporaneity and are not obviously subversive experimentalists, are nonetheless consciously involved in the revitalization of their tradition. Moreover, as I have shown, their methods of "re-making it new" are easily aligned with the more extreme measures of writers like Ashbery and Creeley. Whether or not contemporary authors may be considered avant-garde does not determine whether they can succeed in "ambling on" beyond modernism. As suggested in the Introduction, the considerable overlap among the four contemporaries in their divergence from modernism suggests that the term postmodernist, if used at all, may distinguish from the modernists not only the most radical and subversive recent artists but also a range of more conservative or more subtle innovators who also follow after, build upon, and transform the modernist achievements.

Those who follow immediately after a major artistic revolution inevitably live in the shadow of the great revolutionaries; they recognize the unlikelihood of accomplishing changes as sweeping and strikingly original as their immediate predecessors. Yet the most successful postmodernist writers have turned this situation to their own advantage in locating "The possibility of free declamation anchored / To a dull refrain." Whereas the modernists, to prove their difference from the Genteel Tradition they inherited, had to eschew a range of traditional forms and techniques, the next generation has not been so constrained. Enjoying an eclectic freedom the modernists could not afford, they have availed themselves of the resources of a wide variety of traditions, including those of Romantic poetry and of the nonverbal arts. Rather than competing with the monumental gestures of the modernists – "I don't much care for grand, all out efforts" in art, Bishop says, speaking for many of her peers[4] – the first postmodern generation has created an art more accepting of human limitations and of the world's disorder. In embracing the dull refrain of ordinary living, recent poets are willing to risk flatness and banality in attempting a poetry of credible affirmations through which one might appreciate "the charity of the hard moments."

Their modest acceptance of limitations need not mean diminished achievement or restricted liberty. Ashbery has explained this paradox in "The New Spirit":

One gets the narrowness into one's seeing, which also seems an inducement to moving forward into what one has already caught a glimpse of and which quickly becomes vision, in the visionary sense, except that in place of the panorama that used to be our customary setting and which we never made much use of, a limited but infinitely free space has established itself, useful as everyday life but transfigured so that its signs of wear no longer appear as a reproach but as indications of how beautiful a thing must have been to have been so much prized. (*Three Poems*, p. 27)

The limited field becomes an "infinitely free" one in which the ordinary is revealed as the startlingly valuable. The fictions of contemporary poetry are of a scale with the fictions of life – even if they seem at first tiny, like the painting in Bishop's "Poem," they are "about the size of our abidance." It is the triumph of the contemporary artist that there need be "no oracular amplification." The artist, as Merrill notes of Bishop, needn't "go about on stilts to make her [or his] vision wider."[5] Yet the best contemporaries do achieve a remarkable generosity of vision, equal to or (as in the case of Bishop/Moore) greater than that of their modernist models.

If indeed, as I believe, contemporary poets have engaged a "new spirit," they have done so through their coming to terms with the powerful tradition of modernism – both by drawing upon modernist achievements and by establishing their divergence from those achievements. That is true for an entire generation of poets, not just for the ones examined here. In this study Levertov, Ammons, even Ginsberg, O'Hara, or Lowell might have been paired with Williams; Rich, Nemerov, Hecht, or Hollander with Auden; Merwin or Wilbur with Stevens, and so forth. Whether or not they are easily paired with single modernists, virtually all the significant poets writing since World War II have assimilated multiple technical devices and aesthetic principles from the modernists and given them new life in original contexts. Like Ashbery, Bishop, and Merrill, the strongest of them have not been fettered – as Creeley has been – by excessive reverence for modernist principles or by a narrow sense of usable tradition. Consequently, since the 1950s this generation has accomplished a postmodern renewal; they have done so largely by immersing their art in the dynamic, ordinary present and in fluid consciousness (or subconsciousness), by exploring indeterminacy, by dissolving traditional polarities, by constantly questioning and pushing against the limits of language.

Of course, the four poets examined here can only approximately suggest what the other poets of their generation have made of the modernist tradition. None of them demonstrates, for instance, the transcendental impulses or the neo-surrealism cultivated by the deep image poets such as Bly, Simpson, Wright, and Kinnell. Yet the examples of Ashbery and Bishop do suggest that surrealism, so important to the beginnings of modernism but out of favor in the fifties, has been recently reclaimed. Nor do the four figures in this study suggest how many contemporary poets have undertaken direct political statement, during the Vietnam era and since. But while political writers like Rich or Levertov have explicitly ideological motives for questioning the truth value of language, for pointing to the ways in which language creates the world, even for exploring their personal experiences, they are caught in the same doubleness as the poets discussed here. They, too, are conscious of having to use language contaminated by systems of illusion (including the oppressors' power structures) in attempting to convey the different values of their own experience. Even if numerous recent poets fit some of the trends observed here, I am well aware that the "squamous" generalizations I offer are simplifications, at best approximate outlines of broad tendencies or possible grounds for productive controversy.

Despite the hazards of generalizing, it may be worth speculating about how the development of the poetic generation still coming into maturity follows from these patterns of affinity and divergence. After all, the living members of the generation born in the 1920s are now stately figures approaching their sixties, themselves the poetic establishment. What legacy have those who began publishing in the 1940s and early 1950s bequeathed to the poets born in those years? And what has been the impact of modernism on this younger generation? (Of course, answers offered now can reflect only the early, perhaps more derivative, achievements of the younger generation; they might be compared to speculations based on Ashbery's work only through *Rivers and Mountains*, Bishop's through *A Cold Spring*, or,Merrill's through *Water Street*.)

The most important legacy of the older contemporaries seems to me a permissive field of poetic possibility in which multiple styles can be practiced, varied voices heard. Some of our most promising young poets employ open forms; others contain their free verse within regular stanza and line lengths; and still others prefer exacting traditional forms. Some – like Louise Glück, Mary Oliver, or Robert Hass – use cleanly sculpted language, while others – C. K. Williams, Robert Pinsky, William Matthews, Douglas Crase, James McMichael, Frank Bidart – risk baggy discursive forms and prosaic diction. Some, like Edward Hirsch, Marilyn Hacker, or Alfred Corn, freely invoke a rich artistic tradition; others, more politically minded – say, Judy Grahn, Lucille Clifton, Ishmael Reed,

or Audre Lorde – prefer oral models; still others, like the
L=A=N=G=U=A=G=E poets, would suspend both oral and lyric
traditions in purely linguistic experimentation. Some, like Tess Gal-
lagher or Richard Kinney, tend toward hermeticism, while others like
Sharon Olds and Marge Piercy, are accessible and straightforward.

Those exploring the new discursiveness are widening paths Ashbery
cleared, and those pursuing abstract systems of language follow the lead
of Creeley's experiments. Formalists look to Merrill's example, and semi-
formalists to Bishop's. Yet the example of these contemporaries or others of approximately their generation – Bly, Kinnell, Levertov, Dorn,
Hugo, Van Duyn, O'Hara, Plath, Levine, Merwin, Wright, Kumin, or
older figures like Berryman, Roethke, Lowell, Rukeyser, Stafford, and
so forth – does not appear to have been experienced as an oppression
against which the next generation need rebel. Perhaps that is because of
the older contemporaries' overshadowed position in literary history.
Perhaps it is because they did win in their divergence from modernism a
relatively permissive atmosphere. (Even the sixties anthology wars and
the battles between raw and cooked poetry testify to a healthy sense of
options.) Whatever the reasons, there is now a comfortable continuity
between the poetic generation born in the twenties and the one born in
the forties. Generally, in the younger writers one can observe the same
avoidance of the sensational, the same modest sense of proportion, the
same exploration of the domestic, the personal, the mundane that characterizes the preceding generation.

One does, however, sense gradual changes – for instance, a strength-
ening of the Romantic sensibility. The prosaic, discursive strategies
prevalent today often disguise sweeping Romantic gestures by grounding them in "wastes of wrack and spill" or obscuring them in periphras-
tic structures.[6] The younger writers, like the preceding generation, insist
that we must see through the arbitrariness of fictional orders, but they
are less likely to resist the need for shapely illusions. William Matthews,
for instance, focuses his most recent volume, *A Happy Childhood*, on the
inadequacy and the inevitability of our fictions – not only of labels like
good and bad, but of patterns like causality or narrative coherence. But
he recommends that, rather than undercutting them, we cultivate the
quality of those fictions to which we are always married: "There's no
truth about your childhood, / though there's a story, yours to tend, //
like a fire or garden. Make it a good one, / since you'll have to live it
out, and all // its revisions, so long as you all shall live."[7]

Jorie Graham's "The Lady and the Unicorn and other Tapestries" can
more fully illustrate this younger generation's extension of the modernist
tradition.[8] The poem takes art as its subject, a typically modernist reflex-

ive gesture. Yet the unassuming, personal directness with which the opening lines announce the subject's significance is typically contemporary:

> If I have a faith it is something like this: this ordering of images
> within an atmosphere that will receive them, hold them
> in solution, unsolved.

The phrasing, like Bishop's, is tentative and approximate ("if," "something like"), and what it proposes, as we have come to expect, is an ordering that is not a closed totalizing. The play on "solution" as a solving and a dissolving calls attention to the fluidity of the poem's verbal order, and to the precariousness of oppositional categories. For the poet, as for her quail, the moment "held in place" can only be "a game they enter."

While Graham's proclamation about the ordering of images is "something like" her faith, what she sees in the personal domestic space of "our back field" "is" that faith. The ordinary geography in which she discovers meaning is comparable to Ashbery's "cool shady streets" or "bare fields." At the same time, the backyard quail Graham describes are obviously made of language – a varied diction easily ranging from the prosaic and technical to obviously aestheticized terms. Little attempt is made to represent the birds' palpable presence; what the poet can record is "their role in the design":

> And when they rise, straight up,
> to this or that limb in the snowfat fir, they seem
> – because the body drops
> so far below its wings –
> to also fall,
>
> like our best lies that make what's absolutely volatile
> look like it's weighted down – our whitest lie, *the beauti-*
> *ful.* . . .

Volatile: flying, changeable, transitory – linguistic meanings are necessarily multiple; the only absolute is flux, the only order explicitly fictive. In the descriptive lines, "their faces taupe and indigo and peeking gently out / from under hats like thread / and needle starting to / pull," the simile and the "poetic" delineations of color identify the poet's perspective as inescapably intertextual. The distinction between life and art dissolves, just as the perching quail dissolve into those in medieval tapestry. But that does not distress the contemporary poet; nor does it ultimately alienate her from sensation. For Graham presents the weaving of fictions as an act of love – love for the world as much as for ordering designs – one that has for centuries allowed us to weight down the volatile with physical pleasure:

> it is an ancient tree their eager eyes map out –
> playful and vengeful and symmetry-bound: where out of
> > love
>
>   the quail are woven
> into tapestries, and, stuffed
> with cardamon and pine-nuts
>
>   and a sprig of thyme.

Graham's quail that run "free and clocklike" invite comparison with Stevens' quail that "Whistle about us their spontaneous cries" and with the more famous birds of the same poem: "At evening, casual flocks of pigeons make / Ambiguous undulations as they sink, / Downward to darkness, on extended wings" ("Sunday Morning"). Stevens presents his birds as part of nature; their vitality may enter directly into human experience. Graham's birds, by contrast, are overtly mediated through language and perception. For Stevens it is the brevity of one's physical presence on earth, represented in the birds' flights, that gives life beauty: "death is the mother of beauty." For Graham, it is language – a tissue of lies – that generates beauty. Yet the pleasure of the "sweet berries" that ripen in Stevens' earthly paradise is accessible to her as well, in the naming of "cardamon and pine-nuts"; the effect of her deliberately linguistic tapestry is still to evoke sensations.

Graham's poem seems more immediately responsive to modernist texts like "Sunday Morning" than to poems by Bishop, Rich, Roethke, or Ashbery. For the poets of her generation, it is still the great modernists who stand as the most impressive authorities; their themes and theories, their technical innovations, their great works provide the framework for much contemporary writing. Because the modernist impact is more diffused now, members of the younger generation probably would not lend themselves to extended pairings with single modernists. Yet poets born in the forties, like those who began publishing in the forties, often define themselves by defining their relation to the modernists. And like the older postmodern generation of Ashbery, Bishop, Creeley, and Merrill, they find their own freedom in a revalued "dull refrain." Thus when Robert Hass, in "Songs to Survive the Summer," wonders how to help his daughter and himself deal with their fear of death, he thinks of Wallace Stevens.[9] When questioning the current adequacy of the answers he received from his poetic fathers, he alludes to the modernists:

> Should I whisper in her ear,
> death is the mother
> of beauty? Wooden
>
> nickels, kid? It's all in
> shapeliness, give your
> fears a shape?

Sharing the older postmodern generation's skepticism about escaping into fictive orders, Hass feels "uneasy" with the love of books. Yet by the poem's end, he must acknowledge that he can give his daughter only more stories, and that these "songs" he can bequeath to her, however "curiously shaped," inevitably give form. Their form, however, is distinctively contemporary in being modest and mundane: "every / thing touched casually," "all things lustered / by the steady thoughtlessness / of human use."

# Notes

## INTRODUCTION

1 Robert Pinsky, *The Situation of Poetry: Contemporary Poetry and Its Traditions* (Princeton: Princeton Univ. Press, 1976), p. vii.

2 Wallace Stevens, *The Collected Poems of Wallace Stevens* (New York: Alfred A. Knopf, 1954), p. 423.

3 See David Perkins, *A History of Modern Poetry: From the 1890s to the High Modernist Mode* (Cambridge: Harvard Univ. Press, 1976), p. 297ff.

4 Ezra Pound, "A Retrospect," *Literary Essays of Ezra Pound*, ed. T. S. Eliot (New York: New Directions, 1968), p. 12.

5 Since 1957, when Kermode's *Romantic Image* and Langbaum's *The Poetry of Experience* first appeared, scholars have repeatedly suggested that modernist poetics are in fact outgrowths of Romantic poetics. (For a more recent example, see George Bornstein's *Transformations of Romanticism in Yeats, Eliot, and Stevens* [Chicago: Univ. of Chicago Press, 1976].) Scholars have been slower to look beneath the modernists' anti-Victorian proclamations, but Carol Christ has recently done so in *Victorian and Modern Poetics* (Chicago: Univ. of Chicago Press, 1984).

6 Malcolm Bradbury and James McFarlane, "The Name and Nature of Modernism," *Modernism: 1890–1930*, ed. Bradbury and McFarlane (Harmondsworth: Penguin, 1976), p. 27.

7 Hugh Kenner, *The Pound Era* (Berkeley: Univ. of California Press, 1971), p. 24. See also the chapter "Renaissance II," pp. 41–53.

8 Kenner, *The Pound Era*, p. 67. See the entire chapter, "The Muse in Tatters," pp. 54–75. Some material later in this paragraph derives from the chapter "The Invention of Language," pp. 94–120.

9 T. S. Eliot, "*Ulysses*, Order and Myth," *Selected Prose of T. S. Eliot*, ed. Frank Kermode (New York: Harcourt Brace Jovanovich, 1975), p. 177. This essay first appeared in *The Dial*, November 1923.

10 William Carlos Williams, *The Autobiography of William Carlos Williams* (1951; rpt. New York: New Directions, 1967), p. 174.

268

11  Pound, "A Retrospect," p. 11.

12  Some recent feminist poets, and poets who speak for ethnic minorities, are partial exceptions. They have tried to unearth not only those aspects of past cultures that are responsible for their oppression, but also the suppressed traditions and myths that assert their people's persistent dignity and power. Yet such revisionary archeology, often emphasizing folk arts, differs from Eliot's nostalgic attempts to sustain the tradition of high art by retrieving fragments of earlier dominant cultures to shore up a crumbling civilization.

13  See Walter Jackson Bate, *The Burden of the Past and the English Poet* (Cambridge: Belknap Press of Harvard Univ. Press, 1970) and Harold Bloom, *The Anxiety of Influence: A Theory of Poetry* (New York: Oxford Univ. Press, 1973). Bate emphasizes the increasingly destructive consequences of intensifying pressures upon artists not to follow closely what they admire. Bloom focuses on the individual poet's battles with a particular forerunner and with certain of the forerunner's poems, believing that progress occurs through deliberate misinterpretation of an earlier artist's works. I share these critics' belief that in an era that prizes originality, poets naturally feel anxious that their predecessors may have exhausted the innovative resources of language and poetic form. However, I do not share Bate's belief that this burden is resulting in artistic paralysis, and my interest is in broader affinities than those upon which Bloom bases his theory of influence.

14  John Ashbery, "Willem de Kooning," *Art News Annual*, 37 (October 1971): 120.

15  Marjorie Perloff, *The Poetics of Indeterminacy: Rimbaud to Cage* (Princeton: Princeton Univ. Press, 1981). She distinguishes this tradition from that of Baudelaire and Mallarmé, which "point[s] the way to the 'High Modernism' of Yeats and Eliot and Auden, Stevens and Frost and Crane, and their Symbolist heirs like Lowell and Berryman" (p. 4). In "Contemporary / Postmodern: The 'New' Poetry?" *Bucknell Review*, 25 (1980): 171–9, Perloff's list of postmodern artists essentially duplicates her list of artists in Rimbaud's tradition of indeterminacy. Though Perloff's caution against simplistic chronologizing is valuable, and her definitions of postmodern impulses helpful, her scheme seems to me unrealistically tidy and atemporal.

16  I employ the term to suggest not a cutoff from modernism, but rather the strong continuities between modernist and contemporary writing. Recent artists, even when responding innovatively to poststructuralist theories not articulated or widely circulated in the first half of this century, are often using and developing selected strands from the fabric of modernist poetics.

17  For a bibliography pertinent to this debate as conducted before 1974, see Maurice Beebe, "What Modernism Was," *Journal of Modern Literature*, 3 (July 1974): 1080–4. Ihab Hassan, David Antin, and Majorie Perloff, among others, have since continued to investigate the application of the terms "modernist" and "postmodernist" to contemporary poetry.

18  *Earth Hard* (London: Rapp & Whiting, 1968), p. 10.

19  Irving Howe, *Decline of the New* (New York: Harcourt, Brace and World, 1970), p. 12.

20  "*Ulysses*, Order, and Myth," p. 177.
21  *Corsons Inlet* (Ithaca: Cornell Univ. Press, 1965).
22  Pinsky focuses on this conflict in *The Situation of Poetry*.
23  *Praise* (New York: Ecco Press, 1979), p. 4.
24  This aspect of recent writing is Charles Altieri's focus in *Enlarging the Temple: New Directions in American Poetry during the 1960s* (Lewisburg: Bucknell University Press, 1979). He identifies the postmodern with "immanentist" (as opposed to symbolist) modes of poetic thought; in a poetic of immanence, "poets conceive their work as presenting the action of disclosure rather than of creating order . . . . aesthetic elements have primarily epistemological rather than interpretive functions" (p. 24).
25  Alan Williamson's recent book, *Introspection and Contemporary Poetry* (Cambridge: Harvard Univ. Press, 1984), focuses on subjectivism as the defining characteristic of contemporary poetry.

## CHAPTER 1

1  "A Place for Everything," *Art News,* 69 (March 1970); 33, 73. Ashbery is discussing the work of Anne Ryan.
2  A. Poulin, Jr., "The Experience of Experience: A Conversation with John Ashbery," *Michigan Quarterly Review*, 20 (Summer 1981): 247. The conversation was conducted late in 1972.
3  "An Interview With John Ashbery," *San Francisco Review of Books*, 3 (November 1977): 8.
4  Three hundred copies of *Turandot and Other Poems* were printed by Tiber de Nagy Gallery, New York, in 1953. Almost all the poems in that volume were reprinted in *Some Trees*.
5  The following abbreviations appear as parenthetic citations in this chapter and in Chapter 2:

> CP   Wallace Stevens, *The Collected Poems of Wallace Stevens* (New York: Knopf, 1954)
>
> OP   Wallace Stevens, *Opus Posthumous* (New York: Knopf, 1957)
>
> NA   Wallace Stevens, *The Necessary Angel: Essays on Reality and the Imagination* (New York: Knopf, 1951)
>
> ST   John Ashbery, *Some Trees* (New York: Ecco, 1978)
>
> RM   John Ashbery, *Rivers and Mountains* (New York, Ecco, 1977)
>
> DD   John Ashbery, *The Double Dream of Spring* (New York, Ecco, 1976)
>
> TP   John Ashbery, *Three Poems* (New York: Viking, 1972)

6  See CP 153, 178, 197, 269 for examples of Stevens' use of the adjective "fat" to suggest the potent poet's sensual engagement with reality and his imaginative fecundity. Thinness indicates an alienation from the "physical poetry" in which we live and, consequently, imaginative sterility. Thus the "large red man" who reads from the "poem of life" is contrasted to the ghosts whose hearts are "thin" and "spended" (CP 424). Similarly, the men of

Haddam who are blind to the richness of their world are characterized as "thin" (CP 93).

7  "The Qualified Assertions of Wallace Stevens," *The Act of the Mind: Essays on the Poetry of Wallace Stevens*, ed. Roy Harvey Pearce and J. Hillis Miller (Baltimore: Johns Hopkins Press, 1965), p. 163.

8  *On Extended Wings: Wallace Stevens' Longer Poems* (Cambridge: Harvard Univ. Press, 1969), p. 13.

9  "The Craft of John Ashbery" [an interview by Louis A. Osti], *Confrontations* 9 (Fall 1974): 88.

10  As Vendler has pointed out, questions are "one of the natural forms in which [Stevens'] mind casts its observations" (*On Extended Wings*, p. 20); they "serve as a qualified way to put a premise" (p. 18). For examples of Stevens using questions to suggest an argument, see CP 168, 173, 202–3.

11  For example, the closing stanza of "The Ordinary Women" repeats the opening stanza; the last line of "The Worms at Heaven's Gate" repeats the first line. Variations of phrases repeat in "Anecdote of Men by the Thousand," "Anecdote of the Prince of Peacocks,," "Cortège for Rosenbloom," "Valley Candle," and "Domination of Black."

12  "Craft Interview with John Ashbery," *The Craft of Poetry: Interviews from the New York Quarterly*, ed. William Packard (Garden City: Doubleday, 1974), p. 116.

13  At no point do I intend to imply that Stevens is the only significant influence on Ashbery's work. Auden's strong influence may be detected in *Some Trees*, the influences of Mallarmé, Valéry, Baudelaire, and Eliot (particularly *Four Quartets*) in *Rivers and Mountains*. For discussion of these and other influences see David Shapiro, *John Ashbery: An Introduction to the Poetry* (New York: Columbia Univ. Press, 1979). Alan Williamson discusses Ashbery's "misprision of Baudelaire" in "The Skaters" in *Introspection and Contemporary Poetry* (Cambridge: Harvard Univ. Press, 1984), pp. 128–31.

14  "John Ashbery: An Interview by Ross Labrie," *American Poetry Review*, 13 (May/June 1984): 30.

15  Ibid.

16  *Contemporary Poets of the English Language*, ed. Rosalie Murphy (Chicago: St. James Press, 1970), p. 33.

17  Ibid.

18  The interdependence and ultimate unity of opposites is a recurrent motif in Stevens; see, for instance, CP 215–16, 392. In *On Extended Wings* Vendler points out that Stevens, attached to "paradoxical logic," deceptively employs the language of logical discrimination not to distinguish, but to identify different or alternative categories with each other (p. 37). In this identification, he anticipates what I regard as a central trait of much contemporary poetry.

19  Ashbery discusses the autobiographical aspect of this poem in "Craft Interview with John Ashbery," pp. 119, 123.

20  Bernard Heringman lists Stevens' "stock symbols" as follows: "The moon, blue, the polar north, winter, music, poetry and all art: these consistently refer to the realm of imagination, order, the ideal. The sun, yellow, the

tropic south, summer, physical nature: these refer to, or symbolize, the realm of reality, disorder, the actual" ("Wallace Stevens: The Use of Poetry," *The Act of the Mind*, p. 1). For further discussion of Stevens' symbolism and his seasonal cycle, see Frank Kermode, *Wallace Stevens* (London: Oliver & Boyd, 1960), pp. 34–7; Richard A. Macksey, "The Climates of Wallace Stevens," *The Act of the Mind*, pp. 185–223; Northrop Frye, "The Realistic Oriole: A Study of Wallace Stevens," *Wallace Stevens: A Collection of Critical Essays*, ed. Marie Borroff (Englewood Cliffs, N.J.: Prentice-Hall, 1963), pp. 161–76.

21    Bonnie Costello makes a similar point when discussing Ashbery's "love of surface . . . casting up images for their own sake, redundant in meaning but infinite in texture" in "John Ashbery and the Idea of the Reader," *Contemporary Literature*, 23 (1982): 506.

22    I follow Harold Bloom in using these two quotations to compare the two poets. See "John Ashbery: The Charity of the Hard Moments," *Salmagundi*, 22–23 (Spring–Summer 1973): 112. In that article Bloom presents Ashbery as a descendent of Emerson and of the English Romantics, identifying the Romantic roots on which I focus in discussing *Double Dream*.

23    Originality is also an important criterion by which Ashbery as art critic evaluates others' work. For a few examples from his criticism of the sixties, see "American Sanctuary in Paris," *Art News Annual*, 31 (1966): 164; "Can Art be Excellent if Anybody Could Do It?" *New York Herald Tribune*, European ed., 8 November 1961, p. 11; "Poet-Painter Reflects Self in Paris Show," *New York Herald Tribune*, European ed., 16 February 1965, p. 5.

24    *The Situation of Poetry*, p. 47.

25    Ibid., p. 62.

26    S. T. Coleridge, *Biographia Literaria*, ed. J. Shawcross (1907; London: Oxford Univ. Press, 1973), vol. 1, p. 208.

27    Pinksy makes similar claims about Berryman in *The Situation of Poetry*, especially pp. 25, 36–7.

28    P. B. Shelley, "A Defense of Poetry," *English Romantic Writers*, ed. David Perkins (New York: Harcourt, Brace & World, 1967), p. 1085.

29    Dry academic rhetoric is particularly prevalent in Stevens' *Parts of a World*. See, for example, "Prelude to Objects" (CP 194), "Connoisseur of Chaos" (CP 215–16), "Extracts from Addresses to the Academy of Fine Ideas" (CP 252–9).

30    "Grey Eminence," *Art News*, 71 (March 1972): 64; "Brooms and Prisms," *Art News*, 65 (March 1966): 58; "G. M. P.," *Art News*, 69 (February 1971): 46, 74.

31    See, for example, "Brooms and Prisms," p. 58, and "Willem de Kooning," p. 126.

32    A. Poulin, Jr., "The Experience of Experience: A Conversation with John Ashbery," p. 251.

33    Bloom, "John Ashbery," p. 108.

34    For a detailed reading that includes consideration of the relation of "Fragment" to Stevens' work, see Charles Berger, "Vision in the Form of a Task: *The Double Dream of Spring*," *Beyond Amazement*, pp. 190–208.

35 "Craft Interview with John Ashbery," p. 123.
36 Hugh Kenner, *A Homemade World: The American Modernist Writers* (New York: William Morrow, 1975), p. 51.
37 Ronald Sukenick, *Wallace Stevens: Musing the Obscure* (New York: New York Univ. Press, 1967), p. 3.
38 *On Extended Wings*, p. 21.


## CHAPTER 2

1 John Ashbery, "They Came from Inner Space," *Art News*, 66 (December 1967): 58.
2 Ashbery, "Willem de Kooning," p. 128.
3 Both phrases are from Ashbery, "Can Art be Excellent if Anybody Could Do It?" p. 11.
4 John Ashbery, "Gauguin: The Hidden Tradition," *Art News*, 65 (Summer 1966): 29. Ashbery paraphrases the same statement in "In Memory of My Feelings," *Art News*, 66 (January 1968): 51. He uses Busoni's exact words in "The Invisible Avant-garde," *Art News Annual*, 34 (October 1968): 132.
5 Ashbery states this in his "Introduction" to *The Collected Poems of Frank O'Hara* (New York: Alfred A. Knopf, 1971), p. vii.
6 John Ashbery, "Frank O'Hara, 1926–1966," *Art News*, 65 (September 1966): 45.
7 Ashbery, "Willem de Kooning," p. 120.
8 Ashbery, "Introduction," *The Collected Poems of Frank O'Hara*, p. vii. In this passage Ashbery is actually describing the roots of O'Hara's work, but the two friends followed parallel courses in their early development. Furthermore, as Ashbery says, "poets when they write about other artists always tend to write about themselves" ("G.M.P.," p. 45).
9 In discussing with Moramarco Roussel's influence on his work, Ashbery declared, "I think the main lesson for my work that I have drawn from him is his uniqueness. I would like my work to be as unique (but in other ways, of course) as Roussel's, if that were possible." *Beyond Amazement*, p. 279.
10 John Ashbery, "Growing up Surreal," *Art News*, 67 (May 1968): 41.
11 John Ashbery, "Surrealist Revival May Be on Way," *New York Herald Tribune*, European ed., 30 May 1962, p. 5. Michaux made this remark in an interview with Ashbery recorded in "Henri Michaux: Painter inside Poet," *Art News*, 60 (March 1961): 64.
12 John Ashbery, letter to the author, 15 January 1979, quoted by permission of John Ashbery.
13 Ashbery, "Frank O'Hara," p. 45.
14 For detailed discussion of Ashbery's relation to abstract expressionism, see Fred Moramarco, "John Ashbery and Frank O'Hara: The Painterly Poets," *Journal of Modern Literature*, 5 (1976): 436–62; and Leslie Wolf, "The Brushstroke's Integrity: The Poetry of John Ashbery and the Art of Painting," *Beyond Amazement: New Essays on John Ashbery*, ed. David Lehman (Ithaca: Cornell Univ. Press, 1980), pp. 224-54.

15  "The Craft of John Ashbery," p. 89.
16  Harold Rosenberg, "The American Action Painters," *Art News*, 51 (December 1952; rpt. in *American Art 1700–1960*, ed. John W. McCoubrey (Englewood Cliffs, N.J.: Prentice-Hall, 1965), p. 215.
17  Rosenberg, "American Action Painters," p. 217.
18  Richard Kostelanetz, "How to be a Difficult Poet" [interview with John Ashbery], *The New York Times Magazine*, 23 May 1976, p. 20.
19  Ashbery, "Introduction," *The Collected Poems of Frank O'Hara*, p. ix.
20  Shapiro, *John Ashbery*, p. 27.
21  I employ this phrase in the sense that emerges from Helen Vendler's discussions of Stevens' style in Chapter 1 of *On Extended Wings* and in "The Qualified Assertions of Wallace Stevens," *The Act of the Mind*. In addition, F. O. Matthiessen used the title "In the Optative Mood" for the chapter in *American Renaissance* (New York: Oxford Univ. Press, 1941) devoted to Emerson's poetics, and there are affinities between Stevens' poetics and Emerson's desire that art "create an ideal world better than the world of experience" (p. 52).
22  Richard Kostelanetz, *John Cage* (New York: Praeger Publishers, 1970), p. 133.
23  The title also alludes to Louis David's painting of this historical event. For discussion of the painting's relevance to the poem, see Shapiro, *John Ashbery*, p. 54. Jerome J. McGann also discusses the relation between this title and Ashbery's method in "Formalism, Savagery, and Care; or, The Function of Criticism Once Again," *Critical Inquiry*, 2 (Spring 1976): 620–1.
24  Kostelanetz, "How to be a Difficult Poet," p. 22.
25  Marjorie Perloff has published several articles on Ashbery's "preoccupation with dream structure," including " 'Fragments of a Buried Life': John Ashbery's Dream Songs" in *Beyond Amazement* and Chapter 7 of *The Poetics of Indeterminacy: Rimbaud to Cage* (Princeton: Princeton Univ. Press, 1981).
26  In addition to the abbreviations introduced in Chapter 1, the following abbreviations to works by John Ashbery appear as parenthetic citations in this chapter:

| | |
|---|---|
| TCO | *The Tennis Court Oath* (Middletown, Conn.: Wesleyan Univ. Press, 1962) |
| SP | *Self-Portrait in a Convex Mirror* (New York: Viking Press, 1975) |
| HBD | *Houseboat Days* (New York: Viking Press, 1977) |
| AWK | *As We Know* (New York: Viking Press, 1979) |
| ShTn | *Shadow Train* (New York: Viking Press, 1981) |
| W | *A Wave* (New York: Viking Press, 1984) |

27  For a different view, see Fred Moramarco, "The Lonesomeness of Words: A Revaluation of *The Tennis Court Oath*," in *Beyond Amazement*. Moramarco argues that many of the volume's poems can be approached through rather traditional close readings. His readings, however, are actually untra-

ditional in having to speculate so much about the procession of the poet's associations. Far more persuasive is his claim that Ashbery in this volume is concerned with the generative potential of language.

28 "Craft Interview with John Ashbery," p. 116. Also in Kostelanetz, "How to be a Difficult Poet," p. 30, Ashbery declared, "I'm bored by the automatic writing of orthodox surrealism."

29 John Ashbery (with David Soroushian-Kermani), "Taking Care of the Luxuries," *Saturday Review; The Arts,* 4 November 1972, p. 63.

30 This interest in the effect groupings have on the perceiving mind is also central to Ashbery's 1975 volume, *The Vermont Notebook* (Santa Barbara: Black Sparrow Press, 1978).

31 "The Craft of John Ashbery," p. 87.

32 Kostelanetz, "How to be a Difficult Poet," p. 33.

33 "The Craft of John Ashbery," p. 95.

34 "Craft Interview with John Ashbery," p. 121.

35 "The Craft of John Ashbery," p. 95.

36 Kostelanetz, "How to be a Difficult Poet," p. 26.

37 "Craft Interview with John Ashbery," p. 126.

38 Kostelanetz, "How to be a Difficult Poet," p. 30.

39 "Craft Interview with John Ashbery," p. 127.

40 Ibid., p. 128.

41 In *The Situation of Poetry*, Pinsky complains that the "abstraction" of Ashbery's language is too pure, too nonrepresentational. Though certainly correct that Ashbery's language is often "isolated from all but the ghost of an apprehensible world" (p. 78), Pinsky fails to appreciate the extent to which Ashbery's abstractions represent a genuine transcendence of the Romantic agony over the impossibility of approaching nature through language. Ashbery has freed himself from the Romantic obsession with unreflective physical reality; he places no greater value on portraying or entering that realm than on capturing reflective intellectual experience.

42 "Craft Interview with John Ashbery," p. 128.

43 This is how Ashbery explains the poem in his "Craft Interview," pp. 131–2.

44 In a 1977 interview Ashbery described himself as reading and writing "for escapist purposes," but in the context he seemed only to be differentiating himself from confessional writers: When writing, he wishes to escape from his private suffering and from the intimate details of his personal history. ("An Interview with John Ashbery," *San Francisco Review of Books,* November 1977, p. 8.)

45 "Craft Interview with John Ashbery," p. 122. In a 1982 interview he goes further, declaring that time is "what I have been writing about all these years during which I thought I wasn't writing about anything" ("John Ashbery: An Interview by Ross Labrie," *American Poetry Review,* 13 [May/June 1984] p. 29).

46 See Henri Bergson, *Time and Free Will* (1910; rpt. New York: Harper & Row, 1960), especially Chapter 2.

47    *The Pound Era*, p. 69.

48    This passage echoes the opening of section V of "East Coker," in which Eliot describes himself "trying to learn to use words," finding that

> what there is to conquer
> By strength and submission, has already been discovered
> Once or twice, or several times, by men whom one cannot hope
> To emulate – but there is no competition –
> There is only the fight to recover what has been lost
> And found and lost again and again.

In alluding to this passage written in 1940, Ashbery ironically underlines his own lateness.

49    "John Ashbery: An Interview by Ross Labrie," p. 29.

50    Ashbery, "Taking Care of the Luxuries," p. 63.

51    Knowing that David Kermani – Ashbery's bibliographer, frequent companion, and the man to whom this volume is dedicated – is a Persian scholar reinforces the poem's effect of autobiographical immediacy.

52    This poem is the most frequently and best explicated of all Ashbery's works. See, for example, David Kalstone, *Five Temperaments* (New York: Oxford Univ. Press, 1977), pp. 175–85; Charles Altieri, "Motives in Metaphor: John Ashbery and the Modernist Long Poem," *Genre*, 11 (1978): 676–87; Costello, "John Ashbery and the Idea of the Reader," pp. 501–9.

53    This quotation and all those preceding in this paragraph are from Ashbery, "The Invisible Avant-garde," pp. 131, 132.

54    Ibid., p. 128.

55    Kostelanetz, "How to be a Difficult Poet," p. 30.

56    "John Ashbery: An Interview by Ross Labrie," p. 32.

57    A. Poulin, Jr., "The Experience of Experience: A Conversation with John Ashbery," p. 251.

58    "John Ashbery: An Interview by Ross Labrie," p. 31.

59    Ashbery, "Taking Care of the Luxuries," p. 63.

60    For an excellent discussion of Ashbery's polyvocality, see Lawrence Kramer, " 'Syringa': John Ashbery and Elliott Carter," *Beyond Amazement*, pp. 255–71. Kramer's definition of Ashbery's two dominant voices, the elegiac and the meditative, proves useful for discriminating the "brass" and "silver" voices of "Litany." The right-hand italic column seems to me the elegiac voice, lamenting absence and longing for love.

61    For a provocative critique of this volume, of Ashbery's work in general, and of his critics, see William Harmon, "Orphic Bankruptcy, Deficit Spending," *Parnassus*, 8 (Fall/Winter 1979): 213-20. Harmon considers "Litany" to be "a big nothing."

62    Helen Vendler, "Making It New," *New York Review of Books*, 14 June 1984, p. 33.

63    "John Ashbery: An Interview by Ross Labrie" was conducted in June 1982 in the hospital where Ashbery was "recuperating from major surgery and a

grave spinal infection that had threatened his life earlier in the spring" (p. 29).

## CHAPTER 3

1 Ann Winslow, ed., *Trial Balances* (New York: Macmillan, 1935), pp. 79, 80.
2 Winslow, *Trial Balances*, p. 83.
3 "A Modest Expert," *The Nation*, 28 September 1946, p. 354; rpt. in *Elizabeth Bishop and Her Art*, ed. Lloyd Schwartz and Sybil P. Estess (Ann Arbor: Univ. of Michigan Press, 1983), p. 178.
4 Bishop delightfully portrays Moore and her relationship with Moore in "Efforts of Affection," *The Collected Prose* (New York: Farrar, Straus & Giroux, 1984), pp. 121–56. In that memoir, Bishop claims she invited Moore to the circus at their first meeting, but the correspondence indicates she actually proposed that first outing by mail several weeks later. In "Efforts of Affection" Bishop also insists that Moore offered to write the commentary for *Trial Balances*, but in an interview with George Starbuck she recalls timidly asking Moore to perform the task.

   For a detailed discussion of Moore's impact on Bishop's development as documented in the correspondence, see my article "Words Worth a Thousand Postcards: The Bishop/Moore Correspondence," *American Literature*, 55 (1983): 405–29. For other discussions of the connections between Bishop and Moore, see Bonnie Costello, "Marianne Moore and Elizabeth Bishop: Friendship and Influence," *Twentieth Century Literature*, 30 (Summer/Fall 1984): 130–49 and David Kalstone, "Trial Balances: Elizabeth Bishop and Marianne Moore," *Grand Street*, 3 (Autumn 1983): 115–35.
5 Throughout this chapter I am indebted to Chapters 5 and 6 of Borroff's *Language and the Poet* (Chicago: Univ. of Chicago Press, 1979). In linking Moore's poetry with promotional prose, Borroff does not suggest that Moore is in any crude way an advertiser. Moore uses journalistic techniques to dramatize her subjects so that her readers will share her genuine sense of wonder and her recognition of a link between what is aesthetically or mechanically pleasing and what is morally admirable.
6 Borroff, *Language and the Poet*, p. 82.
7 Letters from Moore to Bishop are in the Elizabeth Bishop Collection, Rare Books and Manuscripts, Vassar College Library; Moore's copies of some of her letters to Bishop are in the Marianne Moore Collection, Rosenbach Museum and Library, Philadelphia. Unpublished work by Marianne Moore is here printed by permission of Clive E. Driver, Literary Executor of the Estate of Marianne C. Moore.
8 The following abbreviations appear as parenthetic citations in this chapter and in Chapter 4:

   CP    Elizabeth Bishop, *The Complete Poems: 1927–1979* (New York: Farrar, Straus & Giroux, 1983)

CPr    Elizabeth Bishop, *The Collected Prose* (New York: Farrar, Straus & Giroux, 1984)

CPM    Marianne Moore, *The Complete Poems of Marianne Moore* (New York: Viking, 1981)

MMR    Marianne Moore, *A Marianne Moore Reader* (New York: Viking, 1961)

9   In comparing passages from *North & South* to Moore's poetry, I have restricted myself to poems that appeared in Moore's *Selected Poems* (1935), which includes almost all of Moore's first book, *Observations* (1924). Bishop wrote many of the poems in *North & South* before the 1941 publication of Moore's *What Are Years*. Bishop followed the publication of Moore's poems in small magazines, but by referring only to early works by Moore, I easily ensure that the lines cited would actually have been seen by Bishop before she composed the poems in *North & South*.

10   Borroff, *Language and the Poet*, p. 111.

11   Jarrell's review of *North & South*, originally published in *Partisan Review* 13, was reprinted in *Poetry and the Age* (New York: Knopf, 1953), pp. 212–14 and in *Elizabeth Bishop and Her Art*, pp. 180–1.

12   Pinsky, *The Situation of Poetry*, p. 76. In this paragraph I make use of Pinsky's notion of the dilemma at the heart of modern poetry, which he presents as an inheritance from the nineteenth-century Romantic poets.

13   Perkins, *A History of Modern Poetry*, p. 556.

14   *A Homemade World*, p. 118.

15   This poem, another of Bishop's personal favorites, was not reprinted in *The Complete Poems*. This quote appears on p. 47 of the 1951 *Collected Poems* (New York: Macmillan).

16   "As We Like It," *Quarterly Review of Literature* (Marianne Moore Issue), 4, no. 2 (1948): 135.

17   "Roosters" was written in 1940, and Bishop has since remarked that "the second world war was going on, and it's about that, more or less" (" 'The Work!': A Conversation with Elizabeth Bishop" [interview by George Starbuck], *Ploughshares*, 3, nos. 3 and 4 [1977]: 19).

18   This phrase is from W. C. Williams' essay "Marianne Moore," which originally appeared in *The Dial*, May 1925, and is reprinted in *Marianne Moore*, ed. Charles Tomlinson (Englewood Cliffs: Prentice-Hall, 1969), p. 54.

19   Ashley Brown, "An Interview with Elizabeth Bishop," *Shenandoah*, 17 (Winter 1966): 5.

20   Kenner, *A Homemade World*, p. 98.

21   Ibid., p. 102.

22   Williams, "Marianne Moore," p. 57.

23   T. S. Eliot, "Introduction" to Moore's *Selected Poems*, reprinted in Tomlinson, *Marianne Moore*, p. 61.

24   *Times Literary Supplement*, 21 July 1921, p. 471. The comment is typical of the reviews her first book received on both sides of the Atlantic.

25   T. S. Eliot, "Book Reviews," *The Dial*, 75 (December 1923): 595.

26  In *Language and the Poet*, p. 110, Borroff lists some of Moore's poems for which the sources are known to be pictures. Even when Moore's scenes do not originate in photographs, Borroff points out that "In poems about places, the content of key passages seems chosen as a professional photographer assigned to illustrate a magazine article might choose scenes in a locale" (p. 112).

27  Borroff discusses this "discrepancy between representation and experience" in Moore's work (*Language and the Poet*, p. 113). On the same page Borroff notes that Moore's "word photographs bespeak an *intellectual* curiosity as readily satisfied by the printed page as by visible phenomena themselves"; I make use of her observation here.

28  Admittedly, Moore's descriptive comparisons that bring together odd and unrelated phenomena might give an impression of arbitrariness. But Kenner is correct that Moore's strange systems of analogies are not analogies for the actual object but for the "eye's act responding" to it (*A Homemade World*, p. 97). Moore found a cubistic approach necessary for creating an object on the page with language; she did not regard that randomness or disjunction as inherent in the thing itself.

29  Of course, such "seeming" may be deceptive. Bonnie Costello argues in *Marianne Moore: Imaginary Possessions* (Cambridge: Harvard Univ. Press, 1981) that there is a dynamic tension in Moore's work between observing and making observations, between representation and association. She claims there is an associational structure to Moore's images, a claim well demonstrated in her reading of "The Fish" (pp. 70–4). She asserts further that "Moore's compositions are trails of associations which conduct the reader to the writer, their source. This identification occurs not only through our vicarious experience of her mental flux, but through her final, and distinct if subtle, self-portraiture" (p. 95). Nonetheless, I would argue (and Costello might well agree) that Moore's poetry is not as personally revealing as Bishop's. Both associational structure and self-portraiture are notably less subtle and less guarded in Bishop's work than in Moore's.

30  See Kenner, *A Homemade World*, pp. 92–4. His entire chapter, "Disliking It," is an excellent essay on Moore.

31  My understanding of Baudelaire's theories derives from the notes by Antoine Adam on pp. 270–7 of his edition of Baudelaire, *Les Fleurs du Mal* (Paris: Garnier Freres, 1961). Quotations in French are from the sonnet "Correspondances," p. 13.

32  Stevenson, *Elizabeth Bishop*, p. 66.

33  Stevens, *The Complete Poems*, p. 383.

34  Borroff, *Language and the Poet*, p. 101. Borroff invokes the grammatical distinction between "stative" and "dynamic" words and discusses the various stative characteristics of Moore's language to demonstrate how her language attempts to hold its subject matter constant; see pp. 96–108.

35  For detailed discussion of this break between Bishop and Moore that followed Moore's meddling with "Roosters," see my article "Words Worth a Thousand Postcards."

36   "Elizabeth Bishop: Influences," *American Poetry Review*, 14 (January/February 1985): 14.

## CHAPTER 4

1   In "Trial Balances: Elizabeth Bishop and Marianne Moore," Kalstone points out that "Many of [Bishop's] best poems of the 1930s can be read as versions of seventeenth-century poems about the soul trapped in the body" (p. 123).

2   Moore's "A Grave" provides one notable exception to this generalization. There the sea is a "rapacious" nullifying force, and human vision cannot penetrate its deceptive surface. In her talk on "Influences" Bishop named "A Grave" as one of her favorite Moore poems.

3   Bishop's affinities with Wordsworth are particularly strong and have been discussed in several essays included by Lloyd Schwartz and Sybil P. Estess in *Elizabeth Bishop and Her Art*; see especially Robert Pinsky, "The Idiom of a Self: Elizabeth Bishop and Wordsworth," pp. 49–60 and Willard Spiegelman, "Elizabeth Bishop's 'Natural Heroism'," pp. 154–71.

4   "Laureate's Words of Acceptance," *World Literature Today*, 51 (Winter 1977): 12.

5   In this chapter I am much indebted to Helen Vendler's article "Domestication, Domesticity and the Otherworldly," *World Literature Today*, 51 (Winter 1977): 23–8 (also reprinted in *Elizabeth Bishop and Her Art*). Vendler points to the centrality of efforts to domesticate in Bishop's poems and to the interpenetration of the domestic and the strange in her world. She provides marvelous readings of "Sestina," "First Death in Nova Scotia," "Poem," "Crusoe in England," and "The Moose." Bishop herself, in her interview with Starbuck, *Ploughshares*, p. 13, referred to Vendler's essay as a "wonderful paper."

6   Moore submitted this review to several journals in the spring of 1937, but it was not published during her lifetime. This passage is quoted in Costello, *Marianne Moore: Imaginary Possessions*, p. 203.

7   "The Art of Poetry XXVII: Elizabeth Bishop" [interview with Elizabeth Spires], *Paris Review*, 80 (Summer 1981): 76.

8   Brown, "An Interview with Elizabeth Bishop," p. 13.

9   Stevenson, pp. 68, 132.

10   The first phrase appears in Brown's interview, p. 10, the second, actually Bishop quoting Coleridge, in "Influences," p. 11.

11   For discussions of Bishop's relation to surrealism, see Richard Mullen, "Elizabeth Bishop's Surrealist Inheritance," *American Literature*, 54 (March 1982): 63–80; and more briefly, Bonnie Costello, "The Complete Elizabeth Bishop," *Poetry*, (July 1983): 233–5 and Kalstone, "Trial Balances," 122–5.

12   In her fine essay, "The Eye of the Outsider," Adrienne Rich links Bishop's themes of marginality and outsiderhood, as well as her preoccupation with inversion, to Bishop's lesbian identity (*Boston Review*, 8 [April 1983]: 15–17). Since Moore did not act out a sexual identity widely regarded as a distortion, she would have been less likely to identify revelation with distor-

tion. Nor did Moore share Bishop's interest in dreams; she once tried (too late) to ward off a dream book Bishop wanted to send her (26 July 1941).

13 Anne Stevenson, "Letters from Elizabeth Bishop," *TLS*, 7 March 1980, p. 261.

14 Many of Bishop's translations of poems by Brazillian poets may also be regarded as tributes to artists who explore the unconscious "market of desires," pushing "into the forbidden / time, forbidden places" more easily than she herself does (CP 246, 247).

15 Similar points have been made by other critics. Kalstone has identified observation as "a kind of life-jacket" in Bishop's poetry (*Five Temperaments*, p. 34); Marjorie Perloff in "Elizabeth Bishop: The Course of a Particular," *Modern Poetry Studies*, 8 (Winter 1977): 177–92 focuses on Bishop's attention to things as a way of steeling herself against suffering and of distancing despair.

16 For a fuller discussion of Bishop's indirect self-scrutiny, see the essay I coauthored with Cristanne Miller, "Emily Dickinson, Elizabeth Bishop, and the Rewards of Indirection," *The New England Quarterly*, 57 (December 1984): 533–53.

17 See pp. 3–11 of *Five Temperaments*.

18 "Domestication, Domesticity and the Otherworldly," p. 23.

19 Stevenson, *Elizabeth Bishop*, p. 66 (from a letter Bishop wrote to Stevenson).

20 "Domestication, Domesticity and the Otherworldly," p. 32.

21 In "The Geography of Gender: Elizabeth Bishop's 'In the Waiting Room' " Lee Edelman has underscored the instability of the inside/outside distinction in this poem, arguing that Bishop's geography "persistently refuses the consolations of hierarchy or placement." In this excellent essay, Edelman suggests that Bishop's dismantling of binary oppositions subverts the patriarchal and heterosexual ideology on which the oppositions are founded (*Contemporary Literature*, 26 [Summer 1985]: 179–96).

22 Kenner, *A Homemade World*, p. 111.

23 Jane Shore, "Elizabeth Bishop: The Art of Changing Your Mind," *Ploughshares*, 5 (1979): 178–91. The quoted phrase is on page 182. Many of these techniques have subsequently been adopted by poets younger than Bishop; see, for instance, C. K. Williams' recent collection, *Tar*.

24 David Perkins, *Wordsworth and the Poetry of Sincerity* (Cambridge: Harvard Univ. Press, 1964), p. 80.

25 While "January First" might suggest that world and poem are equally text ("tomorrow / we shall have to think up signs, / sketch a landscape, fabricate a plan / on the double page / of day and paper"), Bishop's own poems do not go so far in questioning material reality.

26 Borroff, *Language and the Poet*, p. 84.

27 W. C. Williams, "Marianne Moore," in Tomlinson, *Marianne Moore*, p. 57.

28 For statistical evidence of the formality of Moore's language, see Borroff, *Language and the Poet*, pp. 85–90.

29 Stevenson, "Letters from Elizabeth Bishop," p. 261.

30 Borroff, *Language and the Poet*, pp. 95–9.

31   Ibid., p. 102.

32   Brown, "Interview with Elizabeth Bishop," p. 14.

33   For an excellent discussion of Bishop's revisions and the significance of the "interplay of persistence and change" in her successive drafts, see Barbara Page, "Shifting Islands: Elizabeth Bishop's Manuscripts," *Shenandoah*, 33 (1981–82): pp. 51–66.

34   Quoted by Costello, "Marianne Moore and Elizabeth Bishop: Friendship and Influence," p. 139.

35   "The Art of Poetry," *Paris Review*, p. 77.

36   Bishop's proto-proto-dream-houses appear in her early stories, "The Sea & Its Shore" and "In Prison." In many ways "In Prison" anticipates this poem, including the small painted cell, the sunset light "in which any object can be made to look magically significant," and the very dull book which will permit "the pleasure, perverse, I suppose, of interpreting it not at all according to its intent" (CPr 187, 188).

37   In "Shifting Islands," Barbara Page too stresses Bishop's desire to undermine simple oppositions.

38   André Breton, *Manifestoes of Surrealism*, trans. Richard Seaver and Helen R. Lane (Ann Arbor: Univ. of Michigan Press, 1972), p. 123. Breton continues, "Now, search as one may one will never find any other motivating force in the activities of the Surrealists than the hope of finding and fixing this point."

## CHAPTER 5

1   The following abbreviations appear as parenthetic citations in this chapter:

| | |
|---|---|
| Coll | Robert Creeley, *The Collected Poems of Robert Creeley: 1945– 1975* (Berkeley: Univ. of Calif. Press, 1982) |
| CP | Robert Creeley, *Contexts of Poetry*, ed. Donald Allen (Bolinas: Four Seasons Foundation, 1973) |
| QG | Robert Creeley, *A Quick Graph* (San Francisco: Four Seasons Foundation, 1970) |
| WTRP | Robert Creeley, *Was That A Real Poem and Other Essays*, ed. Donald Allen (Bolinas: Four Seasons Foundation, 1979) |
| B2 | *boundary 2*, 6, no. 3; 7, no. 1 (Spring/Fall 1978) |
| CEP | William Carlos Williams, *The Collected Earlier Poems of William Carlos Williams* (New York: New Directions, 1951) |
| CLP | William Carlos Williams, *The Collected Later Poems of William Carlos Williams* (New York: New Directions, 1963) |
| IM | William Carlos Williams, *Imaginations* (New York: New Directions, 1970) |
| PB | William Carlos Williams, *Pictures from Brueghel and Other Poems* (New York: New Directions, 1962) |
| SE | William Carlos Williams, *Selected Essays* (1954; rpt. New York: New Directions, 1969) |

2   W. C. Williams, "Letter to an Australian Editor," *Briarcliff Quarterly*, 3 (October 1946): 207.

3  From a letter to Williams, 11 February 1950, quoted by Paul Mariani, " 'Fire of a Very Real Order': Creeley and Williams" (B2 175). Mariani provides thorough and engaging documentation of the correspondence between Williams and Creeley. As he notes, however, "Williams' most deeply felt influence on Creeley was not the correspondence. It lay, rather, in the fact of Williams' poems" (B2 181). The fact of the poems is my concern here; I have tried to minimize duplication of material Mariani uses.

4  The letters they exchanged between April 1950 and February 1951 have been published in *Charles Olson and Robert Creeley: The Complete Correspondence*, ed. George Butterick (Santa Barbara: Black Swallow Press, 1980, 1981, 1982). Four volumes have appeared so far; the published correspondence will eventually extend to Olson's death in 1970, though fewer letters date from later years.

When the correspondence began, Olson had just drafted his essay on projective verse, which he subsequently revised to incorporate ideas developed in his exchange with Creeley. At that time Creeley was more involved in writing prose fiction than poetry.

5  See, for example, "Guido, i' vorrei che / tu e Lapo ed io" (Coll 22).

6  Cynthia Dubin Edelberg, *Robert Creeley's Poetry: A Critical Introduction* (Albuquerque: Univ. of New Mexico Press, 1978), pp. 7–8. "Hélas" is an example.

7  "Craft Interview with Robert Creeley," *The Craft of Poetry*, ed. William Packard (Garden City, N.Y.: Doubleday, 1974), p. 213.

8  Williams to Creeley, 3 March 1950; quoted in *Poetics of the New American Poetry*, ed. Donald Allen and Warren Tallman (New York: Grove Press, 1973), p. 140. Creeley has echoed these sentiments many times since; see, for example, CP 82–4, QG 3.

9  In his interview with Edelberg in *Robert Creeley's Poetry*, Creeley admits to having "used Williams sadly, unintentionally, as a reassurance that my attitudes in relation to women . . . found company." Recalling the "complacent superiority and distaste" he had once felt toward the woman who is used in *Paterson*, Creeley adds that as he grew older he became more aware of Williams' "tacit hostility" toward women and found it "offensive" (p. 162).

10  "A Critical Difference of View," *Stony Brook*, 3/4 (1969): 362. In "The Literal Activity of Robert Creeley," Paul Diehl, by focusing on bonding strength within and between syntactic units, provides a useful, more technical explanation of how the positioning of line breaks in a sentence creates significance (B2 335–46).

11  In an appreciative review of *The Collected Poems*, "Creeley: His Metric," Robert Hass argues that some of what Creeley took from Williams depended on false assumptions about how his work should be read. According to Hass, Williams' line breaks "where words are most riveted together were intended to speed up the movement," hurrying the reader from one line to the next to imitate "the swiftness of perception." Creeley, in "giving each line a full pause at the end," read those pauses so that they slowed the verse; when read that way "what becomes visible is the strangeness of the struggle

to articulate the fact of the sentence" (*The Threepenny Review* [Winter 1984], reprinted in Hass, *Twentieth Century Pleasures: Prose on Poetry* [New York, Ecco Press, 1984], pp. 150–1).

12   *The Kind of Act of* (1953), *The Immoral Proposition* (1953), *A Snarling Garland of Xmas Verses* (1954), and *All That is Lovely in Men* (whose title may derive from Williams' "All That Is Perfect in Woman" [1949]).

13   *The Whip* contains selections from *Le Fou* as well as from these later volumes. The first section of *For Love* differs from *The Whip* only in including "Naughty Boy," which originally appeared in *A Form of Women* (1959), the collection that constitutes the second section of *For Love*.

14   Pinsky, *The Situation of Poetry*, pp. 11–12.

15   When Olson first read samples of Creeley's poetry, in June 1950, he called Creeley's attention to the inconsistency between the "quick & short" breath with many juxtapositions that Creeley was using in his letters and the long, smooth phrases he was using in his poems; Olson urged him to use in poetry the cadence of his own voice (*The Complete Correspondence*, vol. 1, p. 87).

16   Williams, too, loved blues and jazz, but classic New Orleans jazz rather than Charlie Parker's modern jazz. For a discussion of the importance of jazz to Williams' poetics, see Mike Weaver, *William Carlos Williams: The American Background* (Cambridge: Cambridge Univ. Press, 1971), pp. 71–8.

17   Charles Altieri provides an interesting reading of this poem as Creeley's "most fundamental dramatic statement on the problem of language and its relation to the void" in *Enlarging the Temple: New Directions in American Poetry during the 1960s* (Lewisberg: Bucknell University Press, 1979), pp. 174–5.

18   *Poetic Closure: A Study of How Poems End* (Chicago: University of Chicago Press, 1968), p. 86.

19   Creeley knows all of Williams' works well, and probably learned from works scattered over his entire career. In terms of prosody, however, Williams' early volumes such as *Spring and All* and the short poems of the late thirties and forties (found in CEP as well as in *The Wedge*, *The Clouds*, etc.) are particularly important to Creeley. He has singled out "The Desert Music" as "the loveliest form he left us" (QG 66); that preference probably reflects Creeley's identification with the poet's anguish – his "agony of self-realization" and his need to be reassured about the role of poet (see QG 59–60).

20   Otto Jespersen, "Notes on Metre," *The Structure of Verse: Modern Essays on Prosody*, ed. Harvey Gross (New York: Ecco Press, rev. ed., 1979), pp. 124–5.

21   "On the Function of the Line," *Chicago Review*, 30 (Winter 1979): 33–4.

22   Charles Olson, "Projective Verse," *Selected Writings of Charles Olson*, ed. Robert Creeley (New York: New Directions, 1966), p. 16. The statement "that form is never more than an *extension* of content" is originally Creeley's, from a letter dated 5 June 1950 (*Complete Correspondence*, vol. 1, p. 79); in his essay Olson acknowledges that the formulation is Creeley's.

23   *A Homemade World*, p. 59.

24   Kenner, *The Pound Era*, p. 402.

25 Ibid., p. 400.
26 Creeley, "The Fact of His Life" [review of Williams' *Pictures from Brueghel and Other Poems*], *The Nation*, 13 October 1962, p. 224.
27 *The Pound Era*, p. 403.
28 "How He Knows When to Stop: Creeley on Closure" [interview with Terry R. Bacon], *American Poetry Review*, 5 (November/December 1976): 5. Subsequent quotes in the same paragraph appear on the same page.
29 "An Interview by Emily Keller," *American Poetry Review* 12 (May/June 1983): 27. When asked about the function of his inverted syntax, Creeley replied, "I don't altogether know what you mean by inverted syntax. . . . I use colloquial structure in ways of speaking. Otherwise, I don't like inverted word order at all."
30 Copyright 1981 by the Estate of Florence H. Williams. Used by permission of New Directions Publishing Corporation, agents for William E. and Paul H. Williams. Used also by permission of Robert Creeley and Washington University Libraries. The letter is in the Robert Creeley Papers, Modern Literature Collection, Washington University Libraries, St. Louis, Missouri. Much of the material quoted here was first published by Mariani.
31 23 September 1962, quoted with the permissions of the Collection of American Literature, the Beinecke Rare Book and Manuscript Library, Yale University; of Robert Creeley; and of New Directions, agents for the Estate of Florence H. Williams.
32 *The Complete Correspondence*, vol. 1, pp. 28–9.
33 See J. Hillis Miller, "William Carlos Williams," *Poets of Reality: Six Twentieth-Century Writers* (New York: Atheneum, 1974), pp. 328–33.
34 *A Homemade World*, p. 65.
35 "Craft Interview," p. 211.
36 "How He Knows When to Stop," p. 6.

### CHAPTER 6

1 Although Creeley learned from the rhythms of jazz musicians such as Charlie Parker early in his career, he claims not to have "[taken] instruction from musicians in the way that [he] took it from painters." When asked about John Cage's impact on his work, he expressed admiration for Cage's ability to "locate coherence in the most diverse and random of occasions" by "opening up your sense of perceptive possibilities." Yet Creeley claims not so much to have learned from him as to have been "*reassured*" by his example. ("From the Forest of Language: A Conversation with Robert Creeley," ed. Philip L. Gerber, *Athanor*, 4 [Spring 1973]: 12–13.)
2 The parenthetic abbreviations used in Chapter 5 also appear in this chapter. In addition, the abbreviation L will refer to Robert Creeley, *Later* (New York: New Directions, 1979).
3 *Paterson* (New York: New Directions, 1963), p. 129.
4 In editing his interview "Talking with Robert Creeley" (B2 13–74), William Spanos decided "not to tamper in any radical way with the tape" (B2 74) –

i.e., to preserve syntactic disruptions and to print audible pauses by leaving spaces between words. When quoting from the interview in this chapter, I have eliminated those spaces. Occasionally I have inserted additional words or punctuation in brackets to make the quotations more comprehensible.

5   Several critics have explored the relation between Creeley's thinking and Wittgenstein's. See Linda W. Wagner, "Creeley's Late Poems: Contexts," B2 301–8 and Stephen Fredman, *Poet's Prose: The Crisis in American Verse* (Cambridge: Cambridge Univ. Press, 1983), pp. 71–4. Responding to my inquiries, Creeley explained that he first encountered Wittgenstein through Zukofsky's work in the 1950s, and that while he has never studied Wittgenstein's work carefully, he has in his own "desultory manner" read a number of his texts. He particularly likes *Zettel* and *On Certainty*, along with Wittgenstein's last recorded lecture, on ethics (letter to author, 8 May 1980, used by permission of Robert Creeley).

6   Stephen Fredman, *Poet's Prose*, pp. 67–77. Although concerned specifically with a prose text, *Presences: A Text for Marisol*, Fredman's chapter on Creeley illuminates all his later work.

7   Robert von Hallberg explores Creeley's fascination with systematic organization and links it to the widespread interest in cybernetics in America during the fifties and sixties in *American Poetry and Culture, 1945–1980* (Cambridge: Harvard Univ. Press, 1985), pp. 36–53.

8   "What Makes the Shadows Darker," *The Poet in the World* (New York: New Directions, 1973), p. 240.

9   "From the Forest of Language," p. 14. Creeley is describing what he finds "very intriguing" about Ted Berrigan's work.

10   Ibid., p. 13. "Optative" is Olson's word for Pound's method; Creeley uses Olson's statement to explain his own views.

11   "Stories: Being an Information. An Interview" [interview with Robert Sheppard], *Sagetrieb*, 1 (Winter 1982): 45.

12   "How He Knows When to Stop," p. 6.

13   In the original edition, each "thing" accompanied a collage by Creeley's wife, Bobbie Hawkins.

14   *The Pleasure of the Text*, trans. Richard Miller (New York: Hill & Wang, 1975), pp. 4–5.

15   *The Situation of Poetry*, p. 12.


## CHAPTER 7

1   For a description of this literary generation, see Samuel Hynes, *The Auden Generation: Literature and Politics in England in the 1930s* (Princeton: Princeton Univ. Press, 1976).

2   The following abbreviations for Auden's volumes appear parenthetically in this chapter and in Chapter 8:

>   CP    *Collected Poems*, ed. Edward Mendelson (New York: Random House, 1976)

DH     *The Dyer's Hand and Other Essays* (1968, rpt. New York: Vintage-Random, 1972)

FA     *Forewords and Afterwords* (New York: Random House, 1973)

3   The following abbreviations appear parenthetically in this chapter for citation of Merrill's volumes:

FP     *First Poems* (New York: Knopf, 1951)

CTY     *The Country of a Thousand Years of Peace* (New York: Atheneum, 1959; rev. ed. 1970)

WS     *Water Street* (New York: Atheneum, 1962)

ND     *Nights and Days* (New York: Atheneum, 1966)

DC     *Divine Comedies* (New York: Atheneum, 1976)

M     *Mirabell: Books of Number* (New York: Atheneum, 1978)

S     *Scripts for the Pageant* (New York: Atheneum, 1980)

4   Ashley Brown, "An Interview with James Merrill," *Shenandoah*, 19 (Summer 1968): 5.

5   Donald Sheehan, "An Interview with James Merrill," *The Contemporary Writer*, ed. L. S. Dembo and Cyrena N. Pondrom (Madison: Univ. of Wisconsin Press, 1972), p. 151.

6   J. D. McClatchy, "The Art of Poetry XXXI: James Merrill," *The Paris Review*, 84 (Summer 1982): 207–8.

7   Ross Labrie, "James Merrill at Home: An Interview," *Arizona Quarterly*, 38 (Spring 1982): 24.

8   Humphrey Carpenter, *W. H. Auden: A Biography* (Boston: Houghton Mifflin, 1981), p. 245. Carpenter credits the phrase to Edward Mendelson.

9   Brown, "An Interview," p. 7.

10   Ibid., p. 8.

11   Ibid., p. 9.

12   Merrill has acknowledged this debt, both in McClatchy, "The Art of Poetry," p. 212 and in a note to the author, 22 August 1983.

13   Even *First Poems* contained a few touches of this more comical irony, for example in the third of the "Variations: The air is sweetest that a thistle guards" (FP 28). Playfully revealing human limitations, the amusing and apparently incongruous rhymes point to dark linkages: nursery/mercenary, enticements/basements – exactly the sly use of feminine rhyming that delighted Auden. Loaded line breaks, too, ironically undercut the actors, but without the symbolists' detached cynicism: "We laughed till we died / At her warnings, her funny / Despairs, her enticements."

14   For discussion of the camp and upper-class aspects of Merrill's style and sensibility, see Robert von Hallberg, "James Merrill: Revealing by Obscuring," *Contemporary Literature*, 21 (Autumn 1980): 549–71.

15   Labrie, "James Merrill at Home," pp. 27–8.

16   McClatchy, "The Art of Poetry," p. 214.

17   For discussion of Auden's difficulties with Yeats' influence, see Edward Mendelson, *Early Auden* (New York: Viking Press, 1981), pp. 179–80, 330

and chapter 10 of Edward Callen, *Auden: A Carnival of Intellect* (New York: Oxford Univ. Press, 1983).

18    Writing on Max Beerbohm in 1965, Auden does caution against judging the arts by the rules of social amenity; art must confront the things that matter, he argues, and manners invite us to skirt such things. However, Auden wants those issues confronted in a mannerly, i.e., entertaining and unegotistical, way. ("One of the Family," *New Yorker*, 23 October 1965, p. 243.)

19    See Howard Griffin, *Conversations with Auden*, ed. Donald Allen (San Francisco: Grey Fox Press, 1981), p. 24.

20    Sheehan, "An Interview," p. 148. Merrill's view that manners are essential to personal identity and human emotion is evident in the testimony of 741 as he is about to become the peacock Mirabell: "B4 OUR MEETINGS I WAS NOTHING NO TIME PASSD BUT NOW / YR TOUCH LIKE A LAMP HAS SHOWN ME TO MYSELF & I AM / ME: 741! I HAVE ENTERD A GREAT WORLD I AM FILLD / WITH IS IT MANNERS?" (M 61).

21    Sheehan, "An Interview," p. 149.

22    David Kalstone, "The Poet: Private," *Saturday Review*, 2 December 1972, p. 45.

23    "When We Dead Awaken: Writing as Re-Vision," *Adrienne Rich's Poetry*, ed. Barbara Charlesworth Gelpi and Albert Gelpi (New York: W. W. Norton, 1975), p. 94. Auden chose Rich as winner of the Yale Younger Poets Prize.

24    Sheehan, "An Interview," p. 143.

25    Labrie, "James Merrill at Home," p. 29.

26    Brown, "An Interview," p. 13.

27    The term "anti-Romantic" has appeared often in discussions of Auden. John G. Blair in his first chapter, "The Anti-Romantic Modern," *The Poetic Art of W. H. Auden* (Princeton: Princeton Univ. Press, 1965) links Auden's anti-Romanticism to Eliot's. More recent critics such as Callen and Mendelson see more clearly modernism's roots in Romanticism and present Auden's anti-Romanticism as distinguishing him from the modernists. Callen explores Auden's rejection of Romanticism especially in chapter 10, "Disenchantment with Yeats," and Mendelson emphasizes Auden's departure from the Romantic and modernist traditions in identifying him as a civil rather than a vatic poet.

28    *Early Auden*, p. 61.

29    See chapter 10, "The Insufficient Touch," in Mendelson, *Early Auden*.

30    Griffin, *Conversations*, p. 25.

31    According to Carpenter, the real occasion for this poem was Chester Kallman's twenty-first birthday in January 1942 (p. 321).

32    McClatchy, "The Art of Poetry," pp. 211–12; also Labrie, "James Merrill at Home," pp. 21–2.

33    Brown, "An Interview," p. 14.

34    Ibid.

35    Carpenter, *W. H. Auden*, p. 325.

36    "Craft Interview with W. H. Auden," *The Craft of Poetry*, ed. William Packard (Garden City, N.Y.: Doubleday, 1974), p. 3.

37 "Object Lessons," *New York Review of Books*, 30 November 1972, p. 32.

38 Merrill has said he knew Auden "a little bit" by the mid-fifties and "knew him much better after we began going to Greece [1959] and after Chester Kallman also came to Greece [1963]" (Labrie, "James Merrill at Home," p. 24). Though not claiming to have known the older poet "terribly well, in this world," Merrill acknowledges that Auden liked him, approved of his work, and appreciated his being in Athens to stand by Kallman "when emergencies arose" (McClatchy, "The Art of Poetry," p. 189).

39 McClatchy, "DJ: A Conversation with David Jackson," *Shenandoah*, 30, no. 4 (1979): 36.

40 McClatchy, "DJ," p. 39.

41 Carpenter, *W. H. Auden*, p. 419.

42 "Merrill and Dante" in *James Merrill: Essays in Criticism*, ed. David Lehman and Charles Berger (Ithaca: Cornell Univ. Press, 1983) pp. 152–3 and 311 n4.

43 Sheehan, "An Interview," p. 151.

44 Information from Carlo Izzo, "The Poetry of W. H. Auden," *Auden: A Collection of Critical Essays*, ed. Monroe K. Spears (Englewood Cliffs, N.J.: Prentice-Hall, 1964), p. 127.

45 For discussions of the relation between Merrill's trilogy and Dante's, see essays by Jacoff, Kalstone, and Saez in *James Merrill: Essays in Criticism*.

46 See Merrill, "Divine Poem," *The New Republic*, 183 (29 November 1980): 29–34.

47 *The Contemporary Poet as Artist and Critic*, ed. Anthony Ostroff (Boston: Little, Brown, 1964), p. 186.

48 McClatchy, "The Art of Poetry," pp. 214–15.

49 Marvin Cohen, "An Interview with W. H. Auden," *Arts in Society*, 12 (1975): 366. The interview took place in 1970.

50 Carpenter, *W. H. Auden*, p. 425.

51 Ibid., p. 342.

52 See, for instance, Merrill's presentation of their instruction via 741 as metaphorical fellatio (M 60–1).

53 Brown, "An Interview," p. 10.

54 So say even those who knew Auden personally; in conversation with the author, John Hollander, for instance, remarked that WHA's voice is "uncannily" like Auden's.

55 *Part of Nature, Part of Us* (Cambridge: Harvard Univ. Press, 1980), p. 217.

56 "The Red Eye of God: James Merrill's Reasons to Believe," *Voice Literary Supplement*, March 1983, p. 7.

57 "The Metaphors and Metamorphoses of M," *Parnassus*, 8 (1980): 39.

58 Note dated 22 August 1983, used by permission of James Merrill.

59 Carpenter, *W. H. Auden*, p. 354.

**CHAPTER 8**

1 Auden frequently quoted the passage (see, for example, DH 61); he made this claim in "An Unpublished Interview" conducted by Walter Kerr in

1953, published in the special Auden issue of *The Harvard Advocate*, 108 (Fall 1966): 35. The passage from *The Waves* is reproduced as quoted in that interview.

2 "W. H. Auden," *Writers at Work: The Paris Review Interviews*, fourth series, ed. George Plimpton (New York: Viking Press, 1976), p. 257.

3 He announced his belief in the Devil in "W. H. Auden," *Writers at Work*, p. 268.

4 Helen Vendler, "James Merrill's Myth: An Interview," *The New York Review of Books*, 3 May 1979, p. 12.

5 Labrie, "James Merrill at Home," pp. 30, 31.

6 "The Art of Poetry," p. 200.

7 See Merrill's statement on language and reality in "The Art of Poetry," pp. 196–7.

8 *Early Auden*, p. 21.

9 Ostroff, "The Contemporary Poet as Artist and Critic," pp. 185–6.

10 The following abbreviations appear as parenthetic citations in this chapter:

| | |
|---|---|
| FS | *The Fire Screen* (New York: Atheneum, 1969) |
| BE | *Braving the Elements* (New York: Atheneum, 1973) |
| DC | *Divine Comedies* (New York, Atheneum, 1977) |
| M | *Mirabell: Books of Number* (New York, Atheneum, 1978) |
| S | *Scripts for the Pageant* (New York, Atheneum, 1980) |
| CLS | *The Changing Light at Sandover* (New York, Atheneum, 1982) – cited only for quotes from "Coda: The Higher Keys" |

11 Quotations in this paragraph are from that review, "Object Lessons," *New York Review of Books*, November 1972, pp. 31, 32.

12 Sheehan, "An Interview," p. 146.

13 Critics of Auden's work commonly remark on the doubleness of his allegiances: John Blair, for instance, discusses "a tension between moral seriousness and the inescapable amorality of poetic artifice" (*The Poetic Art of W. H. Auden*, p. 11), and Mendelson remarks on the poetry's "commitment to fact and its deliberate artifice" (*Early Auden*, p. xiv).

14 Auden does acknowledge the truth of opera's portrait of human willfulness; see "Notes on Music and Opera" (DH). Blair quotes from an article in *Vogue*, 1948, in which Auden suggests that one respond to opera by thinking, " 'What psychological insight to construct so many plots around one or the other of the two most uniquely human acts, laying down one's life for one's friend and cutting off one's nose to spite one's face. How realistic to show that, whatever it may be in between, life at its best and its worst is a *performance* that defies common sense.' " (pp. 162–3). To say that opera is "realistic" in this sense, however, is not to deny that its fires are purely fictional.

15 Labrie, "James Merrill at Home," p. 24–5.

16 Sheehan, "An Interview," pp. 144–5.

17 Ibid., p. 146.

18 "W. H. Auden," *Writers at Work*, p. 263.

19 Labrie, "James Merrill at Home," p. 23.

20  The literary ballad had been recently revitalized both by Auden in his late thirties diagnoses of psychological cripples like "Miss Gee," "James Honeyman," and "Victor," and by Elizabeth Bishop in "The Burglar of Babylon."

21  McClatchy, "The Art of Poetry," p. 215.

22  Kalstone, "The Poet: Private"; quotes in this paragraph derive from that interview, pp. 44, 45.

23  Kalstone, "The Poet: Private," p. 45.

24  *James Merrill: An Introduction to the Poetry* (New York: Columbia Univ. Press, 1984), p. 161.

25  The scientific basis of Dante's vision preoccupies Merrill also in his review essay on *The California Dante*, "Divine Poem," *New Republic*, 29 November 1980. He discusses an article by Mark A. Peterson in the *American Journal of Physics*, December 1979, which suggests that Dante's universe "also emerges as a cosmological solution of Einstein's equations in general relativity theory." Merrill's review suggests extensive parallels between Dante's epic undertaking, as Merrill understands it, and his own; in talking about the former he often seems to be describing the latter.

26  I was led to this understanding partly by David Kalstone's essay "Persisting Figures: The Poet's Story and How We Read It" in *James Merrill: Essays in Criticism*. With his customary elegance and insight, Kalstone argues that Merrill's trilogy exemplifies a contemporary trend of long poems that attempt to absorb the instability of the self into the form of the work.

27  "James Merrill's Myth," p. 13.

28  "The Art of Poetry," p. 194.

29  For an excellent discussion of the nature of God and his names in the trilogy as well as of the duality or unicity of Merrill's universe, see Stephen Yenser, "The Names of God: *Scripts for the Pageant*," in *James Merrill: Essays in Criticism*. Yenser has anticipated much of my argument in claiming that "What the trilogy gives us in the end is not a belief but rather a dialectical process of thought and imagination – a process such that it will not tolerate any single belief, or even species of belief, whether monistic or dualistic, materialistic or idealistic" (p. 275).

30  I take issue here with Charles Berger, who argues in "Merrill and Pynchon: Our Apocalyptic Scribes" that the trilogy's "process of revision is grounded in a growing certainty about the truth" and that "the notion of authority remains intact" (*James Merrill: Essays in Criticism*, p. 294).

## CONCLUSION

1  *The Collected Poems of Wallace Stevens*, p. 215.

2  "Second Presentation of Elizabeth Bishop," *World Literature Today*, 51 (Winter 1977): 10.

3  Kramer, "The Age of the Avant-Garde," *The Age of the Avant-Garde: An Art Chronicle of 1956–1972* (New York: Farrar, Straus & Giroux, 1973), p. 12. Kramer himself claims that "What was transmissible [from the avant-

292 Notes to pp. 261–7

garde] was not a 'tradition' but a principle of artistic coherence, gleaned from the work itself. . . . For the roots of this 'tradition,' if we still can call it that, were no longer in the general culture but in the personal culture of the 'individual talent,' and this personal culture . . . could easily be by-passed in favor of those properties of 'style' to which a later generation of artists swiftly reduced all artistic inheritances" (p. 17). Kramer believes the age of the avant-garde to have passed, not because the will to innovation has abated but because it has been "triumphantly institutionalized."

4 Anne Stevenson, "Letters from Elizabeth Bishop," *TLS*, 7 March 1980, p. 261.
5 Don Sheehan, "James Merrill" [an interview], *The Contemporary Writer*, p. 143.
6 The quoted phrase is from C. K. Williams, *Tar* (New York: Vintage, 1983), p. 36.
7 Matthews, *A Happy Childhood* (Boston: Atlantic-Little, Brown, 1984), p. 36.
8 The poem appears in *Erosion* (Princeton: Princeton Univ. Press, 1983) p. 37.
9 The poem concludes *Praise* (New York: Ecco Press, 1978). Quoted lines are on pp. 52, 67, 68.

# Index

293